Lab Manual and Workbook for Physical Anthropology

SEVENTH EDITION

Diane L. France

Colorado State University

WADSWORTH
CENGAGE Learning™

Australia • Brazil • Japan • Korea • Mexico • Singapore • Spain • United Kingdom • United States

WADSWORTH
CENGAGE Learning

Lab Manual and Workbook for Physical Anthropology, **Seventh Edition**
Diane L. France

Anthropology Editor: Erin Mitchell

Developmental Editor:
Liana Monari Sarkisian

Editorial Assistant: Pamela Simon

Media Editor: Melanie Cregger

Marketing Manager: Andrew Keay

Marketing Assistant: Dimitri Hagnéré

Marketing Communications Manager:
Tami Strang

Content Project Manager: Jerilyn Emori

Creative Director: Rob Hugel

Art Director: Caryl Gorska

Print Buyer: Paula Vang

Rights Acquisitions Account Manager, Text:
Roberta Broyer

Rights Acquisitions Account Manager,
Image: Robyn Young

Production Service: Jill Traut / MPS Limited,
A Macmillan Company

Photo Researcher: Megan Lessard /
Pre-PressPMG

Cover Designer: Carole Lawson

Cover Image: © DLILLC/Corbis

Compositor: MPS Limited, A Macmillan
Company

Brief Contents

Contents

Preface

Education in any discipline and at any level should always stress the importance of critical thinking and independent research. Education should offer students the tools to explore their world, seek answers to their questions, and challenge old ways of thinking. My goal in writing this text is, and always has been, to provide a foundation of information about physical anthropology and to encourage independent thinking and research.

Physical anthropology is a fascinating discipline. It encompasses information about humans and their place in nature more completely than any other field. Within this subject, we explore human biology, how humans have evolved, and how and why we know that we are still evolving. We study our primate cousins in their natural (and unfortunately shrinking) environments, and we compare ourselves to other non-primate animals. Within the field of physical anthropology, it is possible to explore (and even celebrate) the differences and similarities of all modern humans. We examine the human skeleton to discover the wide range of natural variation and learn how to provide clues about the identity of unidentified remains in the medicolegal system. How could anyone not be interested in such a vast and exciting field?

NEW TO THIS EDITION

The seventh edition of this book has been almost entirely rewritten and has now added a significant web component. Illustrations and photographs have been improved throughout the book, and more have been added. Specific changes made for the seventh edition include the following:

- The introduction includes a discussion about the scientific method and how to develop a scientific experiment. This is also an introduction to critical thinking and a challenge to thoughtfully evaluate everything within this book and the universe.

- The genetics chapter of previous editions has been divided into two chapters to more thoroughly introduce cellular as well as population genetics. The basics necessary for understanding evolution and our place in the natural world are provided in these chapters, and they incorporate up-to-the-minute developments in the Human Genome Project. The complicated mathematical formulae are now in a web-based section of the book for those instructors or students who want to further study the Hardy-Weinberg formula and statistical indicators of evolution within a population. Real-world situations replace most hypothetical problems.

- Chapter 3 still explores human osteology with the addition of side identification and some tips on what bone fragments can tell us about the individual and the bone. Many more photographs with labels are particularly useful in those laboratories without adequate osteological material.

- Chapter 4 includes more detail about the growth and development of dentition and bone, as well as how various insults to the individual (e.g., nutritional problems) can affect bones and teeth. In this edition, the age at which centers of bone growth appear is discussed in addition to the ages at which those growth centers unite. Additional exercises ask the student to determine the absolute and relative ages of "unknown" individuals.

- Chapter 5 explores the theory and practice of species identification and classification and adds the advances in genetics to the concept of species in primates.

- Chapter 6 discusses biomechanical properties of morphological differences in primates and in quadrupedal mammals, leading to later chapters about how primates move and live. This chapter, as well as the following two (exploring the physical and social characteristics of primates), introduces the primate fossil record. The goal is to give information necessary to analyze the fossil record and not merely memorize species names.

- Chapters 9 through 12 probe the primate fossil record from before the Paleocene era to more recent prehistory. There are more illustrations and charts that facilitate comparisons between the species, and very recent discoveries have been included. Questions and exercises promote discussion about what these fossil discoveries really mean about how humans and our primate cousins evolved.

- The remaining chapters further explore modern humans. How do bones respond to disease, genetic conditions, trauma, and intentional modification? How do we use the differences between human populations, age-related changes, and sexual dimorphism to help us determine who an individual was and what happened to that individual at about the time of death? Forensic anthropology is a hot topic today and is covered in some detail in the final chapter.

Throughout the book, there are ties to a web-based pool of information and exercises and links to outside sites with additional information.

Acknowledgments

As with previous editions of this book, many individuals reviewed the sixth edition and suggested changes and additions for the seventh edition. It was apparent that the reviewers thoroughly read the sixth edition, for their suggestions were very helpful. Where possible, I incorporated their suggestions.

I also thank the following for generously providing photographs and illustrations:

Academic Press; Jayne Bellavia; Brenda Benefit; A. Blackstone; Kathryn Born; David Brill; Peter Brown; Wayne Bryant; Charles Cundiff; J. C. Fleagle; The Human Genome Project and developers of genome.gov; David Haring; M. Y. Iscan; C. Jolly; Robert Jurmain; R. F. Kay; Lynn Kilgore; Mindy Klein; C. S. Larsen and R. M. Matter; Demris Lee generously provided a valuable section on DNA identification; E. Mayr; McGraw-Hill Publications; Mission Paleoanthropologique Franco-Tchadienne; J. R. Napier; National Museum of Health and Medicine; National Museums of Kenya Casting Program; National Museum of Natural History; D. Pilbeam; Plenum Press; F. Plog; J. S. Rhine; W. Saco; E. Simons; Fred Smith; Terrell Smith and Joseph Henry Press; R. Sussman; I. Tattersall; P. Tobias; Rose Tyson from the San Diego Museum of Man; A. C. Walker; Waveland Press; Tim White; D. Ubelaker; and Jay Villemarette from Skulls Unlimited provided photographs and access to skeletal materials in his wonderful museum in Oklahoma City.

David Hunt from the Smithsonian Institution was very generous with his time in helping to find subjects for photography for this and previous editions. I also thank Franklin Damann and Brian Spatola from the National Museum of Health and Medicine for providing access to specimens for photography. I also thank them for their help in obtaining what I needed for this book.

Shane Walker, the manager of France Casting, kept things going swimmingly while I worked on this edition.

I thank all of the people who worked on this book from Cengage Learning including, but not limited to, Lin Gaylord, Jill Traut, Liana Monari, Erin Mitchell, Julie McNamee, Arwen Petty, and Jerilyn Emori.

As always, my husband Art Abplanalp, Jr., was patient and kind through many long days and nights of research, writing, and editing. He is wonderful.

A Note about the Fossil Cast Photographs

Many of the illustrations of fossil primates and hominins in this book are photographs of casts. The National Museums of Kenya Casting Program, the University of Pennsylvania Casting Program, the Werner-Gren Foundation, and the Institute of Human Origins manufactured these casts directly from the original fossils. It is important to understand that these casting programs are assuming all of the risk to the original fossils. It is equally important to understand that a mold made directly from an original specimen will yield the most accurate casts and therefore the most useful casts for instruction.

Money received from the sale of casts produced by the National Museums of Kenya funds research and supports those individuals who are working in the Museum. Without that support, the research into our past will suffer greatly. I encourage instructors to purchase casts from those institutions that make molds directly from the originals.

SUPPLEMENTS FOR INSTRUCTORS

The seventh edition features an updated supplement package to aid instructors.

Companion Website

Log on to the password-protected website to access the *Instructor's Manual with Test Bank*, the *Earthwatch Journal,* InfoTrac College Edition, and more.

Online Instructor's Manual with Test Bank

New to this edition of the workbook, we have developed an online *Instructor's Manual with Test Bank* to help you prepare for lectures, discussions, exams, and quizzes. Each chapter of the *Instructor's Manual* includes learning objectives, a lecture outline, key terms, and concepts with corresponding page number references, lecture suggestions, and InfoTrac College Edition and Internet exercises that can be assigned as homework. The test bank includes 25 multiple-choice and 10 true-false questions, each with the correct answer listed as well as a page number reference and corresponding learning objective. There are also 5 short-answer questions for each chapter, with page-number references.

Introduction to Science and Critical Thinking

OBJECTIVES

1. What is the scientific method?

2. What are the differences between the scientific method and teleological beliefs?

3. How do you set up an experiment with dependent and independent variables?

This book, an introduction to physical or biological anthropology, is based on the scientific method, so we should discuss what is meant by the scientific method.

There are basically two philosophies in understanding the universe and everything in it (although some people combine bits of these philosophies to describe their own belief systems). Those philosophies can be described as "intentional causality" and "natural causality."

Teleology refers to the belief that there is an intentional causality in the universe and that nothing can be explained without reference to the *reasons* why everything exists. The modern form of that assertion is contained within the beliefs of Intelligent Design, which states that the universe and all contained within it are under the intelligent direction of a higher power and that an undirected process such as natural selection cannot explain the final design of living beings or the reason they exist in the first place. In this philosophical model, all change in the world is directed to an end designated by a higher power.

The scientific method (the philosophy followed in this book) does not assume that change is a means to an end nor that the end result is designated by a higher power. It is a *process* of testing hypotheses and theories with certain assumptions as a background.

First, instead of an *intentional* causality to the universe, science assumes that there is a *natural* causality and that events, living organisms, and so on, do not appear without something preceding them (itself there because of natural causality—see "Evolution and Science" box later in this introduction). Natural causality assumes that change is not directed to a final form or purpose. For every effect there was, and is, a natural (not a supernatural) cause.

Further, there is an assumption in science of *uniformitarianism*, or that the same natural processes operate now as they have in the past, and that the same laws of, for example, physics and chemistry apply everywhere and have for all time. Therefore, hypotheses can be tested because the basic laws that govern them exist everywhere and throughout time.

The scientific method also assumes a high level of *transparency* in reports and publications. This is necessary for the process of testing because if researchers do not know the methods and materials used in an experiment, they cannot test the results and conclusions.

EXPERIMENTAL DESIGN: HYPOTHESES AND THEORIES

How many times have you heard: "The theory of evolution is just that . . . a *theory*." This at least implies that it is probably not true, that it is based on false logic, cannot be proven, or perhaps cannot even be adequately described or tested. In fact, a theory is a specific, important step in the scientific method, but it is not the first step.

Before an idea can be said to be a theory, it has to start out as a hypothesis and as a part of the design of an experiment. A hypothesis must be stated in a way in which it can be tested, and it must be stated in a way that it has the possibility of being proven incorrect. Hypotheses are never to be stated as a question but always as a statement with an explanation following it (it states what the experimenter thinks will occur). Hypotheses are usually written in the "if-then" form: If X, then Y. An example of an hypothesis is "*if* I add fertilizer to one set of geraniums, *then* they will grow bigger than the geraniums to which no fertilizer has been added."

A theory is a hypothesis that has been repeatedly tested and the tests have failed to disprove the hypothesis underlying that theory (however, even after a hypothesis has been tested to reach the theory stage, a theory is still testable). A theory is generally recognized as the simplest, most parsimonious explanation (sometimes described as Occam's razor) for a phenomenon, a class of phenomena, or the underlying reality that explains phenomena. In other words, a theory is based on transparent testing of hypotheses. It is based on observations (i.e., something that you and everyone with normal senses can see or measure and something that can be documented) that have been tested.

If a theory that explains a phenomenon has been generally observed for a long enough period of time, it is usually called a "law" or a fact. For example, gravity is explained by the fact (repeatedly tested) that objects with mass attract one another. This is a very simple explanation that can be tested and observed. That objects with mass attract one another has reached the point in scientific testing that it is no longer a hypothesis—it is a theory. In fact, the theories concerning gravity have been tested so many times under so many different controlled conditions that instead of saying that it is the theory of gravity, most people refer to it as the law of gravity. It is generally recognized as a fact. We all understand that gravity exists and affects our lives in countless ways (from how much we weigh to how much fuel rockets must use to escape the earth's attraction).

When designing an experiment that will test the hypothesis, it is important to set up a simple hypothesis based on few variables because it can be more easily tested and potentially falsifiable (naturally, if the hypothesis is tested by experimental design and *not* falsified, it does not always mean that the hypothesis is true!). **Independent variables** are the subject of the hypothesis, the experiment, and the variables. The variables are, by definition, not controlled. The **dependent variables** can be controlled in the experimental design. Experiments are designed to test cause and effect, so a dependent variable is changed to record the effect of the change on an independent variable. When conducting a scientific study, only one variable at a time should be tested (this is part of a practical model—if you change too many variables in one experiment, you don't know which variable is the explanation for the end result).

Independent variables: are the subject of the hypothesis and are, by definition, not controlled.

Dependent variables: are those that can be controlled in the experiment.

EVOLUTION AND SCIENCE

This book discusses evolution on two levels: evolution on a small scale, as can be observed by everyone in everyday life, and evolution as a series of hypotheses and theories used to describe the changes in organisms (in this book, we discuss primates) over time.

Evolution on a small scale is simply a change in gene or allele frequencies from one generation to the next. As we will discuss in the first two chapters of this book, when organisms multiply through the combination of separate genes from two parents, the offspring have frequencies of alleles that differ from the parents. Farmers take advantage of this when they take a cow that produces a high yield of milk and breed that cow more frequently than a cow that produces less milk. Over a few generations of directed breeding, the farmer's herd as a whole likely produces more milk. This change in gene frequency favoring high milk production over generations is *evolutionary change*.

The other, larger aspect of evolution discussed in this book concerns how humans and our primate relatives came to be who we are today. This part of evolution contains hypotheses and theories about specifically which fossil led to other fossils. Those theories are based, in large part, on the principle of uniformitarianism (as discussed earlier); that is, the same basic laws in nature that occurred 20 million years ago occur today. Some of the evidence for the theories of evolution include where the fossil was discovered in the world. What other fossils have come from that geologic layer and geographical location? Are there associated floral, faunal, or artifacts that might give clues about its age? What is the morphology of the fossil? How is that morphology similar to modern animals, and what does that tell us about how that animal moved or what it ate?

When researchers at the National Museums of Kenya discover a new fossil, they cannot "test" it by modifying a dependent variable to observe the changes in the independent variable. It *is* still part of the scientific method, however, because of its transparency and the ability of other researchers to observe the scientific evidence and challenge the conclusions.

The scientific publication should fulfill one of the primary assumptions of the scientific method: *transparency*.

THE SCIENTIFIC PUBLICATION

There are a few different types of papers published in scientific journals. Some publications report the results of a scientific experiment by closely following the format and content of the experiment (as shown in Table I.1). Other publications describe a recent fossil discovery or a forensic case, but they are not based on a scientific experiment *per se*. They may describe an instructive forensic case, an interesting new fossil hominin find, or a new technique in genetic identification, but they usually still describe research related to the topic, the description of the discovery or finding, and the author's conclusions. In these scientific reports, and indeed in any scientific experiment, accurate description is *vital*! In fact, in many reports and publications, a *diagnosis* of, for example, a pathological condition in a skeleton is less important than a precise *description* of the condition. Why? It comes back to the scientific method—it is

Table I.1 Comparisons Between the Scientific Method and the Scientific Publication	
Scientific Method	**Scientific Publication**
1. Ask a question.	1. Abstract and introduction.
2. Do background research: Has this question (or one like it) already been researched?	2. Background.
3. Construct your hypothesis.	3. State the hypothesis (usually stated in the abstract but can be stated at this point).
4. Test your hypothesis with an experiment.	4. Materials and methods.
5. Analyze your data and come up with results.	5. State your results.
6. Draw a conclusion about the hypothesis.	6. Draw a conclusion about the hypothesis.
7. Communicate your results and conclusion.	7. Publications and talks communicate your results.

important to provide enough information so that other researchers are able to take that information and test it (and perhaps develop an alternative diagnosis).

As stated, the publication that reports on the results of a scientific experiment closely follows the format of the scientific enquiry. The outline of a scientific publication is as follows:

- **Abstract:** A short synopsis of the question and a brief summary of the results.
- **Introduction:** A basic description of the problem and a statement of the hypothesis.
- **Background:** A history of studies related to the hypothesis and the results of those studies.
- **Materials and Methods:** What did you observe or measure (bones, teeth, fossils, primates, etc.), and how did you measure or observe your subjects?
- **Results:** What were the outcomes of the measurements, observations, statistical tests, and so on?
- **Discussion:** Were you able to falsify your hypothesis? What are your conclusions about the results? In what way(s) would you want to change your research design, materials, methods, and so on to retest the same or modified hypothesis?
- **References:** List previous work or personal correspondence incorporated in your research.

EXERCISE I.1 **NAME** _____ **SECTION** _____ **DATE** _____

The Scientific Method and Critical Thinking

1. Jean-Baptiste Lamarck (1744–1829), a French scientist who believed in evolution, is known for Lamarckism, or inheritance through acquired characteristics. He argued that environmental influences could put pressure on animals, making them use some characteristics more and some less, and that the changes acquired by the parents would be passed to the next generations. A common example of this theory is that giraffes could actually grow longer necks by straining to get to higher and higher branches for food, and that the offspring of these longer-necked giraffes would have longer necks at birth.

    a. Is this argument at the level of a hypothesis, or is it a theory? Why?

    b. How would you set up an experiment to test Lamarck's beliefs?

    c. What would be your dependent variables?

    d. What would be your independent variable?

2. Design an experiment to test which company sells the best tomato seeds (the first thing you must do is to define "best"). Be specific when answering the following questions.

    a. What is your hypothesis?

    b. What are your dependent variables?

    c. What is your independent variable?

3. Is anecdotal evidence the same as scientific evidence? Why or why not?

CHAPTER 1

●

Cellular Genetics

OBJECTIVES

1. What is DNA?

2. How can we use DNA to identify human remains in a plane crash or prove that someone committed a crime?

3. Can evolution really exist?

Before we can answer these questions, we must understand the basic structure and function of DNA and the basics of molecular genetics. We need to know how genetic information is passed from one generation to the next from DNA in either the nucleus or in the mitochondria in a cell.

Scenario: You are an anthropologist who has been asked to take a sample of bone for DNA analysis (for the identification of the individual, or perhaps to obtain DNA from a Neanderthal), and you are asked to do this using "DNA Protocol." What does this mean, why is it important, and what do you have to do to comply with those procedures?

CELL BIOLOGY

A laboratory manual/workbook is not intended to be a detailed textbook regarding all of the interesting facets of genetics, but we certainly must explore the structures of the cell that incorporate DNA into their structure and function because DNA (deoxyribonucleic acid) determines whether an organism is a plant or an animal, what kinds of nutrients it must take from its environment, what kinds of proteins it creates, and so on. The amount of information we can obtain from studying an organism's DNA has increased exponentially in the past few years, and the importance of that information has grown and will continue to grow at a dizzying speed.

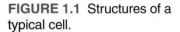

FIGURE 1.1 Structures of a typical cell.

Plasma membrane

Ribosomes

Nucleus

Mitochondria

Cytoplasm

Although DNA is important in all living organisms, we are primarily interested in cells with a nucleus, which include most of the cells of a **eukaryotic** (multi-celled) organism (**prokaryotic** cells are those without a discrete nucleus; e.g., in bacteria). Although we will be primarily interested in structures and events within the nucleus of the cell, some features of the cell and the organelles (small structures within the cell with specific functions) are also important. These include (Figure 1.1) the following:

- **plasma membrane:** The outer surface of the cell that protects the cell from the extracellular environment, but which is selectively permeable to allow some materials into the cell but keep others out.

- **cytoplasm:** The fluid within the cell.

- **mitochondria:** Organelles responsible for the manufacture of energy within the cell. Different cell types have different numbers of mitochondria, depending upon their function. They are located outside of the nucleus, and, interestingly for our discussions, they have their own genome (mitochondrial DNA). As you will see, nuclear DNA is contributed by both parents to the offspring, but mitochondrial DNA is only contributed by the female parent.

- **ribosomes:** Organelles made up of ribosomal RNA (ribonucleic acid) responsible for the translation of the DNA code within the nucleus into specific proteins. As will be discussed later when we explore protein synthesis, messenger RNA (mRNA) is transcribed from a section of DNA within the nucleus, and it takes that protein code to the ribosomes. Transfer RNA (tRNA) recognizes that code and transfers appropriate amino acids to the appropriate location on the mRNA chain.

WITHIN THE NUCLEUS

The nucleus contains **chromosomes**, each of which consists of a series of DNA molecules strung together in long spirals of double strands (called a double helix which might be visualized as sort of a spiral staircase) (see Figure 1.2a–e). Each strand (or **chromatid**) of DNA is composed of smaller molecules (**nucleotides**), each of which is made of one of four chemical bases—**adenine (A), guanine (G), cytosine (C),** or **thymine (T)**—held together with a sugar (deoxyribose) and a phosphate compound (Figure 1.2e and Figure 1.3). A single strand of DNA is held to the other strand in the double helix by hydrogen bonds, but note in the diagram that the molecular shape of the bases are such that adenine can only bind to thymine and cytosine can only bind to guanine. They can be connected in no other way within the nucleus (we will discuss an exception to this rule when the code is carried outside of the nucleus, but within the nucleus, A binds with T and C binds with G).

There are two types of chromosomes in a normal cell: **autosomes** are the chromosomes that carry DNA, which codes for all genetically determined characteristics except for the determination of the sex of the individual. Sex chromosomes (X and Y) determine the sex of the individual (although the presence or absence of only the Y chromosome actually determines sex).

Chromosome numbers vary by species. Most cells in a fruit fly have 8 chromosomes; there are 40 chromosomes in a house mouse, 24 in a tomato, and so on. Every normal human cell that contains a nucleus (except for sperm and ova, which will be explained later) contains 46 chromosomes, which carry all of the genetic information for that cell and, when combined, for the organism. These 46 chromosomes consist of 23 pairs; one of each pair is from the mother and one from the father. These are termed **homologous chromosomes**, meaning that they each carry genetic information for the same trait at the same location (though not necessarily the same specific information for that trait as will be discussed; visit http://learn.genetics.utah.edu/content/begin/traits/karyotype/ for a fun exercise in making karyotypes). Also, information for a single trait may be carried on multiple chromosomes. DNA codes on chromosomes that carry information for the same trait are called alleles. For example, a particular location (**locus**) on each homologous chromosome codes for the condition of earlobe attachment, but one chromosome may carry the genetic code for attached earlobes, and the other chromosome may carry the code for free earlobes. We will discuss this further when we talk about specific genetic traits.

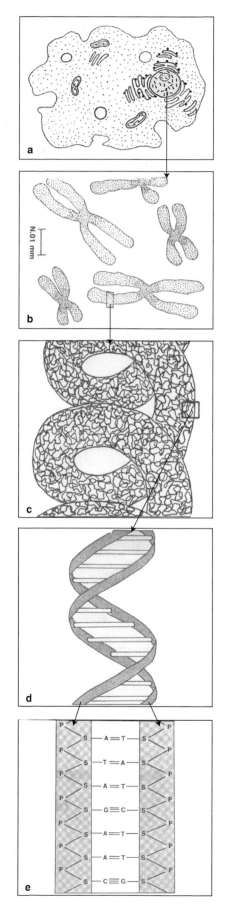

FIGURE 1.2 (a) A generalized cell. Arrow from nucleus; (b) Chromosomes; (c) Closeup of chromosome; (d) Coiled DNA strand; (e) Closeup of single DNA strand showing the base, sugar, and phosphate components of a nucleotide. *Drawing, D. L. France*

FIGURE 1.3 Nucleotides in a DNA double helix.

FIGURE 1.4 Positions of a centromere.

Telocentric (left): centromere at extreme end

Acrocentric (middle): centromere off center

Metacentric (right): centromere in center

FIGURE 1.5 Normal human male karyotype. *Courtesy: National Human Genome Research Institute*

We can look microscopically at the individual chromosomes and match them with their homologues with a **karyotype**. A karyotype is the summary of the chromosomes within a nucleus and is often viewed as an image with the paired chromosomes lined up according to the position of the **centromere** and by size (though to truly be able to recognize the homologues so that they may be paired, a dye is often used to create banding patterns within the chromosomes). A centromere is the place where two sister chromatids are joined together, and its position can vary on the chromosomes (see Figure 1.4).

Notice on the karyotype shown in Figure 1.5 that there are 22 pairs of autosomes and 2 sex chromosomes. In this illustration, there is one X and one Y chromosome, so this karyotype is from a normal male. Karyotyping can also assist in demonstrating abnormal genetic sequences, as we will discuss later.

NUCLEAR DNA REPLICATION

DNA often has to make copies of itself in whole (during cell replication) or in part (during protein synthesis). The specific processes of cell division and protein synthesis will be discussed later, but this is an appropriate location to explore the basic process common to all DNA replication. When DNA replicates or a portion of DNA code is needed for protein synthesis, the hydrogen bonds binding the two strands of DNA are broken by an **enzyme** (**polymerase** and other enzymes control different portions of the replication sequence), and the strands essentially "unzip." These hydrogen bonds were shown earlier as double or triple lines in Figure 1.3. The bases (A, T, C, G) on the single DNA strand attract the bases on free nucleotides within the fluid of the nucleus. Those free nucleotides attach themselves to the appropriate loci of the original (now unzipped) DNA chain (Figure 1.6). Just as in the original DNA chains, adenine can only attach itself to thymine, and cytosine can only attach itself to guanine. Each original single strand of DNA has now paired with a new strand of DNA (called chromatids), and there are twice as many DNA strands in the nucleus. At this point in humans, there are now copies of 46 chromosomes, or 92 chromatids. The cell can now divide, with each new cell receiving one of the two replicas of the chain. As will be discussed later, this process is important in many practical applications involving DNA (such as DNA typing).

Enzyme is a protein that accelerates a specific chemical reaction in a living system.

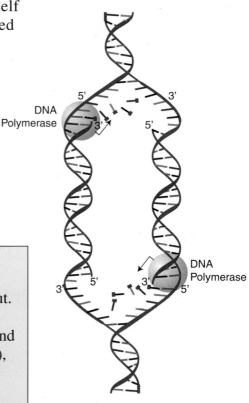

FIGURE 1.6 DNA replication. *Courtesy: National Human Genome Research Institute*

THE HUMAN GENOME PROJECT

www.ornl.gov/sci/techresources/Human_Genome/project/about.shtml
The Human Genome Project was initiated in 1990 to identify and map all of the genes in humans (approximately 20,000–25,000), and to determine the base pair sequences of DNA. Throughout the first two chapters of the book, you will see results from this extraordinary mapping project. Visit the link provided to explore the human genome.

TERMINOLOGY

Allele: Alternative forms of a gene. For example, if the genotype of an individual is Pp for the trait of PTC tasting (see page 39 in Chapter 2), it contains two alleles determining this trait: P and p, one allele for PTC tasting, one for nontasting.

Autosomes: Chromosomes that carry DNA for all characteristics except for the sex of the individual.

Bases: Part of a nucleotide held together with a sugar and a phosphate compound. The bases make up the DNA and RNA chains. DNA bases are adenine, guanine, cytosine, and thymine. RNA bases are adenine, guanine, cytosine, and uracil.

Centromere: The place where two sister chromatids are joined.

Chromatid: One of two identical copies of DNA comprising a replicated chromosome.

Codominant Alleles: Alleles that, when paired in an organism, are both expressed.

Cytoplasm: The fluid within the cell.

Dominant Allele: An allele that is phenotypically expressed in the heterozygote and that prevents the expression of the recessive allele (i.e., masks recessive alleles phenotypically). A dominant allele is written in uppercase letters.

Gene: That section of DNA that defines the specific code for a series of amino acids making up a protein or a part of a protein.

Gene Pool: The total complement of genes in a population.

Genome: A complete set of chromosomes (and genes).

Genotype: All of the genetic information contained in an organism. The genetic constitution (gene makeup) of an organism.

Heterozygote: An organism with unlike members of any given pair or series of alleles at a particular locus. Consequently, this individual produces more than one type of gamete (e.g., Aa or Bb).

Homologous Chromsomes: Carry genetc information for the same trait at the same location.

Homozygote: An organism whose chromosomes carry identical members of a given pair of alleles. The gametes are therefore all alike with respect to this locus. For example, a gamete with the genotypes AA or BB or aa carries only one type of allele for each locus.

Karyotype: The summary of the chromosomes within a nucleus often viewed as an image.

Mitochondria: Organelles within the cytoplasm responsible for energy manufacture within the cell.

Phenotype: Characteristic (or combination of characteristics) of an individual visually observed or discernible by other means; for example, tallness in garden peas or color blindness or blood type in humans. Individuals of the same phenotype appear alike but may not have offspring of the same phenotype because the offspring may have different genotypes.

Plasma Membrane: Outer surface of the cell.

Recessive Allele: An allele that is not expressed when paired with a dominant allele. A recessive allele is written in lowercase letters.

Ribosomes: Organelles made of ribosomal RNA (ribonucleic acid) responsible for protein synthesis.

Sex Chromosomes: Determine the sex of the individual.

Trait: A distinguishing characteristic or quality of a phenotype (i.e., hair color, blood type, eye color, etc.).

MITOSIS

When a cell divides, the DNA must make full copies of itself so that each new cell receives a full complement of the genetic code.

Mitosis is a process of cell replication and division in which two daughter cells, each with a full complement (46 chromosomes in 23 pairs in humans) of genetic information, are produced from a parent cell with a full complement of genetic information as described in the "DNA Replication" section earlier. The cells from this division therefore carry information identical (if there are no mutations) to that of the parent cell. Most of the cells in the body replicate throughout life by this process. Because of this process, bones grow in a developing child, and skin heals itself after a cut.

We are not concerned with describing in detail the different phases of mitosis (interphase, prophase, metaphase, anaphase, and telophase) or meiosis in this book, as the individual phases are not as important in this level of discussion as is the knowledge of the outcome.

As cell division proceeds, the chromatids line up along the "equator" of the nucleus, and the chromatids separate as cell division occurs. As the cell divides, the chromatids move away from each other, each to a different resultant cell, which now contains 46 chromosomes, still in 23 pairs. For a schematic diagram, see Figure 1.7a.

REMEMBER: In mitosis, the cells resulting from cell division carry exactly the same genetic information as the parent cell (as long as there are no mutations).

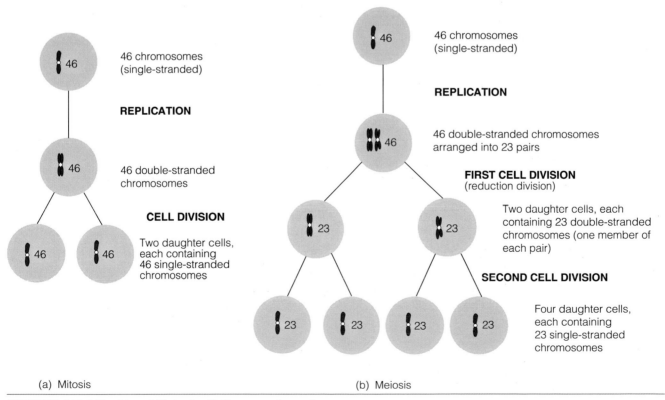

(a) Mitosis

46 chromosomes (single-stranded)

REPLICATION

46 double-stranded chromosomes

CELL DIVISION

Two daughter cells, each containing 46 single-stranded chromosomes

(b) Meiosis

46 chromosomes (single-stranded)

REPLICATION

46 double-stranded chromosomes arranged into 23 pairs

FIRST CELL DIVISION (reduction division)

Two daughter cells, each containing 23 double-stranded chromosomes (one member of each pair)

SECOND CELL DIVISION

Four daughter cells, each containing 23 single-stranded chromosomes

FIGURE 1.7 Mitosis and Meiosis. © Cengage Learning

Gamete: sex cells (sperm or ova) that contain half of the number of chromosomes of the adult of that species.

MEIOSIS

Certain cells participate in the reproduction of the individual by a process of **meiosis,** which creates sex cells, or **gametes** (sperm or ova). Meiosis is the method by which sexually reproducing organisms transfer genetic information through generations; it is therefore important in our discussions of evolution.

The first cell division in meiosis undergoes chromosomal duplication in a manner different from that in mitosis, but it still results in twice the number of chromosomes of a normal cell. After duplication, each set of paired homologous chromosomes (each with two chromatids) lines up along the equator of the nucleus (this is when crossing over or recombination can occur, a process that will be discussed later). As the cell undergoes the first division, each member of a paired homologue segregates (separates) into its own daughter cell. After the first division, then, each daughter cell contains one of the homologous chromosomes, but each of these has two chromatids. Each of the daughter cells, in addition, contains only half of the genetic information that had been contained in the parent cell; hence, this first division is also called reduction division.

The 2 daughter cells next undergo a second mitosis-like division in which the 2 chromatids of each of the 23 chromosomes separate into 2 daughter cells. At the end of this division, then, each of 4 gametes, or sex cells, contains 1 copy of 1 chromosome from the original pair. In other words, each still contains half of the genetic information originally contained within the parent cell, and contains only 1 copy of each of 23 chromosomes (Figure 1.7b).

This sequence in meiosis is typical of spermatogenesis, in that for each meiotic cell division, four sperm are formed. During the first division of oogenesis, however, only one viable, functional cell is produced, and that cell in turn produces only one viable, functional cell after the second division. The other nonviable cells are called polar bodies and give up their cytoplasm (future nutrition for the fertilized zygote) to the one viable cell. The end result of oogenesis, then, is one gamete, the egg, which still has only half of the genetic information of the parent cell (as in spermatogenesis) but which is very much larger than a sperm cell.

Why must the gametes contain only half of the genetic information of an adult body cell? In most cases a "double dose" of DNA in a zygote is lethal. During fertilization of the egg by the sperm, the sperm injects its nuclear genetic information into the egg. That egg now contains half of its genetic information for any trait (except for sex-linked traits, as will be discussed later) from the father and half from the mother. Each half is in the form of one of the homologous chromosomes.

REMEMBER: In meiosis, each daughter cell carries half of the genetic information of the parent cell.

Sometimes chromosomes fail to separate appropriately during meiosis, and that causes problems due to an abnormal number of chromosomes in the fetus. This **nondisjunction** can result in only one of a pair of chromosomes (called **monosomy**) or three chromosomes (**trisomy**).

- Trisomy 21 (formerly called Down Syndrome) is caused when the fetus receives three copies of chromosome 21.

- Monosomy X (Turner Syndrome) occurs in females with only one X chromosome. Most females with Monosomy X die before birth, but if they survive, they are sterile and usually have skeletal deformities and heart and kidney problems.

- Trisomy X occurs in females with an extra X chromosome, although they often appear relatively normal. Males who inherit an extra X chromosome (Klinefelter Syndrome) sometimes show some breast development and reduced testicular development by puberty. They exhibit reduced fertility and sometimes mental retardation.

- Trisomy 13 (Patau Syndrome) have an extra chromosome 13, which causes severe skeletal and organ problems. They are profoundly mentally retarded and usually die at a relatively early age.

EXERCISE 1.1   NAME _____   SECTION _____   DATE _____

Cellular Genetics

1. The following sequence of bases is found on one strand of DNA. What is the sequence of bases of the other DNA strand?

    A A C G T T C C G
    T T G C A A G G C

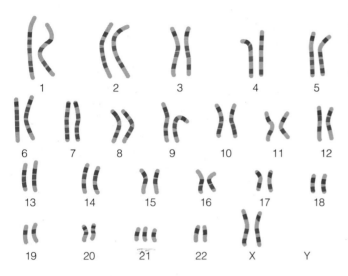

FIGURE 1.8 Karyotype for Question 2.
Courtesy: National Human Genome Research Institute

2. Figure 1.5, shown earlier, illustrates the karyotype of a normal human male. In Figure 1.8, identify the autosomes and the sex chromosomes.

    a. Is this a male or a female?

    b. This is an abnormal genetic sequence. What is abnormal about it?

        3   21st   chromosome

    c. Can you diagnose the syndrome?

        Down Syndrome

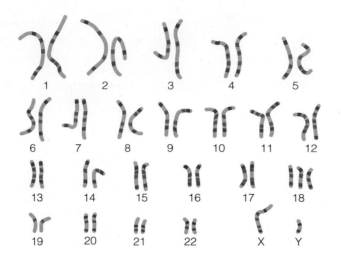

FIGURE 1.9 Karyotype for Question 3.
Courtesy: National Human Genome Research Institute

3. Figure 1.9 is also an abnormal karyotype.

   a. Is this a male or a female?

   b. What is abnormal about this sequence?

   3 of 18

   c. Research this abnormality on the Internet and identify the syndrome as well as its consequences.

   Edwards syndrome

SOURCES OF VARIABILITY

Variability in the genetic code can be at the level of the nucleotides and also at the level of the chromosomes. Before and during the first division of meiosis, several events can occur that can alter the genetic configuration of the gametes and, therefore, potentially alter the evolutionary outcome in a population. Most mutations are deleterious or even lethal, but many are neutral or seemingly neutral (i.e., they will not alter the selected advantages of the individual). For example, a point mutation occurring during meiosis changes the genetic code in the sperm or egg. If that mutation changes a base to another base in an area responsible for protein synthesis, and if the resulting code no longer results in a protein required by the body, then that mutation may be lethal or deletcrious. If that mutation changes the base code from ACA to ACG (guanine is substituted for adenine), the resultant amino acid, cysteine, is the same (see Table 1.1, Amino Acid List), so the mutation may have no natural selection advantage or disadvantage. Mutations that appear to be neutral under one set of environmental circumstances, however, may prove to be beneficial or maladaptive under others. Hence, if an environmental change occurs, a neutral mutation is subjected to different selective pressures and may consequently confer advantage or disadvantage to its carrier.

A point mutation alters one base in a nucleotide.

Chromosome-Level Variation

During the first division, paired homologous chromosomes may exchange genetic material. This exchange, recombination or crossing over, occurs when the chromosomes are arranged in pairs and after they have duplicated themselves (when there are four DNA strands). Before cell division, the "sister" molecules may exchange sections of DNA (Figure 1.10). In addition to recombination, chromosomes can be changed by the deletion, duplication, insertion, or other changes of sections of chromosomes (Figure 1.11). This may alter the specific information carried on a chromosome for a particular trait and can greatly increase the variation of information carried in the gametes.

PROTEIN SYNTHESIS

The DNA in the nucleus of the cell is responsible for more than cell replication in mitosis and gamete formation in meiosis. It is also responsible for providing the blueprint for protein synthesis, which actually occurs outside the cell in small organelles called **ribosomes**. Proteins can be typical structural proteins, enzymes, and hormones, and all are made of smaller molecules called amino acids, which are defined by three bases, or triplets (remember, the bases are adenine, guanine, cytosine, and thymine). Because this synthesis occurs outside of the nucleus, there has to be a way to get the codes from the

Table 1.1   Amino Acids List

DNA Triplets	mRNA Codons	Amino Acid	
ACA, ACG	UGU, UGC	Cysteine	
AAT, AAC	UUA, UUG	Leucine	
AAA, AAG	UUU, UUC	Phenylalanine	Essential
AGA, AGG, AGT, AGC	UCU, UCC, UCA, UCG	Serine	
ACC	UGG	Tryptophan	Essential
ATA, ATG	UAU, UAC	Tyrosine	
CGA, CGG, CGT, CGC	GCU, GCC, GCA, GCG	Alanine	
CTA, CTG	GAU, GAC	Aspartic Acid	
CTT, CTC	GAA, GAG	Glutamic Acid	
CCA, CCG, CCT, CCC	GGU, GGC, GGA, GGG	Glycine	
CAA, CAG, CAT, CAC	GUU, GUC, GUA, GUG	Valine	Essential
GCA, GCG, GCT, GCC	CGU, CGC, CGA, CGG	Arginine	
GTT, GTC	CAA, CAG	Glutamine	
GTA, GTG	CAU, CAC	Histidine	Essential
GGA, GGG, GGT, GGC	CCU, CCC, CCA, CCG	Proline	
GAA, GAG, GAT, GAC	CUU, CUC, CUA, CUG	Leucine	Essential
TTA, TTG	AAU, AAC	Asparagine	
TAA, TAG, TAT	AUU, AUG, AUA	Isoleucine	Essential
TTT, TTC	AAA, AAG	Lysine	Essential
TAC	AUG	Methionine	Essential (usually a start codon)
TCT, TCC	AGA, AGG	Arginine	
TCA, TCG	AGU, AGC	Serine	
TGA, TGG, TGT, TGC	ACU, ACC, ACA, ACG	Threonine	Essential
ATT, ATC, ACT	UAA, UAG, UGA	Terminating triplets	

nucleus to the ribosomes, and that is the job of the messenger RNA (mRNA) (see Figure 1.12). The nuclear DNA unzips (in a way similar to mitosis, though it is called transcription because it "transcribes" the codes), and the bases of the mRNA join with the particular segment of the DNA strand that codes for the prescribed amino acid. The mRNA consists of the bases adenine, guanine, cytosine, and *uracil* (uracil binds with adenine in place of thymine). The strands of mRNA then pass through the nuclear wall and translate the "message" from the nuclear DNA to the ribosome. Only a very small percentage of the

DNA in the nucleus codes for proteins or parts of proteins (these areas are called exons in the DNA and in the RNA molecules). There are areas on the DNA strand that do not code for proteins (called introns); if the mRNA strand "reads" an intron, it will snip it out before leaving the nucleus (see Strachan and Read, 2004). A different RNA—transfer RNA (tRNA)—actually builds the proteins in amino acid blocks. Of the 20 amino acids that exist, 12 are produced by the human body, but 8 (called "essential" amino acids) cannot be directly manufactured by the body. Those amino acids must be obtained from food (this is why vegetarians must be careful to augment their diet with foods that contain those essential amino acids that would readily be supplied in a diet that contains meat).

Specific proteins are created from specific amino acids, and those amino acids are produced according to the code on the DNA strand (and ultimately on the different RNA strands). The codes for each amino acid consist of three bases (called **triplets** on the DNA chain and **codons** on the mRNA chains); however, for some amino acids, there can be several base triplet codes that can code for one amino acid. Likewise, although it has been thought that a specific codon would code for only one amino acid, new research suggests that under certain circumstances, a codon may actually be able to code for more than one amino acid (Turanov et al., 2009).

FIGURE 1.10 Recombination at crossover.

FIGURE 1.11 Types of mutation at the chromosome level. *Courtesy: National Human Genome Research Institute*

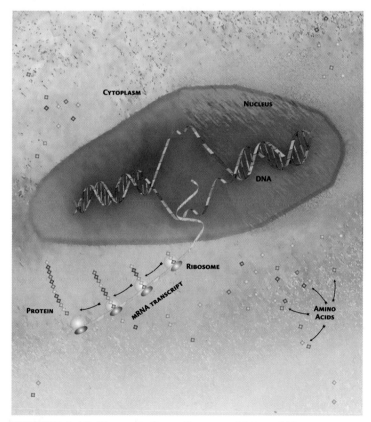

FIGURE 1.12 Transcription. *Courtesy: National Human Genome Research Institute*

In addition to encoding for proteins, parts of the DNA strand may code for the starting and ending point for coding specific base sequences. Other sections of the DNA strand are responsible for regulating the expression of other genes elsewhere in the DNA sequence, in other areas of our bodies, or at different times of our lives. Likewise, only a portion of the RNA in a cell is directly involved in the production of proteins (other RNA molecules are involved in diverse functions in the cells). DNA codes and the proteins produced are extremely conservative, such that the basic sequences for protein synthesis and regulatory genes are basically the same from bacteria to humans (Turanov et al., 2009), which is an important consideration in the analysis of evolutionary relationships.

MITOCHONDRIAL DNA

Mitochondrial DNA (refer to Figures 1.1 and 1.2) is found outside the nucleus of the cell in its own structures (mitochondria; sing.: mitochondrium). The mitochondrial DNA (mtDNA) takes the nutrients we eat and produces energy for the cell. The mtDNA does not divide during meiosis and is not carried by the sperm to the egg during reproduction (only nuclear DNA is injected into the egg). Because of this, all mtDNA passed from generation to generation is the DNA from the female (even that mtDNA in the son's cells), and that mtDNA is an exact copy (barring mutations) from the mother. This form of DNA has become important in discussions about evolution and in the investigation of identity in modern forensic cases. It will be discussed later.

EXERCISE 1.2   NAME _____   SECTION _____   DATE _____

Sources of Variability

1. If a point mutation occurred so that adenine was changed to thymine in the amino acid triplet code CTA, what would the resulting amino acid be?   *Glutamic Acid   CTT*

2. If a point mutation occurred so that thymine was changed to cytosine in the amino acid triplet code TTT, what would the resulting amino acid be?
   TTC   Lysine

3. What is the complementary DNA code for the following base sequence (from a section of DNA)?

   T A C G G G C C G G A A T A A A A G A T G T T G A A
   A T G C C C G G C C T T A T T T T C T A C A A C T T

   T G G T
   A C C A

   b. What is the complementary mRNA code?
      Change all T to U

   c. What is the tRNA code for this sequence?
      Flip of mRNA

4. There are 5,247 base pairs that code for a type of human collagen found in skeletal tissue, located on chromosome 7 (International Human Genome Sequencing Consortium, 2004). If there are significant changes to the normal code for this collagen, it may result in problems with skeletal development. Part of the protein sequence for this code is the following:

ATGCCCGGCC TTATTTTCTA CAACTTTGGT AACTTTAGCA TATACCCCAA

ATCTGTAAGA

Fill out the following table containing the first 10 codes:

DNA	Complementary DNA Triplet Code	mRNA Code	tRNA Code	Amino Acid
ATG	TAC	UAC	AUG	methionine
CCC	GGG	GGG	CCC	proline
GGC	CCG	CCG	GGC	glycine
CTT	GAA	GAA	CUU	leucine
ATT	TAA	UAA	AUU	isoleucine
TTC	AAG	AAG	UUC	phenylalanine
TAC	ATG	AUG	UAC	tyrosine
AAC	TTG	UUG	AAC	asparagine
TTT	AAA	AAA	UUU	phenylalanine
GGT	CCA	CCA	GGU	glycine

DNA TESTING AND TYPING

DNA is found in body fluids (blood, saliva, urine, and semen), soft tissues, bone, teeth, nails, hair roots (nuclear DNA), and hair shafts (mtDNA; see Figure 1.13). Nuclear DNA consists of approximately 3 billion base pairs and is unique between individuals (except identical twins); therefore, it is widely used to identify unidentified human remains. It is also widely used to link trace evidence to individuals and crime scenes, identify victims of mass fatality incidents, and even to identify historical figures, although high temperature, humidity and bacterial activity can degrade the quality of the DNA. DNA typing has been used in the medical arena for years, tracing mutated genes in families with genetic diseases, and now that the Human Genome Project has mapped the entire human genome, the loci of genes controlling other diseases are being researched. DNA typing has even been used in the plant and animal sciences for species identification.

Even though the Human Genome Project has mapped the entire genome, it is currently too expensive and cumbersome to use the entire nuclear DNA sequence to perform DNA testing, but that isn't necessary anyway. There are certain segments of nuclear DNA that vary so much between individuals (again, except for identical twins) that the likelihood of matching sequences between any two individuals on earth is almost nonexistent. The practical difficulties have always been to identify and isolate those segments in a particular DNA sample and to have a large enough sample of those segments to type.

The first technology that overcame most of these practical difficulties and was useful for human identification was restriction-fragment–length polymorphism (RFLP), introduced by Alec Jeffreys

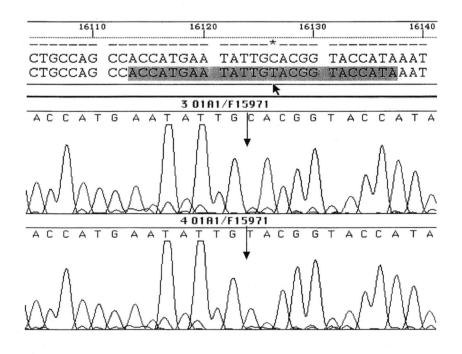

FIGURE 1.13 Mitochondrial DNA sequence analysis. Notice that one allele in the sample (highlighted) is different from the reference sample above it. The reference sample contains a cytosine base at the same location as the thymine base below. *Source: Courtesy of Demris Lee*

in 1984. It is used only for nuclear DNA tests. The DNA is cut with restriction enzymes, which are proteins that bind to and cut DNA at specific sites dictated by the sequence of base pairs there. The restriction enzyme will cut the chromosomal DNA only at a particular base-pair sequence, wherever that sequence occurs, so that different individuals will show different lengths of these chains of DNA, depending on where the base pairs occur. This technique requires a large amount of DNA for sampling, however, so it is usually not suitable for highly degraded samples or for very small samples.

The polymerase chain reaction (PCR), invented by Kary Mullis in 1986, revolutionized DNA analysis. Three main steps occur in PCR analysis: (1) denaturation, in which the two strands of the double helix are separated so that each strand can be used as a template for synthesis of a new strand; (2) annealing, in which primers (short segments of synthetic DNA) bind to the template DNA strands; and (3) extension, in which nucleotides or bases are added to the growing strand of newly synthesized DNA. The three steps are repeated until millions of copies of DNA are created, such that PCR can be used on specimens that were once considered too small or degraded for DNA analysis. There are different types of analyses of the resultant DNA "soup" (DQA1 and Polymarker systems), but the amplified fragment-length polymorphism (AmpFLP) system is becoming more widely used because of its power to discriminate between different samples and because of the small sample sizes needed for analysis. "Touch DNA" is a type of PCR process whereby only a few cells are needed to synthesize enough DNA for typing.

AmpFLPs are similar to RFLPs in that differences are detected based on the length of the DNA segment. Throughout the human genome, there are stretches of DNA sequences that are repeated over and over. These repetitive sequences are commonly known as variable number of tandem repeats (VNTR). These can be divided into two categories: long tandem repeats (LTRs) or short tandem repeats (STRs). These are distinguished according to the number of base pairs that repeat in a series. LTRs have a large number of repeating base pairs (usually more than seven), while STRs have between three and seven repeating units. If several of these analyses are performed simultaneously for different stretches of DNA sequences, the power to discriminate between individuals can exceed the world's population.

In Figure 1.14, a particular DNA sequence of base pairs was repeated three times in Individual 1, four times in Individual 2, and so forth. This segment of DNA is therefore of different lengths in these different individuals. When the segment is labeled with a radioactive substance and submitted to electrophoresis, bands develop on the gel strip. The largest DNA segment is at the top of the strip, and the shortest at the bottom. Electrophoresis is a technique in which a gel is subjected to an electric charge. The molecules (of DNA, in this case) will move a distance across that electrically

FIGURE 1.14 Variable number of tandem repeats (VNTR) samples from four individuals.

charged gel according to their size (molecules in general will move a distance determined by characteristics other than their size).

In Figure 1.15, an unknown sample (U) from four different DNA locations is compared with two known individuals. Note that there are two bands for each sample, denoting one DNA segment length from the mother, and one from the father. If there is only one band, the segment lengths from the mother and father are the same. In this example, S_2 matches the unknown sample and cannot be excluded from further consideration.

The gel used in electrophoresis is either a gelatin made from seaweed, or a compound also used to make soft contact lenses.

Mitochondrial DNA Typing

The mitochondrial genome is a circular double-stranded molecule consisting of approximately 16,500 base pairs. Most of the differences between individuals are found in the control region, which is the region in the DNA strand that controls the actions of the rest of that region. Instead of two copies, as with nuclear DNA, there are hundreds to thousands of copies of mitochondrial DNA per cell. This is advantageous for typing highly degraded samples (refer to Figure 1.13 for an example of how a base pair can differ in the sequence of DNA). In fact, even samples as old and degraded as Neanderthal bones have been typed using mitochondrial DNA. As was stated previously, mitochondrial DNA is maternally inherited, so, assuming mutations have not occurred, all maternal relatives will have the identical mitochondrial DNA sequence.

Similarly, Y chromosomes are only inherited by males in a family. These, too, have the potential to be typed.

The Present and Future of DNA Typing

There is no doubt that DNA typing is a powerful investigative tool, but at present, there is a tendency to overstate its power. Note that to use

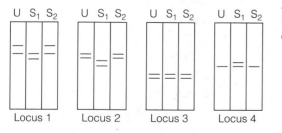

FIGURE 1.15 Unknown "U" compared with two samples.

DNA typing, a reference sample must first be obtained. There is no benefit in typing an unknown fragment of tissue or blood stain if there is no person with whom to compare the sample (except to hold the unknown sample until there is a reference). There is at present no mass DNA reference collection, as there is for fingerprints, for example, although since 1994 all states in the U.S. are required to send DNA samples from many violent criminals after they have been convicted of the crime. The database CODIS (Combined DNA Index System) is searched when unknown DNA is recovered from a crime scene, and if no match is immediately made, it is stored for future comparisons.

DNA "fingerprinting" is increasingly being used to identify the victims of mass fatality incidents, such as victims of a plane crash; the victims of the 9-11 terrorist acts in Washington, DC, New York City, and Pennsylvania; and the victims of Hurricane Katrina. A decision was made early in the recovery process in New York City after 9-11 to take DNA samples from all remains recovered from "Ground Zero" and to have them analyzed to compare to family members or to objects known to have been used only by the victim (such as a toothbrush, chewing gum, etc.). As stated earlier, we must remember that DNA typing is not useful in all situations (e.g., if the remains are badly burned in a plane crash, thereby destroying the DNA). In these situations, family members demand the "best technology" (i.e., DNA typing) for their deceased relatives even when that technology is not practical or possible. In those situations, it is sometimes difficult to convince the public that the "low-tech" means of identification, such as those discussed in Chapter 15, are the most appropriate.

Significant contributions to the discussion of DNA were made by:
Demris A. Lee, Technical Leader
Armed Forces DNA Identification Laboratory

In 1918, after being held captive by the Bolsheviks in the Ipatiev House in Yekaterinburg, Russia, the seven members of the Czar Nicholas II family and four members of his entourage (including his doctor and a maid) were taken to the basement of that farmer's house and killed. In 1991, the Russian government ordered the exhumation of the family members and entourage of the Russian royal family of Czar Nicholas II from a grave outside of Yekaterinburg, where the remains of all but two of the family were finally discovered. The questions before the experts were the following: Are these the remains of the Russian royal family and entourage, and, because two were missing, what members of the family were represented by the remains? No antemortem (before death) dental records or radiographs (x-rays) were available, so the most promising way to identify the skeletons was through comparison of the DNA, but to whom?

The Czar's wife, Czarina Alexandra, was related to Prince Philip, the husband of England's Queen Elizabeth II, in that Prince Philip's maternal grandmother was the Czarina's sister. By testing, the researchers discovered that the mitochondrial DNA from the Czar's wife and daughters was a match to the DNA from Prince Philip (this information is used to answer questions later in the chapter).

The identification process for some of the individuals within the family will be explored in Chapter 15.

EXERCISE 1.3   NAME _____   SECTION _____   DATE _____

DNA Typing

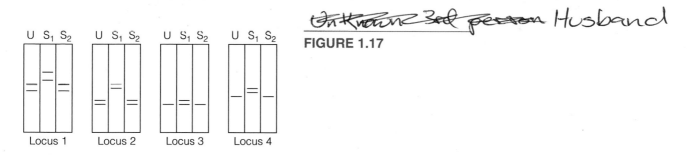

Match? Woman to gate

FIGURE 1.16

1.   In Figure 1.16, blood samples are taken from a gate (U), an injured woman (S_1), and her former husband (S_2). The woman claimed that she was attacked by her former husband. The man had a cut on his hand, which he explained as a cut from a broken water glass. Is the unknown sample from her wound, from her former husband, or from an unknown third person?

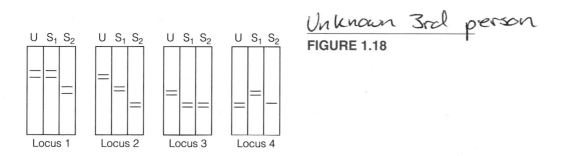

~~Unknown 3rd person~~ Husband

FIGURE 1.17

2.   From the same case, a second blood sample was collected from a stain on the floor of the former husband's home (Figure 1.17). Is this stain from the woman, her former husband, or an unknown third person?

Unknown 3rd person

FIGURE 1.18

3.   A third blood sample was collected from a knife in the alley two blocks from the woman's home (Figure 1.18). Is this stain from the woman, her former husband, or an unknown third person?

4. What do the preceding tests tell you about the case?

Missing evidence & the woman was not attacked by her husband

5. Refer to the text box about identifying the remains of the Russian royal family earlier in this chapter. What kind of DNA was used to identify the Czar's family's remains? Why was it possible?

Prince Philip's mitochondrial DNA

6. Would it have been possible to identify which of the Czar's daughters was which by using DNA? Why or why not?

No. Because they have the same mom their mitochondrial DNA is identical

TALKING POINTS

- Now that the Human Genome Project has successfully mapped the human genome, there are debates about what to do with the information that now can be obtained about a person's DNA.

  What is your opinion about the following scenarios and why (most of these have actually been suggested by lawmakers and/or insurance companies)?

  - Individuals *convicted* of a felony (homicide, rape, etc.) should have their DNA on file to link them to past and future criminal activity.

  - Individuals *arrested* for a felony should have their DNA on file to link them to past and future criminal activity.

  - Everyone should have their genome mapped.
    - So that health or life insurance companies can analyze the risk of insuring that individual
    - For identification purposes in mass fatality incidents (plane crashes, etc.)
- Because the technology is available to perform DNA typing for identification purposes in a mass fatality incident, every element (bodies or body parts, skeletons or skeletal elements and fragments) should be typed, regardless of the cost.
  - Should the families of the victims make the decision about how much money should be spent to identify everyone in a mass fatality incident, or should the medical examiner make that decision? At what point do you draw the line on the amount of money being spent (thousands? tens of thousands? hundreds of thousands?—the costs can easily reach these points in a large disaster).

CHAPTER 2

●

Population Genetics

OBJECTIVES

1. How does your genetic code express itself in your physical characteristics?

2. How do genetic counselors use these physical characteristics to advise their clients about the genetics of children they may have?

3. How can we determine that evolution is occurring in a population?

In the previous chapter, you studied genetics at the cellular level. You saw how mutations in one base in a nucleotide chain can alter codes for amino acids and proteins. You also explored different kinds of mutations at the chromosome level and how those can have an effect on the individual. You learned how DNA typing can be possible through an understanding of cellular genetics.

In this chapter, you will explore genetics at the individual and population levels and discuss how evolution at a larger scale can occur. You will explore your own genetic codes for certain traits based on how those traits are visibly expressed and learn how to trace the genes and gene frequencies through several generations.

GREGOR MENDEL

Gregor Mendel was an Augustine monk who was born in 1822 in Moravia (the southeastern part of Czechoslovakia). He was interested in the characteristics of plants and animals and how those characteristics would be inherited through the generations. At the time he was doing his research, Jean-Baptiste Lamarck proposed a theory of evolution in which characteristics acquired by the parents are inherited by the offspring. A different theory of evolution stated that characteristics of the parents would be blended in the offspring. Mendel's most famous experiments involved pollinating pea plants with, for example, gray and round seeds with plants with white and wrinkled seeds to determine whether or not the resulting "daughter" seeds were a blend of the colors and smoothness of the parent generation (which would be expected if Lamarck's theories were correct). In fact, Mendel discovered that there was no blending. He found that a certain percentage of the offspring had wrinkled peas and a certain percentage had round peas. Through experimentation and mathematical calculations, he developed his principles concerning segregation and independent assortment—the principles we use today. Even though his work did not become well known until after his death, he is still considered an important figure in modern genetics. For more information, research the many important works about Gregor Mendel.

PRINCIPLES OF INHERITANCE

We return to the discussion of gamete production in meiosis to understand how traits are passed from one generation to the next. The key to understanding the principles of inheritance resides in remembering Gregor Mendel's **Principle of Segregation** and the **Principle of Independent Assortment**. Remember that during meiosis, or the formation of gametes (sex cells), the number of chromosomes in a cell is reduced from 46 to 23 (see Chapter 1). Each pair of chromosomes thus separates, and one chromosome goes to one gamete while the other goes to the other gamete. With the separation of chromosomes, the alleles on those chromosomes also separate.

This is essentially Mendel's Principle of Segregation, that during meiosis the alleles separate. The Principle of Independent Assortment states that the members of different pairs of alleles assort independently into gametes. Obviously, these principles are true *only* if the alleles in question are on separate chromosomes, so we will assume this fact in all of the following examples and exercises.

TERMINOLOGY

Allele: Alternative forms of a gene. For example, if the genotype of an individual is Pp for the trait of PTC tasting (see page 39), it contains two alleles determining this trait: P and p, one allele for PTC tasting, and one for nontasting.

Autosomes: Chromosomes that carry DNA for all characteristics except for the sex of the individual.

Chromatid: One of two identical copies of DNA comprising a replicated chromosome.

Codominant Alleles: Alleles that are both expressed when paired in an organism.

Dominant Allele: An allele that is phenotypically expressed in the heterozygote and that prevents the expression of the recessive allele (i.e., masks recessive alleles phenotypically). A dominant allele is written in uppercase letters.

Gene: That section of DNA that defines the specific code for a series of amino acids making up a protein or a part of a protein.

Gene Pool: The total complement of genes in a population.

Genome: A complete set of chromosomes (and genes).

Genotype: All of the genetic information contained in an organism; the genetic constitution (gene makeup) of an organism.

Heterozygote: An organism with unlike members of any given pair or series of alleles at a particular locus. Consequently, this individual produces more than one type of gamete (e.g., Aa or Bb).

Homologous Chromosomes: Carry genetic information for the same trait at the same location.

Homozygote: An organism whose chromosomes carry identical members of a given pair of alleles. The gametes are therefore all alike with respect to this locus. For example, a gamete with the genotypes AA or BB or aa carries only one type of allele for each locus.

Phenotype: Characteristic (or combination of characteristics) of an individual visually observed or discernible by other means; for example, tallness in garden peas or color blindness or blood type in humans. Individuals of the same phenotype appear alike but may not have offspring of the same phenotype because the offspring may have different genotypes.

Principle of Independent Assortment: Paired chromosomes and the alleles on those chromosomes separate into gametes independently of one another. For example, the way in which the genetic information on chromosome #1 separates into gametes has no influence on how the genetic information on chromosome #3 separates into gametes.

Principle of Segregation: During meiosis, paired chromosomes (and therefore alleles) separate into different gametes.

Recessive Allele: An allele that is not expressed when paired with a dominant allele. A recessive allele is written in lowercase letters.

Sex Chromosomes: Determine the sex of the individual.

Trait: A distinguishing characteristic or quality of a phenotype (i.e., hair color, blood type, eye color, etc.).

Question: Why do we use uppercase and lowercase letters for alleles?

Answer: To keep track of the alleles under discussion, we must follow certain conventions in terminology. Any symbol can be used to designate the alleles, but the letters A, B, C, and so on, or the first letters of the traits being discussed (e.g., "P" for PTC tasting) are common. The alleles determining the same trait are written together (e.g., PpTt), and the dominant form of the allele is written first. Capital letters designate the dominant form of the allele, and small letters are used for the recessive forms.

Suppose an individual possessed the two alleles Rr for the trait earwax type (we will explore the specific traits later). In the production of sex cells, these two alleles segregate and go into two different gametes:

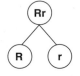

These are the gametes, or sex cells.

If you wanted to determine the genetics of an individual for two different traits, earwax type and PTC tasting, for example, we could say that his genotype is RrPp. The alleles would separate into gametes as follows:

These are the gametes.

This second example uses the Principle of Independent Assortment; that is, regardless of how the alleles for earwax type segregate, the alleles for PTC tasting will segregate independently, so that every combination possible will occur in different gametes.

SAMPLE PROBLEMS

1. An individual with a genotype Aa would create what kinds of gametes?
2. An individual with a genotype AaBb would create what kinds of gametes?
3. An individual with a genotype AaBbCc would create what kinds of gametes?

Answers:

1. The gametes would be

   Aa
   A   a

2. The gametes would be

   AB Ab aB ab

3. The gametes would be

   ABC ABc AbC Abc aBC aBc abC abc

Simple Punnett Square:

	A	a
A	AA	Aa
a	Aa	aa

After you have determined the gametes possible for each individual in your mating pair, it is easy to figure out the results of matings between individuals because you simply put the different gametes into all of the possible combinations. One of the easiest ways to do this is by using the Punnett Square.

HINT: Another method sometimes used to predict the gamete combinations:

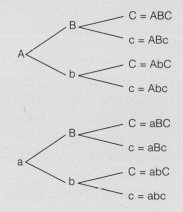

A
├─ B
│ ├─ C = ABC
│ └─ c = ABc
└─ b
   ├─ C = AbC
   └─ c = Abc

a
├─ B
│ ├─ C = aBC
│ └─ c = aBc
└─ b
   ├─ C = abC
   └─ c = abc

Example:

What are the possible outcomes of a mating between individuals AaBb and AaBb? *Hint:* Put the gametes along the top and side of the square and then cross-multiply.

Answer:

The **genotypes** for this cross are:

	AB	Ab	aB	ab
AB	AABB	AABb	AaBB	AaBb
Ab	AABb	AAbb	AaBb	Aabb
aB	AaBB	AaBb	aaBB	aaBb
ab	AaBb	Aabb	aaBb	aabb

The results in this case are shown here:

AABB (1)
AaBB (2)
AABb (2)   There are nine different
AaBb (4)   genotypes for a cross
AAbb (1)   between individuals who
Aabb (2)   are heterozygous for two
aaBB (1)   traits.
aaBb (2)
aabb (1)

What are the **phenotypes** for the preceding cross?

AB(both traits dominant) = 9

Ab = 3

ab (both traits recessive) = 1

Any time you cross two individuals who are heterozygous for two traits, the phenotype ratio will be 9:3:3:1. If you cross two individuals who are heterozygous for three traits, the phenotype ratio will be 27:9:9:9:3:3:3:1 (try it!).

SURVEY OF SOME GENETIC TRAITS

Most phenotypic traits are the results of a combination of effects of heredity and the environment. For example, skin color in an individual is determined to a large extent by genetic and ancestral background but is also affected by the sun and even by diet. A small number of traits have been used traditionally to demonstrate simple Mendelian genetic patterns, although many of these are now known to be affected by much more complex hereditary patterns than once thought. Traits such as tongue rolling and folding (also called "tongue gymnastics"), interlocking fingers and thumbs, and the presence or absence of the palmaris longus tendon are not completely understood but are likely not simply determined by a single allele.

1. **Sickle-cell anemia (S, s)** is a condition in which the red blood cells are sickle-shaped (like a "C") instead of disc-shaped. Hemoglobin is a protein molecule in red blood cells that contains iron, which transports oxygen and carbon dioxide in the blood. In sickle-cell anemia, the hemoglobin and the shape of the red blood cells are abnormal, which causes problems because the cells cannot deliver sufficient oxygen to the tissues and because the abnormal shape of the cells causes them to get stuck in blood vessels. This causes pain in various areas in which these cells get stuck; they can cause a stroke by prohibiting blood flow in areas of the brain, and, in general, the victim suffers from hypoxia (insufficient oxygen). Those individuals with the genotype heterozygous for the sickle trait carry the trait but do not show classic sickle-cell anemia (although under certain conditions, the red blood cells can become sickle-shaped). Those individuals carrying both recessive alleles will show the trait.

Although sickle-cell anemia is a terrible disease, there is an interesting benefit to being heterozygous for the trait. Malaria is caused by a parasitic organism (*P. falciparum*), which is transmitted by mosquitoes. When a mosquito carrying the

FIGURE 2.1 Attached earlobe (recessive). *Photo, D. L. France*

parasite bites a human, the parasite is injected into the human bloodstream and into the red blood cells. The parasite consumes the hemoglobin in a normal red blood cell and ultimately kills the cell. If enough of these red blood cells are destroyed, the victim can die. As we have already discussed, a person with the homozygous genotype for sickle-cell anemia can die of the disease, but if a person who is heterozygous for the sickle-cell trait is injected with the *P. falciparum* parasite, the red blood cells attacked by the parasite become sickle-shaped and cannot support the parasite. Those sickled red blood cells are taken out of the body's circulation. Therefore, people who are heterozygous for the trait are protected against malaria. This is a *balanced polymorphism*, the gene for which is located on chromosome 11.

2. **Earwax Type (R, r):** There are two basic types of earwax: wet and dry. The dry type is frequent in East Asians, while wet earwax is more frequent in other populations around the world. Yoshiura et al. (2006) have demonstrated that the dry earwax occurs with a homozygous recessive state of a gene on chromosome 16 (locus 16q12.1). This trait does seem to be inherited as a simple Mendelian trait. The maps for this trait can be seen at www.ncbi.nlm.nih.gov/mapview/map_search.cgi? taxid=9606&build=current&advsrch=off&query=earwax+ideo gram.

3. **The ability to taste PTC (phenylthiocarbamide or phenylthiourea) (P, p):** This bitter-tasting, synthetic chemical is believed to be an approximation of a naturally occurring substance that is present in plants such as turnips, kale, and Brussels sprouts. Individuals who can taste the chemical are therefore more likely to reject large amounts of those foods and to be less subject to goiter, which is caused by substances contained in these foods (Kitchin et al., 1959). Kim et al. (2003) found a small area on chromosome 7 that accounts for much of the variation in PTC tasting. It is inherited as a dominant. Though this region has been discovered to directly influence PTC tasting, it is unlikely inherited as a simple Mendelian trait. Mangold et al. (2008) have found a connection between the inability to taste PTC and nicotine dependence in African Americans.

4. **Earlobes (E, e):** Attached earlobes are characterized by the attachment of the lower part of the lobe to the skin of the head (Figure 2.1), whereas free-hanging lobes are not attached (Figure 2.2). The attached earlobe is inherited as a recessive.

5. **Darwin's tubercle (D, d):** This is a projection on the helix of the ear, or a pointed thickening of the cartilage of the ear

FIGURE 2.2 Free-hanging earlobes (dominant). *Photo, D. L. France*

FIGURE 2.3 Darwin's tubercle (dominant). *Photo, D. L. France*

FIGURE 2.4 Hitchiker's thumb (recessive). *Photo, D. L. France*

FIGURE 2.5 Hair whorl direction. *Photo, D. L. France*

(Figure 2.3). The size of the projection varies, and it may be seen only on one of the ears. This trait is inherited as a dominant.

6. **Hitchhiker's thumb (T, t):** If, in the hitchhiker's position (Figure 2.4), one can bend the thumb back at an angle of 50 degrees or greater, one has inherited the trait as a recessive.

7. **Hair whorl (H, h):** Observe this trait while standing behind and above an individual: a hair pattern that whorls clockwise is dominant, whereas a counterclockwise whorl is inherited as a recessive (Figure 2.5). Interestingly, Klar (2003) found a connection between handedness and hair whorl rotation (and believes that it is caused by a gene at a single locus). He found that nonright-handers (left and ambidextrous) displayed a random pattern of hair whorl rotation, while right-handers showed clockwise hair whorl as a dominant.

8. **Palmaris longus tendon (A, a):** Place your fingertips under the table edge and move to lift the table with your fingertips. If two flexor tendons arise at the wrist, this is inherited as a recessive. If there is a third (palmaris longus) tendon in the middle, it is inherited as a dominant (although it is actually the less frequent genotype).

9. **Tongue rolling (B, b):** For years, it was reported that ability to roll the edges of one's tongue upward was inherited as a dominant, although Martin (1975) disputes that the trait is genetically determined at all.

EXERCISE 2.1   NAME _____   SECTION _____   DATE _____

Gamete Formation

Show your work.

1. What are the gametes that can be produced by the following individuals?

    a. AABB? AB

    b. AaBB?

    $AB,\ Ba$

    c. AABBcc?

    $100\%\ ABc$

    d. AAbbCc?

    $AbC,\ Abc$

2. What are the possible genotypes of the offspring from a mating of the following individuals?

    a. EE x ee

    heterozygous

    b. Ee x Ee

    $EE,\ Ee,\ Ee,\ ee$

    c. AaBb x AAbb

    $AABb,\ AAbb,\ AaBb,\ Aabb,$

	AB	Ab	aB	ab
Ab	AABb	AAbb	AaBb	Aabb
Ab	AABb	AAbb	AaBb	Aabb
Ab	AABb	AAbb	AaBb	Aabb
Ab	AABb	AAbb	AaBb	Aabb

4 Aabb

EXERCISE 2.2   NAME _____   SECTION _____   DATE _____

Phenotype Summary

Survey a sample of about 30 to 50 individuals for one or more of the traits listed. Fill in the following chart; the information will be used in later exercises.

Summary of Genetic Data for Sample

Trait	N	Number Dominant Phenotype	Number Recessive Phenotype	% Dom	% Rec	Yourself Dom/Rec	Letters to Be Used in Exercise
Earwax type	20	11	9	55%	45%	Dom	R, r
PTC taste	2	7	13				P, p
Earlobes	20	67	13	35%	65%	Dom	E, e
Darwin's tubercle	20	86	14	30%	70%	Rec	D, d
Hitchhiker's thumb	20	72	18	10%	90%	Rec	T, t
Hair whorl	20	77	13	35%	65%	Rec	H, h
Palmaris longus	20	1	19	5%	95%	Rec	A, a
Tongue rolling	20	16	4	80%	20%	Dom	B, b

EXERCISE 2.3 **NAME** _____ **SECTION** _____ **DATE** _____

Genotype Formations

1. What are the possible genotypes for each of the phenotypes tested in the survey?

   Homozygous Dominate, heterozygous, homozygous recessive

2. Investigate the relationship between handedness and hair whorl direction described by Klar (2003) and defined on page 40. Do you see a correlation?

   All right handers 50% dom 50% rec

3. What are the genotype possibilities for those individuals in your survey who have hitchhiker's thumb?

   Tt; TT

4. What are the genotype possibilities for those individuals in your survey whose hair whorls in a clockwise direction?

   HH; Hh

5. What percentage of the offspring from a mating of two individuals, each heterozygous for earlobes and PTC tasting, will be able to taste PTC and have free-hanging earlobes?

   25%

6. What percentage of the offspring from the preceding mating will not be able to taste PTC but will have attached earlobes?

   12%

7. What percentage of the offspring from the preceding mating will be heterozygous for both traits?

   25%

PEDIGREE ANALYSIS

When a researcher comes across a subject who phenotypically shows a trait that the researcher knows to be dominant, as we have seen, the subject can genetically be either homozygous dominant or heterozygous for that trait. With the advances in gene mapping, we are getting closer to the time when it will be practical to determine the complete genotype of an individual for any given trait, but for now, a person's genotype for a trait is still usually determined by researching the phenotypes of a person's family. By reconstructing the "family tree" for the expression of phenotypes of a trait, we can, to an extent, even predict the expression of that trait in descendants.

The steps for determining whether a trait is dominant or recessive and for determining the genotypes in a family are listed here:

1. In the case of dominant inheritance, the individual who exhibits a trait must have at least one parent who also shows it.

2. If only one parent shows the trait, the individual in question must be heterozygous for it. Because of the rule of dominant inheritance, an individual who exhibits the dominant trait will have at least one parent who also shows it (assuming there are no mutations).

3. If an individual showing a recessive trait has two parents neither of whom shows the trait, both parents must be carriers of one recessive and one dominant allele (i.e., heterozygous).

The recessive traits are, therefore, not found in every generation. *Note:* A recessive condition with a substantial gene frequency will sometimes mimic a dominant trait in a pedigree chart. In the following exercises, however, assume the typical situation just described.

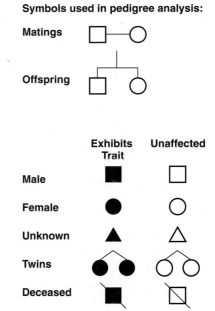

Symbols used in pedigree analysis:

Matings

Offspring

	Exhibits Trait	Unaffected
Male		
Female		
Unknown		
Twins		
Deceased		

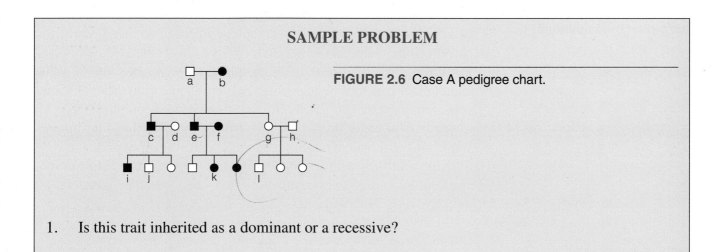

SAMPLE PROBLEM

FIGURE 2.6 Case A pedigree chart.

1. Is this trait inherited as a dominant or a recessive?

2. What are the probable genotypes of individuals a and b?

   a.

   b.

3. If individual **a** had married an individual of the same genotype as himself, how many of the children from this mating would show the trait (what percentage)?

Answers:

1. In the case of dominant inheritance, any individual who shows the trait must have at least one parent who shows the trait. Notice that this is true in this problem; therefore, the trait is inherited as a dominant.

   a. homozygous recessive

   b. heterozygous

2. None of the children would show the trait.

SEX LINKAGE

Sex-linked traits occur on the chromosomes that determine the sex of the individual.

Several genes are said to be **sex linked** when the genes that influence them are located on the X or Y chromosome. A female receives two X chromosomes from her parents, while a male receives an X chromosome from his mother and a Y from his father. Remember that during meiosis, the paired chromosomes segregate so that each gamete receives half of each paired chromosome, and those chromosomes may exchange genetic information before separating (described on page 21). This is also true in the paired X chromosomes of the females, but because the Y chromosome carries few of the loci of the X chromosomes, it can only exchange information at its ends. For this reason, most of the Y chromosome is passed directly from fathers to sons.

Because the Y chromosome carries few of the loci of the X chromosome, most of the sex-linked genes are carried on the X chromosome. For most traits, therefore, a female with two X chromosomes will carry a pair of alleles for a trait, while a male, who

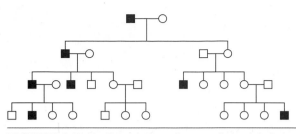

FIGURE 2.7 Pedigree chart for sex-linked trait.

has an XY configuration, will carry only one allele of a trait. Hence, the male has a greater chance of phenotypically showing a sex-linked trait. Males are referred to as being **hemizygous** for X-linked traits, and in this situation, recessive alleles behave as dominants in males.

Notice in the pedigree chart in Figure 2.7 that no women in the family group expressed the trait shown. However, females can show sex-linked traits if the father is affected, and the mother carries the trait on at least one of her X chromosomes.

Defective color vision, or color-blindness, is a sex-linked trait, as is hemophilia, or bleeder's disease. One type of night blindness, a form of nystagmus (an involuntary oscillation of the eyeball), and more than 1,500 other conditions and diseases are now known to be sex linked. A red–green color-blind man has a single recessive allele on his X chromosome. The Y chromosome carries no locus for this trait, so whatever allele form is carried by the X chromosome will determine the man's phenotype. If this man has children with a woman who is homozygous dominant (i.e., normal), all of the daughters will be carriers of the trait but will be phenotypically normal. The sons will all be normal and will not carry the trait.

Hemizygous: usually refers to males in sex-linked traits because most of these traits are contained on the X chromosome and have no corresponding locus on the Y chromosome.

SAMPLE PROBLEM

Why will all of the sons of a marriage between a red–green color-blind man and a woman who is homozygous dominant for the trait (i.e., normal) be normal?

Answer:
The homozygous normal woman can give only a normal allele to any offspring, sons or daughters. The Y chromosome passed by the father to the sons carries *no* allele for the trait, so the mother's normal allele passed to the son will be expressed. The color-blind man will, however, pass a recessive allele on the X chromosome inherited by his daughters, making them carriers.

EXERCISE 2.4   NAME _____   SECTION _____   DATE _____

Pedigree Exercises

1. Clark and Cindy have two grown sons and two infant daughters. On a separate sheet of paper, draw the pedigree chart for this family.

2. Clark and Cindy were once married to Margaret and John, respectively. Clark and Margaret had one daughter, now deceased. Cindy and John had one son. Combine this pedigree chart with the previous one for Clark and Cindy.

3. Jack and Betty are married, and they have two sons and one daughter. Jack's mother is deceased, but his father is still living. Betty's parents are both still alive. Jack's mother showed trait A, but his father does not. Jack and one of his sons show trait A, but the other son and daughter are free of the trait. No one on Betty's side of the family shows the trait. The trait is inherited as a recessive. Determine the genotypes of each member of the extended family.

4. In Case A (page 45), what are the genotypes of individuals c through l?

    c.   e.   g.   i.   k.

    d.   f.   h.   j.   l.

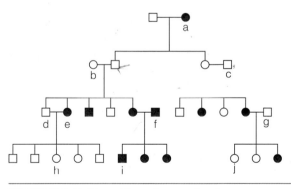

FIGURE 2.8 Case B pedigree chart.

5. Is the trait indicated in Case B (Figure 2.8) dominant or recessive? Is it a sex-linked trait?

6. What are the possible genotypes of individuals a through j? *recessive sex linked*

    a.   c.   e.   g.   i.

    b.   d.   f.   h.   j.

FIGURE 2.9 Case C pedigree chart.

7. Is the trait in Case C (Figure 2.9) dominant or recessive? Is it inherited as a sex-linked trait?

    recessive   sex linked

8. What are the possible genotypes of individuals a through o?

    a.   c.   e.   g.   i.   k.   m.   o.

    b.   d.   f.   h.   j.   l.   n.

BLOOD TYPING

The ABO blood group system is one of the best understood multiple allele systems. All of the ABO blood types are determined by two genetically determined proteins called **antigens,** the A antigen and the B antigen. These proteins occur on the surface of the red blood cells. An individual's blood may contain one, both, or neither of these antigens, giving rise to the four blood groups: A, B, AB, and O, as shown in Table 2.1.

Antigens: as used in this book, proteins that occur on the blood cells of the individual.

Table 2.1 Blood Groups

Blood Group (phenotype)	Genotype
A	AA or AO
B	BB or BO
AB	AB
O	OO

As you can surmise from Table 2.1, the A and the B alleles are dominant to the O allele, while the A and B alleles are codominant with one another. How? If the A or B allele is paired with O, only the A or B is displayed phenotypically. Because the AB genotype is displayed phenotypically as AB blood type, the two alleles are codominant.

Individuals with blood group A have the A antigen on the red blood cells, those with group B have the B antigen, those with AB blood type have both the A and B antigens, and those with genotype OO have neither blood group antigen. **Antibodies** destroy antigens, resulting in the destroyed red blood cells clumping together, or **agglutinating,** so in this case, the anti-A antibodies cause agglutination of the A and the AB blood types, as both have the A antigen on the red blood cells.

Antibodies: a protein produced by the body in response to, and in an attempt to neutralize, a foreign antigen.

Agglutination: clumping of red blood cells as a result of the destruction of blood antigens by antibodies.

Likewise, the anti-B antibodies will cause agglutination of the B and the AB blood types. Neither anti-A nor anti-B antibodies will cause agglutination of type O blood, as neither antigen is present on those red blood cells.

Table 2.2 should make these combinations easier to understand.

Table 2.2 Blood Group Phenotypes and Genotypes

Blood Group	Contains Antigens	Can Donate to	Can Receive
A	A	A or AB	A or O
B	B	B or AB	B or O
AB	A or B	AB	A, B, AB or O
O	Neither	A, B, or O	O

REMEMBER: You inherit antigens that create antibodies against other antigens.

For example: If you are given a transfusion of blood from a person with a different blood type, the antigens you inherited will interpret the foreign antigens as threats to your body and will create antibodies to destroy them.

Blood group O is referred to as a universal donor (contains no antigens).

Blood group AB is referred to as the universal recipient (produces no antibodies against A or B).

Blood group O, as can be seen in Table 2.2, contains neither antigen, so is commonly referred to as the "universal donor" because the host antibodies can find nothing against which to react. Conversely, individuals with blood group AB will create antibodies against neither antigen (because it contains both antigens on its blood cells and would not make antibodies against its own type). Because of this, type AB is commonly referred to as the "universal recipient."

The distribution of blood groups varies in different areas of the world and among different groups. Europeans most commonly have either blood group A or O (about 40% each), about 15% have type B blood, and about 5% show type AB blood. The highest frequency of type A blood occurs in the Blackfoot Native Americans of North America and the Lapps in northern Scandinavia. The lowest frequency of type A blood occurs in Central and South American natives. In most of the world, the frequency of type A blood is about 10% to 35%. The highest frequency of type B blood occurs in central Asia, and it is virtually absent among American Indians and Australian Aborigines. In most of the world, the frequency of type B blood is about 5% to 25% (Mourant, 1954, Mourant et al., 1958).

SAMPLE PROBLEM

A man has been taken to trial in a paternity suit by a woman who claims that he is the father of her son. The man claims innocence. At the trial, the expert witness disclosed the blood types of all three, as follows:

> Woman: Type A
>
> Man: Type B
>
> Child: Type O

Could the man be the father of the child?

Answer:

First list the possible genotypes of each of the above blood types, as follows:

> Woman: Genotypes AA or AO
>
> Man: Genotypes BB or BO
>
> Child: Genotype OO

If the woman possessed genotype AO, and if the man had BO, then the cross could look like this:

	B	O
A	AB	AO
O	BO	OO

Because 25% of the offspring are likely to be genotype OO, or blood type O, then the man *could* be the father. However, any other man with blood types B, A, or O (though not AB: why?) could be the father, so this case cannot be decided on this evidence alone.

EXERCISE 2.5   NAME _____   SECTION _____   DATE _____

Blood-Type Genetics

1. You have been testing blood samples to determine blood type and have found that sample one agglutinates with anti-A serum, but you haven't tested it against any other serum.

    a. What is (are) the possible blood type(s)?

    Ao or AB

    b. What antigen(s) is (are) present?

    A antigen

    c. What are the possible genotypes?

    AA, Ao, AB

2. A different blood sample agglutinates with anti-A and anti-B serum.

    a. What is (are) the possible blood type(s)?

    AB

    b. What antigen(s) is (are) present?

    anti A & Anti B

    c. What are the possible genotypes?

    AB

3. If a baby has blood type AB, and the mother has blood type A, what genotypes could the father be?

    AB, BB, Bo

4. Should a person with blood type A accept an offer of a blood transfusion from someone with blood type O? Why or why not?

    Yes, universal doner

5. Should a person with blood type O accept an offer of a blood transfusion from someone with blood type A? Why or why not?

    No, O can only accept O

EVOLUTION AND THE HARDY–WEINBERG FORMULA

As you have learned in The Scientific Method section of this book, and in Chapter 1, evolution occurs when allele frequency changes from one generation to the next in a population. Even though the specific sequence of the evolutionary process in humans contains theory, the general processes of evolution can be documented every day in, for instance, the success of farmers to select for milk production in cattle and in the increased success of bacteria to resist the effects of many of our antibiotics. Factors that produce and redistribute variation in a population include the following:

- **Mutation:** An actual alteration in genetic material either at the level of the base or at the level of the chromosome. This is the basic creative force in evolution and is the only way to produce new variation in a population.

- **Gene Flow:** A movement of genes from one population to another; also termed migration (although that can imply that individuals are migrating, when in fact only the genes may remain in the new area).

- **Genetic Drift** (random genetic drift)**:** An effect of sampling error and chance fluctuations in gene frequency based simply on a variation from a statistically expected outcome. This is a function of population size in that a shift in gene frequencies will have a proportionately greater effect in a small mating population than in a large mating population. The traits involved in genetic drift must have no selective advantage or disadvantage because if there is selective pressure, the change in frequencies is due to natural selection (described a few paragraphs down) and not to genetic drift.

- **Founder Effect:** A newly isolated sample from the original population soon diverges genetically from the parent population. For example, if 10 people from a normal population started a new population on a deserted island, and if all of those individuals had attached earlobes, the new population and all of the offspring would be very unlike the original population.

All of the preceding forces act to produce variation in a population.

- **Natural Selection:** A process that acts on this variation. If there is variation in a population, some of these variations may influence reproductive success (numbers of offspring successfully raised to have offspring of their own). Natural selection may, then, be defined as *differential net reproductive success.* The unit of natural selection is the individual; the unit of evolution is the population. The individuals best adapted to an environment will be the ones who survive to pass their genetic information to the next

Evolution occurs when allele frequency changes from one generation to the next in a population.

Mutation, gene flow, genetic drift, and founder effect act to produce variation in a population. Natural selection acts on that variation.

generation, while those who are not so adapted will not be selected and will not pass their genes to the next generation. Adaptation is therefore a shift in gene frequencies due to selection.

All of these factors in a particular environment define situations in which gene frequencies change in a population from generation to generation (i.e., the population is evolving). If a population wasn't evolving, we could define that the population was in genetic equilibrium, and we could describe it in terms of a mathematical model, the **Hardy–Weinberg Equilibrium formula.** Naturally, it would be very complicated to look at every trait possible in a population to see if the gene frequency was in equilibrium, so the simplest way to proceed is to look at one trait at a time. If that trait is determined by two alleles (in simple Mendelian inheritance), the equation contains two allele frequencies, p and q (which might, for example, stand for H and h, the alleles that control hair whorl direction). These two alleles are the only determinants of the trait, so the frequencies are represented by $p + q = 1$ (or $p + q = 100\%$ of the population). If we looked at all of the possible genotypes that represent hair whorl, we see the following:

$$HH + Hh + hh = 1$$

In the Hardy–Weinberg formula, this would be represented by the general **binomial** ("two names") equation:

$$p^2 + 2pq + q^2 = 1$$

P (or p) denotes the dominant allele, q denotes the recessive, and the preceding general equation reflects the potential outcomes of crosses between the dominant and recessive forms of the allele (remember the Punnett square).

> Remember in the following discussions:
> $p^2 = pp = p \times p$
> p = the frequency of the dominant allele
> q = the frequency of the recessive allele
>
> Convention uses p and q to denote the frequencies of the dominant and recessive alleles, and this convention will be followed in this book.

In our studies so far, we have used both the two-allele traits (or those traits determined by two alleles such as attached earlobes, PTC tasting, etc.) and the three-allele traits, such as the ABO blood-grouping system. We could look at more traits than this, but of course the equation becomes more complicated.

The Hardy–Weinberg formula is a mathematical model in which genetic equilibrium is defined.

In a two-allele system, the formula for allele frequencies is

$$p^2 + 2pq + q^2 = 1$$

The genotype frequencies are represented by p^2, pq, and q^2.

p is the frequency of the dominant allele; q is the frequency of the recessive allele.

REMINDER: A binomial formula always equals 1 (100%)! This is an important fact for calculating the allele and genotype frequencies.

SAMPLE PROBLEM

We have stated before that people who exhibit clockwise hair whorls inherit the trait as a dominant (HH or Hh), whereas people who exhibit counterclockwise whorls inherit the trait as a recessive (hh).

Suppose we have taken a survey from campus and have found that 75 of 100 students (75%) have clockwise hair whorl patterns. Our genotypes are the following:

hh = 25%, or .25 (100 students minus the 75 students who have the dominant genotypes)

HH and Hh = 75% or .75

The first step in determining the frequencies of the genotypes (p^2, 2pq, q^2) in a population is to calculate the allele frequencies (p, q). To do this, begin with the homozygous recessive genotype frequency (the frequency of the homozygous recessive [qq] is known from the sample data collected, so calculations start with this number, and you always work from the known to the unknown in any mathematical problem).

The following loop is a reminder of the sequence to follow in calculating gene and genotype frequencies:

Start with qq

1. In this method, you calculate the frequency of the homozygous recessive allele q first. We want the allele frequency, q, and we know the pp genotype frequency, q^2.

    Because $q = \sqrt{q^2}$, in this case, t = $\sqrt{.25}$, or .5. This, remember, describes the allele t in our formula, so we have determined the frequency of one allele.

2. Determine p (in this case, the frequency of H).

    Since p + q = 1,

    then 1 − .5 = p,

    so p = .5

3. Determine the observed genotype frequencies.

    We just plug these numbers into our formula:

	p^2	+	2pq	+	q^2	=	1
so	$(.5)^2$	+	2(.5)(.5)	+	$(.5)^2$	=	1
and	(.25)	+	(.50)	+	(.25)	=	1

    which corresponds to our genotypes

    HH   Hh   hh

REMEMBER: The Hardy–Weinberg formula gives expected frequencies when the population is in genetic equilibrium. The real frequencies may vary. We can determine whether the population is in genetic equilibrium by testing whether the observed frequencies match the frequencies expected from the calculation of the Hardy–Weinberg formula.

Click!

To use the chi-square (χ^2) test to determine whether or not your results are statistically significant, go to the companion website: www.cengage.com/anthropology/france.

While we can observe whether or not the observed allele frequency is different from the expected allele frequency from one generation to the next, to test whether or not that difference is statistically significant enough *not* to have been the product of chance, we would use a chi-square (χ^2) test. In this chapter, we will simply look at the expected and observed frequencies, but you can check whether or not those differences are statistically significant by going to the link provided.

As an example of the difference between observed and expected frequencies, the frequency of male to female students in a population (which can be a classroom) is expected to be 50% males and 50% females (although in reality there are slightly more females than males on earth). If the observed frequency is significantly different from the expected frequency, the population is not in equilibrium, and the researcher can begin to question the forces at work that create that difference. That is, if that frequency is actually 45% males and 55% females, is that deviation caused by sampling error, or is the difference statistically significant and perhaps linked to a specific cause or event? In a real-life example, the expected frequency of males to females within a university program can be expected to be equal if it represents random sampling of the larger population. However, 30 years ago, many more males than females pursued a career in forensic anthropology, while today more females than males are in forensic anthropology classes. It seems unlikely that the original male-to-female ratio was strictly due to chance, and it is equally unlikely that the shift in frequency is due to chance, but the exact reason for the shift is unknown.

EXERCISE 2.6 **NAME** _____ **SECTION** _____ **DATE** _____

Hardy–Weinberg and Evolution

1. If the frequency of the dominant allele (P) for PTC tasting is 50% in a population, what are the genotype frequencies for that trait in that population?

2. You have sampled 550 college students and found that 352 have Darwin's tubercle.

   a. What are the frequencies of alleles T and t?

   b. What are the genotype frequencies (TT, Tt, and tt)?

   c. If the *expected* allele frequencies are equal, what are the expected genotype frequencies?

   d. What does this tell you about the population?

3. Using the numbers obtained in your survey of individuals for the sample Mendelian traits (page 42), what are the probable genotype frequencies of your sample for these traits?

POPULATIONS IN EQUILIBRIUM AND POPULATIONS EVOLVING

As a reminder, we have discussed various forces that work on gene frequencies in populations, including mutations, gene flow, genetic drift, founder effect, and natural selection. Let's take a closer look at some of these forces and how the allele frequencies can change from one generation to the next (thereby meeting our definition of evolution).

NATURAL SELECTION

Remember that natural selection can be defined as net differential reproductive success, which means that the "fittest" individuals are those who pass their genetic information to subsequent generations. Individuals who do not mate or who do not have offspring that successfully have offspring of their own are not "fit" in an evolutionary sense and are at a genetic dead-ends. Note that in this definition, the individual can live to a very old age and be able to run marathons, but if he does not pass his genes to the next generations, he is not "fit" in a natural selection sense. Conversely, if an individual has a fatal disease that kills him *after* he passes the genes to the next generation, he is "fit" in a natural selection sense.

Sickle cell anemia is a classic example of natural selection at work. As was stated earlier (page 38), individuals who inherit two recessive alleles (homozygous recessive) for the trait develop sickle-cell anemia. Those who inherit a dominant and a recessive allele (heterozygous) do not show symptoms of the disease but are resistant to malaria. Those who inherit two dominant alleles (homozygous dominant) are more susceptible to malaria in those geographical areas with the disease-carrying mosquitoes. There is a natural selection disadvantage in malaria-prone areas to being homozygous dominant or homozygous recessive but a strong natural selection advantage to being heterozygous for the trait. Those individuals are more likely to pass their genes to the next generations. It is a balanced polymorphism.

To experiment with the effects of natural selection on a disease, however, a more dramatic effect can be seen with classic (infant onset) Tay-Sachs disease. Infants who are homozygous recessive for this terrible disease show onset of physical and mental disabilities due to abnormalities in the nerve cells caused by insufficient activity of an enzyme (beta-hexosaminidase A), that acts to reduce fatty acids around nerve cells (NINDS Tay-Sachs Disease Information Page at http://www.ninds.nih.gov/disorders/taysachs/taysachs.htm). Symptoms appear at about six months of age, and the infant usually dies by the age of four. The disease is caused by a mutation at a single locus on chromosome 15 (therefore, it is an autosomal mutation).

EXERCISE 2.7   NAME _____   SECTION _____   DATE _____

Evolving Populations

1. Tay-Sachs disease is actually very rare, but for this demonstration, assume that the frequency of the dominant and recessive alleles are equal in your population. Take 50 red beans (representing the dominant allele) and 50 black beans (representing the recessive allele) and put them into a can. Without looking, draw pairs of beans out of the can and place each pair together on the table.

    What are the genotype frequencies in your study population?

2. Because the homozygous recessive condition is fatal early enough in life that no offspring are possible from that genotype, remove all of the homozygous black bean pairs.

    What are the frequencies of dominant and recessive alleles after this step?

3. Put all of the remaining beans into the can and, again without looking, draw pairs of beans out of the can and place each pair together on the table (if you end up with a single bean at the end, place it back in the can if it is a red bean and remove it if it is a black bean).

    a. What are the genotype frequencies of this generation?

    b. What are the allele frequencies of this generation?

4. Repeat these steps for three to five generations. How do the genotype and allele frequencies change from generation to generation? This is natural selection (and evolution) in action.

ASSORTATIVE MATING

We don't have to use an example as dramatic as a fatal disease to demonstrate the effects of natural selection on a population. Assortative mating is a type of *intentional* selection in which individuals select mates because those mates have certain traits (or lack undesirable traits). Birds mate with other birds that know the correct song (even within species) and avoid mates that do not know the correct songs. Humans also make selections of mates because of certain desirable traits. Even though this is intentional selection, those individuals with traits undesirable to potential mates do not have as great a chance to pass their genetic information to the next generations.

MIGRATION OR GENE FLOW (HYBRIDIZATION)

Migration has occurred for millions of years in millions of species. In a book such as this, we would naturally talk about genetic trait transfer between humans as individuals from one geographic region migrate and mate with individuals around the world. What would happen to genotypes and phenotypes if, for example, a group of individuals carrying the sickle-cell trait migrated from a malarial zone to an area in which there was no malaria? If the trait is a balanced polymorphism in a malarial zone (there is a selective advantage to the heterozygous state but disadvantages for individuals with either homozygous state), what are the genotypes with the selective advantage in the new nonmalarial zone? What then happens to the allele and genotype frequencies over generations in the new population?

REMEMBER: Evolution is said to be occurring when the allele frequencies change from generation to generation within a population.

EXERCISE 2.8   NAME _____   SECTION _____   DATE _____

Gene Flow

Suppose 10 individuals who were all heterozygous for sickle-cell anemia migrated into a population of 30 individuals in which everyone was homozygous dominant for normal red blood cells. How would the gene frequencies of the next generation from random matings of the new population be different from the original population?

1. How many red beans (representing the dominant S allele) and how many black beans (representing the recessive s allele) should you put into the can?

2. Blindly draw pairs of beans out of the can, and place each pair together on the table.

   a. How many homozygous dominant genotypes do you have?

   b. How many homozygous recessive genotypes do you have?

   c. How many heterozygous genotypes do you have?

   Remove all homozygous recessive genotypes as they will have sickle-cell anemia. (Although with treatments today, many will survive to reproductive age and pass their genes to the next generation. This is for demonstration purposes.)

3. Repeat this experiment, and document the changes to the genotype and phenotype frequencies over generations.

MATHEMATICAL APPROACH TO GENOTYPE, PHENOTYPE, AND ALLELE FREQUENCY CHANGE

Example: Suppose that 10 individuals who were all homozygous for Darwin's tubercle migrated into a population of 100 individuals in which 36 individuals had no Darwin's tubercle. How would the allele frequencies of the next generation (from random matings) be different from the original population?

DD, Dd = Darwin's tubercle

dd = no tubercle

Answer: In the original population, 36% of the individuals were genotype dd, so the frequency for $d = \sqrt{.36} = .6$, therefore $D = 1 - .6 = .4$. The genotype frequencies for the original population would be

$$DD + 2Dd + dd = 1$$
$$(.4)^2 + 2(.4)(.6) + (.6)^2 = 1$$
$$.16 + .48 + .36 = 1$$

The number of individuals for each genotype is

$$DD = .16(100) = 16 = 16\%$$
$$Dd = .48(100) = 48 = 48\%$$
$$dd = .36(100) = 36 = 36\% \text{ dd (already discovered)}$$

If the individuals who migrated into the population are all genotype DD (discovered from their past records), then the numbers for the new population are as follows:

$$DD = 16 + 10 = 26/110 = 24\%$$
$$Dd = 48 + 0 = 48/110 = 44\%$$
$$dd = 36 + 0 = 36/110 = 33\%$$

New allele frequencies are

$$d = \sqrt{.33} = .57$$
$$D = 1 - .57 = .43$$

GENETIC DRIFT AND FOUNDER EFFECT

Genetic drift and founder effect (a more dramatic form of genetic drift) are situations in which a very small sample of individuals (and therefore genes) are removed from a larger population and start new populations.

The fact that many species of plants and animals are becoming extinct (because of encroachment by humans on their habitat, global warming, or other human and nonhuman causes) is common knowledge. Unfortunately, many animals such as the gorilla and orangutan will almost certainly become extinct in the wild and will only live in zoos and wildlife centers. This is a disturbing fact in and of itself, but it is also of concern because of the diminished gene pool in these species.

The California Condor is a success story about bringing a species back from the brink of extinction. In 1982, there were fewer than 25 left in the wild (because of a combination of habitat encroachment, pesticides, poaching, etc.), and the problem was exacerbated because a mating pair only produced an egg every two years (see National Parks Conservation Association at www.npca. org). In an attempt to save the species in the wild, condor eggs were gathered from cliff sites and other nesting sites and hatched by wildlife officials (sometimes the mating pair would lay another egg if the first egg was taken), and today, through the breeding programs, about 160 condors are alive in the wild.

Although this is a great success story, think of the limited gene pool in the population of condors today because the wild population dwindled to so few mating pairs. This is an example of founder effect, and with limited variation inherent in the genotypes for many traits comes a potential limit in the ways in which the population and individuals can react to changes in environment.

► Click!

For a mathematical model of genetic drift and founder effect, go to www.cengage.com/ anthropology/france.

EXERCISE 2.9 NAME _____ SECTION _____ DATE _____

Population Genetics

1. Suppose that out of a population of 100 individuals, 25 could not taste PTC and that the individuals in that population who could taste this chemical decided to marry only other individuals who could taste PTC. How would the genotype and allele frequencies change in the second generation?

    This is an example of what evolutionary force?

2. Suppose that a small island population of 100 individuals is visited by 25 sailors who decide to stay and raise families. Suppose also that 36% of the original population had a counterclockwise hair whorl and that all of the sailors had a counterclockwise hair whorl. What will be the genotype and allele frequencies of the next generation?

    This is an example of what kind of evolutionary force?

3. Suppose that 35% of a population of 100 individuals has hitchhiker's thumb, which is inherited as a recessive. Suppose also that 10 individuals, 5 of whom have hitchhiker's thumb, decide to go deep-sea fishing and are stranded on a deserted island for at least a generation, and that all stranded individuals mate. What are the genotype and allele frequencies of both new populations in the next generation?

    This is an example of what kind of evolutionary force?

4. What would you say to someone who says "bacteria are learning how to survive today's antibiotics"?

5. What is the genetic reason why farmers can increase milk production in their cows?

REEXAMINING THE ISSUES

In this chapter, we have learned:

- How genetic information from both parents is passed from generation to generation in the nuclear DNA and how that is important in understanding how allele frequencies can change in populations.
- Sources of genetic variability in populations are produced by mutation, gene flow, genetic drift, and founder effect, and that natural selection acts on that variability.
- How to determine whether or not a population is in stasis, and how to track changes in allele frequency in populations through time.

●

CHAPTER 3

Human Osteology

OBJECTIVES

1. What is bone?

2. How do muscles attach to bone?

3. How do you figure out what bone you have if you only have a fragment?

Much of what physical anthropologists do involves bone morphology in some way. Current theories about fossil hominins start with comparisons of the fossils with modern bones. Human identification and even the differentiation between human and nonhuman bones involve skeletal clues. Likewise, understanding primate locomotion begins with a study of the biomechanics of the bones, joints, and muscle attachments. To build on our knowledge of these (and many more) interesting aspects of physical anthropology, we must have a foundation in skeletal anatomy.

INTRODUCTION

Bone is a living, dynamic tissue that responds to its environment. Many of the clues to learning about this environment, and therefore learning about the life of the individual, will be covered later in this book, but you can begin to learn about the functional interrelationships between the specific bones and muscles of the body in this chapter. During this laboratory period, you will learn terminology of the skeleton and dentition (Figures 3.1–3.3) and the names of the bones and of the major landmarks of the skeleton. Although this task requires some memorization, the landmarks discussed have functional significance and are easier to learn if you think of that function, especially as you think of how your own body operates. To

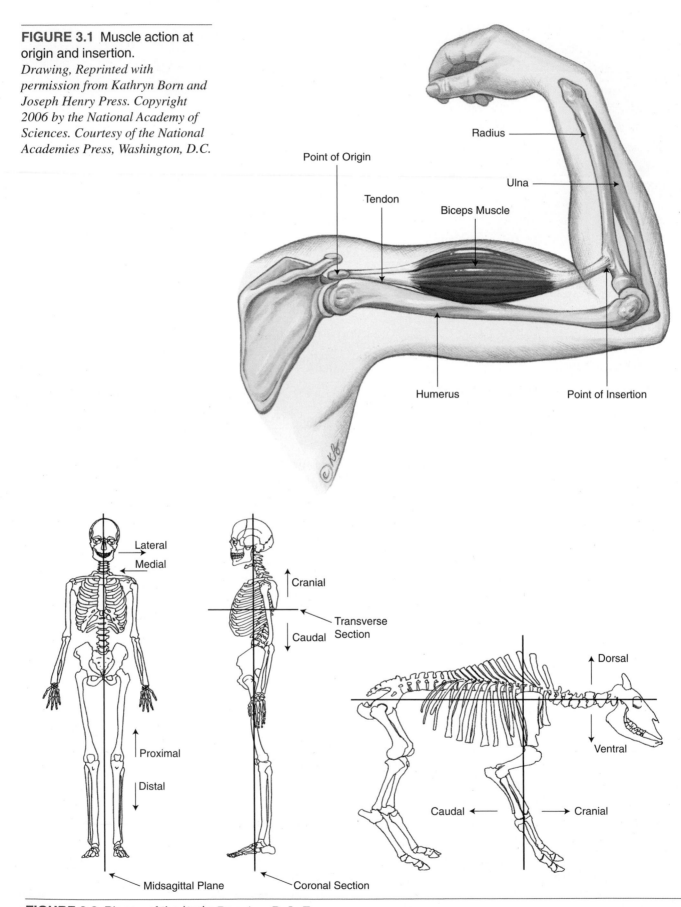

FIGURE 3.1 Muscle action at origin and insertion.
Drawing, Reprinted with permission from Kathryn Born and Joseph Henry Press. Copyright 2006 by the National Academy of Sciences. Courtesy of the National Academies Press, Washington, D.C.

Radius

Ulna

Point of Origin

Tendon

Biceps Muscle

Humerus

Point of Insertion

Lateral

Medial

Cranial

Transverse Section

Caudal

Proximal

Distal

Dorsal

Ventral

Caudal

Cranial

Midsagittal Plane

Coronal Section

FIGURE 3.2 Planes of the body. *Drawing, D. L. France*

a large extent, the form of the bone is determined by its function, and its function is limited by its form.

Some of the best clues for determining the function of a particular bone are also just common sense. For instance, in healthy bone, the area of **articulation** between two bones that are designed to move against each other will have a smooth surface. This surface will be separated from the articular surface of the other bone by a layer of cartilage, which is soft tissue able to withstand the movements and impacts of the bones.

The joints are held together by **ligaments** that sometimes completely envelop the joint capsule (as in the humeral head). Most movable joints capsules are filled with a slippery (somewhat like raw egg whites) lubricant called **synovial fluid** ("syn" means "together" and "ovia" means egg!) that helps keep the joint and cartilage healthy and moving freely with little friction. If the cartilage or articular surface of the bone is damaged, or if there is insufficient synovial fluid, the bone may show areas in which the bones rub against each other and polish the surface of each bone (as described in later chapters), or the bone may break down altogether at those surfaces. If too much synovial fluid is produced in the joint capsule, a condition popularly known as "water" on the joint is produced, which is evidenced by swelling at the joint.

Two other kinds of joints occur in the body. **Synarthroses** (sing.: **synarthrosis**) are joints in which the two bones are so tightly bound by cartilage that there is virtually no movement between them (such as in the sutures of the cranium). Later in this chapter, we will briefly discuss the spheno-occipital synchondrosis, which is a form of synarthrosis. These types of joints often disappear in adulthood, when the bones they join fuse. This information will become useful to us later in the determination of age.

The third type of joint is called an **amphiarthrosis** (pl.: **amphiarthroses**), which is a joint in which some movement is allowed. The bones in these joints are held together by disks of fibrous cartilage, such as in the pubic symphysis and between vertebral bodies (the intervertebral disks). Another type of this joint is seen at the ankle, where the tibia and fibula articulate.

While healthy bony surfaces are smooth at the areas of movement, they are generally not smooth at synarthroses or amphiarthroses. Also, the area of **origin of a muscle** or **insertion of a muscle** (or muscle **tendon**) or ligament on bone is rough and often raised (though not all rough areas are locations of muscle attachment). Generally, the larger and more powerful a muscle is, the more area of the bone it needs on which to anchor itself (see Figures 3.4a and 3.4b).

Muscle fibers only actively contract and then relax. Therefore, when you flex (or bend) your lower arm to your shoulder, the anterior muscles of the arm are contracting, and the muscles of the posterior arm are passive. When you extend (or straighten) your

FIGURE 3.3 Terminology in the mouth. *Photo, D. L. France*

Articulation: in osteology, this occurs when two or more bones are joined, whether they move at that point or not.

Ligament: flexible fibrous tissue connecting the articular ends of bones (and sometimes making up a capsule that envelops them).

Synovial fluid: a slippery lubricant that fills most joint capsules.

Synarthrosis: a joint in which there is virtually no movement.

Amphiarthrosis: a joint in which there is some movement.

Origin of a muscle: area of its attachment to bone that remains relatively fixed during the contraction of that muscle.

Tendon: a band of dense fibrous tissue that forms the ends of muscles, particularly at the insertion, and attaches the muscle to the bone.

arm, the posterior muscles of the arm are contracting, while the anterior muscles are passive. A general observation in gross anatomy, when describing the action of a muscle, is that the insertion of muscle is pulled toward the origin—that is, the point of origin remains fairly stationary, while the insertion moves. The muscle tendon at the insertion point must move through a greater angular range of motion than does the origin and must therefore be a smaller point on the bone (Figure 3.1). If muscle fibers covered a large area, some fibers at the extreme edge of the insertion would stretch farther during muscle contraction and might be strained or torn. The origin may be attached over a greater area of bone as it travels through a very limited range of motion, and the muscle fibers in general remain more parallel to the bone. The same force is acting on each end of the muscle, but since the insertion is typically smaller, more force per unit area is placed on the insertion than at the origin, both at the muscle tendon and at the bone. Since bone reacts to the amount of force applied by increasing both the density and the amount of roughening on the bone, the area of insertion will show more of the effects of a large muscle than will the origin.

These general rules can be used to decipher the significance of large crests or other areas of muscle attachment on bone. For instance, the large sagittal crest on the male gorilla (Figures 3.4a and 3.4b) is produced by a combination of a very large temporal muscle (one of the major chewing muscles) with a relatively small cranium. This temporal muscle becomes more powerful in the male gorilla as the gorilla matures (in part because the large teeth are developing) and gradually requires more bone on which to anchor itself. As the muscle becomes larger, it spreads out over the bone of its origin until it becomes so large that it literally runs out of cranium. The bone is then stimulated to produce more bone in order to provide

Insertion: area of attachment of a muscle to bone that usually moves through a greater range of motion when a muscle contracts.

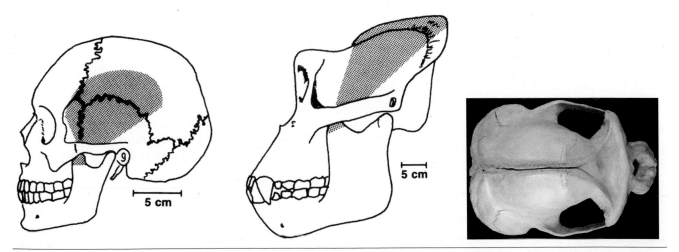

FIGURE 3.4 Origin of temporal muscle in modern humans and gorilla. *Photo, D. L. France*

FIGURE 3.5 Bison humerus.
Photo, D. L. France

FIGURE 3.6 Human humerus.
Photo, D. L. France

this attachment area (a muscle does not anchor itself to another muscle) and will produce the crests you see in the sagittal region of the gorilla cranium.

The results of muscle origin and insertion need not be as spectacular as the sagittal crest in a gorilla to be useful to us as indicators of function. Even relatively small raised areas of muscle attachment can be useful in determining, even from small fragments, which bone we are holding, the side of the body, and many features about the individual.

It should be noted that after learning the morphology of human bones, it is also possible to identify most nonhuman bones because they are often very similar in shape, though they may differ in function. For example, the femur and humerus have very similar gross morphology in the human and bison (Figures 3.5 and 3.6) even though the humerus performs different functions.

INSTRUCTIONS FOR HANDLING BONE: Skeletal material is irreplaceable. Each skeleton is the only copy of a "book" of unique information. Treat it with the respect with which you would want your own skeleton to be treated.

EXERCISE 3.1 **NAME** _____ **SECTION** _____ **DATE** _____

Comparing Muscles, Cartilage, and Bone

This exercise will give you a chance to explore the relationship among muscles, cartilage, and bone, and will introduce the basics of growth and development in bone. It is intended to be a fun exercise that will no doubt influence the way you look at some of your food!

FIGURE 3.7
Chicken leg without skin. *Photo, D. L. France*

FIGURE 3.8
Chicken leg with muscle being removed. *Photo, D. L. France*

FIGURE 3.9
Chicken leg, bones separated. *Photo, D. L. France*

FIGURE 3.10
Chicken leg with cartilage. *Photo, D. L. France*

FIGURE 3.11
Chicken leg without soft tissue. *Photo, D. L. France*

FIGURE 3.12
Proximal chicken leg. *Photo, D. L. France*

FIGURE 3.13
Cut proximal chicken leg. *Photo, D. L. France*

FIGURE 3.14
Cut deer tibia. *Photo, D. L. France*

FIGURE 3.15
Deer tibia, closeup of trabeculae. *Photo, D. L. France*

Safe food handling practices should be used during this exercise!

Materials:

- Chicken drumsticks, preferably cooked (it is safer to handle cooked meat). Each student should have a drumstick.
- Paper plates or paper towels, moist towelettes.
- Knife (does not have to be a sharp knife, and the class can share one or two knives).

At the beginning of this exercise, remove the skin from the drumstick very carefully (Figure 3.7)! If the meat (or muscle as we will call it from now on) begins to tear away, leave the skin on in that area.

Using blunt dissection (meaning just with your fingers—do not use a knife!), gently investigate the muscles (Figure 3.8).

1. Are the muscles in layers, or are they side-by-side?

2. Are the muscles larger near the proximal end or near the distal end?

3. What do you notice about the characteristics of the muscles at each end (proximal and distal)? Carefully remove the top muscle (meaning the muscle nearest the surface). Describe it.

4. Is the muscle smooth? Slippery? Why do you think this is true?

5. Pull that muscle apart. Which way do the muscle fibers run (from proximal to distal or medial to lateral)? Given the earlier discussion about the function of a muscle, why do the muscle fibers run in this direction?

   Gently pull all of the muscles off of the drumstick, being careful to leave the cartilaginous ends (proximal and distal).

6. How many bones are there (Figure 3.9)? Describe each of the bones (size and shape). You will be asked to determine which bones of the body you are studying at the end of this chapter.

7. As was described earlier, muscles originate and insert on bone. They cannot originate on other muscles. As you are pulling the muscles away from your drumstick, where are the muscles originating and inserting? Are they all originating on bone, or are some of them originating on cartilage? You will be asked to talk about this in more detail later in this book.

After you have cleaned the muscles from the bone, gently pry the proximal cartilage from the bone as completely and as neatly as possible (Figures 3.10 and 3.11). Your goal is to remove the entire cartilage cap in one piece. If you are successful, there will still be some cartilage remaining on the bone, but it will be more or less interwoven into the bone itself. Set the cartilage cap aside.

Use your fingernail to scrape the bone near the midshaft. Can you remove a very thin, delicate layer of soft tissue (it is so delicate that it will not come off in a continuous layer)? This is the periosteum, the thin soft tissue layer surrounding the bone. This will be discussed in more detail later, but it is important to know that the periosteum plays a large role in the development and continuing health of a bone.

Now concentrate on the bone itself. Notice the differences in external texture in different areas of the bone (also see Figures 3.12 and 3.16). In fact, texture differences throughout the bone is just as important as gross morphological differences for diagnosing whether or not what you are observing is actually bone, which bone of the skeleton you have, which part of that bone, and often even the species you have.

FIGURE 3.16 Human femoral neck.
Photo, D. L. France

The internal and external texture of bone is often as important in your diagnoses as the general shape of the bone itself!

Use your thumb and forefinger and try to pinch the bone at the proximal aspect, and then in the middle of the bone.

8. Describe the differences in the "pinch" test at the proximal end and near the midshaft (you may have to use a pair of pliers to pinch the bone).

9. Use the knife and split the proximal third of the bone in half along its long axis. Describe the morphological differences between the proximal end and the midshaft in the split bone.

   a. Do you see differences in the quantity of the soft, reddish-brown material in the proximal aspect relative to the midshaft (Figure 3.13)? This soft, fatty material is the bone marrow and is responsible for the production of red and white blood cells.

   b. Do you see differences in bone type between the proximal end and the midshaft? What are those differences (it may help to rinse the marrow off and out of the proximal end of the bone)?

The type of bone typically seen near articular surfaces is called trabecular, cancellous, or spongey bone (Figures 3.14 and 3.15). Cortical or compact bone is typically seen in long bone shafts (though not exclusively) and is, as the name implies, very compact and dense bone.

10. Inspect the section of cartilage that you removed from the proximal aspect of the drumstick. There may be some bone residue on the inner surface of the bone, and if there is, gently scrape this off so that you are looking at a relatively clean cartilage surface. Hold the cartilage up to light, and look into its translucent center. What do you see? This feature will be discussed in more detail in Chapter 4, Growth and Development. You can also go to Chapter 3 on the book companion website at www.cengage.com/anthropology/france for an online version of the exercise.

Even though you are looking at a chicken drumstick, the elements you have described translate to mammalian (including human) bone. As we proceed through the chapter, we will use these characteristics to understand the biomechanics of human bone and even to help us identify bone fragments.

As we explore growth and development and forensics, we will occasionally come back to the drumstick exercises!

▶ Click!

The entire chicken bone exercise includes additional elements of osteology, human vs. nonhuman bone identification, growth and development, and fracture characteristics of wet and dry bone.

FIGURE 3.17 Common long bone. *Photo, D. L. France*

FIGURE 3.18 Cranial cross section. *Photo, D. L. France*

The morphology and terminology of bone discussed to this point are typical of most of the bones of the body. The morphology seen and terminology used to discuss the cranium differ, however (see Figure 3.18), as do the patterns of growth and development (discussed in Chapter 4).

FIGURE 3.19 The human skeleton. *Photo, D. L. France*

Cranium

Mandible

Hyoid

Clavicle

Sternum

Scapula

Humerus

Ribs

Vertebra

Os Coxa (Innominate)

Sacrum

Radius

Ulna

Carpals

Metacarpals

Phalanges

Femur

Patella

Tibia

Fibula

Tarsals

Metatarsals

Phalanges

TERMINOLOGY

Anatomical Position:	Body with arms by side, palms forward
Anterior:	In front (similar to ventral)
Appendicular:	The skeleton of the limbs
Axial:	The skeleton of the head and trunk
Caudal:	Toward the tail
Coronal Plane:	Parallel to the coronal suture
Cranial:	Toward the head
Distal:	Away from trunk of body along a limb
Dorsal:	In back (similar to posterior)
External:	Outside of
Inferior:	Lower
Internal:	Inside of
Lateral:	Perpendicularly away from midsagittal plane
Longitudinal:	Coursing or placed lengthwise
Medial:	Perpendicularly toward the midsagittal plane
Posterior:	Behind, to the back (similar to dorsal)
Pronation:	Rotation of the hand and forearm so that the palm faces dorsally or toward the body
Proximal:	Toward the trunk of the body along a limb
Sagittal Section:	Any section of the body parallel to the sagittal suture of the cranium (refer to Figure 3.2)
Superficial:	Near the surface
Superior:	Above, top
Supination:	Turning the palm of the hand anteriorly
Transverse:	Any crosswise section
Ventral:	In front (similar to anterior)
Vertex:	Top, highest point

In mouth:

Buccal:	Toward the cheek
Distal:	At greatest distance from the anterior midline of the mouth

Labial: Toward the lips

Lingual: Toward the tongue

Mesial: Toward the anterior midline of the mouth

Occlusal: The chewing surface of the teeth

(*Note:* many dentists are now referring to positions in the mouth only as buccal or lingual.)

Frankfort Plane: A standard plane of reference on the cranium in which the upper border of the external auditory meatus is on the same level as the lower border of the eye (also called the Frankfort Horizontal)

FEATURES OF BONE

Feature (plural):	**Definition:**
Cavity (cavities):	An open area
Condyle (condyles):	Rounded process at the point of articulation with another bone
Crest (crests):	A projecting ridge
Diaphysis (diaphyses):	The shaft of bone
Epiphysis (epiphyses):	A process of bone initially attached to another piece of bone by cartilage and usually later consolidated with it by bone
Fontanelle (fontanelles):	Membranous space between cranial bones in fetal life and infancy
Foramen (foramina):	A hole or opening
Fossa (fossae):	A pit, depression, or cavity
Meatus (meatuses):	A canal
Process (processes):	Any outgrowth or prominence of bone
Sinus (sinuses):	Bone cavity lined with mucous membrane
Suture (sutures):	Areas of articulation between cranial bones
Torus (tori):	An elevation or prominence
Tubercle (tubercles):	A small, knob-like projection on bone
Tuberosity (tuberosities):	A large, rough eminence or projection on bone

BONES OF THE SKULL

Skull

The skull, consisting of cranium and mandible, is a complex set of bones that protect and support the functioning of the brain, eyes, ears, nose, and mouth.

Cranium The cranium articulates with the first cervical vertebra (the atlas) by means of the occipital condyles (Figure 3.34). The **occipital condyles** lie on the anterolateral borders of the foramen magnum ("large hole"). The spinal cord passes through the **foramen magnum** on its way from the brain to the vertebral column.

The **nuchal (neck)** muscles are actually a group of muscles positioned on the neck. The posterior nuchal muscles have as their uppermost point of insertion a raised line on the posterior portion of the occipital bone, the **superior nuchal line** (also sometimes called the *superior nuchal crest,* especially in certain other animals, as we will discuss later). One large anterior nuchal muscle, the *sternocleidomastoid* (or sternomastoid), inserts on a large, downward-projecting process of bone, the **mastoid process** (Figure 3.34).

The temporal muscle, one of the major muscles of mastication (chewing), originates on the **temporal line** (Figure 3.35)**,** on the frontal and parietal bones of the skull.

Locate the **external auditory meatus** (external opening of the ear shown in Figure 3.34) and the **zygomatic arches** (which, along with the zygomatic [also called zygoma or malar] bone, form the bony prominence of the cheek and can be felt just below and lateral to the eye; see Figure 3.34). Another protrusion that can be felt through the skin is the **supraorbital torus** (as will be discussed in Chapter 15, this is a rounded ridge above the eyes that is usually more prominent in males than in females; see Figure 3.34). An additional feature cannot be felt through the skin but is nevertheless important. The **foramen ovale** is an opening on either side of the basilar portion of the occipital bone on the sphenoid bone (see Figure 3.34). This opening allows the passage of a small artery and one or two nerves (varies by individual).

The sagittal suture is a long straight suture "tying together" the two parietal bones, running anteroposteriorly along the top of the cranium. The coronal suture runs laterally from the top of the cranium and ties together the frontal and two parietal bones. The lambdoidal suture ties together the occipital and two parietal bones on the posterior cranium. The squamosal suture is an area in which the squamosal section of the temporal bone is beveled and overlaps the parietal bone.

FIGURE 3.20 Frontal bone (single bone). *Drawing, D. L. France*

FIGURE 3.21 Parietal bone (paired). *Drawing, D. L. France*

FIGURE 3.22 Temporal bone (paired). *Drawing, D. L. France*

FIGURE 3.23 Palatine bone (paired). *Drawing, D. L. France*

FIGURE 3.24 Occipital bone (single). *Drawing, D. L. France*

FIGURE 3.25 Vomer bone (single). *Drawing, D. L. France*

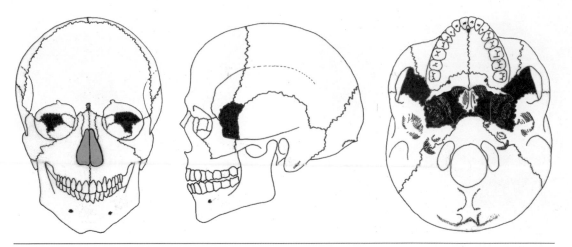

FIGURE 3.26 Sphenoid bone (single). *Drawing, D. L. France*

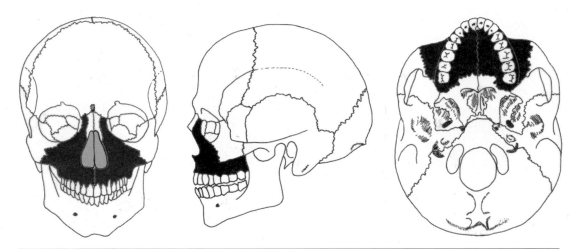

FIGURE 3.27 Maxilla (paired). *Drawing, D. L. France*

FIGURE 3.28 Zygomatic bone (paired). *Drawing, D. L. France*

FIGURE 3.29 Mandible (single). *Drawing, D. L. France*

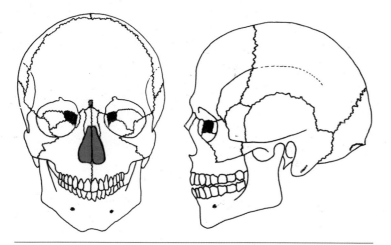

FIGURE 3.30 Ethmoid bone (single). *Drawing, D. L. France*

FIGURE 3.31 Lacrimal bone (paired). *Drawing, D. L. France*

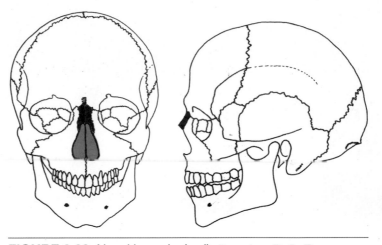

FIGURE 3.32 Nasal bone (paired). *Drawing, D. L. France*

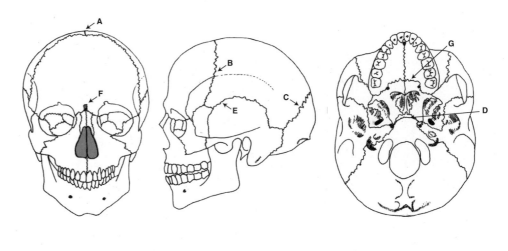

Sutures of the cranium

A. Sagittal

B. Coronal

C. Lambdoidal

D. Spheno-occipital synchondrosis (basilar suture)

E. Squamosal suture

F. Metopic suture (remnant)

G. Palatal suture

Most other sutures are named for the two bones joined by the suture (e.g., zygomaxillary).

FIGURE 3.33 Sutures of the cranium. *Drawing, D. L. France*

The spheno-occipital synchondrosis, sometimes called the basilar suture, is the point of articulation by synchondrosis (a joint in which the surfaces are connected by a growth of cartilage) of the basilar portion of the occipital bone with the body of the sphenoid bone. As early as mid-teens in males and probably earlier in females (Rhine and Sperry, 1991), there is complete bony union of the two bones. Occasionally one sees a **metopic suture** dividing the frontal bone. The metopic suture is a remnant of a suture that is usually united and obliterated by the time a child reaches 4 years of age (Scheuer and Black, 2000). The occurrence of the metopic suture well into adulthood is not pathological but is one of the many variations of the human skeleton in different individuals and in different populations.

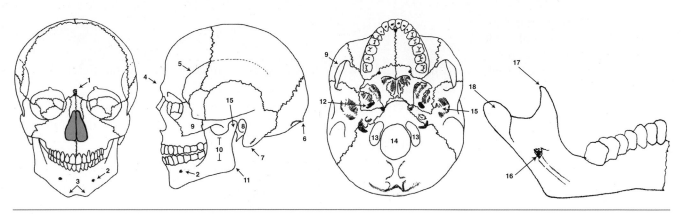

FIGURE 3.34 Features of the skull. *Drawing, D. L. France*

Mandible The mandible (or lower jaw) articulates with the cranium at the **temporomandibular joint** (refer to Figure 3.34) by its **mandibular condyles**. The **mental eminence** (chin) shows some sexual dimorphism (to be discussed further in Chapter 15), in that in males it is usually more squared, with slight projections on either side of the midline, and in females, the mental eminence usually has only a single point at the midline. Of course, as with many other aspects of the human skeleton, there is variation in this feature. The **mental foramen** allows passage of the mental nerve and blood vessels on either side of the midline (refer to Figure 3.34), while the **mandibular foramen** (refer to Figure 3.34) is on the lingual (tongue) side of the mandible about midway in the ascending ramus (the rising part of the mandible above the mandibular angle) (refer to Figure 3.34). The **ascending ramus** bifurcates into the mandibular condyles and the **coronoid process** (which is the area of insertion of the **masseter muscle**, one of the muscles used in chewing) (refer to Figure 3.34).

Teeth Each tooth has three areas, the **crown, neck**, and **root** (Figure 3.35 on the next page). The crown is covered with very hard, white enamel and is that part of the tooth above the gum line. The neck is a constricted area just below the crown. The root is below the neck and is contained within the tooth socket of the mandible or maxilla.

There are 20 deciduous (baby) teeth in children, and 32 permanent teeth in adults. A **dental formula** is a count of the number and kinds of teeth an animal has, written in shorthand form. Only the teeth in one upper quadrant and often a lower quadrant are counted (see Figure 3.38 on the next page).

In each adult quadrant (upper left, upper right, lower left, lower right) there are two **incisors** (one central, one lateral), one **canine,** two **premolars** (third, fourth*), and two or three **molars** (first, second, and third or wisdom tooth) (see Figure 3.38). Hence the dental formula of the maxilla and mandible for a modern human adult is

Features of the skull

1. **Metopic suture**
2. **Mental foramen**
3. **Mental eminence**
4. **Supraorbital torus (brow ridge)**
5. **Temporal line**
6. **Superior nuchal line**
7. **Mastoid process**
8. **External auditory meatus**
9. **Zygomatic arch**
10. **Ascending ramus**
11. **Gonial angle**
12. **Foramen ovalis**
13. **Occipital condyle(s)**
14. **Foramen magnum**
15. **Temporomandibular joint**
16. **Mandibular foramen**
17. **Coronoid process**
18. **Condyle**
19. **Sella turcica**
20. **Crista galli**
21. **Cribiform plate**
22. **External occipital protuberance**

Primitive mammals have four premolars. In the line of evolution leading to humans, the first two premolars were lost, leaving the third and fourth.

$$\frac{2:1:2:3}{2:1:2:3}$$

if upper and lower quadrants are counted, or abbreviated 2:1:2:3 if upper and lower quadrants are the same.

In each quadrant of the child (ages about 2–6 years) mouth, there are two incisors (one central, one lateral), one canine, and two molars (first, second). The dental formula is therefore

$$\frac{2:1:0:2}{2:1:0:2}$$

After about 6 years of age, there is a mixture of deciduous and permanent dentition.

FIGURE 3.37 Maxillary dentition left two rows; mandibular dentition right two rows. *Photo, D. L. France*

FIGURE 3.35 Features of the skull. *Photo, D. L. France*

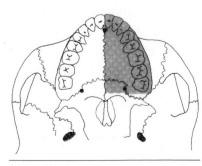

FIGURE 3.38 Tooth row. Shaded area is one quadrant. *Drawing, D. L. France*

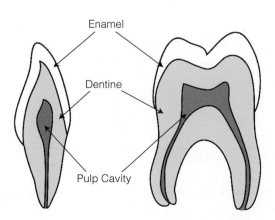

FIGURE 3.36 Cross section of teeth. *Drawing, D. L. France*

POSTCRANIAL BONES

Hyoid

The hyoid bone (Figure 3.39) is a very small bone that does not articulate directly with any other bone but is suspended below the mandible by many muscles acting on the tongue, pharynx, and neck.

Vertebrae

The vertebral column is divided into five sections: **cervical** (7 in number), **thoracic** (12), **lumbar** (5), **sacral** (4–6 but fused in the adult to form sacrum), and **coccygeal** (3–5, also often fused in the adult). The bodies of the cervical, thoracic, and lumbar vertebrae increase in size from the head toward the feet. The numbers of each type of vertebra may vary slightly from the number given. See Figure 3.40 for features common to all vertebrae.

Cervical Vertebrae Cervical vertebrae (Figure 3.41) are the smallest weight-supporting vertebrae. The coccygeal and terminal sacral vertebrae are smaller, but they support no weight. The cervical vertebrae are also recognizable in that

FIGURE 3.39 Hyoid bone.
Photo, D. L. France

FIGURE 3.40 Typical vertebra, superior view. The anterior is at the top of the photograph, the posterior at the bottom. *Photo, D. L. France*

FIGURE 3.41 Cervical vertebrae, superior view. The atlas is at the top, axis in the middle, and a typical cervical vertebra at the bottom. *Photo, D. L. France*

The spinous processes are sites of attachment of various muscles and ligaments.

- There is a foramen in the **transverse process.** These foramina transmit the vertebral arteries that help supply blood and therefore oxygen to the brain.
- The spinous processes are often bifurcated (forked).
- The body is oval in shape with the long axis in the transverse direction (except the first and second cervical vertebrae, discussed later).
- The articular processes (between vertebrae) are nearly flat. The cranial articular processes face dorsally and cranially, and the caudal face ventrally and caudally.

The first cervical vertebra, the atlas (it holds the "world," that is, cranium, on its shoulders), has no body. The second cervical vertebra, the **axis,** has a prominence on its body, called the **dens** or **odontoid process** ("tooth," as it looks like a tooth). The atlas (and hence the cranium) rotates around the dens.

Thoracic Vertebrae Thoracic vertebrae (Figure 3.42) are easy to recognize because

- They have facets for the articulation of the ribs. These articulations are also called **costal pits.**

- The articular processes (between vertebrae) are parallel to each other, vertical, and flat (except for the 12th, which has a lumbar vertebra–type process on the inferior surface). These articular processes face dorsally.
- Most of the spinous processes are long, pointed caudally, and tend to overlap the spinous process on the subjacent (below or next) vertebra.
- There is no transverse foramen.

Lumbar Vertebrae Lumbar vertebrae (Figure 3.43) are the largest of the movable vertebrae because they carry the most weight. In addition,

- The processes for articulation with the other vertebrae are angled, vertical, and curved to interlock with each other, giving a much stronger intervertebral articulation.
- The spinous processes are short and blunt.
- Lumbar vertebrae have no rib facets.
- Lumbar vertebrae have no transverse foramina.

Note: Occasionally, loose lower coccygeal vertebrae are confused with the body of the unfused hyoid bone.

A note about general side identification in paired post-cranial bones: It is easiest to identify the side the bone is from if you visualize how the bone is positioned in your own body. The hints given will include how prominent features of the bone are related to the function of the bone in the body or to other anatomical features easily recognized in your own body.

FIGURE 3.42 Thoracic vertebra, superior view (left), lateral view (right). *Photo, D. L. France*

FIGURE 3.43 Lumbar vertebra, superior view (left), lateral view (right). *Photo, D. L. France*

Sacral Vertebrae Sacral vertebrae, usually five but sometimes four or six in number, are fused in the adult to form a single bone, the sacrum (Figures 3.44, 3.45, 3.46). The weight of the upper body in humans is passed to the os coxae (innominate bones) and femora (plural for femur—the thigh bone) through the upper part of the sacrum, so this bone must be strong and stable.

The sides of the upper sacral vertebrae are flared into wings, or **alae** (sing.: ala), to form a large surface that articulates with the ilium.

Coccygeal Vertebrae Coccygeal vertebrae (Figure 3.47) give no support to the vertebral column but are the site of origin of a few muscles and ligaments.

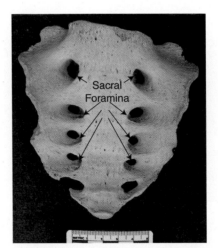

FIGURE 3.44 Sacrum, anterior view. *Photo, D. L. France*

FIGURE 3.45 Sacrum, anterior view. *Photo, D. L. France*

FIGURE 3.46 Sacrum, superior view. *Photo, D. L. France*

FIGURE 3.47 First coccygeal vertebra, anterior view. *Photo, D. L. France*

Clavicle

The **clavicle** is a long bone that maintains a constant distance between the scapula and the sternum and thereby adds strength to the shoulder girdle. In generalized quadrupeds that use their fore-limbs primarily for support or striding locomotion, that strength is supplied by the musculature (without a clavicle), while animals that use their forelimbs for manipulation or more complicated forms of locomotion often have a clavicle. The medial end is rounded for articulation with the sternum; the lateral end is flattened (and rough-ened inferiorly) for articulation with the scapula (Figure 3.48). The conoid tubercle is inferior and posterior and is part of the area of attachment for the conoid ligament that secures it to the scapula (Figure 3.49).

To determine on which side a clavicle resides in the body, position the rounded sternal end medially, and let the bone round out anteriorly as it progresses laterally. If you hold the sternal end medially and the bone rounds out posteriorly, you have it on the wrong side. Also, since the conoid tubercle is the point of attachment for the conoid ligament, make sure that the roughest flat side of the lateral aspect is positioned inferiorly (because muscle and ligament attachment points are rougher).

FIGURE 3.48 Left clavicle, superior view.
Photo, D. L. France

Scapular
Articulation

Sternal
Articulation

FIGURE 3.49 Left clavicle, inferior view.
Photo, D. L. France

Conoid Tubercle

FIGURE 3.50 Sternum, anterior view. *Photo, D. L. France*

Sternum

The **sternum** is composed of three segments and is similar to a broadsword (Figure 3.50):

- **Manubrium** ("handle"), articulates with the clavicle and the first two ribs.
- **Body** ("blade, gladiolus"), articulates with ribs (3 to 7 directly, 8 to 10 indirectly).
- **Xiphoid process** ("tip"), often a cartilaginous tab, becomes bony in later years (the exact time of ossification varies).

The three segments of this bone are sometimes separate but are usually fused in adults.

Scapula

The scapula is a triangular flat bone that rests on the upper back (Figures 3.51, 3.52, 3.53). It has two major projections on the proximal lateral angle: the **coracoid process** (anterior projection) and the **acromion process** (posterior projection), which are both points of origin of muscles of the upper back and arm. The acromion process articulates with the clavicle and is one of the points used by a tailor to calculate sleeve length.

The **scapular spine** is posterior and supports several muscles of the back, including the trapezius. The **glenoid fossa** is lateral and is the point of articulation of the head of the humerus.

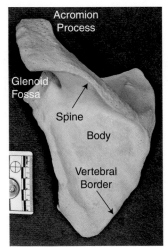

FIGURE 3.51 Left scapula, dorsal surface. *Photo, D. L. France*

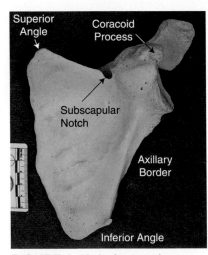

FIGURE 3.52 Left scapula, ventral surface. *Photo, D. L. France*

FIGURE 3.53 Left scapula, lateral view. *Photo, D. L. France*

To determine on which side a scapula resides in the body, position the glenoid fossa laterally and the inferior angle caudally with the scapular spine posteriorly. It is easy to mistakenly put the scapular spine anteriorly, but remember that there are no *prominent* muscle insertion areas between the scapula and the ribs!

Ribs

The ribs are in general easy to recognize (Figures 3.54 and 3.55). The superior surface is rounded, the inferior surface is rather sharp, and the rib is flat dorsoventrally. The head articulates with the lateral vertebral body, and the tubercle articulates with the transverse process of the thoracic vertebra.

The first rib, however, is flat craniocaudally and is very much shorter than the other ribs. The superior surface shows grooves for the subclavian artery and vein (which, as its name implies, runs under the clavicle). To determine on which side a first rib resides in the body, then, be sure that the groove (which

FIGURE 3.54 Left ribs, superior view; first rib (bottom), standard rib (top). *Photo, D. L. France*

FIGURE 3.55 Left ribs, superior view. *Photo, D. L. France*

is sometimes more easily felt than seen) is positioned superiorly, the sternal end medially, and the vertebral articular surface posteriorly.

The first seven ribs are *true* ribs, in that they articulate with the sternum at the readily observable costal (rib) notches.

The 8th, 9th, and 10th ribs are *false* ribs in that they do not articulate directly with the sternum but to a common cartilage, which itself articulates with the distal sternum.

The 11th and 12th ribs are *floating* ribs, so named because they have no connection at all to the sternum.

To determine on which side a second rib resides in the body, make sure that the sternal end is positioned medially, the vertebral end posteriorly, and the rougher convex side superiorly. To determine on which side ribs 3 through 12 reside in the body, place the rib so that the sternal end is medial, the vertebral end is lateral, and the more rounded surface is superior.

All ribs except the first rib are rounded on the superior surface and exhibit a costal ("rib") groove on the inferior surface.

Humerus

The **humerus** (Figures 3.56, 3.57, 3.58) is the largest bone of the upper limb. The rounded head at the proximal end articulates with the glenoid fossa of the scapula, and the distal end articulates with the radius and ulna. The deltoid muscle, a large muscle of the upper arm and shoulder, inserts at the deltoid tuberosity and **abducts** (or draws away from—think of the abduction of someone) the arm and hand when contracted. Think of the action of the muscle, and it makes sense that the deltoid tuberosity is on the lateral aspect of the humerus. The medial epicondyle, a point of origin of major muscles of the forearm and hand, is, as its name implies, medial. The ulnar nerve (the nerve insulted when you hit your "funny bone") passes under the medial epicondyle just medial to the trochlea. The trochlea articulates with the medial bone of the forearm, the ulna, and the rounded capitulum articulates with the rounded head of the radius, which is the lateral bone of the forearm.

To determine on which side a humerus resides in the body, hold the bone as it is in the body (head is proximal), and the medial epicondyle is medial. This is the position of the bone in the body. If you have only the distal section of the humerus, make sure that the medial epicondyle is medial, and the olecranon fossa is posterior. Then align it with your body. If you only have the proximal section, make sure that the articular surface is medial and the bicipital groove is anterior.

Pronation: the rotation of the hand and forearm so that the palm faces dorsally or toward the body; the hand is in the anatomical position at supination with palm up. Think of holding a cup of soup ("supination") on your palm.

Radius

The **radius** (Figures 3.59–3.62) is the lateral bone of the forearm and "follows" the thumb in the movements of the forearm in **pronation** and **supination.** The radius crosses over the ulna in

FIGURE 3.56 Left humerus, anterior view. *Photo, D. L. France*

FIGURE 3.57 Left humerus, posterior view. *Photo, D. L. France*

FIGURE 3.58 Humerus head.
Photo, D. L. France

pronation. The proximal surface is rounded for articulation with the capitular surface of the humerus, so think of the "radius of a circle" when remembering the radius (Figure 3.61). A roughened projection just below the proximal articular surface on the antero-medial surface is the radial tuberosity and is the point of insertion for the biceps muscle (when you think of the action of the biceps, it makes sense that the point of insertion is anterior). Distally, the radius articulates with navicular and lunate (description to follow in the "Wrist and Hand" section) via a concave articular surface

FIGURE 3.59 Left radius, anterior view. *Photo, D. L. France*

FIGURE 3.60 Posterior radius. *Photo, D. L. France*

FIGURE 3.61 Radial head (proximal radius). *Photo, D. L. France*

FIGURE 3.62 Distal radius. *Photo, D. L. France*

(Figure 3.62). Just above this articular surface is the ulnar notch, a concave articular surface that accommodates the rounded head of the ulna.

To determine on which side a radius resides in the body, make sure that the rounded head is proximal and that the radial tuberosity is anterior. Distally, the radius is roughened on the posterior surface and has a smoother, slightly concave surface anteriorly. Make sure that the smoother anterior surface is placed anteriorly, and align it with your body.

Ulna

The **ulna** (Figures 3.63, 3.64, 3.65) is the medial bone of the forearm when the body is in anatomical position, and it articulates proximally with the humerus and laterally with the radius. The **semilunar notch** ("half moon notch") at the proximal end forms a "U" (which should help you remember "ulna") and articulates snugly at the trochlea. The olecranon process slides into the olecranon fossa of the humerus when the forearm is extended.

The proximal area of articulation with the radius is at the radial notch, just below the semilunar notch. Distally, the ulna ends with a small, rounded articular surface (the head) and the styloid process that is on the posteromedial surface. The rounded head of the ulna articulates with the distal radius.

To determine on which side an ulna resides in the body, place the semilunar notch in the proximal position with the open part of the "U" facing anteriorly. Then make sure that the radial notch is lateral (remember that the radius is the lateral bone in the body when it is in anatomical position), and align it with your body.

FIGURE 3.63 Left ulna, lateral view. *Photo, D. L. France*

FIGURE 3.64 Left ulna, medial view. *Photo, D. L. France*

FIGURE 3.65 Proximal ulna and radius articulated. *Photo, D. L. France*

Wrist and Hand

The wrist and hand consist of many different kinds of bones (Figures 3.66, 3.67, 3.68). The **carpals** are the eight wrist bones. From medial to lateral when the wrist is in the anatomical position, the proximal row consists of **pisiform, triquetral** (sing.: triquetrum)**, lunate,** and **navicular** (or **scaphoid**), and the distal row of **hamate, capitate, lesser multangular** (or **trapezoid**), and **greater multangular** (or **trapezium**).

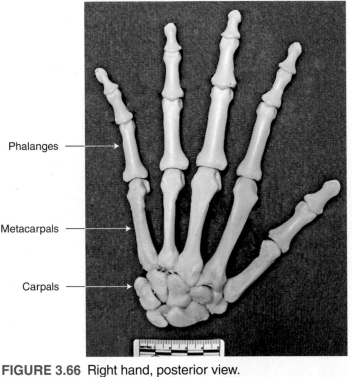

Phalanges

Metacarpals

Carpals

FIGURE 3.66 Right hand, posterior view.
Photo, D. L. France

FIGURE 3.67 Left hand, palmar view.
Photo, D. L. France

FIGURE 3.68 Carpals, left hand. *Photo, D. L. France*

The **metacarpals** make up the body of the living hand between the wrist and the projection of the fingers. They are simply numbered 1 through 5, beginning at the thumb (lateral or radial) side.

The **phalanges** are the bones of the fingers. The thumb has two (proximal and distal); all other fingers have three each (proximal, middle, and distal).

Os Coxa (Innominate)

The **os coxae (innominata)** (sing.: os coxa, or innominate) are the two large bones of the pelvis, which join with the sacrum to form the pelvic girdle (Figures 3.69, 3.70, 3.71).

Although the os coxa is one unit in the adult, it actually consists of three separate bones, all coming together in the **acetabulum,** the large cup-shaped cavity that articulates with the head of the femur (Figure 3.69).

- **Ilium:** upper portion. The **iliac crest** is the most superior edge of the ilium and can be felt through the skin. Posteriorly, the **greater sciatic notch** is a deep incurve. The auricular surface (so called because it looks like an ear) is the point of articulation with the sacrum, forming the sacroiliac joint.
- **Ischium:** the most posterior bone of the coxa. The **ischial tuberosity** supports the body in the sitting position. The area is roughened because of the attachment of many muscles and ligaments, including the origin of the powerful hamstring muscles that extend the thigh.
- **Pubis:** the most anterior portion. It articulates with the pubic bone from the opposite side at the **pubic symphysis** to form the anterior wall of the pelvis.

To determine on which side a complete os coxa resides in the body, make sure that the acetabulum is lateral (as it articulates with the head of the femur) and that the ischial tuberosity is posterior and caudal. It is tricky at first to determine which part of the os coxa is the ischial tuberosity and which is the pubic symphysis. Remember that the ischial tuberosity is a muscle insertion area, so it is larger and more rounded, and has a more roughened surface than seen on the pubic symphysis. Often the pubic symphysis has a flatter surface (except in very young individuals), as will be seen in Chapter 15.

Femur

The femur is the largest and longest bone in the human body (not so for all other animals, as we will see later). The head of the femur articulates proximally with the acetabulum, and the condyles articulate with the condyles of the tibia distally (Figures 3.72–3.75).

FIGURE 3.69 Left coxa, lateral view. *Photo, D. L. France*

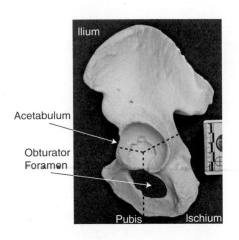

Ilium

Acetabulum

Obturator Foramen

Pubis   Ischium

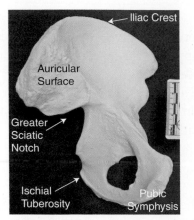

Iliac Crest

Auricular Surface

Greater Sciatic Notch

Ischial Tuberosity

Pubic Symphysis

FIGURE 3.70 Left coxa, medial view. *Photo, D. L. France*

FIGURE 3.71 Articulated pelvic girdle. *Photo, D. L. France*

Head

Greater Trochanter

Shaft

Patellar Articular Surface

FIGURE 3.72 Left femur, anterior view. *Photo, D. L. France*

Lesser Trochanter

Linea Aspera

Condyles

FIGURE 3.73 Left femur, posterior view. *Photo, D. L. France*

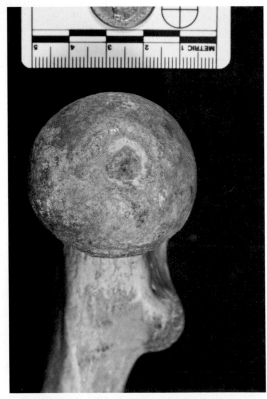

FIGURE 3.74 Right femoral head. *Photo, D. L. France*

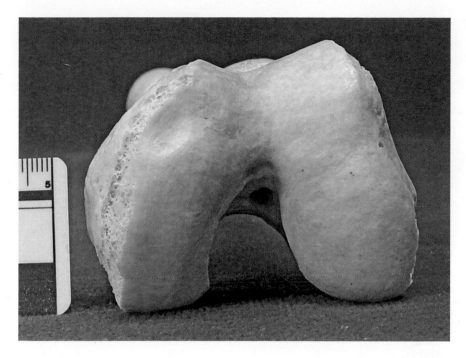

FIGURE 3.75 Distal femur.
Photo, D. L. France

The head of the femur is a more complete ball than is the head of the humerus. The head exhibits a pit, the **fovea capitis** (Figure 3.75)**,** in the center, at which the very strong **ligamentum teres** connects the femur to the acetabulum and carries blood to the femur. The femur is much more difficult to dislocate than is the head of the humerus in the living person. The greater trochanter is a large projection on the lateral proximal surface, roughened because of the insertion of muscles that, among other actions, abduct the thigh. The lesser trochanter is a posteromedial conical projection distal to the greater trochanter.

The **linea aspera** is a long raised and roughened line along the posterior aspect of the femur. It is the area of insertion of many muscles, including the powerful hamstring muscles that extend the thigh. The condyles of the distal femur are more extensive posteriorly, to allow the tibia to flex.

To determine on which side a femur resides in the body, make sure that the head faces medially (as it articulates with the acetabulum) and that it is proximal. The lesser trochanter is posterior, as are the more rounded aspects of the condyles. If you have only the proximal aspect, use the lesser trochanter. If you have only the distal aspect, make sure that the condyles are more rounded posteriorly and that they are distal. Also, notice that the distal aspect of the medial condyle is larger and has more of a curve anteroposteriorly. The lateral condyle is shorter (anteroposteriorly) and straighter.

FIGURE 3.76 Patella, anterior view. *Photo, D. L. France*

FIGURE 3.77 Patella, posterior view. *Photo, D. L. France*

Patella

The **patella** is the kneecap, which rests just anterior to the distal femur (Figures 3.76 and 3.77). The patella points distally and is rounded proximally. It is generally recognized as the largest of the **sesamoid bones.** A sesamoid bone is one that develops within a tendon (in this case, the patellar tendon) and acts as a pulley to enhance the mechanical force or action of the tendon that passes over it. Other smaller sesamoids occur in the hands and feet associated with the (usually first) metacarpals and metatarsals.

Determining on which side a patella resides in the body is easy. Simply place the bone on a table with the apex pointing away from you. The bone will fall to the side it is from. Also, the lateral articular surface is larger than the medial articular surface.

Tibia

The **tibia** (Figures 3.78–3.81), the second largest bone of the lower limb, has a **tibial tuberosity** and a sharp shin, both of which can be palpated anteriorly in the living subject. The tibial tuberosity is the point of common insertion (through the patellar tendon) of many of the muscles that flex the thigh at the hip and extend the leg. The articular facet for the fibula can be seen on the posterolateral tibia just below the condyles. The **medial malleolus** of the distal tibia forms the medial projection of the ankle felt in the living person.

To determine on which side a tibia resides in the body, make sure that the condyles are proximal, the medial malleolus is on the

FIGURE 3.80 Proximal left tibia. *Photo, D. L. France*

FIGURE 3.81 Distal left tibia *Photo, D. L. France*

FIGURE 3.78 Left tibia, anterior view. *Photo, D. L. France*

FIGURE 3.79 Left tibia, posterior view. *Photo, D. L. France*

medial side, and the tibial tuberosity is anterior. Then align the bone with your body.

Fibula

The **fibula** (Figures 3.82, 3.83, 3.84) is, with the tibia, the analog of the radius and ulna of the arm, although the leg has lost most of the pronation–supination function (see the earlier discussion). The **lateral malleolus** of the distal fibula forms the lateral projection of the ankle felt in the living subject. Distally, the fibula is grooved on the posterior surface (the malleolar fossa, Figure 3.84), where a tendon crosses from the posterior leg to the plantar surface of the foot, and acts to, among other things, extend the foot.

To determine on which side a fibula resides in the body, make sure that the styloid process is proximal and that the articular surface is medial (to articulate with the tibia). Also, make sure that the malleolar fossa is posterior, and place it in anatomical position.

FIGURE 3.82 Fibula, lateral view. *Photo, D. L. France*

Styloid Process

Shaft

Lateral Malleolus

FIGURE 3.83 Proximal left fibula. *Photo, D. L. France*

FIGURE 3.84 Malleolar fossa. *Photo, D. L. France*

Ankle and Foot

The **tarsals** are the seven bones that make up the ankle: the **calcaneus, talus, navicular, first cuneiform, second cuneiform, third cuneiform**, and **cuboid** (Figure 3.87).

The **metatarsals** are analogous to the metacarpals of the hand and make up the body of the foot. Again, they are simply numbered 1 (medial) through 5 (lateral).

The **phalanges** of the foot are again analogous to the phalanges of the hand (see Figure 3.85 and 3.86).

Phalanges

Metatarsals

Tarsals

FIGURE 3.85 Left foot, dorsal view.
Photo, D. L. France

FIGURE 3.86 Left foot, plantar view.
Photo, D. L. France

Cuboid

Second cuneiform

Third cuneiform

First cuneiform

Navicular

Calcaneus

Talus

FIGURE 3.87 Tarsals, left foot.
Photo, D. L. France

EXERCISE 3.2 NAME _____ **SECTION** _____ **DATE** _____

The Human Skeleton

1. Why do we usually see trabecular bone near articular surfaces of bone? To answer this question, think about the biomechanics of the areas around joint surfaces (in other words, what kinds of stresses/forces are applied to bone in these areas?).

2. Why do we see dense cortical bone in the midshaft of the femur (again, think about the biomechanics of this area of the femur)?

3. What bones were you looking at in the drumstick?

4. Short Answer

   Raised, rounded areas just above the eye orbits are the:

   The suture that joins the two parietal bones is the:

   The skull articulates with the vertebral column by means of:

   The place where the scapula that articulates with the humerus is:

   The rotation of the hand and forearm so that the palm faces downward is:

   The medial bone of the forearm (in the anatomical position) is:

5. What is the definition of a dental formula?

6. How many deciduous premolars are there in humans?

7. What is the dental formula of

   a. an adult human?

   b. a human child of 5 years?

   c. an adult chimpanzee?

FIGURE 3.88 Unknown. *Photo, D. L. France*

FIGURE 3.88 Unknown. *Photo, D. L. France*

8. What vertebra is in Figure 3.88 (cervical, thoracic, lumbar, sacral, or coccygeal)? What leads you to this conclusion?

FIGURE 3.89 Unknown. *Photo, D. L. France*

FIGURE 3.89 Unknown. *Photo, D. L. France*

9. What bone is shown in Figure 3.89? What leads you to this conclusion? From what side is it?

FIGURE 3.90 Unknown. *Photo, D. L. France*

10. What are the three segments of this sternum (Figure 3.90)?

    a.

    b.

    c.

FIGURE 3.91 Unknown. *Photo, D. L. France*

11. Is the bone in Figure 3.91 the head of a femur or of a humerus? How can you tell?

12. How is the first rib different from the other ribs?

13. How are the 11th and 12th ribs different from the other ribs?

FIGURE 3.92 Unknown
Photo, D. L. France

14. What bones are shown in Figure 3.92? This is from what side of the body? How can you tell?

BONE FRAGMENT IDENTIFICATION

The identification of bone fragments is likely the single best way to really learn about the skeleton. To identify fragments, you have to pay attention to the gross morphology of the entire bone, the different parts of each bone, and the texture of the different areas in bone (refer to Figure 3.16).

Identifying the Bones of the Cranium

The cranium is a complicated set of bones. There are smooth, gently curved sections (such as the parietals and frontal), very small with relatively sharp edges such as the lacrimals and ethmoids, morphologically complicated such as the sphenoid, rough muscle insertion areas such as the mastoids, and so on.

Here are a few hints (these are not at all exhaustive—there are so many different shapes and textures within the cranium that it would take an entire book to list all of the traits of each section):

- If you see sutures, you are looking at a section of cranium. Some sutures are extremely complex and isolate little sections of bone (called extra-sutural or Wormian bones). Those sutures can occur in many areas of the cranium, but if the sutures are large and complex, they are more likely on or near the lambdoidal suture (Figure 3.93).
- Very thin bones are often in the cranium (although the scapula has a thin section, so be careful if you have a small fragment).
- The parietal bones are relatively smooth on the outside surface but have grooves for the middle meningeal arteries on the inside surface. Those grooves run from the lower anterior to the upper posterior cranium, so they can be used not only for bone identification but also for side identification (Figure 3.94).
- The bones of the superior orbits are very thin and gently curved next to the eye and wavy on the inside of the cranium (Figure 3.95).
- The occipital bone is thick and has a set of raised surfaces internally that form the shape of a cross. This is the cruciform eminence and is the point of separation of the occipital lobes of the cerebral hemispheres and the lobes of the cerebellum (Figure 3.96).

Identifying Long Bones

Following are some hints for identifying long bones:

- Be alert for areas of articulation, particularly those areas with freely movable joints. Note the shape of that articular surface. Is it round like a ball (suggesting the head of the humerus or femur)? Is it a hinge joint (suggesting, for example, the distal humerus)?

FIGURE 3.93 Closeup of posterior cranial sutures.
Photo, D. L. France

FIGURE 3.94 Intracranial view of parietal bone.
Photo, D. L. France

FIGURE 3.95 Intracranial view of orbits. *Photo, D. L. France*

FIGURE 3.96 Intracranial view of occipital bone. *Photo, D. L. France*

FIGURE 3.97 Cross-section of femur. *Photo, D. L. France*

- Do you have a section of trabecular bone (see Figure 3.97)? Where do you normally see trabecular bone (this was discussed earlier in this chapter)?
- Look for compact bones typical of a long bone shaft. Is it robust and large in cross section (suggesting perhaps a femur)? If so, look for evidence of the linea aspera.
- Notice the texture of the bone. Is it full of foramina (perhaps like the femoral neck)? Is it rough, suggesting an area of muscle or ligament insertion?
- Do you have a bone that is relatively small in cross section but has cortical bone at midshaft? It might be a bone of the hand or foot (the metacarpals, metatarsals, or proximal and middle phalanges).

The hints for irregular bones (such as the scapula, sternum, os coax, vertebrae, etc.) are just modifications of the hints for the other areas of the body. Keep an eye out for areas of articulation, areas of muscle attachment (insertion or origin), thick cortical bone, trabecular bone, and general morphology. If the bone wasn't broken, what shape would it be just beyond the break?

The following exercises will help you practice fragment identification, intact bone identification, and the biomechanics of the skeleton (human and nonhuman). If you have bone fragments in your laboratory, practice on them. Also try putting bones in other students' hands behind their back or in a box covered with cloth so that the bone cannot be seen. Figure out what bone you are holding just by the sense of touch.

EXERCISE 3.3 **NAME** _____ **SECTION** _____ **DATE** _____

Fragment Identification

FIGURE 3.98 Unknown. *Photo, D. L. France*

1. Are all human cranial sutures the same? Figure 3.98 shows a section of cranium. Where on the cranium could this be located?

FIGURE 3.99 Unknown. *Photo, D. L. France*

2. What bones are represented in Figure 3.99? From what side of the body?

FIGURE 3.100 Unknown. *Photo, D. L. France*

3. What bone is represented in Figure 3.100? From what side of the body?

FIGURE 3.101 Unknown. *Photo, D. L. France*

4. What bone is represented in Figure 3.101? From what side of the body?

FIGURE 3.102 Unknown. *Photo, D. L. France*

5. What bone is represented in Figure 3.102? From what side of the body?

FIGURE 3.103 Unknown. *Photo, D. L. France*

6. What bone(s) is/are represented in Figure 3.103? From what side of the body?

FIGURE 3.104 Unknown. 7.
Photo, D. L. France

7. What bone is represented in Figure 3.104? From what side of the body?

REEXAMINING THE ISSUES

In this chapter, we learned the following:

- The names of the bones and the relationship of those bones to adjacent bones in the body.
- Bone is a living, dynamic tissue that responds to its environment.
- If you want to learn about an animal's skeleton and what it does for a "living" (i.e., its locomotor modes, etc.), the first step is to learn about the bones themselves.

CHAPTER 4

●

Growth and Development

OBJECTIVES

1. How can we determine a person's age at death by looking at the skeleton?
2. If someone claims that he can legally drink alcohol because he is 21 years of age, how can we determine whether or not that person is likely telling the truth?
3. How confident can we be in using modern standards to diagnose the age at death of a fossil hominid?

We will build on our understanding of the skeleton by investigating how humans (and, to some extent, other animals) grow and develop. Knowing the *relative* ages at which certain milestones occur in the development of the skeleton gives us the tools we need to identify the age at death of a fossil hominid as well as a modern young victim of crime. By studying the rate at which other animals (particularly primates) grow and develop and by comparing those ages to modern humans, we may better understand the aging process in fossil hominids. By learning that the rates vary at which certain bones develop in different individuals, we may avoid the common mistake of stating an exact age at death of fossil hominids or modern humans (we should instead state the age as a range). And as we learn the effects of nutritional and disease status of an individual during this growth process, we may use those clues to more effectively determine the history of an unknown individual.

We will delve into the morphological (primarily degenerative) changes in the adult skeleton and dentition in Chapters 14 and 15.

INTRODUCTION

When we talk about growth and development, we often assume that they mean the same thing. However, *growth* is defined as the increase in size (of a cell, bone, etc.), while *development* can mean a morphological change that does not necessarily occur with absolute growth. Also, we must observe that not only is an individual becoming taller and more developed through time (until the late teens or early twenties in a healthy, well-nourished individual), the *rate* at which these factors proceed increases and decreases during certain periods. The growth and development of the body proceeds very quickly in the uterus, where the fertilized egg produces cells at a rapid rate and differentiation of those cells into different kinds of tissues can be marked in days (or less). The rate of growth slows somewhat during the last 3 months before birth but becomes rapid again after birth. Although growth and development continues, the rate spikes again during the adolescent growth spurt around the time of puberty. At this time, males and females undergo rapid growth in height and development of the skeleton and soft tissues and rapid differentiation in sexual features. In other words, at birth there is very little sexual dimorphism (differences between males and females) in the skeleton, while at puberty the skeleton becomes very different between males and females. This is a very important fact in human-identification cases because it is very difficult to diagnose the sex of an individual much before puberty (this will be discussed in more detail in Chapter 15). Also, females at about this time grow and mature more quickly than males (by about two years), an important feature to remember.

It is important to note that bone is composed of both an organic and inorganic component—that is, bone is not entirely mineral; there is a soft-tissue component as well. The mineral component is a compound of calcium and phosphates called hydroxyapatite that is formed in and around an organic matrix containing collagen. Collagen is similar in consistency to very thick, relatively hard gelatin (like a hard Jell-O® made with much less water than normal). This is important to understand not only because it helps to explain the way in which bone develops, but it also helps to explain the way bone decomposes and the way it reacts to various stresses (fractures, cuts, diseases, etc.). These will be discussed in more detail in Chapters 14 and 15.

The growth and development of the skeletal elements is also interesting. Most bones will grow and develop from primary centers (which occur first within a particular bone and are approximately midshaft in long bones) and often from one or more secondary centers (which usually occur on the ends of long bones or on projections such as the greater trochanter of the femur). Different bones will develop at different rates and ages throughout the body, which is particularly useful in determining age because the age can be bracketed by the age of appearance and union of the different elements.

At the very earliest stages, the centers of bone growth start as a single bone cell and, for a time, are indistinguishable from other centers of bone growth of the same size in the body. Of course, their location in the body can be determined if the body is intact, and this can give valuable information about the age of the individual. But if the amorphous centers are discovered archaeologically when the position within the body is not known, they are, naturally, considerably less useful in age determination (if they are found at all).

SKELETAL DEVELOPMENT FROM THE FETUS TO THE ADULT

Dental and skeletal tissues arise from **mesenchymal cells** (see, for example, Carlson, 2004), which are unspecialized cells in the embryo that give rise to all connective tissue (including cartilage, bone, and elements of the teeth, but also including blood vessels, blood, the heart, and other tissues). Interestingly, the mesenchymal cells within the embryo migrate to different locations and receive signals from other tissues and growth factors, which dictate the type of cell into which they will develop; that is, mesenchymal cells have different points of origin and develop from different cells and into different cells in the embryo. For example, in the cranium, some of the bones originate from mesenchymal cells derived from one part of the embryo, while the facial bones and cranial vault bones are from mesenchymal cells from a different part of the embryo (from Carlson, 2004).

Some areas of the cranium are ossified (turned into bone) from membranes transformed from mesenchymal tissues and are called **intramembranous bones.** These bones include the cranial vault, facial bones, mandible, and, in part, the clavicle (remodeling bone also involves intramembranous ossification). Other bones in the body are developed from mesenchymal tissues that develop into cartilage models first and are then overtaken by osteogenic (bone-forming) cells that develop that cartilage into bone. These are called **endochondral bones** (this is a simplified version of the complex nature of intramembranous and endochondral bone formation, and some bones, such as the clavicle, are a mixture of the two processes). Figure 4.1 shows a six-month-old fetus stained to show the developing skeleton.

Throughout these processes of bone development in the embryo through adulthood, some mesenchymal cells differentiate into osteogenic cells called **osteoblasts**. In intramembranous ossification, the osteoblasts begin to lay down a network of fine bone (very small spicules of bone) in the membrane. Initial bone formation occurs very quickly and produces loosely woven bone (more a collection or weaving of those spicules of bone). A significant amount of cartilage remains within these areas of rapid bone growth, and if dry bone (in which much of the organic

Mesenchymal Cells: unspecialized cells in the embryo that give rise to all connective tissue, including cartilage, bone, and teeth (as well as some other types of cells).

Endochondral means "inside cartilage." Chondral tissue is cartilage tissue.

Intramembranous means "inside membrane."

Membranous bone = specialized mesenchymal cells → membrane → bone

Endochondral bone = specialized mesenchymal cells → cartilage → matrix bone

FIGURE 4.1 Stained six-month human fetus. *Photo, D. L. France of specimen courtesy of National Museum of Health and Medicine*

Osteoblasts: bone-forming cells.

Osteoclasts: bone-removing cells.

Chondroblasts: cartilage-forming cells.

Chondroclasts: cartilage-removing cells.

Odontoblasts: dentin-forming cells.

Periosteum: a thin layer of soft tissue that surrounds bone.

component is removed) is observed at this stage, it will appear to be very porous (Figure 4.2). This is true in intramembranous or endochondral bone. This bone growth is so rapid that it traps osteoblasts, which then become **osteocytes** (bone cells).

FIGURE 4.2 Porous nature of infant bone.
Photo, D. L. France

 Click!

For the chicken drumstick exercise. See the collagen matrix surrounding the proximal epiphysis, and what bone looks like during rapid growth.

THE CHICKEN DRUMSTICK EXERCISE

In Chapter 3, Human Osteology, you were introduced to the chicken drumstick exercise (you can read about or perform the initial parts of the exercise on pages 81, or you can go to Chapter 3 on the book companion website at www.cengage.com/anthropology/france for an online version). The growth and development part of the exercise involves the cartilage at the proximal and distal ends of the drumstick (by now you know that this is the tibia and fibula of the chicken) and in the nature of the bone itself.

The cartilage at the proximal end was removed to study the proximal aspect of the bone and to view the very porous nature of the tibia. Compare the chicken bone in Figure 4.3 to the porosity of the human infant femur shown in Figure 4.2. It is useful to compare the proximal aspect of the tibia from an older chicken than the one we have been studying.

After studying the bone itself, clean the bits of proximal tibia off of the inside (or distal aspect) of the cartilage so that you are looking at a relatively clean surface (Figure 4.4). Look through the cartilage at a relatively strong light. Do you see the small dark spot? You will be asked about this dark spot in the exercises.

FIGURE 4.3 Proximal chicken tibia. *Photo, D. L. France*

FIGURE 4.4 Chicken proximal tibia epiphyseal cartilage. *Photo, D. L. France*

The porous nature of infant bones somewhat mimics some pathological conditions (such as an inflammation of the periosteum, or periostitis) in which the bone reacts to stress by rapidly laying down bone. It is important to recognize that infant bones are very porous in a healthy, well-nourished individual, as well.

FIGURE 4.5 Developmental stages of the human femur. *Drawing, Reprinted with permission from Kathryn Born and Joseph Henry Press. Copyright 2006 by the National Academy of Sciences. Courtesy of the National Academies Press, Washington, D.C.*

FIGURE 4.6 Nutrient foramen in infant femur.
Photo, D. L. France

Nutrient foramen

FIGURE 4.7 Normal adult femur (left), shortened femur from an achondroplastic dwarf.
Photo, D. L. France

FIGURE 4.8 Femur at two stages of development. Note that the shape of the two femora changes with age, necessitating removal of bone in some places with deposition of bone in others.
Photo, D. L. France

A bone may have several secondary centers of growth (see Figure 4.5). In endochondral bone, each secondary center of bone growth (termed **epiphysis;** pl.: epiphyses) will grow and develop and eventually fuse to the growing and developing primary center (termed **diaphysis;** pl.: diaphyses). Bone growth in a shaft begins where bone-forming cells enter the matrix of cartilage and begin to secrete a substance that is quickly mineralized (the hydroxyapatite crystals). The primary blood vessel that initially carries these osteoblasts into the diaphysis becomes surrounded by bone and becomes the nutrient foramen (Figure 4.6). This process proceeds away from the initial site of bone growth toward both ends of the bone; and the growth is the most rapid at the ends of the bone formation.

At about this time, different mesenchymal cells are differentiating into a thin layer of soft tissue called **periosteum,** which coats the bone and is filled with blood vessels. This layer will be active in bone formation throughout the life of the individual and will itself react to various stresses (bacterial, trauma, etc.).

The area of rapid growth between the diaphysis and the epiphysis (or epiphyses) is the growth plate or metaphysis. As the cartilage matrix is turned into bone at the diaphysis and the epiphysis, the cartilage between the two continues to grow and add new cells. In this way the bone growth between the diaphysis and epiphysis can continue. When the bone formation at the diaphysis meets the formation of bone at the epiphysis, the two unite, and longitudinal bone growth ceases (that bone will not grow longer; see Figures 4.9 to 4.11 for information about what epiphyseal union looks like and the approximate ages at which it occurs in various bones). If this happens too quickly, the bones may be shorter than normal (refer to Figure 4.7). If it happens too late, bones may be longer than normal.

It makes sense that as the bone is growing in length in the infant and beyond, the size of the initial bone is infant-sized, so it has to have a way to increase its diameter as it grows in length. It does this by appositional growth (or putting layers over the older layers) and taking away some bone from the areas to be reshaped. There is a constant process of remodeling of bone practically from the very

FIGURE 4.9 Stages of epiphyseal union at the iliac crest: (a) unfused with no epiphysis present, (b) unfused with separate epiphysis, (c) partially united, (d) obliterated line with complete union. These are part of an epiphyseal age determination system developed by P. O. Webb and J. M. Suchey (1985). *Photo, D. L. France*

FIGURE 4.10 Epiphyseal surface on proximal tibia. *Photo, D. L. France*

FIGURE 4.11 Epiphyseal union in various bones. *Photo, D. L. France*

beginning of bone formation, and it proceeds throughout life. This process is undertaken by osteoclasts taking bone away from where it is not useful and additional osteoblasts putting bone down where it is needed (refer to Figure 4.8).

After birth, girls mature at an earlier age than do boys (this is very important!). The adolescent growth spurt occurs later in boys than in girls, which means that the skeletons in boys have somewhat more time to increase in size before the spurt in maturity (Tanner, 1978).

Adults

As was discussed in Chapter 3, the areas of cranial sutures are actually joint surfaces, though not the same kind of highly movable joint as in, for example, the knee or shoulder. In adults, those sutures may eventually disappear, and the bones separated by them will fuse in a way similar to the fusion of epiphyses to diaphyses. Cranial bones will often fuse at different rates *endocranially* (inside the cranium) and *ectocranially* (outside the cranium). Although the age at which this occurs varies from suture to suture, it also varies considerably between individuals, making it somewhat problematic for use in age determination in the adult. This will be discussed further in Chapter 15.

Table 4. 1 Appearance of Ossification Centers and Epiphyseal Union in Various Postcranial Bones (IU = In Utero)

Bone	Element	Appearance	Union	Notes
Clavicle	Diaphysis	Week 5 IU		
	Sternal epiphysis		17–30 for males, 16–33 females (Webb and Suchey, 1985)	
	Acromial epiphysis		19–20	
Sternum	Manubrium	Month 5 IU		
	Body sections	1: week 5 IU	All sections to manubrium 15–20 yrs.	
		2 & 3: by week 8 IU	Body section 2 fuses to 3 & 4 at 11–16 yrs.	
		4: after 1 yr	Body section 3 fuses to 4 at 4–10 yrs.	
Cervical vertebrae	Atlas	Week 7–10 IU	Three major sections 5–6 yrs.	
	Axis	Week approx. 8 IU	Major elements 9–10 yrs.	

continues

Table 4. 1 (Continued)

Bone	Element	Appearance	Union	Notes
	Axis dens tip	Approx. 2 years	To dens approx. 12 yrs.	
	C7–C3 (progressing cranially)	By month 4 IU	Neural arches 2–3 yrs.; arches to centrum 3–4 yrs.	
Thoracic vertebrae	Centrum and both neural arches	By week 10 IU	Fuse from caudally to cranially neural arches 1–3 yrs.; arches to centrum 5–6 yrs.	
Lumbar vertebrae	Centrum and both neural arches (progressing caudally)	By month 4 IU	Progressing caudally, arches 1–5 yrs.; arches to centrum 2–4 yrs.	
Ilium	Primary center	Months 2–3 IU		
	Iliac crest	12–13 yrs. in females; 14–15 yrs. in males	Completed 18–24 yrs. in females, 17–24 in males (Webb and Suchey, 1985).	
Ischium	Primary center	Months 3–5 IU	Fuses with pubis 4–8 yrs.	
	Ischial tuberosity	13–16 yrs.	Completed by 21–23 yrs.	
Pubis	Primary center	Months 4–6 IU	Fuses with ischium 4–8 yrs.	
Os coxa	All major elements		11–15 yrs. in females, 15–17 yrs. in males	
Sacrum**	Centra (center) for S1–S3	Month 3 IU	S1–3 centra to arches and alae 2–5 yrs.	
	Neural arches for S1–S3	Months 4–6 IU		
	Alae for S1–S3	Months 6–8 IU		
	Centra for S4, S5	Months 4–5 IU	S4, S5 centra to arches 2–6 yrs.	
	Neural arches for S4, S5	Months 6–8 IU		
	Sacral elements		At spinous processes 7–15, alae and centra approx. 12–20 yrs., years from S5 to S1; S1–S2 in the 20s.	
	Auricular surface and lateral epiphyses	15–16 yrs.	to sacrum late teens	
Scapula	Body	Week 7–8 IU		
	Coracoid process	Birth–1 yr.	To body 16–17 yrs.	
	Acromion process	13–16 yrs.	18–20 yrs.	

Table 4. 1 (Continued)

Bone	Element	Appearance	Union	Notes
	Inferior angle	15–17 yrs.	20–23 yrs.	
	Vertebral margin	15–17 yrs.	20–23 yrs.	
Humerus	Diaphysis	Week 7 IU		
	Head epiphysis	Birth–6 mos.	To diaphysis: 15–19 in females; 18–22 in males	
	Distal epiphyses	6 mos. to 2 yrs.	To diaphysis: 11–15 in females; 12–17 in males	
	Medial epicondyle	After 4 yrs.	To diaphysis: 13–15 in females; 14–16 in males	
Radius	Diaphysis	Week 7 IU		
	Proximal epiphysis	Approx. 5 yrs.	To diaphysis: 11–15 in females; 14–17 in males	
	Distal epiphysis	1–3 yrs.	To diaphysis: 14–17 in females; 16–20 in males	
Ulna	Diaphysis	Week 7 IU		
	Proximal epiphysis	8–10 yrs.	To diaphysis: 12–15 in females; 13–17 in males	
	Distal epiphysis	5–7 yrs.	To diaphysis: 15–17 in females; 17–20 in males	
Hand	Carpals	After birth		
	Metacarpal diaphyses	Week 8–10 IU		
	Metacarpal distal epiphyses 2–5	10 months–2.5 yrs.	to diaphysis: 14–15 in females, 16–17 in males*	
	Phalanges vary			
Femur	Diaphysis	Week 7–8 IU		
	Head	Birth–1 yr.	To diaphysis: 12–16 in females; 14–19 in males	
	Greater trochanter	1–5 yrs.	To diaphysis: 14–16 in females; 16–18 in males	
	Lesser trochanter	7–12 yrs.	To diaphysis: 16–17 yrs.	
	Distal epiphysis	Week 36–40 IU (usually before birth)	To diaphysis: 14–18 in females; 16–20 in males	
Tibia	Diaphysis	Week 8 IU		
	Proximal epiphysis	Near birth	To diaphysis: 13–17 in females; 15–19 in males	
	Distal epiphysis	Approx. 2 yrs.	To diaphysis: 14–16 in females; 15–18 in males	

continues

Table 4. 1 (Continued)

Bone	Element	Appearance	Union	Notes
Fibula	Diaphysis	Week 8 IU		
	Proximal epiphysis	Approx. 4–5 yrs.	To diaphysis: 12–18 in females; 15–20 in males	
	Distal epiphysis	1–2 yrs.	To diaphysis: 12–16 in females; 15–18 in males	
Foot	Calcaneus	Varies: week 3–28 IU		
	Calcaneus posterior epiphysis	4–12 yrs.	Beg. 10–12 in females; 11–14 in males; and completed by 16 in females and 22 in males	
	Metatarsal diaphysis	Week 8–10 IU		
	Metatarsal distal epiphyses	2–3 yrs.	To diaphysis: 11–13 in females; 14–16 in males; and completed by 16 in females and 18 in males	

*Scheuer and Black, 2000.
**Sacral elements fuse at spinous processes first, then lateral borders, and then centra.
These ages are approximations and are compiled from Scheuer and Black (2000) (who often report narrower age ranges than other sources); Baker et al., 2005; Webb and Suchey, 1985; Bass, 1996; and McKern and Stewart, 1957. Also, see hand-wrist radiographs from Greulich and Pyle, 1959. Females usually mature more quickly than males by about 1 to 2 years.

EXERCISE 4.1   NAME _____   SECTION _____   DATE _____

Skeletal Development

FIGURE 4.12 Two stages of femur development superimposed. *Photo, D. L. France*

1. In Figure 4.12, would you expect greater action by osteoblasts or osteoclasts in the shaded area?

FIGURE 4.13 Unknown for Question 2. *Photo, D. L. France*

2. In Figure 4.13, what is the feature designated by the arrow, and what is the significance of that feature in growth and development?

3. Why is it important to know the sex of the individual before estimating the skeletal age?

4. How do you change your reported estimated age if you do not know the sex of the individual?

FIGURE 4.14 Distal radius.
Photo, D. L. France

5. What is the age range of the individual represented in Figure 4.14? On what are you basing that estimate?

FIGURE 4.15 Unknown for
Question 6. *Photo, D. L. France*

6. What is the age range of the individual represented in Figure 4.15? On what are you basing that
    estimate?

FIGURE 4.16 Unknown
for Question 7. *Photo,
D. L. France*

FIGURE 4.17 Unknown for
Question 7. *Photo, D. L.
France*

7. Is the individual represented in Figure 4.16 younger or older than the individual represented in
    Figure 4.17? How can you tell? What cautionary notes would you put into your report concern-
    ing this determination?

DENTAL DEVELOPMENT FROM THE FETUS TO THE ADULT

Dental tissue also arises from mesenchymal cells. **Ameloblasts** are the cells that secrete enamel.

Odontoblasts secrete the dentin of the tooth (Carlson, 2004). Hydroxyapatite (also the mineral component of bone) is the dominant inorganic component of enamel (Carlson, 2004).

As was discussed in Chapter 3, there are two sets of teeth in humans: the deciduous (or baby) teeth followed by the permanent dentition. All teeth develop from the crown to the tip (apex) of the root (Figure 4.18) and begin to develop deep inside the maxilla or mandible before reaching a point in their development at which they erupt beyond the gum line (or the alveolus in bone) and become noticeable in the mouth. Note that in a young mandible, there are large voids (called crypts) in which the crown of the tooth develops, and those voids close around the root of the tooth as it erupts beyond the alveolus. If you find that large void, you know that a tooth was developing in that void (Figure 4.19), but be careful you do not mistake it for a void caused by a disease process such as an abscess or mistake it for a fracture before or after death.

Beneath (in the mandible) or above (in the maxilla) the deciduous tooth, the permanent tooth is forming, and while it is expanding in size, the root of the deciduous tooth begins to resorb (Figure 4.20).

Ameloblasts: cells that secrete enamel.

Odontoblasts: dentin-forming cells

FIGURE 4.18 Partially developed molar. *Photo, D. L. France*

FIGURE 4.19 Developing dentition in crypts. *Photo, D. L. France*

FIGURE 4.20 Cutaway mandible showing dental development. *Photo, D. L. France*

FIGURE 4.21 Dental eruption chart. *Courtesy, D. Ubelaker*

When enough of the deciduous root is gone, the deciduous tooth falls out.

Dental Eruption

The determination of the ages at which the deciduous and permanent dentition erupts is useful in identifying age to approximately 15 years. The third molar (wisdom tooth) erupts after this time, but the age at its eruption (if it erupts, as many never do) is so variable that it is not a very reliable indicator of age. The chart shown for dental eruption times (Figure 4.21) is based on a Native American population, so be aware that other populations will vary from these time frames.

Dental Development

FIGURE 4.22a Unknown.
Photo, D. L. France

FIGURE 4.22b Unknown.
Photo, D. L. France

1. Concerning Figures 4.22a and 4.22b:

    a. Do the cranium and mandible represent an adult or subadult?

    b. How can you tell?

    c. What is the approximate age of this individual?

FIGURE 4.23a Unknown.
Photo, D. L. France

FIGURE 4.23b Unknown.
Photo, D. L. France

2. There are two individuals represented in Figures 4.23a and 4.23b.

    a. Which tooth is the most developed? How can you tell?

    b. Which individual is the oldest? How can you tell?

FIGURE 4.24a Unknown. *Photo, D. L. France*

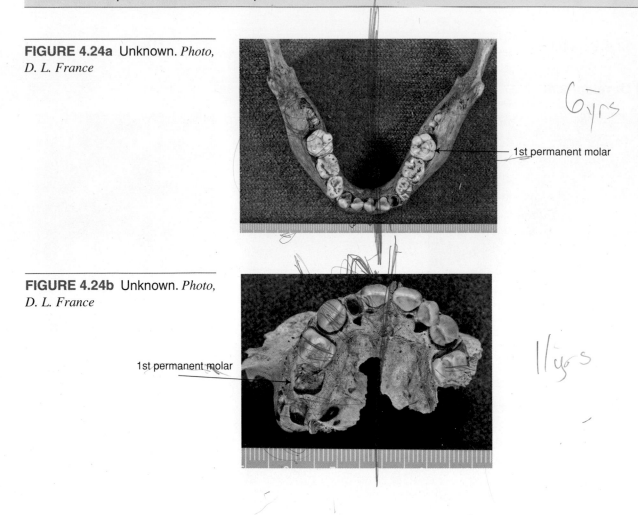

6 yrs

1st permanent molar

FIGURE 4.24b Unknown. *Photo, D. L. France*

1st permanent molar

11 yrs

3. There are two individuals represented in Figures 4.24 a and 4.24b.

    Which individual is the oldest? How can you tell?

THE EFFECTS OF VARIOUS INSULTS
ON BONE AND TEETH

The rate and degree of growth and development in a young individual is largely determined by genetics and the timing of the release of hormones. We know that the actual rate at which an individual develops is influenced heavily by other factors of the environment, the nutritional status of the individual, and disease.

It is commonly known that there are secular changes throughout recent decades in adult size (we are taller than our parents and grandparents), but there is also a decrease in the age at which adult size is achieved in many societies (Tanner, 1962; Floud et al., 1990; Hoppa and Garlie, 1998). The age at menarche and the age of the adolescent growth spurt tend to occur earlier as well (Tanner, 1978; Roede and Van Wieringen, 1985; Hoppa and Garlie, 1998). The effects on human children of hormones fed to cattle and chickens, and in other foods are becoming widely known (primarily in earlier maturation ages).

A low socioeconomic status of an individual may result in compromised nutrition and greater exposure to disease. Garn et al. (1973a, b) found that lower socioeconomic status resulted in smaller babies, smaller children, and delayed maturation. Many different kinds of osteological and odontological insults can occur when bones and teeth are growing. These can be genetic (a mutation of the gene or chromosome, for instance), problems during pregnancy (including nutritional deficiencies, disease agents, or "environmental" problems within the womb), or nutritional, health, or traumatic insults as the body is developing. These insults can result in the bone or tooth growing or developing abnormally (the recognition and diagnosis of the abnormality *may* be traced back to one of these agents, but, as will be seen later, there are a limited number of ways in which bones and teeth can react to stress). Some insults will result in slowed growth and development of bones and teeth, but it has been known for some time that dental development is more resistant to these stresses than is bone development, so the diagnosis of age from dental development is somewhat more accurate (see Saunders and Katzenberg, 1992, and Hillson, 2003, for good discussions of dental formation and eruption).

A commonly described result that has been linked to disease or nutritional problems in the growing bone is called "growth-arrest lines" or "Harris lines" (after the person who described them). These are lines of bone where the bone cells are denser than in other areas of bone, and they occur at the point at which the cartilage matrix is being overtaken by bone. The osteoblasts are still laying down bone, but the cartilage matrix is adversely affected to a greater degree and does not allow the formation of bone to advance forward as quickly, so the bone is denser. These insults can be linked to nutritional

FIGURE 4.25 Radiograph of radius showing growth arrest line.
Photo, D. L. France

FIGURE 4.26 Enamel hypoplasia.
Photo, D. L. France

problems or even a child's high fever. After the body has recovered to the point at which normal bone growth can occur, growth proceeds beyond the growth-arrest line, but that line may exist for years and can be seen both in radiographs and by the naked eye in cross sections of the bone. It will potentially disappear with continuous remodeling that occurs in a normal, healthy body (Figure 4.25).

A similar effect takes place in dentition with enamel hypoplasias. If an insult similar to those described previously occurs when a tooth is developing, the enamel of that tooth takes on a wrinkled or ribbed appearance (Figure 4.26). If that occurs while a permanent tooth is developing, that effect will stay with that tooth forever because unlike bones, teeth do not remodel throughout the life of the individual.

THE USE OF SERIATION TECHNIQUES

Seriation in age estimation involves placing an individual within a series of individuals based on age. Placing an individual in a series is, of course, easy when you know the absolute ages of a group of people, but when used on undocumented skeletal remains in a mass grave, a mass fatality incident, or an undocumented cemetery, it can be difficult, particularly if the remains are fragmentary. In reality, as much as the biological profile (age, sex, stature, ancestry, etc.) and nutrition and disease states of individual skeletal elements are used to assist in reassociating remains, age is almost always an important variable.

A FINAL COMMENT

At least in part because of the variables in the life of an individual before death (insults, nutrition and health status, etc.), there is a range of variation in the dental or skeletal maturity, stature, and other aspects of individuals studied (here we are talking primarily about skeletal samples, but this applies as well to living subjects). When the anthropologist develops standards (age, stature, etc.) for a population from a sample of individuals, there is a temptation to throw out the measurements from those individuals who are on the outer edges of the normal range. If this is done, the standards developed from that sample have narrower ranges of variation than normal. This practice might make the standards look more *precise* (and might make it more attractive for use in court, for example), but it artificially narrows the age range and therefore makes the standards less *accurate*. Researchers must resist this temptation and embrace the variation that makes us human. We can explain the natural variation within the human species far more convincingly than we can explain away the fact that the individual we just studied remains unidentified because we wanted narrow age ranges, for instance, and our victim falls outside that range.

EXERCISE 4.3   NAME _____   SECTION _____   DATE _____

Growth and Development

1. Why should skeletal age be reported as a range instead as of a single age?

2. What problems can you identify in developing stature reconstruction formulae from collections of skeletons established in the 1940s for use in modern populations?

3. When developing age-determination standards for use in modern populations, what variables in the population would you like to control?

4. When using modern age-determination standards on early fossil hominids, what cautionary notes would you want to include in your analysis?

5. In many countries, different punishments for crime are applied to adults and to those under 18 years of age. If you were asked by the court to identify whether or not someone was over 18 years of age,

   a. What tests would you perform (i.e., what features of the body would you use)?

   b. What would you want to know about the individual?

   c. What would you say to the court if you discovered Harris lines in a radiograph of the individual?

6. What would cause a difference between the biological age (the age of the body) and chronological age (the time since birth) of an individual?

7. If you are trying to identify the individual skeletal (including dental) elements of two individuals aged 10 and 16 years of age, what specific clues would you be trying to find?

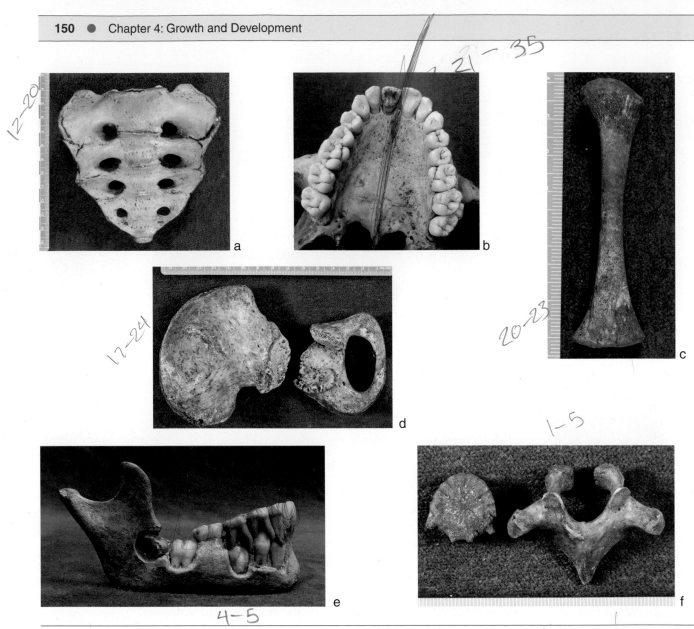

FIGURE 4.27a-f Unknown. *Photo, D. L. France*

8. In Figures 4.27a through 4.27f, seriate the individuals from youngest to oldest, and include why you made those decisions.

REEXAMINING THE ISSUES

- Bones and teeth are ultimately derived from mesenchymal tissues.
- The rate and age at which individual bones and teeth develop differ within a body and between individuals but are predictable enough that they are useful for determining the biological and chronological age of an individual.
- There are secular changes in the maturation rate and age over time.
- The growth and development of an individual will react to different stresses.

●

CHAPTER 5

Biological Classification

OBJECTIVES

1. Why do we talk about all living creatures in terms of genus and species?

2. What does the classification system we use tell us about the relationships between all living creatures?

3. How have recent comparisons of genomes changed the way we classify primates (including the genetic distance between humans and nonhuman primates)?

Classification systems are developed because they improve communication. There are many classification systems based on common names of items, people, events, and so on, but at some point, scientists need an unambiguous language to speak to each other about their studies (think about the scientific method and how much more difficult it would be for scientists to test hypotheses and theories without being certain that they are studying the same animal!). If scientists did not have a way to organize individuals (or new fossils discovered by paleoanthropologists) into species, it would be more difficult to know how that fossil compares with other previously described fossils or with contemporary or extant species. That we can talk about "species" and "genera" in modern and fossil organisms is made possible by early classification systems.

How do those classification systems make sense of the biological world? Which classification system is the most logical given the variation in that biological world? Are these systems completely arbitrary? This chapter will introduce some of the tools necessary for answering these questions.

Phylogenetic: a classification system based on evolutionary relationships, usually including a time line.

Cladistics: a classification system based on homologous derived characteristics. This system does not always include a time line.

INTRODUCTION

Biological classification is based on the system established by the Swedish naturalist Carolus Linnaeus (Karl von Linné, 1707–1778). Linnaeus used the Latin language in his biological classification system and assigned each organism a Latin **binomial** ("two names"): a genus and species. Our biological name, for example, is *Homo sapiens* (Latin for "wise man").

Linnaeus established a formal hierarchy for establishing taxa (sing.: taxon, a general term for any Linnaean category) above the level of species. Although Linneaus devised this hierarchy more than a century before Darwin and Wallace proposed the theory of evolution, most taxonomists today classify organisms according to their evolutionary relationship (phylogeny). Table 5.1 shows many of the higher levels of classification and the classification of our species. As you can see, in some groups of animals and plants, these levels are further subdivided into other categories such as suborders, subfamilies, subgenera, and subspecies. Species within the same genus are more closely related to each other than they are to species in other genera. Genera are grouped into related families, families into related superfamilies, superfamilies into related orders, orders into related classes, and so on. For example, the genus for chimpanzees contains two closely related species, *Pan troglodytes* (common chimpanzee) and *Pan paniscus* (bonobo chimpanzee), while the genus *Homo* contains only one surviving species, according to most (but not all) taxonomists.

Rules for using Linnaean Classification:

1. The first letter of the genus (pl.: genera) is capitalized.
2. The species begins with a lowercase letter.
3. The genus and species are underlined or italicized in print.
4. The genus name may be abbreviated by using only the first letter (e.g., *H. sapiens*).

Table 5.1 A Biological Classification of Humans	
Kingdom:	Animal
Phylum:	Chordata
Class:	Mammalia
Order:	Primates
Suborder:	Haplorhini
Infraorder:	Anthropoidea
Superfamily:	Hominoidea
Family:	Hominidae
Subfamily:	Homininae
Tribe:	Hominini
Genus:	*Homo*
Species:	*sapiens*

Although most of the rules and conventions of biological classification are well established, there remain many differences of opinion among the classifiers. Even the species concept, which is the basis of the Linnaean Classification system, is still debated. Most biologists today agree to the following definition of species: "species are groups of interbreeding natural populations that are reproductively isolated from other such groups" (Mayr, 1970). However, one primary criterion of this definition, the potential to interbreed, is often impossible to determine in natural populations, particularly when those populations are separated geographically. Furthermore, there are many degrees of interbreeding potential among natural populations in that some animals may be able to interbreed but their offspring are infertile (e.g., if a horse crosses with a donkey, the resultant offspring, the mule, is almost always infertile), or the fertility of offspring may be less than the offspring of "true species."

In practice, most species determinations in fossils are made on the basis of the similarity or dissimilarity of morphological traits, or **characters.** To be useful in biological classification, the similarity of these characters must have resulted from common descent, or **homologies**. We can see that, whether we are looking at the humerus of a horse (Figure 5.1) or the humerus of a squirrel (Figure 5.2), there are characteristics of those bones that make them recognizable as a humerus and not a femur or a radius. They are homologous because they are shared by millions of living and extinct species and have ultimately resulted from a common ancestor; therefore, they are useful to us in producing a classification scheme.

Homologies: characters shared through common descent.

FIGURE 5.1 Horse humerus, posterior view. *Photo, D. L. France*

FIGURE 5.2 Squirrel humerus, posterior view. *Photo, D. L. France*

Analogies: characters similar in appearance and with common function but through separate descent.

Interestingly, the humerus of a bird and the humerus of a bat are homologous (see Figure 5.3 for a schematic representing ancestor-descendant relationship) but the entire wing structure of a bird is **analogous** to the wing structure of a bat because they have common functions (flight), but *those structures* are derived from different evolutionary descent, even though the bat and bird once shared a common ancestor in the Phylum Chordata. Therefore, those wings would not be useful in a classification scheme.

Classifiers have often disagreed on what morphological criteria should be used in their classifications. For example, should the shape of the skull, the morphology of the teeth, the color of the coats, or biomolecular data be weighted more in making species designations? Should genetic distance be the final determinant?

Designations of fossil species, called paleospecies, are even less "exact." Obviously, nothing can be determined about the interbreeding potential of paleospecies, and often, because of the condition of the remains, DNA has not been available for study. Furthermore, the morphological variation of fossils reflects not only geographic variation but also variation over time. Although scientists who study fossils do their best to designate paleospecies in a manner that approximates the designation of living species, there is obviously an arbitrary factor in the designation of species and paleospecies.

Disagreements arise in making classifications above the species level as well. Most, but by no means all, biologists believe that the higher taxonomic categories of organisms should be determined on the basis of the organism's evolutionary history: Organisms that are more closely related should be placed in the same taxa, whereas those more distantly related should be placed in different taxa. This phylogenetic approach to classification is divided into two schools:

FIGURE 5.3 Cladogram of hypothetical taxa A, B, and C. *Adapted from E. Mayr, "Biological Classification: Toward a Synthesis of Opposing Methodologies." Science, 214: 510–516.*

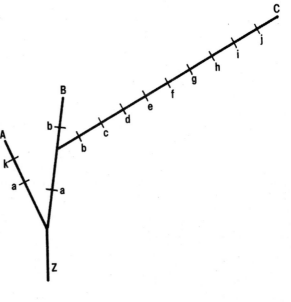

cladistics and evolutionary classification (Mayr, 1981). Cladistic classification (cladism) is based exclusively on genealogy (and branching order), regardless of the time scale—that is, a genus should include a group of species all descended from the same common ancestor (see Figure 5.3). Cladistic classification is also usually focused on more recently shared characters, or "derived" characters.

Derived characters evolve from more primitive characters of more ancient ancestors. For example, the presence of five digits on human hands and feet are actually a primitive condition, as many other animals share that condition, regardless of their evolutionary distance from humans. Cows and many other hooved animals share the derived condition of two digits (two hooves), while horses exhibit an even more derived characteristic of only one digit (one hoof). In primates, one example of a shared-derived character in anthropoids is that they have nails on all of their digits. Prosimians, on the other hand, do not have nails on all of their digits, as they retain at least one grooming claw. The presence of grooming claws on prosimians is a "primitive character." The fact that monkeys, apes, and humans have nails on all their digits is an example of one shared-derived character used by taxonomists to classify them together in the suborder Anthropoidea (see Chapter 7 for more discussion). These shared-derived (or shared-specialized) characters are usually assumed to be derived from a common ancestor. Organisms that share these derived characters are grouped into a **clade,** or a group of related organisms. Scientists must be careful, however, because organisms frequently have evolved morphological similarities independently through parallel or convergent evolution. On the other hand, even though evolutionary taxonomy or evolutionary classification is the same as cladism in that it is based on evolutionary history, it also takes into account the time factor and the different rates of evolution in different lineages (see Mayr, 1981, for discussion). Many classification schemes will start out as cladistic schemes, and a time scale will be added later. In Figure 5.3, cladists would combine A and C into one taxon because they shared a common ancestor: Z. Evolutionary taxonomists, on the other hand, would put A and C into separate taxa because C has many derived characters (b through j) not shared with A.

Recent DNA studies and genome maps are refining the taxonomic relationships established by taxonomists. We are most interested in the way these relationships are now understood in primates, but first we must explore the way primates are classified in the class Mammalia and the way in which primates differ from other mammals.

Clade: a group of organisms related through a common ancestor.

Cladistic classifications are based on shared, derived characters to establish a lineage. It does not include a time scale.

Primitive characters are found with phylogenetically older organisms and are usually shared with many organisms in an evolutionary group.

Derived characters evolved from more primitive characters and are usually acquired by few members of an evolutionary group.

GENERAL MAMMALIAN CLASSIFICATION

Before we delve into primate classification schemes, it is useful to briefly discuss the characteristics that define a mammal (Class

Mammalia). These are the elements that separate mammals from reptiles, amphibians, birds, and so on, and are also characteristics of the Order Primates.

Mammals:

- Have hair at some point in their lives (some marine mammals lose most of their hair)
- Have mammary glands (these are specialized sweat glands)
- Give birth to live young (this is true in most mammals, although monotremes such as the platypus lay eggs)
- Possess three middle ear bones (the malleus, incus, and stapes) Figure 5.4 shows these bones in humans.
- Are characterized by heterodonty, which means that the teeth are in different forms (e.g., incisors, canines, premolars, and molars, although the combinations of these forms vary considerably in different mammals). Many marine mammals, including some whales, have homodonty (which means that the tooth shape is the same throughout the mouth). See Figures 5.5 and 5.6 for examples of heterodonty and homodonty in mammals.

FIGURE 5.4 Malleus, Incus, Stapes. *Photo, D. L. France*

FIGURE 5.5 Heterodonty, the most common form in mammals. *Photo, D. L. France*

FIGURE 5.6 Homodonty is the exception to the rule in mammals. *Photo, D. L. France*

PRIMATE CLASSIFICATION

Traits common to all primates include (we will look at specific groups of primates and primate behavior in subsequent chapters)

- Retention of pentadactyly (five digits on the hands and feet).
- Sensitive tactile pads.
- Nails instead of claws on at least one digit.
- Trend toward opposable thumb, and, except for humans, a trend toward opposable big toe.
- Trend toward precision grip.
- Trend toward a reduction in olfaction and, with that, a reduction in the size of the nose. This is accompanied by the eyes becoming closer together in the front of the face and an accompanying overlap in visual fields (which creates binocular vision and a good depth perception).
- Color vision in diurnal primates (those who are active during daylight hours). Nocturnal primates do not have color vision.
- A retention of a more omnivorous diet (one with a wide assortment of foods), and a retention of a generalized dentition for processing those foods.
- Increased complexity of the brain.

The most recent and widely accepted primate classification scheme differs from the traditional scheme (Figure 5.7) in the representation of the relationship of tarsiers, lemurs, and lorises to all

Diurnal: active during daylight hours

Nocturnal: active during the night

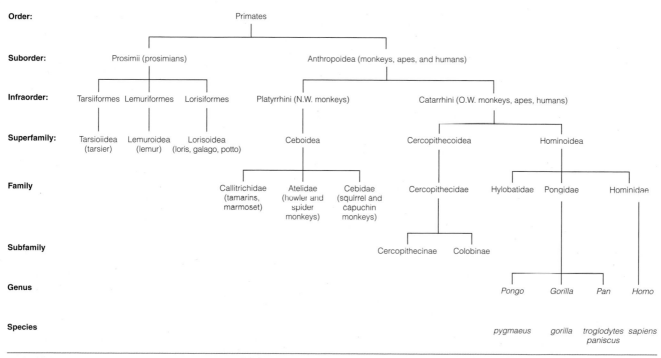

FIGURE 5.7 A traditional primate classification.

other primates. Traditionally, all lorises (Infraorder Lorisiformes), lemurs (Infraorder Lemuriformes), and tarsiers (Tarsiiformes) were classified in the Suborder Prosimii, with the understanding that tarsiers, lemurs, and lorises were more closely related to each other than to any other primate (Suborder Anthropoidea). In the recent classification scheme (Figure 5.8), primates are divided into two suborders: Strepsirhini (with wet noses) and Haplorhini (with dry noses). The tarsiers are now grouped into the Haplorhines, with the understanding that they are less closely related to lemurs and lorises than to any other primate (though not all primatologists agree with this classification).

Tarsiers today live only in island areas of Southeast Asia. They share a number of characteristics with other prosimians (lemurs and lorises), including a primitive dental pattern and social behavior,

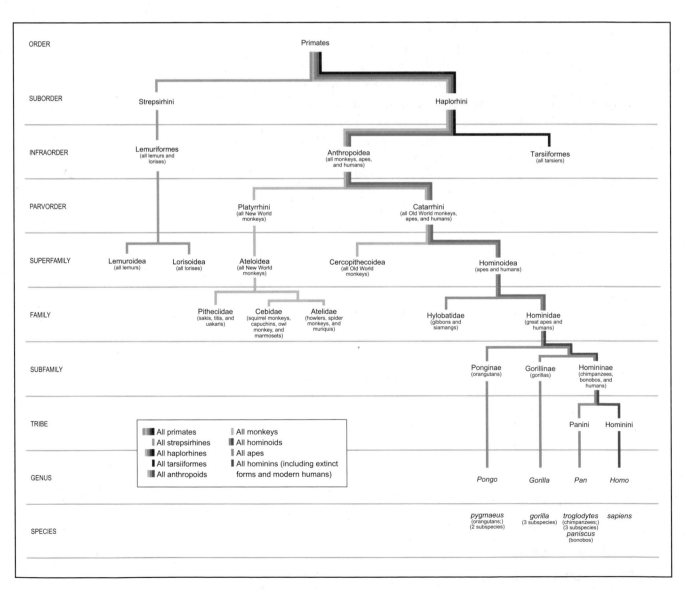

FIGURE 5.8 Updated primate classification. © Cengage Learning

small bodies, and large ears. However, tarsiers also show many similarities to the higher primates. Their eye orbits are mostly enclosed by bone (unlike other prosimians: see Figures 5.9a–5.9d and Chapter 8); they possess a bony ear canal more like that of anthropoids; and they lack a rhinarium (a wet, naked portion that surrounds the nostrils, possessed by all other nonanthropoid land-living mammals). Decades ago (Dene et al., 1976) reported that the biomolecular data show the tarsiers to be more closely related to anthropoids than to other prosimians. With the explosion of research into the genomes of primates, there is evidence that tarsiers are more closely related to anthropoids than to the other prosimians, though not all research (e.g., Matsui et al., 2008) is unambiguous at this point.

In the higher primates, comparative morphology, comparative biomolecular and fossil data, and more recently research on the genetic sequence data strongly suggest that African apes shared a common ancestor with humans after both taxa had shared a common ancestor with the Asian great ape, the orangutan, and that chimpanzees and humans shared a common ancestor after gorillas branched off. Therefore, the more recent primate classification system lumps humans and chimpanzees in the same subfamily (Homininae) and into different genera (*Pan* and *Homo*). Largely because of the recent genome research, some researchers (Wildman et al., 2003, and others) propose one *Homo* genus with three species: *Homo sapiens* (humans), *Homo troglodytes* (common chimpanzees), and *Homo paniscus* (bonobo chimpanzees).

FIGURE 5.9a Skull of a mammal (badger). *Photo, D. L. France*

FIGURE 5.9b Cranium of a prosimian. *Photo, D. L. France*

FIGURE 5.9c Skull of a tarsier. *Photo, D. L. France*

FIGURE 5.9d Skull of a monkey. *Photo, D. L. France*

EXERCISE 5.1 NAME Brianna Sanders SECTION _____ DATE _____

Biological Classification

1. Some of the differences between the two primate classification systems were listed in the text. What are some of the other differences (Figures 5.7 and 5.8)?

    Strepsirhini (wet noses)
    primitive dental pattern
    dental comb

    Haplorhini (dry noses)
    enclosed eye orbitals
    no dental comb

2. Evolutionary, or phylogenetic, relationships of organisms are represented graphically by branching diagrams. These diagrams are usually known as phylogenies or cladograms if cladistic analysis is used. Figures 5.3, 5.7, and 5.8 are examples of phylogenies and cladograms.

    Construct a cladogram (using cladistic analysis) for the following hypothetical organisms with the following hypothetical characters. Lowercase letters signify primitive characters, or characters of more ancient members of a lineage (an evolutionary line linked by common ancestry). Uppercase letters signify derived states of those same characters.

Organism	Character
1	Abcdefgh
2	ABCDEfgh
3	abCDefGh
4	abcdeFgh
5	abCDefgH
6	abCDefgh

Example: Suppose we have five organisms with the following primitive and derived characters:

Organism	Character
1	Abcd
2	Abcd
3	aBcd
4	aBCd
5	aBcD

A cladogram for these organisms would look like this:

FIGURE 5.10 Unknown specimens for Question 3. *Photo, D. L. France*

FIGURE 5.11 Unknown specimens, inferior view, for Question 3. *Photo, D. L. France*

a

3:1:2:3

b

3:1:3:3

3. If you were a paleontologist and had to try to classify the specimens in Figures 5.10 and 5.11a and 5.11b, would you put them into the same or different species, based only on the features you can see in the photograph?

Based on detal record, skull size & shape, apperance of sagittal & (sp?) neval crest, length of pallet & size of eye orbitals

Give several reasons why you would classify them in this way.

& foramen magnum I'd say the species are NOT the same but they share common ancestory

4. Name some derived characters of humans not shared with the apes.

Non opposable toes & advanced tool making soley bipedal walking & smaller teeth due to cooked foods control of environment & fire

5. Do you favor classifying humans in a separate or in the same biological family as the African apes? Based on scientific evidence, discuss the pros and cons of each system.

I would classify humans in the same family because it is clear on social & physical attributes we decended from apes not monkeys however some cons of the system include streching sapien ancestory all the way back 4.4 million years of growth (when bipedal apes began) & tweeking some familiy characteristics to still include humans

6. Do you favor classifying humans in the same genus as chimpanzees? Based on scientific evidence, why or why not?

I do not favor them in the same genus because while dna is similar the palatte & teeth as well as the locomotion of chimps show a desicive split of ancestory. I don't think chimps belong in homo if even the bipedal Lucy (Australopithicus Afarences) does not.

7. Consult the textbook you use in this course (or the lecture if the lecture and lab are combined). Does it use evolutionary classification or cladistic classification?

Both, more evolutionary though

8. Could scientists confuse the differences in size and morphology between the sexes with the differences between species in identifying fossils? What might be the causes of their confusion?

Sexual dimorphism & things like bigger teeth or features for fighting in males may make it hard to reconize species members of opposite sex

9. Could scientists confuse **intraspecies variation** (e.g., age, sex, individual differences) with **interspecies** differences while identifying fossils? What might cause them to be confused?

Yes. Look at humans an african man averaging 7ft with lean bones & slightly varied skull maybe considered a different species from an eskimo woman who is 4ft & stockily built if no other fossils are found to bridge the gap btwn the two (physical & geographical attributes may be misleading)

FIGURE 5.12 Unknown specimens for Question 10.
Photo, D. L. France

10. If you were a paleontologist and had to classify the specimens in Figure 5.12, would you put them into the same or different species, based only on the features you see in the photograph? Why would you classify them this way?

> Very similar possibly even different sexes, same species. eye orbitas are shaped differently but features dental record, slope of head & shape of chin/mandable are variations found in sexual dimorphism & are the only real differences btwn the two. If I had to say I'd guess same species.

FIGURE 5.13 Unknown specimens for Question 11. *Photo, D. L. France*

11. Would you put the hand bone specimens shown in Figure 5.13 into the same or different species (they are the corresponding bone in two individuals)? Why?

> Different species, size can be overlooked (sexual dimorphism) but curvatur & tips of bone shouldn't vary that much btwn sexes.

FIGURE 5.14 Unknown specimen for Question 12.
Photo, D. L. France

12. Would you classify the animal in Figure 5.14 as a mammal?

Hard to tell but odd teeth & skull shape position of nose & pallete I'd guess no.

FIGURE 5.15 Unknown specimens for Question 13.
Photo, D. L. France

2:2:3:3

2:2:3:3

13. Would you place the animals shown in Figures 5.15 in the same species? Why or why not?

No, features almost identical except streched but odd feature in faamien magnum suggest varied locomotion & therefore may indicate different species but a similar genus of family

REEXAMINING THE ISSUES

In this chapter, we learned the following:

- Classification systems improve communication.
- Biological classification systems are based on the work of Carolus Linnaeus.
- Phylogenetic classification systems are based on evolutionary relationships and include a time component.
- Cladistic classification systems are based on homologous derived characteristics and do not always include a time line.

Two primate classification systems were presented: a more traditional scheme and one that differs in the relationship of higher primates and in the relationship of great apes to humans.

CHAPTER 6

●

Comparison of the Skeletons of Quadrupeds, Bipeds, and Brachiators

OBJECTIVES

1. How are patterns of locomotion reflected in the skeleton?

2. Some animals (such as dogs) rely on their sense of smell, while other animals (notably most primates) have a reduced sense of smell and increased reliance on vision. How is this illustrated in the skeleton?

3. Can we determine dietary patterns from the skeleton?

Before we get into the specifics of skeletal morphology in humans and our ancestors, it is important to understand the basic differences between living quadrupeds (such as horses and dogs), bipeds (humans), and brachiators (such as gibbons). In addition to interpreting skeletal fragments of primates and primate ancestors, we may also use the information from this chapter to determine the forensic significance of skeletal remains. If you found a skeleton of a cow in a cornfield, for instance, you know that the bony structures are inappropriate for a human skeleton. But if you found only a fragment of that cow skeleton, would you still be able to recognize the clues? Much of this chapter concentrates on the locomotor patterns, but a part of it also includes dietary patterns and other differences not related to locomotion. All of these characteristics vary greatly in each group, so they are given here only for general comparative purposes. The information in this chapter is a compilation of data from Campbell (1976, 1985), Clark (1959), and Schultz (1937, 1973) and from observations by the author.

THE VERTEBRAL COLUMN

It usually makes sense to start discussions of anatomy with the cranium and move caudally. As discussed in this chapter, however,

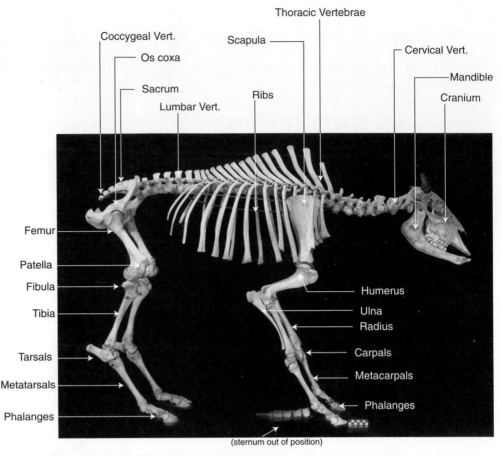

FIGURE 6.1 Bison skeleton. *Photo, D. L. France*

Quadruped: an animal that habitually walks on four limbs.

Biped: an animal that habitually walks on two limbs.

Brachiator: an animal that habitually swings under branches in arm-over-arm locomotion.

the skeletal differences between the animals with different locomotor patterns are due in large part to a shift in the center of gravity in the animal. In the typical **quadruped** the center of gravity is roughly over the forelimbs, while in the **biped,** the center of gravity is closer to the hindlimbs. The center of gravity in **brachiators** is low (sort of like a clock pendulum) in their body. Changes in the rest of the skeleton can be followed relatively easily from a discussion of the changes in the thoracic region of each animal and working toward each end.

In typical large quadrupeds (horses, cattle, etc.) the vertebral column is a single curve from the cervical to the sacral vertebrae, somewhat like a cantilever bridge. The thorax is relatively narrow from side to side but deep anteroposteriorly, and ligaments hold the intestinal contents in suspension from the lumbar region. The vertebral bodies are cylindrical in shape and similar in size from the neck to the pelvis. The head is also affected by gravity, as it is suspended from the nuchal vertebrae. To counter the effects of gravity, large muscles originate on the occipital region of the cranium and insert on the spinous processes of cervical and

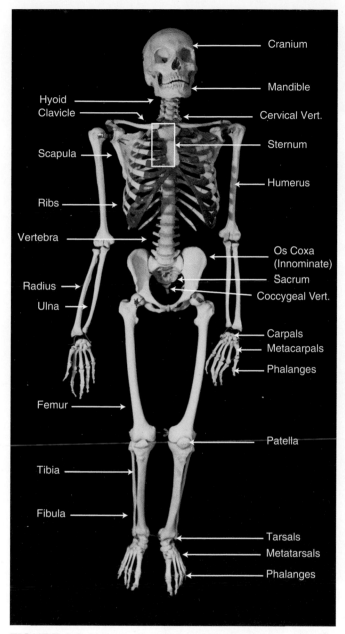

FIGURE 6.2 Human skeleton. *Photo, D. L. France*

FIGURE 6.3 Gibbon skeleton. *Photo courtesy of Jay Villemarette*

FIGURE 6.4a Bison thoracic vertebra. Note very long spinous process. *Photo, D. L. France*

FIGURE 6.4b Wolf thoracic vertebra. *Photo, D. L. France*

FIGURE 6.4c Chimpanzee thoracic vertebra. *Photo, D. L. France*

FIGURE 6.4d Human thoracic vertebra. *Photo, D. L. France*

Table 6.1   Comparative Anatomy: The Vertebral Column and Thorax

	Typical Quadruped (e.g., dog or bison)	Typical Biped (human)	Typical Brachiator (gibbon)
Shape of the vertebral column	Single curve from neck to pelvis; similar to cantilever bridge	S-shaped curve	Single gentle curve from neck to pelvis
Shape of vertebral bodies	Cylindrical, relatively regular in shape from neck to pelvis (see Figure 6.4)	More wedge-shaped, differences in shape between neck and pelvis greater than in quadrupeds (see Figure 6.4)	Intermediate
Size of spinous processes	Large, particularly those at the origin of nuchal (neck) muscles	Small, as the large area for the origin of "nuchal" muscles is not needed; cranium is more balanced over the vertebral column	Fairly small
Size of vertebral bodies	Similar in size from neck to pelvis	Great differences in size between neck and pelvis	Intermediate
Center of gravity of animal body	Over the forelimbs: the forelimbs catch the body in locomotion and aid in propulsion	Closer to the hindlimbs: propulsion through the hindlimbs	Intermediate
Shape of thorax	Narrow, deep thorax, narrow sternum	Shallow, broad thorax, wide sternum	Shallow, broad thorax, wide sternum
Tail	Occurs in some quadrupeds, not in apes	Caudal vertebrae curved ventrally, aid in support of viscera	No tail

FIGURE 6.5 Origin of nuchal muscles in modern humans and gorilla. The arrows represent the center of gravity through the skull. *Drawing, D. L. France*

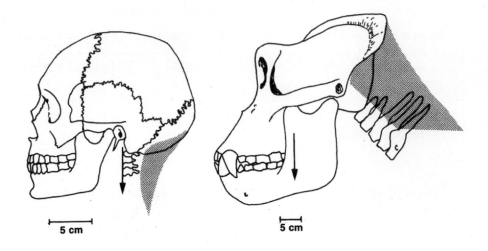

thoracic vertebrae. These large muscles must attach to a relatively large area at the origin and insertion, so the nuchal area of the cranium and the affected spinous processes are very large (proportional to the weight carried) (Figures 6.1, 6.5). Whereas most large quadrupeds have very large spinous processes because of the large heads to be suspended, most small quadrupeds (small monkeys, for instance) have smaller spinous processes that allow increased range of motion in the spinal column (also, their heads are typically smaller, and the muscles used to support them against gravity can be relatively smaller).

In bipeds, the center of gravity runs from approximately the vertex of the head through the center of the sacrum, and the vertebral column is S-shaped. This double curvature of the spinal column is perfect for balancing the body around the center of gravity and allowing a smooth bipedal locomotion, but it creates associated differences throughout the skeleton. For example, the vertebral bodies are larger as one moves caudally (they support more weight), and they are wedge-shaped (refer to Figure 6.4). Although this is a more flexible arrangement, it is less stable and results in back problems in humans. The nucleus pulposus, the fluid of toothpaste consistency inside the intervertebral disks (the cushions between the vertebrae), can be more easily extruded beyond its normal limits with downward force, often exerting pressure on a spinal nerve root and causing pain. In addition, while the abdominal contents in the quadruped are suspended relatively evenly from the lumbar vertebrae, the abdominal contents suspended from the same ligaments in bipeds are working against gravity, pulling the contents caudally (instead of ventrally). This makes them more difficult to support and increases the likelihood of herniation of the abdominal wall (in which the abdominal contents erupt through the abdominal muscles).

In brachiators, the center of gravity is intermediate (Figure 6.6); think of a swing on a long chain versus that on a short chain. It is

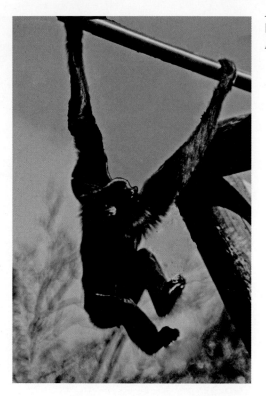

FIGURE 6.6 Siamang brachiating. *Photo, D. L. France*

easier to get good distance on the swing seat if you have much of your weight near the base of a long pendulum. The vertebral column has a gentle curve from the neck to the pelvic girdle, and, although there is some difference in the size of the vertebral bodies as one moves caudally, the difference is not as great as in bipeds.

THE CRANIUM

As stated previously, the area of the occipital region of large quadrupeds is modified for the attachment of large nuchal muscles devoted to counteracting the effects of gravity on a large skull. The foramen magnum of a typical quadruped (Figure 6.7a) is located more posteriorly (which makes sense because the skull is in front of the spinal column). The foramen magnum in a biped (Figure 6.7b) is more centrally located under the cranium, which helps in balancing the cranium on the vertebral column. Figure 6.7c is a photograph of the position of the foramen magnum in a siamang. Because of the center of gravity and the placement of the foramen magnum, the nuchal region of a biped is not as extensive as in a quadruped. See the differences between quadrupeds and bipeds in muscle insertions shown in Table 6.2.

The form of the dentition of an animal (and the associated morphology of the bone supporting the dentition) is different with different diets. As the dentition (and maxilla and mandible) of an animal becomes larger, larger muscles are needed to operate that

FIGURE 6.7a Elk cranium inferior view. Note position of the foramen magnum. *Photo, D. L. France*

FIGURE 6.7b Human cranium inferior view. Note position of foramen magnum. *Photo, D. L. France*

FIGURE 6.7c Gibbon cranium inferior view. Note position of foramen magnum. *Photo, D. L. France*

FIGURE 6.7d Chimpanzee cranium inferior view. Note position of foramen magnum. *Photo, D. L. France*

Table 6.2   Comparative Anatomy in the Cranium

	Typical Quadruped (dog or bison)	Typical Biped (human)	Typical Brachiator (gibbon)
Prognathism (projection of lower face)	Extensive prognathism, very long tooth row, very long snout	Reduced prognathism, short tooth row, nasal area and tooth row more directly under forehead	More similar to biped than to quadruped
Foramen magnum (see Figures 6.7a–6.7c)	Near rear of cranium	More centrally located under cranium; cranium almost balanced on spinal column	Intermediate
Nuchal crest (area for origin of nuchal muscles on occiput)	Very large, rough area indicating origin of substantial nuchal muscles	No nuchal crest, only a slightly roughened area on the occiput, often difficult to see	Similar to biped
Mastoid process (insertion of sternocleidomastoid muscle) (see Figures 6.8 a–6.8c)	Very small, as there is little need to bring the cranium from a dorsal to a ventral position with muscles when gravity will function as well	Fairly large, as now the cranium is more balanced on the spinal column, and if skull is tilted dorsally, these muscles may bring it to upright position	Not pronounced
Supraorbital torus (Figure 6.9)	Sometimes present, particularly in great apes	Sometimes present, particularly in early humans and to some degree in modern males	Not pronounced
Sagittal crest (origin of temporal muscle which is major mastication muscle)	Very large, notably in gorilla	Absent: temporal muscle originates alongside cranium on parietal bones	Not pronounced

FIGURE 6.8a Mastoid area in human. *Photo, D. L. France*

FIGURE 6.8b Mastoid area in siamang. *Photo, D. L. France*

FIGURE 6.8c Mastoid area in wolf. *Photo, D. L. France*

FIGURE 6.9 Supraorbital torus in chimpanzee. *Photo, D. L. France*

dentition. In young male gorillas, the temporal muscle (one of the major muscles for chewing) originates on the sides of the cranium in a way similar to that in humans (Figure 6.10a), but as the dentition and associated bony structure become larger as the animal becomes larger, the muscle literally runs out of bone on which to anchor itself. The bone is then stimulated (possibly by the **piezoelectric effect,** which is a slight electric charge) to produce more bone to provide this area for attachment, thus producing the crests seen in the occipital and sagittal regions of the gorilla cranium (Figures 6.10a and 6.10b). Note that, although most of the features of the skeleton listed in the tables in this chapter relate to locomotion, the size of the supraorbital torus and the sagittal crest are *not* directly related to the differences in locomotor patterns!

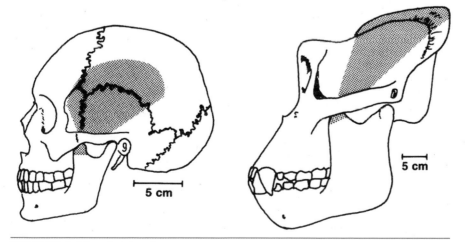

FIGURE 6.10a Origin of temporal muscle in modern humans and gorilla. *Drawing, D. L. France*

FIGURE 6.10b Young gorilla male with temporal muscle insertion areas in development (before reaching center of cranium). *Photo, D. L. France*

THE PELVIS

The pelvic girdle (os coxae and sacrum) in quadrupeds is long and narrow and reflects the function of the leg muscles that attach to the pelvis. The lower limbs in the large quadrupeds move anteroposteriorly with very little lateral motion, so the strength of the muscles of the leg that make this movement possible are benefited by a long lever arm (see Table 6.3 and Figures 6.12 and 6.13). The pelvic girdle in humans has become shorter and wider, reflecting the different locomotion patterns (balancing the weight over each leg independently as forward movement occurs) as well as the difference in support of the abdominal contents and the need for a large pelvic outlet for childbirth in females (see Chapter 15 for a more extensive discussion of this feature of sexual dimorphism). The auricular surface of the sacrum and ilium in humans has moved until it is closer to the acetabulum, which brings the weight from the spinal column closer to the femur head.

THE LIMBS

The concept of lengthening certain bones (and therefore muscle attachment areas) to increase the power of the muscle is easy to understand if we use an analogy of using a jack to lift a car. If you are trying to use a jack to lift a car, would you use more energy if you used a short handle or a long one? Naturally a long handle would use less of your energy, and it would move through a greater distance to get the car the same distance off the ground. The biomechanics of a long lever arm in animal locomotion works

Table 6.3	Comparative Anatomy in the Pelvis		
	Typical Quadruped (dog or bison)	**Typical Biped (human)**	**Typical Brachiator (gibbon)**
Ilium (Figure 6.11)	Long and narrow, greater sciatic notch is very wide, forming an obtuse angle.	Short and splayed, greater sciatic notch is more acute.	Intermediate
Gluteus muscles	Gluteus maximus, medius, and minimus are all abductors (draw leg away from midline of body).	Gluteus maximus is an extensor (see Figure 6.12).	

FIGURE 6.11a Pelvic girdle of a quadruped (deer).
Photo, D. L. France

FIGURE 6.11b Pelvic girdle of a chimpanzee.
Photo, D. L. France

FIGURE 6.11c Pelvic girdle of human.
Photo, D. L. France

FIGURE 6.12 Biped gluteal muscles: gluteus maximus (left), gluteus
medius (middle), gluteus minimus (right). *Drawing, Courtesy of Jayne Bellavia*

the same way. The animal uses less energy to move what is on the end of the long lever arm (i.e., parts of the leg). In addition (and this is particularly important in animals that run at high speed), that lever (or leg) moves through a greater range of motion than a leg that is shorter or that has a shorter lever arm. See Figures 6.13a and b and Table 6.4 for examples of differences in the limbs in the various locomotor patterns.

In general the articular surfaces of the limbs of quadrupeds such as dogs, cats, and horses are more sculpted than those of primates (and higher primates and humans in particular). Observe the articular surfaces of the distal femur of two quadrupeds (the moose and dog), and compare those to the human distal femur (Figures 6.16a, 6.16b, and 6.16c).

There are three distinct functions of the forelimbs in most mammals: They support the body in a quadruped, suspend the body in brachiators, and manipulate objects in bipeds.

Figure 6.1 and Figures 6.17 through 6.26 show skeletons of various quadrupeds (nonprimate and primate). Figures 6.3 and 6.23 show the skeleton of a brachiator, and Figure 6.2 demonstrates a human skeleton. The principles discussed in this chapter can be seen in these photographs.

FIGURE 6.13a Achilles area in quadruped (bison). *Photo, D. L. France*

FIGURE 6.13b Achilles area in human. *Photo, D. L. France*

Table 6.4 Comparative Anatomy of the Hind Limbs

	Typical Quadruped (dog or bison)	Typical Biped (human)	Typical Brachiator (gibbon)
Intermembral Index (to be measured; formula given later)	In typical primitive mammals, the forelimbs and hindlimbs are of equal length; there are notable variations in primates.	Hindlimbs are longer than forelimbs.	Forelimbs are longer than hindlimbs.
Tibia and fibula	Many primitive mammals and most primates use both bones for rotary movement of the foot: The tibia transmits weight while the fibula allows rotation. In large quadrupeds, the fibula is greatly reduced, and there is virtually no rotary movement of the foot.	Humans have lost most lateral rotation of the foot afforded by the fibula.	Rotary movement of the foot is retained.
Foot	Highly variable; differences between monkeys and apes are noted later.	Transmits weight through the triad: heel, outside of foot, and then roll off of great toe.	Grasping ability is retained.

DISTINGUISHING HUMAN FROM NONHUMAN BONE AND DENTITION: ADDITIONAL FEATURES

Articular Surfaces

As was stated before, nonprimate quadrupeds (particularly large quadrupeds) tend to have more "sculpted" articular surfaces than do humans, allowing for more stability but decreased range of motion in the joint (see Figures 6.27a–6.26e). The metacarpals and metatarsals of many nonprimate animals demonstrate this fact, as well (and are frequently mistaken for humans in forensic cases).

Table 6.5	Comparative Anatomy of the Forelimbs		
	Typical Quadruped (dog or bison)	**Typical Biped (human)**	**Typical Brachiator (gibbon)**
Scapula	Located on the side of the body, the glenoid fossa is more nearly in line with the lateral line of the scapula; points downward.	Located on the dorsum of body, the glenoid fossa is more open, allowing wider movement of the arm.	Located on the dorsum, the glenoid fossa is fairly open; points more cranially than in humans.
Clavicle	Absent in many quadrupedal mammals in which there is very little lateral movement of forelimbs. The clavicle is present in primates.	Present, allows stable lateral motion of the humerus.	Relatively longer than in humans.
Forearm	In large quadrupeds, the distal shaft of the ulna is reduced, and often the proximal ulna is fused to the radius. In smaller quadrupeds, the radius and ulna are distinct bones and often allow for some pronation and supination.	The radius and ulna allow pronation and supination, increasing the ability to manipulate materials in the hands.	The radius and ulna allow pronation and supination.
Hands (Figures 6.14, 6.15)	The form of the hands varies from one digit present, as in the horse, to five digits in monkeys and humans. The specific characteristics of brachiators, quadrupedal monkeys, apes, and humans will be discussed in a later chapter.		Hands are hook-like with very long curved fingers and a reduced thumb.

In Figures 6.27a, notice that the distal articular surface of the human metacarpal is smooth and rounded, and notice that there is a ridge that runs through the center of the articular surface in the wolf and bear (also animals with the primitive five-digit arrangement). The deer (Figure 6.27d) and moose (Figure 6.14b) have a derived condition in the forelimbs and hindlimbs of two digits instead of five.

FIGURE 6.14a Primitive condition in digit number (5). *Photo, D. L. France*

FIGURE 6.14b Derived condition in digit number (2). Notice vestigial digits on the moose, often absent in other large quadrupeds. *Photo, D. L. France*

FIGURE 6.15 Siamang hand. Notice the long fingers and short thumb characteristic of a brachiator. *Photo, D. L. France*

FIGURE 6.16a Distal femur of moose.
Photo, D. L. France

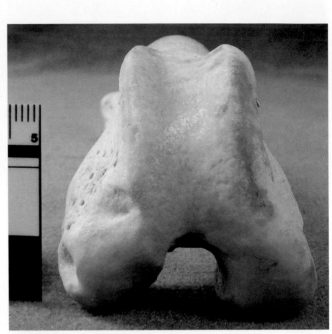

FIGURE 6.16b Distal femur of dog.
Photo, D. L. France

FIGURE 6.16c Distal femur of
human. *Photo, D. L. France*

FIGURE 6.17 Domestic dog. *Photo, D. L. France*

FIGURE 6.18 Bushbaby (Galago sp.). *Photo, D. L. France*

FIGURE 6.19 Lemur skeleton. *Photo, D. L. France; access to specimen courtesy Jay Villemarette, Skulls Unlimited*

FIGURE 6.20 New World monkey (squirrel monkey). *Photo, D. L. France*

FIGURE 6.21 Old World monkey (macaque). *Photo, D. L. France*

FIGURE 6.22 Old World monkey (common baboon). *Photo, D. L. France*

FIGURE 6.23 Gibbon (Hylobates). See additional view in Figure 6.3. *Courtesy: Jay Villemarette, Skulls Unlimited*

FIGURE 6.24 Orangutan (Pongo pygmaeus).
Photo, D. L. France of cast by France Casting

Further, the two metacarpals have fused into one bone, but notice that the distal articular surface still shows the individual distal metacarpals with the central ridge on each! The horse has a further derived condition of only one digit, also reflected in the single metacarpal. Notice that the distal articular surface in the metacarpal of the horse also shows the central ridge.

Interestingly, the diaphyseal and epiphyseal surfaces on many large nonprimate mammals are more sculpted as well (Figure 6.28).

The biomechanical differences go far beyond that fact, however. It is interesting to try to determine the lifestyle of an animal by looking at the morphology of the skeletal elements. Three radii from

FIGURE 6.25 Gorilla male. *Photo, D. L. France*

three different animals are represented in Figures 6.29a–6.29c.
Note the differences in morphology that represent differences in the
patterns of use of those skeletal elements, the interrelationship
between skeletal elements in that area of the animal's body, and in
muscle use (remember that more powerful muscles require more
robust areas onto which to attach to bone). Figure 6.29c is a radius
from a horse. Notice that the proximal radius and ulna are fused and

FIGURE 6.26 Adult male chimpanzee. *Photo, D. L. France*

that the distal ulna no longer exists. Look at the large olecranon process, and remember that the muscles that insert on the olecranon process are responsible for the extension of the radius and ulna. Notice also that the shaft of the radius is robust, reflecting a heavy animal that requires massive support with a limited range of motion. The radius in Figure 6.29a is from a coyote. Notice that the shaft is long and slender, and the ulna (not shown) is a separate bone. The radius from a harbor seal (Figure 6.29b) increases distally toward the wide flipper.

FIGURE 6.27a Human hand (left) and metacarpal (right). Notice smooth surface on distal aspect of metacarpal. *Photos, D. L. France*

FIGURE 6.27b Wolf metacarpals. Note ridge on the distal articular surface (right). *Photos, D. L. France*

FIGURE 6.27c Bear metacarpals. Note ridge on the distal articular surface (right). *Photos, D. L. France*

FIGURE 6.27e Horse metacarpal. Note the single metacarpal with a single ridge on the distal aspect. *Photo, D. L. France*

FIGURE 6.27d Deer metacarpal. Note fused metacarpals (2) and central ridge on each original distal metacarpal. *Photos, D. L. France*

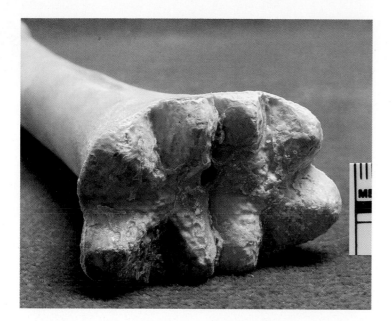

FIGURE 6.28 Nonhuman epiphyseal surface showing "crown" effect. *Photo, D. L. France*

FIGURE 6.29b Radius of a seal. Notice that the radius widens distally. *Photo, D. L. France*

FIGURE 6.29c Radius of a horse. Notice that the radius and ulna are fused and that the ulna has been reduced to the point where it disappears distally. *Photo, D. L. France*

FIGURE 6.29a Radius of coyote. *Photo, D. L. France*

EXERCISE 6.1 NAME _____ SECTION _____ DATE _____

Quadrupeds, Bipeds, and Brachiators

1. If you found a fossil with a very large sagittal crest, what would that feature indicate about the animal's masticatory apparatus relative to its cranial size?

2. a. If you found a fossil that had a very large nuchal crest, what would you expect of the size of the spinous processes of the thoracic vertebrae? Why?

   b. What might this large nuchal crest tell you about that animal's pelvic girdle?

      Its legs?

      Its vertebrae?

      The position of the foramen magnum?

      The scapula?

      The shape of the thorax?

3. a. If a fossil had very long hook-like fingers with a short thumb, what would this probably indicate about its locomotor ancestry?

   b. What might this tell you about the rest of the animal's skeletal morphology?

FIGURE 6.30 Os coxa. *Photo, D. L. France*

4. What does the morphology of the os coxa shown in Figure 6.30 tell you about the locomotor pattern of the individual?

FIGURE 6.31a Unknown.
Photo, D. L. France

FIGURE 6.31b Unknown.
Photo, D. L. France

FIGURE 6.31c Unknown.
Photo, D. L. France

5. Look at the hands represented in Figures 6.31a–6.30c. What does each "hand" tell you about the lifestyle and/or ancestry of the animal (arboreal, terrestrial, other)?

FIGURE 6.32 Unknown.
Photo, D. L. France

6. The local sheriff has brought you these bones (Figure 6.32) and has asked you whether or not they are human. Are they? How can you tell?

FIGURE 6.33 Unknown.
Photo, D. L. France

7. The local sheriff has brought you this bone (Figure 6.33). Are they human? How can you tell?

MEASUREMENTS AND INDICES

Although Chapter 13 contains a more complete discussion of measurements and indices, it is important to introduce some of those measurements at this point. We use indices to help us compare the ratio of one measurement to another, and, in this chapter, to numerically compare the skeletons of quadrupeds, brachiators, and bipeds. We then use these comparisons to analyze fossil remains to determine their likely modes of locomotion.

Postcranial Measurements

Maximum length of long bone: With all except the tibia, this is the maximum measured length taken on the osteometric board (Figure 6.34). On the tibia, length is taken from the most prominent part of the lateral half of the lateral condyle to the distal end of the medial malleolus. This length does not include the intercondylar eminence.

FIGURE 6.34 Osteometric Board. *Photo, D. L. France*

Cranial landmarks (descriptions from Bass, 1987). The following points are illustrated in Figure 6.35.

FIGURE 6.35 Landmarks on the cranium. *Drawing, D. L. France*

Basion (Ba)	The midpoint of the anterior margin of the foramen magnum
Inion (I)	An intersection in the midline with a line drawn tangent to the uppermost convexity of the right and left superior nuchal lines.
Opisthocranion (Op)	The most posterior point on the cranium not on the external occipital protuberance
Orale (Or)	A point on the hard palate where a line drawn tangent to the curves in the alveolar margin in back of the two medial incisors crosses the midline.
Prosthion (Pr)	The most anterior point on the upper alveolar process in the midline.
Staphylion (St)	The midpoint of a line drawn connecting the most forward points on the curves in the posterior margin of the palate.
Vertex (V)	The uppermost point on the midline of the cranium when it is in the Frankfort plane.*

Condylar Index: measures the position of the foramen magnum (see Figure 6.35).

$$\frac{\text{Basion to Opisthocranion}}{\text{Basion to Prosthion}} \times 100$$

Palatal Index: measures the shape of the palate (and hence of the mouth and lower face). Palatal length is taken from orale to staphylion (see Figure 6.35), while palatal width is the greatest transverse breadth between the inner borders of the alveolar arch at the second molars.

$$\frac{\text{Palatal Width}}{\text{Palatal Length}} \times 100$$

---

*A standard plane of reference on the cranium in which the upper border of the external auditory meatus is on the same level as the lower border of the eye. This is also called the Frankfort Horizontal.

Supraorbital Index: measures the height of the skull.

$$\frac{\text{Vertex to Superior Border of Eye}}{\text{Vertex to Inferior Border of Eye}} \times 100$$

Nuchal Index: measures the area given for origin of nuchal muscles.

$$\frac{\text{From a line level with inferior border of eye to a line with inion}}{\text{From vertex to a line with inferior border of eye}} \times 100$$

Postcranial Indices

Brachial Index: measures the relative lengths (using the osteometric board) of the upper and lower arm.

$$\frac{\text{Length of Radius}}{\text{Length of Humerus}} \times 100$$

Crural Index: measures the relative lengths (using the osteometric board) of the thigh and leg bones. The bicondylar length of the tibia is measured with both condyles resting flat against the upright part of the osteometric board.

$$\frac{\text{Length of Tibia}}{\text{Bicondylar Length of Femur}} \times 100$$

Intermembral Index: measures the relative lengths of the upper and lower limbs.

$$\frac{\text{Length of Humerus + Radius}}{\text{Bicondylar Length of Femur + Tibial Length}} \times 100$$

[handwritten annotations: spider monkey, 5.4, human 5.9/5.4, 241/296, SM 412, 398/409, 226/271, 573/402, 483/713, 176]

Metric Comparison of Skeletons

The measurement descriptions used in the following exercises can be found in the indices just described.

Note: In several of these exercises, measurements may be taken from the photographs if the skeletal material is unavailable. This is not a rigorous method and not recommended for research purposes but is intended to give general observations of the relationships between different animals.

1. Fill in the following chart using Figures 6.1–6.3 and 6.17–6.26.

	Quadruped		Brachiator	Biped
	Bison	Monkey	Gibbon	Human
Brachial Index				
Crural Index				
Intermembral Index				

2. Describe what the differences in the brachial, crural, and intermembral indices between these groups mean.

3. a. Take appropriate measurements of the skeletal elements in Figure 6.36a–6.36d, and determine the probable pattern of locomotion in this animal.

   b. Can you determine anything else about this animal when comparing it with the other skeletons shown in this chapter?

FIGURE 6.36a Unknown humerus. *Photo, D. L. France*

FIGURE 6.36b Unknown radius. *Photo, D. L. France*

FIGURE 6.36c Unknown femur. *Photo, D. L. France*

FIGURE 6.36d Unknown tibia. *Photo, D. L. France*

4. Is there a significant difference between an arboreal and a terrestrial quadruped in the crural and intermembral indices? What are they?

REEXAMINING THE ISSUES

In this chapter, we learned the following:

- If form follows function, then skeletal morphology provides important information about how an animal lives.
- We can gain insights about the general locomotor patterns from the vertebral column, the head, the pelvic girdle, and the hands and feet. In fact, changes in one area of the body often significantly affect other areas of the body, so that it is possible to deduce (within reason) what one element of a fossil looked like even if that element is never discovered.

CHAPTER 7

●

Comparing the Living Primates

OBJECTIVES

1. Why are primates classified into the specific groups in the classification schemes?

2. What are some of the clues for classifying fossil primates into different taxonomic groups?

3. What are the major differences between primates?

We have made very general comparisons of the anatomies of quadrupedal, brachiator, and bipedal animals (Chapter 6). Now we will take a closer look at the anatomical similarities of and differences between the major primate groups. With this information, we will not only know more about living primates, but we will also be better prepared to interpret the fossil record. We will first discuss the morphological differences between Strepsirhini and Haplorhini primates; then we will study the evolutionary trends of primates. We will examine the dental trends, which will be interesting in our comparison of fossilized material, and finally, we will compare the postcranial area of primates to correlate certain characteristics with their primary locomotor modes.

INTRODUCTION

Chapter 5 introduced taxonomic classification schemes and the place of primates in them. We noted the differences between primitive (pleisomorphic) and derived (apomorphic) characters, and that primitive characters are found with phylogenetically older organisms. All living primates retain some primitive characters of our ancient ancestors. For example, all living primates retain five digits on the hands and feet, the same number of digits found on the first primates in the fossil record. Derived characters evolve beyond more primitive characters, and they are usually classified in the same clade by cladists because they are usually acquired by a few members of an evolutionary group. In this chapter, we will look more closely at some of the primitive and derived characters in our primate classification models.

As was discussed, recent cladistic classifications divide the primates into two suborders, the Strepsirhini and the Haplorhini (see Figure 7.1). Strepsirhini primates include lemurs and lorises, which are the most primitive primates. Lemurs are only found naturally on the island of Madagascar (and adjacent islands) off of the southeast coast of Africa. There are around 60 species of lemurs, and they fill many different niches. There are nocturnal and diurnal species and species that eat insects while others eat a greater variety of vegetation. Lorises are much more widely distributed and, like the lemurs, occupy many different niches.

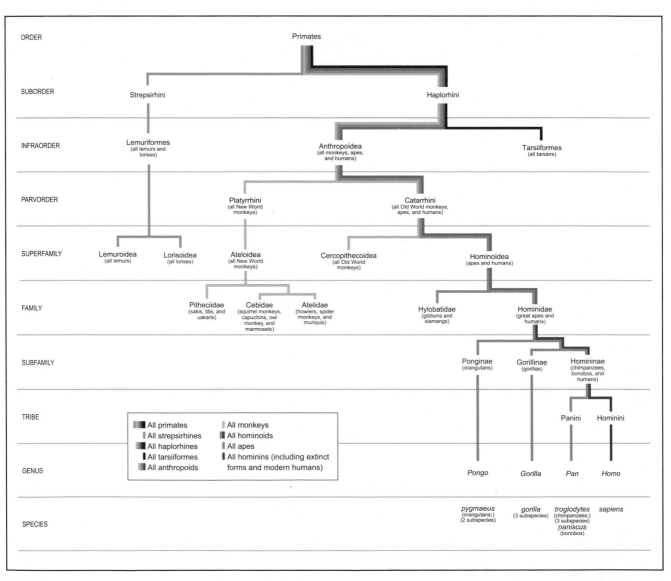

FIGURE 7.1 Updated primate classification. © Cengage Learning

The Haplorhini suborder is divided into two infraorders (Figure 7.1): Tarsiiformes and Anthropoidea. Members of the genus *Tarsius* are grouped with the Haplorhini because, although they are in many respects very primitive primates, they share a few derived characters with monkeys and apes. We will explore a few of those traits in this chapter (and you will have a chance to explore them in more detail in the first exercise of this chapter) and compare them to other Haplorhini primates as well as the more primitive Strepsirhini primates. To begin this discussion, Table 7.1 lists a few of the evolutionary trends in all primates, while Table 7.2 is a list of some of the more primitive traits of the Strepsirhini compared to the more derived traits of the Haplorhini.

The Anthropoids include all New World and Old World monkeys, apes, and humans. The New World monkey species (around 70) are all in the Parvorder Platyrrhini (or "flat nose" as shown in

---

Table 7.1   Primate Evolutionary Trends (Shared Derived Characters or Synapomorphy Among Primates)

1. Retention of five digits on hands and feet (pentadactyly).
2. Nails on all digits (exceptions occur in some Strepsirhini) (Figures 7.2, 7.5, 7.8).
3. Primate hands and feet are usually prehensile (the first digit on the hand or foot can touch the other four digits). This is an adaptation for grasping (Figure 7.2).
4. Tactile pads on the digits are expanded and more sensitive (Figure 7.2).
5. Reduction in the importance of the sense of smell. Primates usually have shorter snouts and a smaller area of the brain (the olfactory bulbs) devoted to the sense of smell. Some primates have long snouts, but in the upper primates this is often related to the size and configuration of the dentition.
6. An increase in the importance of vision. Primate eyes are usually close together in the front of the face, allowing overlapping vision (binocular vision), which enhances depth perception. Most higher primates also possess color vision (Figure 7.3).
7. Primates usually have large brains relative to their body size.

In part because of these trends, the following behavioral trends are also involved:

8. Primates usually have only one infant at a time. Twins are rare, except in one of the New World monkey families, the Callithricidae (tamarins and marmosets), in which twins are the rule.
9. An increase in the time of infant dependency. Primate infants are born in a more helpless and dependent condition and remain so for a longer period of time relative to most other mammals. There is, therefore, an increased learning and socialization period. Other life phases are similarly extended.
10. Primates usually live in social groups consisting of both sexes and all age grades (infants, juveniles, and adults). Some other mammalian groups show this tendency (e.g., elephants, wolves, dolphins), but it is the rule in primates.

Table 7.2   Anatomical Characteristics in Strepsirhini and Haplorhini

1. Rhinarium (fleshy, wet nose) on a relatively long snout. This indicates an increased importance in the sense of smell. (Figures 7.4, 7.5).	1. Shortened snout, no rhinarium (Figure 7.3).
2. Unfused mandibular symphysis (unfused in the middle).	2. Fused mandibular symphysis.
3. Eyes placed more on side of face (Figure 7.5).	3. Eyes facing more forward on face (Figure 7.3).
4. Smaller brain relative to body size.	4. Larger brain relative to body size.
5. Postorbital bar (partial orbital closure) (Figures 7.6 and 7.7).	5. Postorbital closure (see Figures 7.6 and 7.7).
6. Retention of grooming claws on the second toe (Figure 7.8).	6. Nails on all digits (Figure 7.2).
7. Specialized dentition with high-cusped molars.	7. More generalized dentition for more varied diet.
8. Dental comb formed by small, forward-projecting lower incisors (Figure 7.12).	8. No dental comb.
9. Shortened gestational and maturation periods.	9. Increased gestation and maturation periods.

FIGURE 7.2 Saki hand. Notice nails on all digits and opposable thumb. *Photo, D. L. France*

Figure 7.3) and are found in southern Mexico, Central America, and South America. They differ in several ways (other than the flat nose) from those primates in the Parvorder Catarrhini (or "narrow nose").

Just as in the Strepsirhini, there are some exceptions to the general primate classification trends in the more primitive Platyrhines. The marmosets and tamarins are the smallest of the New World monkeys, and they differ from the primate norm in that they have claws instead of nails, and they usually give birth to twins. New World monkeys in

FIGURE 7.3 Saki monkey (a New World monkey). *Photo, D. L. France*

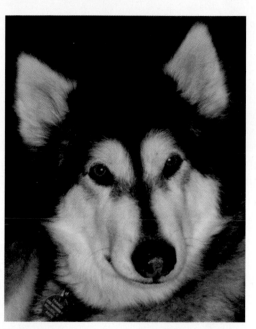

FIGURE 7.4 Notice the wet rhinarium in a dog. *Photo, D. L. France*

FIGURE 7.5 Lemur. Notice the shape of the face, the rhinarium, and the hands. *Photo, D. L. France*

FIGURE 7.6 Lack of postorbital closure in cat (left), postorbital bar in prosimian (right). *Photo, D. L. France*

general have a dental pattern that is different from the Catarhines in that New World monkeys have an extra premolar in each quadrant (see page 213). The sizes of the monkeys as well as their diets, locomotion patterns, and behavioral patterns differ. All New World monkeys have tails, and a couple of species have prehensile tails (or tails that can be used to grip, e.g., tree branches for extra support).

Old World monkeys are grouped in the superfamily Cercopithecoidea and are found in much of the Old World, including southern Africa (sub-Saharan), southern Asia, and Japan. They occupy even more varied niches than do the New World monkeys in that New

FIGURE 7.7 Unenclosed orbits in prosimian (right), postorbital closure in monkey (left). *Photo, D. L. France*

FIGURE 7.8 Lemur foot. Notice grooming claw on second toe. *Photo, D. L. France; access to specimen courtesy Jay Villemarette, Skulls Unlimited*

World monkeys inhabit arboreal areas while Old World monkeys inhabit arboreal areas as well as savannah, the temperate climates of Japan, and even urban areas! Their social groups are extremely varied as well, from the smaller groups of the arboreal colobine monkeys to the larger groups of the terrestrial baboons. We will discuss some of the dental and locomotion differences shortly.

The primates in the superfamily Hominoidea include the "lesser apes" in the family Hylobatidae (the gibbons and siamangs) and the great apes and humans in the family Hominidae. The gibbons and siamangs are the smallest of the hominoids. The great apes and humans are classified in an interesting way: the orangutans (subfamily Ponginae) are the most distantly related of the hominids; that is, there is good evidence (morphological as well as biochemical and genetic) that they split off of the line leading to gorillas, chimpanzees, and humans before any of those other groups split from the line. They have an interesting pattern of locomotion, as we shall soon see, and they exhibit great sexual dimorphism (different morphology in males and females). Orangutans are confined to the forested areas of Borneo and Sumatra (both islands in Indonesia), and they are in danger of extinction because of their shrinking habitat and the fact that they are the targets of poachers. Likewise, gorillas, the largest of all living primates, are confined to forested areas of western and eastern equatorial Africa. They, too, are the victims of poachers and shrinking habitat. They are believed to have split from the line leading to chimpanzees and humans before the lines leading to chimpanzees and humans diverged.

Note in Figure 7.1 shown earlier that the current classification scheme puts the two species of chimpanzee (*Pan troglodytes* and *Pan paniscus*, or Bonobos) in the same subfamily (Homininae) with humans. Some researchers (with some pretty strong genetic evidence) argue that chimpanzees are even more closely related than this classification scheme shows. Currently humans are in a different tribe (Hominini) than chimpanzees (Panini).

EXERCISE 7.1   NAME _____   SECTION _____   DATE _____

Living Primate Clades

FIGURE 7.9 Living tarsier.

FIGURE 7.10 Tarsier skeleton. Notice elongated tarsals (arrows show limits) and large orbits. *Photo, D. L. France; access to specimen courtesy Jay Villemarette, Skulls Unlimited*

1. Tarsiers (Figures 7.9 and 7.10) are newly classified with higher primates in the suborder Haplorhini, although they do not share enough characteristics with the monkeys, apes, or humans to be classified with them in the infraorder Anthropoidea.

   a. Using the following traits for tarsiers, do you think they should be placed in the suborder Strepsirhini or Haplorhini (or do you think they are so different from either that they should be in their own suborder)?

Characteristics of Tarsiers	Strepsirhini?	Haplorhini?
Very large brain to body size.	~~X~~	X
Very large eyes for nocturnal habitat. Eyes do not move within sockets, but head can rotate 180 degrees.		X
No dental comb on mandible.		X
Presence of grooming claws on feet.	X	
Lack of rhinarium.		X
Enclosed eye sockets.		X
Social unit is mated pair and offspring.		

b. What other information would you want to see that would help you decide whether to put the tarsiers in the suborder Strepsirhini or Haplorhini?

Locomotion, eating habits, pallette size, appearance or absense of the crests & brain case size

---

FIGURE 7.11 Unknown skeleton. *Photo, D. L. France*

2. Using the photograph in Figure 7.11, would you put this primate into the Strepsirhini or Haplorhini? Why?

Haplorhini because there is no dental comb, the eye sockets are enclosed & the brain case is large.

3. What information, if any, might convince you that humans and chimpanzees should share the same genus? Why? If you could not be convinced, then what *scientific* evidence leads you to that conclusion?

I wouldn't be convince a chimp could share the same genus as humans - I admit their similar & share the same family but if not even Lucy is under the genus 'homo' I don't think a chimp could ever share that genus.

DENTAL TRENDS THROUGH PRIMATE EVOLUTION

We discussed dentition in humans in Chapter 3, including the definition of a dental formula. Deciduous dentition in humans has a dental formula of 2:1:0:2 (two incisors, one canine, zero premolars, and two molars), while adult humans have the formula: 2:1:2:3 (two incisors, one canine, two premolars, and three molars). Why is the dental formula important for us to know? The different dental formulae of the New World monkeys (2:1:3:3) and Old World monkeys (2:1:2:3) gives us some important information about the sequence of divergence of those primate groups from each other. In a somewhat related way, the dental formula can give us some information about where to place a fossil primate in the taxonomic scheme.

Incisors

Most generalized mammals have four incisors in each quadrant, while most primates have two. Most living primates have at least somewhat procumbent (forward-projecting) incisors, but incisors generally became more vertically oriented through hominid evolution.

An interesting characteristic of the incisors of lemurs and lorises (Strepsirhini) is the "tooth comb" (Figure 7.12) on the mandible. This tooth comb is used for grooming their own fur or the fur of another member of the social group. It is also used to take tree gum off of trees for eating.

Canines

We have seen that a reduction in the importance of the sense of smell and accompanying reduction in the size of the snout are features in the evolutionary trends of primates. In fact, small canines are one of the distinguishing characteristics in humans and our closely related ancestors, as through hominid evolution the canines have become more incisor-like and extend only very little beyond the occlusal line of the other teeth.

In some primates, however, the size of the dentition, and in some primates such as the baboon, gorilla, and chimpanzee, the size of the canines, dictates the size and shape of the dental arcade and of the snout. In primates such as these, the canines are used for gripping and for defense. Note the diastema (the gap that receives the canine of the opposite jaw), which accommodates the very large canines (Figures 7.13 and 7.14).

Premolars

Very early mammals had four premolars in each quadrant. The first premolar in the tooth row was lost first to give some of the New World monkey formula: 2:1:3:3. The second premolar in the tooth

FIGURE 7.12 Bushbaby tooth comb. *Photo, D. L. France*

FIGURE 7.13 Sectorial lower first premolar in baboon. *Photo, D. L. France*

FIGURE 7.14 Diastema. *Photo, D. L. France*

row was lost next to give the dental formula of Old World monkeys, apes, and humans: 2:1:2:3. The practice by paleontologists is, therefore, to state that our dental formula includes premolars 3 and 4.

Modern pongids and some monkeys have a **sectorial lower first premolar** (P3), a single-cusped premolar that forms a cutting, slicing complex with the cutting edge of the upper canine (Figure 7.13 and 7.14). Note that the upper canine of these forms is honed by the sectorial premolar. Later in human evolution, this premolar is a true "bicuspid" ("two cusps," the term dentists frequently use for these teeth). A trend through much of hominid evolution includes "molarization" of the premolars; that is, the premolars in many hominids became wider, with a more effective grinding surface.

Molars

Many of the major differences of molar morphology among primates reflect differences in their diets. Primates who primarily eat insects have high, pointed cusps, which enables them to better puncture and digest the insect's body. Similarly, folivore primates have high shearing crests or blades on their molars that enable them to break up leaves and other plant material more easily. In contrast, the frugivore primates have low, rounded cusps for crushing fruit, and primates who eat a lot of tough, hard foods such as seeds and nuts have low, rounded cusps on their molars for grinding the materials. Primates who eat tough food objects also have thick enamel (the hard outer layer of a tooth) on their molars to help them withstand the strong chewing forces (this is an important feature in human evolution).

A clear distinction can be made between the morphology of the molars of Old World monkeys and apes. The cercopithecoids have **bilophodont molars** (Figures 7.15 and 7.16), which usually have four cusps situated in two parallel rows (sometimes a fifth cusp is present). Hominoids, on the other hand, often have two or

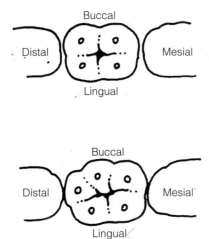

FIGURE 7.15 Bilophodont (X-4) molar (left); Y-5 molar (right). *Photo, D. L. France*

FIGURE 7.16 X-4 Bilophodont molars in baboon (two views). *Photo, D. L. France*

more 5-Y (or Y-5) molars in their mandibles. The 5-Y molars have five cusps in a pattern that resembles a "Y" (Figures 7.15 and 7.17).

Tooth Row Shape (Dental Arcade)

Very early primates have tooth rows that are divergent toward the back. Throughout evolution, the shape of the tooth row has changed from those like the modern gorilla (rectangular, long tooth row), to a parabolic shape as in modern humans (Figure 7.18). As a coincident change with this difference in tooth row form, the entire face has become less prognathic (in which the lower part of the face protrudes forward). The snout has become generally smaller, and the cranial vault has expanded out over the face. Throughout hominid evolution, then, the parabola of the tooth row has become wider.

FIGURE 7.17 Y-5 molar in chimpanzee. *Photo, D. L. France*

FIGURE 7.18a Gorilla dental arcade.
Photo, D. L. France

FIGURE 7.18b Baboon dental arcade.
Photo, D. L. France

FIGURE 7.18c Chimpanzee dental arcade.
Photo, D. L. France

FIGURE 7.18d Human dental arcade.
Photo, D. L. France

EXERCISE 7.2   NAME _____   SECTION _____   DATE _____

Dental Trends

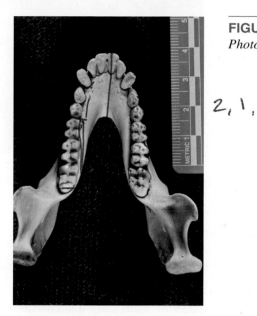

FIGURE 7.19 Unknown.
Photo, D. L. France

2, 1,

1. Are the molars shown in Figure 7.19 bilophodont, Y-5, or some other form?

Bilophodont X 4

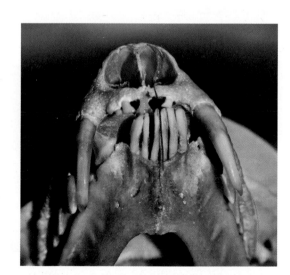

FIGURE 7.20 Unknown.
Photo, D. L. France

2. What do the incisors shown in Figure 7.20 tell you about the taxonomic classification of this animal? Why?

Strepsirhini because it has a dental comb

FIGURE 7.21 Unknown.
Photo, D. L. France

3. What characteristics of the mandible shown in Figure 7.21 tell you about the taxonomic classification of this animal?

> Primate that eats either fruits or cooked foods because of palatte size

4. If you found a section of a mandible with only a sectorial first premolar, what would that tell you about the other dentition in the mouth?

> It would tell us it is either a modern pongid or some type of monkey

FIGURE 7.22 Unknown.
Photo, D. L. France

5. The individual in Figure 7.22 is a fossil from the Miocene (a time period roughly 23 to 10 million years ago). How would you classify this fossil? Is it a primate? Be as specific as possible, and give reasons for your decision.

> 2:1:2:3   Primate dental record
>
> Palette lengut

3:1:3:0

FIGURE 7.23 Unknown.
Photo, D. L. France

6. How would you classify the mandible shown in Figure 7.23? Is it a primate? Give reasons for your decision, and be as specific as possible.

No, not primate

3:1:3:0 probably a cat

POSTCRANIAL COMPARISONS AND LOCOMOTION

We will discuss seven modes of primate locomotion:

- *Slow quadrupedal climbing (SQC):* pottos of Africa and lorises of South Asia
- *Vertical clinging and leaping (VCL): Galago* sp. of Africa and some other Strepsirhines
- *Quadrupedal walking, running, leaping:* many monkeys and some Strepsirhines
- *Brachiation:* gibbons and siamangs
- *Knuckle-walking:* a subcategory of quadrupedalism found in African apes (chimpanzees and gorillas)
- *Slow quadrumanual climbing:* orangutan
- *Bipedalism:* humans

Primates exhibit great variety and versatility in their locomotor behavior, particularly in the trees, where most of them spend all or part of their existence. Simply stating that a primate is a quadruped or a brachiator, for example, hardly describes all of the movements a primate must make to earn a living in natural habitats. Siamangs, for example, while generally classified as brachiators (using the forearms to swing beneath branches), tend to move primarily by climbing when feeding (Fleagle, 1976) and may sometimes move bipedally on top of branches.

Slow Quadrupedal Climbing

This specialized mode of locomotion is seen only in the pottos of Africa and lorises of South Asia. Unlike all others, these primates never run or leap in their arboreal habitat but always move very slowly and deliberately. These Strepsirhines are nocturnal, and their slow, quiet mode of locomotion allows them to stalk prey (insects, birds, and lizards) and to avoid predators in the trees. Slow quadrupedal climbers are characterized by robust musculature and limb bones; mobile ankle, wrist, and hip joints; and short or absent tails.

Vertical Clinging and Leaping

The bushbaby (*Galago* sp.) (Figure 7.24) of Africa and other prosimians of similar anatomical structure exhibit a locomotor mode that has been called vertical clinging and leaping (VCL) (Napier & Walker, 1967). Prosimians that typically move in this way push off with their powerful hindlimbs from a vertical or near-vertical support to which they were clinging, turn around while in midair, and then land feet first on another branch or tree trunk (Figure 7.25).

FIGURE 7.24 Bushbaby (*Galago* sp.). *Photo, D. L. France*

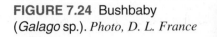

FIGURE 7.25 Vertical clinging and leaping. *Photo, A. Blackstone, with permission, from J. R. Napier and A. C. Walker, "Vertical Clinging and Leaping: A Newly-Recognized Category of LocomotorBehavior of Primates," Folia Primat., 1967, 6:204–219.*

Recent analysis of the anatomy of VCL prosimians indicates that vertical clinging and leaping cannot be considered as one coherent locomotion category. For example, Anemone (1990) argues that there may have been two or three separate evolutionary pathways among prosimian groups to arrive at a VCL locomotor mode. Nevertheless, for the purposes of this introductory course, VCL is considered as one locomotor mode.

Quadrupedal Walking, Running, and Leaping

Most monkeys and many Strepsirhines are quadrupeds (Figure 7.26 shows a quadruped lemur), and those that are primarily arboreal (a majority of them) can be called quadrupedal runners and leapers; that is, they move on top of the branches quadrupedally and leap from tree to tree when there is a break in the forest canopy by using their strong hindlimbs to propel themselves and using their tails as stabilizers. There are subtle differences between the skeletons of terrestrial Old World monkeys (e.g., baboons) and those that are completely arboreal. The Old World monkeys are adept at moving their limbs in a relatively limited plane, and they rarely suspend themselves beneath a branch by hanging from their forelimbs. There are many similarities between the New World and Old World monkeys thought to be a result of parallel evolution. These are adaptations to a similar way of life in similar habitats, in this case, in the canopy of tropical rain forests. There are a few differences, however, between the two groups. Some of the New World monkeys (but no Old World monkeys) have prehensile tails, used as a "fifth hand" in manipulating objects or hanging from branches. Ground-living behavior is

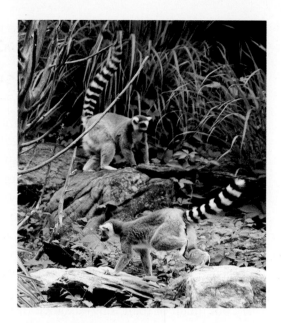

FIGURE 7.26 Ring-tailed lemurs. *Photo, D. L. France*

rare among New World monkeys but is more common in the Old World monkeys. There are no monkeys adapted to the savanna in the New World, whereas there are a few such species in the Old World (e.g., baboons).

Brachiation

The small apes (gibbons and siamangs of Southeast Asia) habitually swing, or brachiate, beneath the branches (Figure 7.27), and sometimes feed while hanging by their forelimbs. This activity is aided by the position of their scapulae, by the upward orientation of their glenoid cavities, and by their hook-like hands with small thumbs and long fingers (Figure 7.28). When climbing in the trees, they use their forelimbs and strong upper bodies much more than their legs. In short, the locomotion and posture habits of the small apes can be said to be forelimb and upper-body dominated (Fleagle, 1976).

Knuckle-Walking

Although the great apes share most of the morphological characteristics of the small apes and occasionally brachiate for short distances, they are too large to brachiate habitually through the forest canopy.

African apes (chimpanzees and gorillas) carry out most long-distance movements on the ground by "knuckle-walking." The knuckle-walkers (Figures 7.29 and 7.30) are characterized by tough, hairless skin on the dorsum of the middle fingers, and their wrists are strengthened by differences in the carpals. When these apes climb trees, however, they, like the lesser apes, use their

FIGURE 7.27 Brachiation in a siamang. *Photo, D. L. France*

FIGURE 7.28 Siamang hand. *Photo, D. L. France*

FIGURE 7.29 Knuckle-walking (and holding on for dear life). *Photo, D. L. France*

FIGURE 7.30 Skeleton of a knuckle-walker. *Photo, D. L. France*

forearms and strong upper bodies more than their hindlimbs and often use a variety of hanging or suspensory postures.

Slow Quadrumanos Climbing

The orangutans of Sumatra and Borneo move through the forest canopy by a locomotor mode that has been called slow quadrumanos climbing. Figure 7.31 shows an orangutan at the National Zoological Park in Washington, D.C., on the "O" line. Note that he is using cables in a quadrumanos manner. Note the morphology of the hands and foot of the orangutan in Figure 7.32 (also note the grasp as she inspects her finger). These large great apes use their hands and feet to grasp branches and other supports as they slowly move through the trees. The female orangutans are almost exclusively arboreal. The huge males, which are about twice as large as females (about 120 kg), carry out much of their long-distance movements on the ground. These males move quadrupedally on the ground with their hands held in a fist, not in the knuckle-walking posture of the African apes.

Bipedalism

The anatomical modifications for habitual bipedal locomotion found in humans are unique among extant primates. These anatomical modifications are observed mostly in the pelvis and feet of humans.

However, anatomists have long recognized the similarities between humans and apes in the upper body: a short, inflexible trunk (relative to most monkeys), the position of the scapula on the dorsum of the thorax, the triangular shape of the scapula, and the relative anteroposterior shallowness of the thorax. These upper-body similarities are not due to similarities in locomotor behavior but to the long period of evolutionary relatedness.

FIGURE 7.31 Orangutan quadrumanos climbing on "O" line. *Photo, D. L. France*

FIGURE 7.32 Orangutan. Note hands and foot. *Photo, D. L. France*

EXERCISE 7.3 NAME _____ SECTION _____ DATE _____

Comparing Extant Primates

1. Which of the three bones that make up the os coxae has changed most in humans, compared with monkeys and apes? In what way has it changed?

   Illium of chimps has squashed & widened in humans; obturator foramen has widen in humans & the greater sciatic notch has shortend & compressed in humans

FIGURE 7.33 Unknown. *Photo, D. L. France*

2. Is the skeletonized hand in Figure 7.33 from a primate? What characteristic(s) lead(s) you to that conclusion?

   Yes, primate (orangutan)

FIGURE 7.34a Orangutan hand.
Photo, D. L. France

FIGURE 7.34b Gorilla hand.
Photo, D. L. France

FIGURE 7.34c Human hand.
Photo, D. L. France

3. Compare the phalanges of the hands of the orangutan, gorilla, and human in Figure 7.34. What are the differences, and what does that tell you about the ways these animals use their hands differently?

   Orangutan has elongated fingers for grasping (braciating) Gorilla's bones are thickest at first knuckle (knuckle-walking)

4. What are four differences between the skeletons of an Old World monkey and an ape?

Smaller brains, tails, palette sizes, (old world monkey), → vertebrae smaller

FIGURE 7.35 Unknown.

Photo, D. L. France

5. How would you classify the individual in Figure 7.35? Is it a primate? Is it a New World monkey? Old World monkey? Ape? Human? Why would you classify it the way you did? Be specific in your answer.

2:1:2:2   New world monkey because it has 4-5 molars

FIGURE 7.36a Squirrel monkey.

Photo, D. L. France

FIGURE 7.36b Old World monkey (macaque).

Photo, D. L. France

FIGURE 7.36c Gibbon. *Photo courtesy of Jay Villemarette*

FIGURE 7.36d Chimpanzee skeleton. *Photo, D. L. France of cast from France Casting*

FIGURE 7.36e Human skeleton. *Photo, D. L. France*

FIGURE 7.37a *Galago* maxilla. *Photo, D. L. France; access to skeleton courtesy Jay Villemarette, Skulls Unlimited*

FIGURE 7.37b Squirrel monkey. *Photo, D. L. France; access to specimen courtesy Jay Villemarette, Skulls Unlimited*

FIGURE 7.37c Macaque maxilla.
Photo, D. L. France

FIGURE 7.37d Gibbon dental arcade.
Photo, D. L. France

FIGURE 7.38a *Galago* skull.
Photo, D. L. France; access to specimen courtesy Jay Villemarette, Skulls Unlimited

FIGURE 7.38b Squirrel monkey skull. *Photo, D. L. France; access to specimen courtesy Jay Villemarette, Skulls Unlimited*

FIGURE 7.38c Macaque skull.
Photo, D. L. France

FIGURE 7.38d Gibbon skull.
Photo, D. L. France

FIGURE 7.38e Chimpanzee skull. *Photo, D. L. France; access to specimen courtesy Jay Villemarette, Skulls Unlimited*

FIGURE 7.38f Human skull.
Photo, D. L. France

6. Fill out the following chart for the prosimians, a New World monkey, an Old World monkey, an ape, and a human. If you do not have these skeletons in your laboratory, use Figures 7.18, 7.24, and 7.36–7.38.

Comparisons of Extant Primates

	Prosimian	New World Monkey	Old World Monkey	Ape	Human
Intermembral index					
Condylar index					
Brachial index					
Dental formula					
Enclosed eye orbits?					
Location of scapula on thorax					
Location of scapula on thorax					
Nails on all digits?					
Tail?					

REEXAMINING THE ISSUES

In this chapter, we learned the following:

- Extant primate dentition gives us clues about the diet of the primate.
- Extant primate locomotion is reflected in their skeletons and in turn gives us information about the environment in which the primate lives.
- The morphological differences in the skeletons of primates offer clues about their evolutionary relationships.

With this information, we are now prepared to begin to interpret the fossil record. In future chapters, you will be asked to do just that.

CHAPTER 8

●

Observation of Living Primate Behavior and Morphology

OBJECTIVES

1. Do different species of animals exhibit different behaviors?

2. Do different species of primates exhibit different interpersonal behaviors?

3. What role does the environment in which they live influence interpersonal behavior?

Primates are interesting to us for several reasons: They are fascinating individuals in their own right, and their behavior and their interactions with other primates help us to understand our own behavior and our roles in society. Also, because we cannot deduce all we need to know about the behavior of our ancestors by studying their skeletal morphology, we can obtain some of the information we need by studying the social behavior of primates.

After learning about general behavioral categories and ways to observe and record primate behavior in a zoo or in the wild, we will practice our techniques at a dog park.

INTRODUCTION

This chapter involves exercises in observing behavior and morphology of zoo primates. Before visiting the zoo, we will review the typical locomotor behavior and other physical characteristics and classification of major groups of primates discussed in previous chapters. In addition, there are links on the Internet to short video clips of primates in various situations.

Naturally, primate morphology is not greatly different between the zoo and the wild (although there are some differences in many primates because of the sedentary lifestyle and different foods), but the behavior of primates in zoos can be atypical. Studies of baboons in a very crowded enclosure in the London Zoo in the 1930s gave the impression that primate societies were centered on sex and violence. Studies of primates in their natural habitats that began in earnest in the 1950s and 1960s have shown that although sex and violence are certainly parts of the behavioral repertoire of primates, they are exhibited rarely relative to other aspects of their behavior, such as foraging for food, grooming behavior, and mother–infant interactions.

The locomotor behavior of primates in zoos obviously depends to a large extent on what they have available in their cages and enclosures. An arboreal primate will not be able to exhibit its full repertoire of arboreal agility, for example, if its cage consists only of bars and a concrete floor. Also note that many of the behaviors listed next will be season-specific and will be determined to some extent by the number, ages, and sexes of individuals present within each enclosure. The zoo personnel will often provide some of the information needed to complete the checklist, such as the species and common names and their distributions.

BEHAVIOR CATEGORIES

There are basically two methods for observing primates:

- Specific behavioral categories
- All behavior of a specific (focal) animal or group of animals

If, for example, a female in the zoo has recently given birth, the researcher may wish to concentrate on mother–infant interactions. If, on the other hand, a group of primates includes many juveniles, research may focus on play behavior.

To fully understand the behavior sequences observed, one must usually be familiar with the individual and group histories. For example, an adult female may interact with another adult female to which she is closely related quite differently than to one to which she is not related. Again, zoo personnel may be able to give some information on the relationships between different individuals. Following is a short list of behavioral categories to choose from:

1. Mother–infant interactions

2. Play behavior

3. Sexual behavior/mounting behavior

4. Adult male–adult female interactions (including nonsexual)

5. Adult male–juvenile interactions

6. Adult male–adult male interactions

7. Adult female–adult female interactions

8. Adult female–juvenile interactions

9. Agonistic behavior (combative or contestant)

10. Dominance behavior

SAMPLING TECHNIQUES

To try to record all behavior for each animal over a long period of time is impractical and overwhelming, so sampling techniques are used. The following is a brief summary of three of the more common techniques.

1. **Scan sampling:** The researcher records the behavior of a group of primates or an individual at regular time intervals, usually 30 seconds, 1 minute, or 5 minutes. If you want to use this method with a group of primates, the group should not be too large, and all members should be visible at all times.

2. **Focal sampling:** The researcher records the behavior of a specific animal.

3. **Ad-lib sampling:** The researcher records any behavior of a group of primates that is observable and that seems interesting. Recordings are made on a blank sheet of paper or in a field notebook. Even though regular time intervals are not used in ad-lib sampling, the time should be recorded often. Also, the researcher usually develops a form of abbreviations because this method involves much writing.

Your instructor may divide the class into groups, which may use different sampling techniques to compare the results.

If your class does not have access to zoo primates, but your campus has a tree squirrel population, observe the behavior of the squirrels. This has one advantage in that you will be exposed to the difficulties of observing animals in a "wild" habitat. Tree foliage at times makes observing the animals impossible. Keep in mind that the trees in a tropical rain forest, where most primates live, are two to five times taller than most trees found in temperate zones. A disadvantage to observing squirrels is that they are often observed alone, whereas one rarely observes a solitary primate in the wild.

EXERCISE 8.1   NAME _____   SECTION _____   DATE _____

Observation Skills at a Dog Park

As an introduction to observing primate behavior, visit a dog park where dogs are allowed to be off of a leash (you probably do not want to take your own dog at this point so you can observe other dogs without being distracted). Take a notebook, and observe the following behaviors:

- Play behavior
- Aggressive behavior
- Dominance displays around other dogs (stiff posture, tail erect, ears up, etc.)
- Submissive displays around other dogs (slumped posture with tail down or tucked between the legs or lying on back)

1. When do these displays occur? How far was the dominant dog from its owner?

> Every time new dog arrived/play began/
> something interesting appeared
>   Dominant dog strayed from owner abt
> at least 10ft or more any given time

2. If there is a dominant dog, how many times did he display dominance to another dog within 10 minutes?

> At least 5 times & showing every
> new dog he was boss

3. Did the submissive dog display submission to more than one other dog?

> Yes, showed belly to dominant dog &
> hid behind owner when pack started
> to get rough

4. Did a certain breed show dominance more often than other breeds?

> Huskey & chivawa (sp?) showed most
> dominance - older dogs & labs more
> submissive

5. Did very young dogs display dominance? How often? Were they more likely to show dominant or submissive behavior?

Tried & were rolled onto backs were more likely to start dominant & then became more submissive in dominant dog's presences

6. What other behaviors did you witness?

Belly showing, face liking, whimpering wagging tail

7. When did those other behaviors occur?

In presence of dominant dog

Classification, Morphology, and Locomotion of Primates

Provide the following information for one to four primates at the zoo, from videotapes, or from library or internet research.

Common name _____

Scientific name _____

Infraorder _____

Superfamily _____

Family _____

Subfamily _____

Genus _____

Species _____

Distribution _____

Number of animals in cage _____

Tail? _____

Prehensile tail? _____

Nails on all digits? _____

Relative length of forelimbs to hindlimbs _____

Hand grip used _____

Habitual mode of locomotion _____

Sexual dimorphism in body size? _____

Common name _____

Scientific name _____

Infraorder _____

Superfamily _____

Family _____

Subfamily _____

Genus _____

Species _____

Distribution _____

Number of animals in cage _____

Tail? _____

Prehensile tail? _____

Nails on all digits? _____

Relative length of forelimbs to hindlimbs _____

Hand grip used _____

Habitual mode of locomotion _____

Sexual dimorphism in body size? _____

Common name _____

Scientific name _____

Infraorder _____

Superfamily _____

Family _____

Subfamily _____

Genus _____

Species _____

Distribution _____

Number of animals in cage _____

Tail? _____

Prehensile tail? _____

Nails on all digits? _____

Relative length of forelimbs to hindlimbs _____

Hand grip used _____

Habitual mode of locomotion _____

Sexual dimorphism in body size? _____

Common name _____

Scientific name _____

Infraorder _____

Superfamily _____

Family _____

Subfamily _____

Genus _____

Species _____

Distribution _____

Number of animals in cage _____

Tail? _____

Prehensile tail? _____

Nails on all digits? _____

Relative length of forelimbs to hindlimbs _____

Hand grip used _____

Habitual mode of locomotion _____

Sexual dimorphism in body size? _____

Additional Comments

EXERCISE 8.3 NAME _____ **SECTION** _____ **DATE** _____

Primate Observation

Scan Sampling (Record the behavior of a group of primates or an individual at regular time intervals, usually 30 seconds, 1 minute, or 5 minutes.)

Beginning Time: _____

Ending Time: _____

Species: _____ Common name: _____

Composition of group: Number of adult males _____ Adult females _____

Immature individuals _____ Group size _____

Brief description of weather:

Focal Sampling (Record the behavior of a specific animal.)

Description of the focal animal:

Age grade (adult, juvenile, infant):

Sex:

Additional Observations

Checklist of Primate Behaviors

Choose a focal animal. Using a watch, observe what this animal is doing during the relevant time intervals, and make a check in the appropriate category. Feel free to use behavioral categories you have created in addition to those presented.

Interval used: ___ 30 seconds ___ 1 minute ___ 2 minutes ___ 5 minutes

	Number of occurrences during time interval																			
	1	2	3	4	5	6	7	8	9	10	11	12	13	14	15	16	17	18	19	20
Walking																				
Sitting																				
Prone																				
Standing																				
Eating																				
Scratching																				
Vocalizing																				
Sleeping																				
Autogrooming																				
Grooming/Groomed																				
Displaying																				
Threat/Threatened																				
Chase/Chased																				
Attack/Attacked																				
Inspecting																				
Playing																				
Courtship/Courted																				
Mount/Mounted																				
Present																				
Displace/Displaced																				
Other																				
Other																				

REEXAMINING THE ISSUES

In this chapter, we learned the following:

- In previous chapters, we have seen that we can determine how an animal moves by looking at the skeletal morphology. There are serious limits, however, to what we can surmise about behavior from the skeleton, so we must look to living models for behavior.
- The behavior of living animals (from squirrels to dogs to primates) depends in part upon the environment in which they are observed and in part upon the behavior of the surrounding animals.

CHAPTER 9

●

The First Primates

OBJECTIVES

1. Why did primates evolve?

2. When we examine a fossil primate, how do we know it is a primate?

3. When did the earliest primates show up in the fossil record?

Geological Time	Dates
Paleozoic Era	570–225 M.Y.A.
Mesozoic Era	225–65 M.Y.A.
Cenozoic Era	65 M.Y.A. to present
Paleocene Epoch	65–55.8 M.Y.A.
Eocene Epoch	55.8–33 M.Y.A.
Oligocene Epoch	33–23 M.Y.A.
Miocene Epoch	23–5.3 M.Y.A.
Pliocene Epoch	5.3–1.8 M.Y.A.
Pleistocene Epoch	1.8 M.Y.A.–10 K.Y.A.
Holocene (Recent)	10 K.Y.A.–present

M.Y.A. = millions of years ago
K.Y.A. = thousands of years ago

INTRODUCTION

In this book (and in any introductory text in physical anthropology), the differences between species of extant primates and between extant and extinct primates must focus on some of the major characteristics. It must be stated, however, that many researchers are studying minute but significant morphological differences between species to try to place them into the appropriate taxonomic classification. As only one example, many researchers (Kay et al., 1992; Silcox, 2003; Bloch and Silcox, 2001; Bloch and Silcox, 2006) are studying the anatomy of the middle ear in extant primates (as well as their sister orders, discussed shortly) and of the earliest primate-like ancestors in the Paleocene to try to find a tiny canal through which the internal carotid artery and nerves are transmitted. If that canal is present, it is an indication that the fossil is more similar to primates than to the sister orders. This is a demonstration that evolutionary changes do not have to be huge to be significant for species differentiation!

In this chapter, we will explore the earliest appearances of primates in the fossil record (including the appearance of lemurs and other strepsirhines through the first appearance of haplorhines). To do this, we have to look all the way back to when the dinosaurs became extinct (at about 65 M.Y.A.) and the Age of Mammals began. With the absence of the dinosaurs, many groups of mammals (including the earliest primate ancestors) were free to explore the newly vacated niches, and at about that time, primates began to diverge from other mammalian lineages, and further evolution of mammals continued. We should, of course, expect that the very earliest primates would share many primitive traits with generalized mammals and perhaps a few of the more derived traits of later primate descendants (in particular, the strepsirhines, or lorises, lemurs, and galagos).

WHY PRIMATES?

Why did the earliest primates evolve? The evolutionary circumstances surrounding the origin of primates may never be known for certain, but a couple of theories are worth considering. The first is known as the **arboreal theory**, which dates from the early part of this century. Briefly, this theory states that the characteristics found on most primates are adaptations that allow primates to pursue an arboreal lifestyle and to compete with other arboreal animals. These characteristics include an increased reliance on vision with binocular vision, a reduction in the importance of the sense of smell, and prehensile hands and feet with nails instead of claws (claws get in the way of the precision grip: see Figure 9.1).

FIGURE 9.1 Prairie dogs. Their claws interfere with a precision grip. *Photo, D. L. France*

Table 9.1 Anatomical Characteristics in Strepsirhini and Haplorhini

1. Rhinarium (fleshy, wet nose) on a relatively long snout. This indicates an increased importance in the sense of smell. (Figures 7.4, 7.5 in Chapter 7).	1. Shortened snout, no rhinarium (Figure 7.3).
2. Unfused mandibular symphysis (unfused in the middle).	2. Fused mandibular symphysis.
3. Eyes placed more on side of face (Figure 7.5).	3. Eyes facing more forward on face (Figure 7.3).
4. Smaller brain relative to body size.	4. Larger brain relative to body size.
5. Postorbital bar (partial orbital closure) (Figures 7.6 and 7.7).	5. Postorbital closure (see Figures 7.6 and 7.7).
6. Retention of grooming claws on the second toe (Figure 7.8).	6. Nails on all digits (Figure 7.2).
7. Specialized dentition with high-cusped molars.	7. More generalized dentition for more varied diet.
8. Dental comb formed by small, forward-projecting lower incisors (Figure 7.12).	8. No dental comb.
9. Shortened gestational and maturation periods.	9. Increased gestation and maturation periods.

This theory had become dogma in anthropological thought by the 1950s, but in the early 1970s, Matt Cartmill of Duke University criticized the arboreal theory and proposed the **visual predation theory** (Cartmill, 1972, 1974, 1992). He pointed out that there are many mammals (e.g., tree squirrels) that make their living partially or fully in the trees and that do not possess these primate characteristics. He suggests that prehensile extremities with precision grip, reduced claws, and binocular vision evolved in the very first primates to enable them to prey on insects on the terminal branches of the lower layers of tropical rain forests. Indeed, most of the primates of the early Eocene are quite small, a clear benefit for moving on the outermost limbs of trees. Today, primates that specialize in eating insects weigh less than 500 g, or about 17.5 oz (Kay, 1984). Furthermore, the molar morphology of these early primates is functionally similar to extant insectivorous primates. Sussman (1991), however, added that some primate traits (including color vision) developed because of the occurrence of flowering plants (angiosperms), and that the different beneficial aspects of those plants (fruits, seeds, etc.) contributed to the new niches exploited by various animals. This seems to be supported by theories proposed by Dominy et al. (2003) that eyes of catarrhines, platyrrhines, and strepsirhines were modified through evolution to be attracted to figs and palms. However, Kirk and Simons (2001) state that probably all late Eocene Fayum (we will discuss the Fayum in more detail in the section on the Oligocene) anthropoids were probably fruit eaters, but that late Eocene prosimians were diverse eaters (some were insectivores, some leaf eaters, and some fruit and insect eaters). They state that this dispels the notion that diet was one of the major driving factors in the evolution of anthropoids. Further, they say that anthropoids probably developed in Africa, and that the resemblance to Asian primates is probably not a result of a direct ancestral line to anthropoids in Asia, but rather a "dietary convergence." In fact, at least parts of all of these hypotheses may be true at the same time or in different times along the evolutionary paths in primates.

WHEN DID THE EARLIEST PRIMATES APPEAR?

A superorder term used to describe the very earliest mammals that show primate characteristics in the late Mesozoic Era is "Euarchonta," which includes the tree shrew (Order Scandentia) (Figure 9.2), flying

FIGURE 9.2 Tree shrew (Order Scandentia). *Photo, D. L. France*

PALEOCENE PRIMATES

Semiorder	Plesiadapiformes (late Cretaceous, Paleocene)
Superfamily	Plesiadapoidea
Family	Plesiadapidae
Genus	*Plesiadapis (North America, Europe: Late Paleocene)*
Family	Purgatoriidae
Genus	*Purgatorius (Montana: early Paleocene–early Eocene)*
Family	Carpolestidae
Genus	*Carpolestes (Wyoming: 55.8–60.2 M.Y.A.)*

EOCENE PRIMATES

Suborder	Strepsirhini
Infraorder	Adapiformes
Superfamily	Adapoidea
Family	Notharctidae
Genus	*Cantius (North America and Europe 50 M.Y.A.)*
Family	Adapidae
Genus	*Adapis (Europe: 33.9–40.4 M.Y.A.)*
Genus	*Afradapis (Egypt: 37 M.Y.A.)*
Genus	*Darwinius (Germany: 47 M.Y.A.)*
Family	Amphipithecidae (Burma and Thailand: late Eocene)
Infraorder	Lemuriformes
Superfamily	Lemuroidea
Family	Archaeolemuridae
Genus	*Archaeolemur*

Superfamily   Lorisoidea
 Family   Galagidae
  Genus   *Wadilemur elegans (northern Egypt: 37.2–33.9 M.Y.A.)*
  Genus   *Saharagalago (northern Egypt: 37.2–33.9 M.Y.A.)*
Suborder   Haplorhini
 Infraorder   Omomyiformes
  Superfamily   Omomyoidea
   Family   Omomyidae (North America, Pakistan, China: Eocene)
    Subfamily   Anaptomorphinae
     Genus   *Teilhardina (Asia, Europe, N. America: early Eocene)*
    Subfamily   Microchoerinae
     Genus   *Necrolemur (Europe: middle to late Eocene)*
    Subfamily   Omomyinae
     Genus   *Shoshonius (North America: 46.2–55.4 M.Y.A.)*
 Infraorder   Anthropoidea (Middle to late Eocene)
  Superfamily   Parapithecoidea
   Family   Unsure placement
    Genus   *Algeripithecus (Algeria: 45 M.Y.A.)*
   Family   Parapithecidae
    Genus   *Biretia (Fayum, Egypt: 37 M.Y.A.)*
 Parvorder   Catarrhini
  Superfamily   Propliopithecoidea
   Family   Oligopithecidae
    Genus   *Catopithecus (Fayum, Egypt: 37–35 M.Y.A.)*

OLIGOCENE PRIMATES

Suborder   Haplorhini
 Infraorder   Omomyiformes
  Superfamily   Omomyoidea
   Family   Afrotarsiidae (not everyone agrees with this classification)
    Genus   *Afrotarsius (Fayum, Egypt: Oligocene)*
 Infraorder   Anthropoidea
  Superfamily   Parapithecoidea
   Family   Parapithecidae (also in Eocene)
    Genus   *Apidium (Fayum, Egypt: 30 M.Y.A.)*
 Parvorder   Platyrrhini
  Superfamily   Ateloidea
   Family   Unsure placement
    Genus   *Branisella (South America–Bolivia: 27 M.Y.A.)*
    Genus   *Homunculus (Argentina: 16.5 M.Y.A.)*
 Parvordere   Catarrhini
  Superfamily   Propliopithecoidea
   Family   Oligopithecidae
    Genus   *Catopithecus (Fayum, Egypt: 35 M.Y.A.)*
   Family   Propliopithecidae
    Genus   *Aegyptopithecus (Fayum, Egypt: 28.4–33.9 M.Y.A.)*

A FURTHER LOOK AT EVOLUTIONARY THEORY

When Charles Darwin first proposed and refined the theory of evolution through natural selection in the latter part of the 19th century, he envisioned a constant, gradual process in which organisms would be evolving characteristics that would enhance their survival. In the 1930s and 1940s, when Darwinism was combined with genetics (called the Modern Synthesis, or neo-Darwinism), this constant, gradual evolutionary process was still believed to be the norm (with a few exceptions, such as genetic drift). In the 1970s, two paleontologists claimed that data from the fossil record does not support gradual continuous morphological evolution (Eldredge and Gould, 1972; Gould and Eldredge, 1977). They stated that many fossil records indicate that the morphology of a species is often in **stasis** (no morphological change in an organism for long periods of time). They argued that the fossil record indicates that this stasis is "punctuated" by the appearance of one or more new species. Further, they theorized that new species would evolve in a small peripheral population that was genetically separated from the parent population. After the new species appears, it may replace the parent species if the new morphological characters possessed by the new species give its members survival advantages over the parent species. These paleontologists called their new ideas **"punctuated equilibria."** Much debate has occurred over the past few years about this new model of the rate of evolutionary change. Later, when we examine hominid evolution, we will review examples that some believe are stasis and punctuation and those that others believe are examples of gradualism.

A process called **adaptive radiation** (or radiation) is also important in evolution. Radiation occurs when organisms come into an area with many empty ecological **niches** (the environment to which a species is adapted, including diet, habitat preference, activity pattern, and other features) or when an organism evolves a character or characters that allow it to prevail over another organism for its ecological niche. When this happens, a species is said to "radiate." Usually the species that radiates has shared characteristics. The fossil evidence indicates that many species of such a radiation soon become extinct, but some survive and continue to evolve.

lemurs (Order Dermoptera), and living and extinct primates (Order Primates), which are all thought to be relatively closely related. We are, of course, interested in the Order Primates as the lineage that leads to modern primates. Also, it should be noted that the term "flying lemurs" for one of the orders of the Superorder Euarchonta could be misleading because they are not really lemurs (they were so named in part because their head looks lemur-like). Also, they don't fly; they glide on membranes between their limbs. They and the Order Scandentia are, however, being studied as close relatives of the earliest true primates.

For a look at the first indisputable primates, we must go to the Paleocene.

PALEOCENE (65–55.8 M.Y.A.)

The search for the first primates has traditionally started in the late Paleocene with a group of mammals classified as plesiadapiforms

(Semiorder Plesiadapiformes), thought to represent the first radiation of primates, and a very diverse group (Bloch and Silcox, 2006). They were considered to be primates because of certain morphological characters of their molars (which had somewhat more rounded cusps than did mammalian insectivores in general) and because of the morphology of the internal ear, as well as a handful of other derived characters they were thought to have shared with primates. However, other parts of their bodies were distinctly unlike modern primates, including that their eyes are not completely enclosed by a bony ring (a postorbital bar), they have enlarged (somewhat rodent-like, though not ever-growing nor self-sharpening) incisors, and some of them have a diastema (Szalay, 2000), unlike later primates. Many authors today put the plesiadapiforms into their own **semiorder** within the Order Primates, but separate from later true primates. Observe *Plesiadapis,* one of the best known of the plesiadapiforms (Figure 9.3), and thought to be among the most successful.

semiorder: taxonomic classification between suborder and order

Purgatoriidae is the most primitive family of the plesiadapiforms. The genus *Purgatorius* was described in 1979 by Szalay and Delson as a mouse-sized probable insectivore that was discovered in what is now Montana. It was described at that time as possibly the earliest primate because it was discovered in deposits that dated to 65 M.Y.A., although the origin of the genus may be earlier—some time in the late Mesozoic (the animal represented by a fossil didn't suddenly appear at that moment; the close relatives would have developed earlier). Only teeth and jaws are currently known for this genus.

Also in the New World, a fossil discovered in Wyoming (*Carpolestes simpsoni*) (Bloch and Gingerich, 1998, Bloch and Boyer, 2002) is described as a nearly complete skeleton with characteristics consistent with early primates. They still have the enlarged incisors and greatly modified premolars possibly adapted to process a high-fiber vegetable diet. Interestingly, their thumbs and big toes are opposable, the morphology of the hands and feet make them

FIGURE 9.3 *Plesiadapis tricuspidens.*

Drawing, I. Tattersall, from Man's Ancestors: An Introduction to Primate and Human Evolution, *Levittown, NY: 1970*

better adapted to life in the trees (Kirk et al., 2008), and their big toe has a nail instead of a claw. Sargis et al. (2007) do not believe that this animal was a vertical clinger and leaper like later (Eocene) primates, to which we will now turn.

EOCENE (55.8–33 M.Y.A.)

The climate of the world inferred from paleobotany indicates that the Eocene was the warmest and wettest epoch of the Cenozoic era. Consequently, rain forest habitats extended into the northern continents even more than they did during the Paleocene era. A gradual cooling and drying trend began in mid-Eocene times, a trend that continues, with many fluctuations. This climate was ideal for the spread of the **"euprimates"** (or primates of modern aspect—a term first used by E. Simons in 1972) around the world. The plesiadapiforms gradually disappeared during the Eocene. Until the middle of the Eocene, North America was connected to Europe, and in the middle to late Eocene, North America was at times connected to Asia, so many of the Eocene primates are represented in these continents (as well as Africa).

In the past few years, the studies of fossils from the Eocene deposits around the world have yielded exciting information concerning the branching of the lemurs and lorises from the tarsiers as well as the very early development of anthropoids. The primary questions in primate evolution are: Where did the first strepsirhines develop, and where did the anthropoids first appear? Did the first anthropoids come from Africa or Asia? We will begin our discussion of Eocene primates with the two superfamilies that represent the most lemur-like (**Adapoidea**) and the most tarsier-like (**Omomyoidea**) lines. These superfamilies are further divided into many families and subfamilies, and there are more than 40 proposed genera of Eocene primates, which ranged in size from 70 to 10,000 g (2.25 oz to 20 lb), the latter figure larger than some of the smaller modern monkeys. Both superfamilies possess the postorbital bar (although the eyes are not completely enclosed in bone), eyes that are more toward the front of the face, digits with nails that are opposable for grasping, and in general, dentition that shows movement toward a more generalized diet.

Adapoidea

The superfamily Adapoidea includes more than 35 genera, and, by dental evidence, these are the most primitive of the euprimates. They have a primitive dental formula of 2:1:4:3 (remember that the dental formula for a general mammal is 3:1:4:3; most strepsirhines are 2:1:3:3; a New World monkey is 2:1:3:3; and the Old World monkey, ape, and human are 2:1:2:3), and, in general, they do not yet show the derived trait of a tooth comb.

The adapoids are divided into families primarily based on their geographic distribution (although there are differences in morphology between them): In North America they are represented by the **notharctids**, in Europe they are the **adapids**, and in Asia they are the **amphipithecids**. The interesting question is how these relate to each other, and which, if any, gave rise to later primates.

Cantius (primarily from North America with a couple of species in Europe) is the earliest notharctid (see Figure 9.4 for a drawing of *Notharctus*). Dental morphology and a dental formula of 2:1:4:3 have led some researchers to think that *Cantius* was likely a fruit eater.

The adapids (represented in Europe in the late Eocene by *Adapis*) (Figure 9.5) have a dental formula of 2:1:4:3 but may have an incipient tooth comb. Cranial elements indicate a reduction in the importance of smell and an increase in the importance of vision (small orbits that face forward) (Gingerich and Martin, 1981).

FIGURE 9.4 *Notharctus. Drawing, Jolly and Plog,* Physical Anthropology and Archeology, *5th ed., 1988, Copyright © 1988 The McGraw-Hill Companies. Reprinted by permission of the publisher*

FIGURE 9.5 *Adapis. Drawing, Jolly and Plog,* Physical Anthropology and Archeology, *5th ed., 1988, Copyright © 1988 The McGraw-Hill Companies. Reprinted by permission of the publisher*

Skeletal elements suggest that it was a slow arboreal quadruped (Bacon and Godinot, 1998; Gebo et al., 2008).

The amphipithecids from Burma and Thailand have some traits that can be potentially confusing (Marivaux et al., 2005, 2008). They have a mix of very primitive adapoid traits in the postcranial skeleton along with some characteristics of the dentition that are similar to the anthropoids (monkeys) (Ciochon and Gunnell 2002). They are currently thought to have been adapoids who developed some anthropoid dental traits but are not in the line of anthropoids.

This convergent evolution (in which similar traits in different species evolve independently—they are homologies and not shared derived traits) occurred in other lemur ancestors.

In May 2009, a fossil was brought to the attention of the public with what most scientists believe was great theatrics. The primate skeleton, named *Darwinius masillae* (nicknamed "Ida" for the daughter of one of the researchers) by Franzen et al. was described as "not simply a fossil lemur, but part of a larger group of primates, Adapoidea, representative of the early haplorhine diversification" (2009). The preservation of this complete fossil is extraordinary, to be sure, as even the contents of the digestive tract were preserved (although there have been other well-preserved fossil adapoids). The skeleton has nails on all of the digits (no grooming claw) and a tooth comb (link to online publication with photographs: www.plosone.org/article/info%3Adoi%2F10.1371% 2Fjournal.pone.0005723). Many researchers believe the claim that this fossil is a close relative of anthropoids and a distant relative of tarsiers is incompatible with the current thinking (supported by most genetics and morphology) that tarsiers are more closely related to anthropoids than to lemurs and lorises (although in a very recent paper, Chatterjee et al. (2009) stated that their genetic research places tarsiers as a sister group to strepsirhines and not to haplorhines, a position that is inconsistent with most current taxonomic information).

In fact, Seiffert et al. (2009) have discovered a poorly preserved fossil that they have named *Afradapis* near the Fayum Depression in northern Egypt. They believe that this fossil (dated to about 37 million years ago) and *Darwinius* are more closely related to the lemurs and lorises than to anthropoids.

Archaeolemur has bilophodont molars and a few other traits characteristic of monkeys (Fleagle, 1999; Martin, 1990). The form of its brain (Martin, 1990) was more like that of a monkey and less like a lemur, which is interesting because it is found on the island of Madagascar, where lemurs have resided and where monkeys did not! They seem to have taken up the niche that would have been occupied by monkeys. Current DNA analysis suggests that *Archaeolemur* may be closely related to the extant Indri, which is one of the largest living lemurs (Orlando et al., 2008).

In Pakistan, Marivaux et al. (2002) have described an adapiform fossil from early Oligocene formations as having a morphology that is between the Eocene and Miocene adapiform primates from Asia. Ciochon and Gunnell (2002) have also evaluated fossils from Pakistan dating as far back as the Eocene and have suggested that they are not closely related to the African anthropoids. They suggest that the true anthropoids did not reach Asia until the Oligocene or perhaps even the Miocene (see Chapter 10). However, Marivaux et al. (2002) have suggested that primate fossils from deposits in Pakistan show that stem anthropoids survived in South Asia even during the climatic changes that made the Oligocene cooler and drier. Arguing for the Asian origin of anthropoids, they state that the fossils in Pakistan are so diverse (and some are similar to the morphology of early anthropoids) that anthropoids likely arose in Asia. Beard and Wang (2004) studied fossils of eosimiids (Anthropoidea) from China and stated that, because of dental similarities, the later anthropoids were probably more likely derived from these eosimiids than from adapiforms (see also the current discussion about *Algeripithecus* later).

Poux et al. (2005) used DNA data to suggest that lemurs had arrived in Madagascar, the limits of their current natural habitat, between 60 M.Y.A. (when they split from lorises) and approximately 50 M.Y.A. If this date proves to be accurate, it pushes the prosimian line back further than previously thought and may change the current thinking about strepsirhine and haplorhine origins.

Seiffert et al. (2005) describe a late Eocene primate, *Wadilemur elegans,* from northern Egypt as a probable early galagid (or galago-like species). They suggest that this shows that by middle Eocene times, the lines leading to modern galagos and lorises had split. Seiffert et al. (2003) found an even older (circa 37 M.Y.A.) galagid fossil, *Saharagalago,* in northern Egypt.

Omomyoidea

Omomyoids are the earliest haplorhine group (leading to modern tarsiers). They have a dental formula of 1.1.3.3, very large eye orbits, and small snouts. There is a wide range of morphology in the omomyoids, from very generalized forms (thought by Ross, 2000, to be a generalized ancestor for all haplorhines) to more specialized forms with more derived traits.

The genus *Teilhardina* is found on three continents (Asia, Europe, and North America). It is thought that they originated in Asia and probably migrated west from there.

Shoshonius (in North America) and *Necrolemur* (in Europe) (see Figure 9.6 for comparison of *Adapis* and *Necrolemur* skulls) have eye orbits and characteristics of the ear and olfactory regions of the brain that are very similar to tarsiers (Fleagle, 1999). Also,

FIGURE 9.6 *Adapis* compared to *Necrolemur*. *Drawings by Hugh Nachamie. This figure was published in* Primate Adaptation and Evolution, *Fleagle, J.C., Academic Press, p. 307. Copyright Elsevier (1988).*

FIGURE 9.7 Hindfoot of tarsier. Notice the elongated tarsals (arrow) that are advantageous for leaping. *Photo, D. L. France; access to specimen courtesy Jay Villemarette, Skulls Unlimited*

Necrolemur is thought to have had a fused tibia and fibula and an elongated calcaneus that acts like a lever-arm for great leaping abilities like modern tarsiers (Figure 9.7) (Rasmussen et al., 1998) (see Chapter 6 for an explanation of the biomechanical advantages of this arrangement).

Anemone and Covert (2000) and Gunnell (1997) have described the tarsier-like primate (*Omomyidae*) from Wyoming, which probably moved in an "active quadrupedal and leaping" manner. Tarsier-like primates have also been discovered in Eocene deposits in Pakistan (Thewissen et al., 1997). Rossie et al. (2006) state that a facial fragment found in China in middle Eocene deposits is very similar to modern tarsiers. It is likely that tarsiers had evolved to nearly their modern morphology in the Eocene.

ANTHROPOIDS

One might expect that anthropoids came onto the scene later than the strepsirhines if the adapoids or omomyoids were ancestral to monkeys, apes, and humans, but some evidence places early anthropoids in the middle to late Eocene (Miller et al., 2005). Whether they arose from the adapiform primates of the early Eocene is still a matter of debate, although Beard and Wang (2004) described a late middle Eocene anthropoid in China that, because of derived dental features (not generalized primitive features that would make it a likely ancestor to strepsirhines and haplorhines), seems to place it in its own ancestral line (not shared with strep-sirhines or tarsiers).

Also, a fossil that was an undisputed anthropoid (*Algeripithe-cus*, dated to more than 45 million years ago) from Algeria appears about 3 million years before the middle Eocene anthropoids in Asia and may be an early ancestor to anthropoids (Godinot and Mah-boubi 1992; Godinot 1994). However, Tabuce et al. (2009) now describe evidence from additional fossils that points to *Algeripithe-cus minutus* (a tiny animal) as having a tooth comb, which, if true, would mean that it is not an anthropoid.

Biretia is a species of anthropoid dated to 37 M.Y.A. from the Fayum Depression in Egypt. It is represented by a nearly complete fossil (Seiffert et al., 2005b). Simons has placed this into the extinct superfamily Parapithecoidea, and it is thought to be the root stock for all New World anthropoids.

Again from the Fayum, *Catopithecus* (Seiffert, 2005b), from the family Oligopithecidae, possessed complete postorbital closure and a 2:1:2:3 dental formula (see Figure 9.8). With *Biretia*, this shows that by 37 to 35 M.Y.A., different species of anthropoids are living in the Fayum Depression in Egypt.

The climate at the beginning of the Oligocene was becoming cooler and drier, and many primate species had appeared and disappeared by this time. The anthropoids become much more prevalent in the Oligocene, so we will turn to that epoch now.

OLIGOCENE (33–23 M.Y.A.)

We will discuss the fossil evidence, but, as DNA testing becomes more widely used in all contexts, it is also becoming more widely used to investigate the relationships and genetic distances between extant primates. This leads to theories about the dates of divergence of the ancestors of various primates.

FIGURE 9.8 *Catopithecus.*
Photo, Elwyn Simons

The Biomolecular Data

The basic premise in biomolecular analysis of the phylogenetic relationship of organisms is that the closer organisms are biochemically and genetically, the more closely they are related. Many different techniques of biomolecular analysis have been used over the years to classify extant hominoids, including immunodiffusion, DNA hybridization, and, more recently, DNA sequencing and animo acid sequencing. These techniques can be briefly and simply explained as indirect (immunodiffusion and hybridization) and direct (sequencing) comparisons of various proteins or DNA.

Data from such studies on hominoids have shown a fairly consistent branching sequence among the hominoids and all anthropoids (the classification scheme presented in Chapter 5 gives you an idea of the branching sequence). First, these data show that the Cercopithecoidea (Old World monkeys) branched off of the ancestral tree before the living apes diverged. Steiper et al. (2004) have used DNA data to estimate this hominoid-cercopithecoid divergence at between 29.2 and 34.5 M.Y.A., although Janecka et al. (2007) estimated the split at about 27 M.Y.A. Among the hominoids, gibbons and siamangs branched off before the orangutan, the orangutan before the gorilla, and chimpanzees and humans were the last to share a common ancestor (Figure 9.9). Since the time of Charles Darwin and Thomas

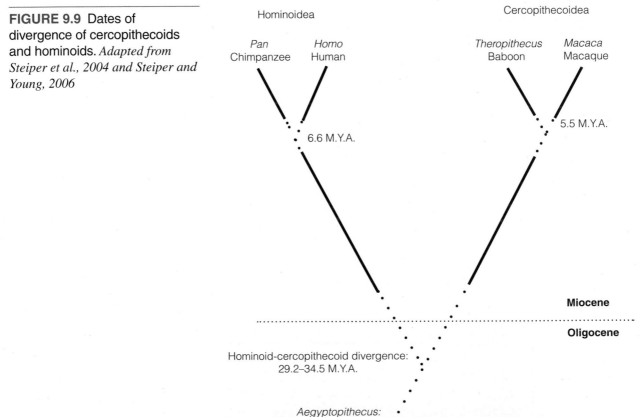

FIGURE 9.9 Dates of divergence of cercopithecoids and hominoids. *Adapted from Steiper et al., 2004 and Steiper and Young, 2006*

Huxley, most comparative morphological studies have supported the view that the African apes are more closely related to humans than are any of the other primates. The biomolecular studies have strongly supported this view. We will discuss this issue more thoroughly as it relates to the great apes and humans in the next chapter.

The Fossil Data

Most of our knowledge of the Oligocene primates still comes from one site, the Fayum Depression (or badlands) of Egypt (Figure 9.10), but we will discuss a few fossils found elsewhere that are adding to our information about this epoch.

The Fossil Primates of the Fayum

The Fayum is on the eastern edge of the Sahara Desert (Figure 9.10) and contains not only Oligocene primates but also late Eocene primates. Although the area is now on the edge of a desert, during Oligocene times, the Fayum was much wetter, with mixed habitats of freshwater swamps bordered by grasslands and woodlands (Olson and Rasmussen, 1986).

There were tarsier-like primates at the Fayum. Significantly, the genus *Afrotarsius* was initially represented by a mandible with five teeth and classified with the generalized anthropoids because of similar dentition (Simons and Brown, 1985; Kay et al., 1997). Simons (1995, 1998), however, thought that the teeth were not similar enough to anthropoids to declassify them as tarsier ancestors. *Afrotarsius* has the modified tibiofibula and tarsals, and on that basis, researchers classify *Afrotarsius* with extant tarsiers instead of with the generalized anthropoids.

Roos et al. (2004) used genetic markers in living strepsirhines to conclude that this suborder originated in Africa, and that Madagascar and Asia were colonized by migration. Madagascar, they state, was inhabited between the late Cretaceous and middle Eocene (by "rafting" across the Mozambique channel), and Asia was colonized between the early Eocene and middle Oligocene by land.

Obviously, the anthropoids would be expected to appear more like extant primates as time goes by. The eyes face more forward (the ranges of vision overlap to allow stereoscopic vision) and are completely enclosed in bone. The mandible is fused in the front, and there appear to be nails on all digits (instead of a grooming claw).

The Fayum anthropoids are usually classified in two families and at least six genera. A handful of fossils are of uncertain status. These anthropoids are roughly between 35 and 40 million years old. They are mostly known by teeth and jaws, but there are some skulls and postcranial fossils. Their postcranial material suggests that they were all arboreal and ranged in size from that of a New World marmoset (300 g, or 9.6 oz) to that of a gibbon (6000 g, or 12 lb).

FIGURE 9.10 Fayum, Egypt.
Drawing, D. L. France

Strepsirhines = lemurs, lorises, galagos

Haplorhines = tarsiers and anthropoids (New World and Old World)

Catarrhines = Old World anthropoids

Platyrrhines = New World anthropoids

Fayum anthropoids possess most of the anthropoid characteristics noted in Table 5.1 in Chapter 5.

The Parapithecidae resemble Eocene prosimians, yet they possess the diagnostic characters of anthropoids, including fused mandibular symphyses. They are the most primitive of all known higher primates (Fleagle, 1988). *Apidium* possesses a primitive dental arrangement (retention of a 2:1:3:3 dental formula) that some paleontologists have suggested puts it in the likely ancestry of both New World and Old World anthropoids (Simons, 1995). South America was much closer to Africa during the Oligocene, and oceanic ridges were probably exposed during Oligocene times. These exposed ridges as well as other islands are believed by some to have provided primates a series of "stepping stones" across the Atlantic (Tarling, 1980), although this idea is not universally accepted. At any rate, fossil primates represented by the genus *Branisella*, first appeared in South America (Bolivia) during the late Oligocene (about 27 M.Y.A.), and they resembled the parapithecids. *Homunculus* was another of the early platyrrhine ancestors, appearing in Argentina in the middle Miocene (about 16.5 M.Y.A.). Molecular evidence suggests that the platyrrhines shared a common ancestor about 20 M.Y.A. (Hodgson et al., 2009a).

The dental form of *Apidium* suggests that they ate primarily fruit and some seeds. From their postcranial skeleton, it is thought that they were arboreal quadrupeds. *Apidium* is the most common primate from the early Oligocene, according to Fleagle and Simons (1995) and may be similar enough to platyrrhines to be an ancestor (see Figure 9.11). Simons (2001) described a Parapithecid from the early Oligocene from Egypt that he says is larger than *Apidium*. He states that it is the most complete higher primate skull yet found for this time and place. The cranial and dental characteristics place it in the anthropoid line.

For ancestors to later Catarrhines, we have to look to members of the Propliopithecidae (Figure 9.12). The propliopithecids have a

FIGURE 9.11 *Apidium* postcranial elements showing primate characteristic and adapdation for quadrupedal running and leaping. *Drawings by Hugh Nachamie. This figure was published in* Primate Adaptation and Evolution, *Fleagle, J.C., Academic Press. P. 333, Figure 12.9. Copyright Elsevier (1988).*

dental formula of 2:1:2:3. For this reason and because their dentition morphologically resembles those of later apes, they are usually classified in the superfamily Hominoidea. Otherwise, they possess none of the specializations of Old World monkeys or apes. Postcranially, they resemble primitive platyrrhine morphology more than they resemble catarrhine morphology (Fleagle, 1988), but cranially, Rossie (2005) believes they are more like catarrhines. Studies of the postcranial remains of *Aegyptopithecus* (Figure 9.13) suggest that it was a robust arboreal quadruped (Ankel-Simons et al., 1998). Also compare the orbits of *Aegyptopithecus* to the orbits of a cat and monkey (Figure 9.14), noting that they are very similar to the monkey. Studies of propliopithecid dentition suggest that they primarily ate fruit.

In 1990, a skull was found in the Fayum of possibly very late Eocene age that was named *Catopithecus browni* (Simons, 1990). This specimen had a fused frontal bone, postorbital closure, and features of the ear that are all characteristics of higher primates. However, a possibly unfused mandibular symphysis of this specimen and some details of its teeth resemble certain Eocene prosimians. One would expect, however, a combination of prosimian and anthropoid characters in a primitive anthropoid, and researchers believe that this species could be the earliest catarrhine.

Elsewhere, a couple of jaw fragments of late Eocene age have been found in Burma, each containing two molars. The dental morphology suggests that these may have been anthropoids, but the material available is insufficient to confirm this possibility.

These first anthropoids are too primitive to draw direct ancestral-descendent relationships from them to any extant primate. Also, their fossil record, while considered "good," is not refined enough to specify which genus or species is ancestral to a specific genus or species of the primitive hominoids of the early Miocene. We can say, however, that the propliopithecids are broadly ancestral to the hominoids of the Miocene. They are likely in, or very close to, our own line of descent.

FIGURE 9.12 *Propliopithecus* mandible. *Photo, J. C. Fleagle and R. F. Kay, "New Interpretations of the Phyletic Position of Oligocene Hominoids," in* New Interpretations of Ape and Human Ancestry, *R. Ciochon and R. Corruccini (eds.), 1983, Plenum Press*

FIGURE 9.13 *Aegyptopithecus* mandible. *Drawing, J. C. Fleagle and R. F. Kay, "New Interpretations of the Phyletic Position of Oligocene Hominoids," in* New Interpretations of Ape and Human Ancestry, *R. Ciochon and R. Corruccini (eds.), 1983, Plenum Press*

FIGURE 9.14 Unenclosed eye orbits in cat (left), enclosed in monkey. *Photo, D. L. France*

EXERCISE 9.1   NAME _____   SECTION _____   DATE _____

Early Evolution of Primates

FIGURE 9.15 Unknown animal.
Photo, D. L. France

1. Is the animal in Figure 9.15 likely a primate? How do you know?

FIGURE 9.16 *Plesiadapis tricuspidens. Drawing, I. Tattersall, from* Man's Ancestors: An Introduction to Primate and Human Evolution, *London J. Murray, 1970*

2. Observe the Paleocene-age plesiadapiform pictured in Figure 9.16.

   a. Make a short list of characteristics in which it does not resemble lemurs.

   b. Are there ways in which it does resemble lemurs?

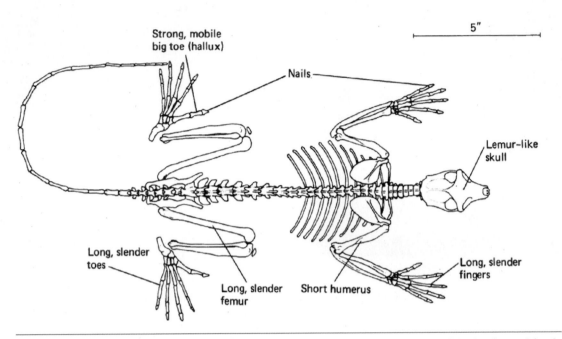

FIGURE 9.17 *Notharctus. Drawing, Jolly and Plog,* Physical Anthropology and Archeology, *5th ed., 1988, Copyright © 1988 The McGraw-Hill Companies. Reprinted by permission of the publisher*

FIGURE 9.18 *Adapis. Drawing, Jolly and Plog,* Physical Anthropology and Archeology, *5th ed., 1988, Copyright © 1988 The McGraw-Hill Companies. Reprinted by permission of the publisher*

  3. Observe the two Eocene primates of Figures 9.17 and 9.18. Make a short list of characteristics in which these fossils are like Figure 9.16. How are they different?

FIGURE 9.19 Bushbaby skull. *Photo, D. L. France*

4. Do you think that the animal in Figure 9.19 is nocturnal or diurnal? Why?

5. Why is it significant that there were tarsier-like primates among the primate fauna of the Fayum?

6. Given all of the information about the fossils in the Eocene and the potential dates of divergence of the primate groups (based on genetic information), draw a phylogeny of the Eocene primates. Realize that some of the information is contradictory, depending upon the evidence and points of view of the researchers.

FIGURE 9.20 *Aegyptopithecus. Drawing, J. C. Fleagle and R. F. Kay, "New Interpretations of the Phyletic Position of Oligocene Hominoids," in* New Interpretations of Ape and Human Ancestry, *R. Ciochon and R. Corruccini (eds.), 1983, Plenum Press*

7. What do the cranial characteristics of *Aegyptopithecus* (Figure 9.20) suggest about the relative importance of the senses of smell and sight?

8. What are the similarities of *Aegyptopithecus* (Figure 9.20) orbits (in size, relative enclosure, and position) with those of living prosimians, monkeys, apes, and humans?

9. *Aegyptopithecus* has been found in two sizes, both in skull and canine size, and in canine shape. What might this suggest about their social structure?

10. In describing *Darwinius masillae* (page 252), Franzen et al. (2009) concluded that the fossil was representative of Adapoidea and also an early haplorhine diversification. Why would that be incompatible with the belief that tarsiers are more closely related to anthropoids than to lemurs?

11. If you found cranial remains from the Paleocene, what features would you look for to classify it as a primate?

REEXAMINING THE ISSUES

- Eocene primates are found in North America, Europe, and Asia.
- Adapoidea fossils are lemur-like.
- Omomyoidea fossils are tarsier-like.
- *Aegyptopithecus* could be the ancestor of Old World monkeys, apes, and hominins, and they are found in Oligocene deposits in the Fayum Depression in Egypt.

CHAPTER 10

●

Miocene Hominoid Evolution

OBJECTIVES

1. What did the last common ancestor of apes and humans look like?

2. When did we last share a common ancestor with apes?

3. Where did hominins first appear?

The Miocene (23–5 m.y.a.) is the epoch during which the ape and human lineages diverged, according to most evidence. It is an epoch, therefore, of primary interest and importance to paleoanthropologists and to anyone curious about human evolution. In previous editions of this book, the Miocene was described only in terms of **hominoid** evolution, with the idea that as yet undescribed **hominins** probably branched off of the hominoid line just before the end of the Miocene. It is now apparent that the Miocene may be more richly populated with hominins than even recently believed, as will be discussed in the next chapter.

Hominoid: lesser apes, great apes, and humans

The Miocene hominoid fossil record has improved considerably over the past two decades, and researchers continue to discover exciting new fossils. In addition, the refinement of DNA sequencing and the work by the Human Genome Project have added a great deal of genetic information to the discussion. Before we discuss the fossil data, it will be helpful to continue the discussion of the current biomolecular data introduced in the previous chapter.

THE BIOMOLECULAR DATA

Biomolecular studies of hominoids have indicated for years a surprising genetic similarity between humans and the great apes. Recent studies of the entire genomes of humans and chimpanzees have estimated a nuclear DNA difference between humans and chimpanzees of between 2.7 percent (Cheng et al., 2005) and 6.4 percent (Demuth et al., 2006). This is surprising because the behavioral, ecological, and morphological differences between humans and our nonspeaking, quadrupedal, forest-living relatives suggest a larger difference (although the more we study our ape cousins, the more similarities we find). This indicates that only a small amount of the genome is responsible for the differences observed between humans and apes. The significance of this as a basis for a "molecular clock" is discussed later, but the researchers in various studies argue that because of the genetic similarities, chimpanzees and humans should be in the same genus (*Homo*) with two subgenera, *Pan* and *Homo!*

THE MOLECULAR CLOCK

Not only have the branching sequences of taxa been derived from the biochemical–molecular techniques, but the dates of the separation of the taxa have been estimated as well. At one time, molecular clocks relied on the premise that the biochemical (or molecular) differences between taxa accumulate at a constant rate when averaged over geologic time, so that a greater molecular difference implies an earlier divergence date of the taxa in question. Now researchers understand that the rates of genetic change are not necessarily constant.

Steiper and Young (2006) studied the differences in chromosome 7 of many species of hominoids (including humans and the great apes), Old World monkeys, New World monkeys, strepsirhines, and several nonprimate species. They calibrated the split between humans and common chimpanzees with *Sahelanthropus tchadensis* (discussed later in this chapter), which has been dated between 6 and 7 M.Y.A. using faunal comparisons (Brunet et al., 2002; Vignaud et al., 2002), and other fossil data. Other primate divergence times were calibrated in similar ways. Steiper and Young (2006) developed the following divergence times (all of these are listed here as single dates, whereas the original article gives a range of dates) based on their research (see Figure 10.1): strepsirhines from haplorhines at 77.5 M.Y.A.; New World monkeys from Old World monkeys, apes, and humans at 42.9 M.Y.A.; Old World monkeys from apes and humans at 30.5 M.Y.A.; the orangutan diverged from the other great apes and humans at 16.3 M.Y.A.; the gorillas diverged at 8.6 M.Y.A., and chimps from humans at 6.6 M.Y.A. It should be noted that there are several molecular clocks with somewhat different dates (Wildman et al., 2003; Kumar et al., 2005; Arnason et al., 1998; Sibley and Ahlquist, 1984, 1987). See also Steiper and Young (2008) for an interesting discussion on why the estimated dates between molecular and paleontological don't always agree.

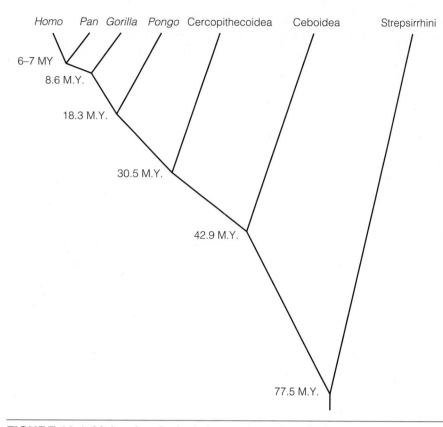

Homo   *Pan*   *Gorilla*   *Pongo*   Cercopithecoidea   Ceboidea   Strepsirrhini

6–7 MY

8.6 M.Y.

18.3 M.Y.

30.5 M.Y.

42.9 M.Y.

77.5 M.Y.

FIGURE 10.1 Molecular clock phylogeny based on Steiper and Young, 2006.

THE FOSSIL DATA

MIOCENE TAXONOMY

Superfamily	Pliopithecoidea
Family	Unsure placement
Genus	*Lomorupithecus* (Uganda, 19–20 M.Y.A.)
Family	Pliopithecidae
Genus	*Pliopithecus* (Europe, 12.5–13 M.Y.A.)
Superfamily	Cercopithecoidea
Family	Victoriapithecidae
Genus	*Victoriapithecus* (northern and eastern Africa, 19 M.Y.A.)
Family	Cercopithecidae
Genus	*Theropithecus* (Kenya, 3.3 M.Y.A.)
Superfamily	Proconsuloidea
Family	Proconsulidae
Genus	*Proconsul* (Africa, 20–17 M.Y.A.)
Genus	*Micropithecus* (Uganda, 20 M.Y.A.)

Superfamily	Hominoidea
Family	Hylobatidae
Genus	*Yuanmoupithecus* (China, 9 M.Y.A.)
Family	Hominidae
Subfamily	Kenyapithecinae
Genus	*Kenyapithecus* (Kenya, 14 M.Y.A.)
Subfamily	Ponginae
Genus	*Sivapithecus* (Europe and Asia, 12 M.Y.A.)
Genus	*Gigantopithecus* (Asia, 8–1 M.Y.A.)
Genus	*Lufengpithecus* (southern China, 9–5 M.Y.A.)
Subfamily	Homininae
Genus	*Dryopithecus*
Genus	*Ouranopithecus* (Greece, 9.6–8.7 M.Y.A.)
Genus	*Nakalipithecus* (Kenya, 9.9–9.8 M.Y.A.)
Genus	*Chororapithecus* (Kenya, 10.5–10 M.Y.A.)
Genus	*Sahelanthropus*
Species	*tchadensis* (Chad, 6–7 M.Y.A.)
Genus	*Orrorin*
Species	*tugenensis* (Tugen Hills, central Kenya 6 M.Y.A.)
Genus	*Ardipithecus*
Species	*ramidus* (Afar Rift, northeastern Ethiopia, 4.4 M.Y.A.)

OLD WORLD MONKEYS

Old World monkeys appeared in the early Miocene (Rossie and Maclatchy, 2006; Rae, 2004; Conroy et al. 1996), primarily from Asia and Europe, though the origin of the line was thought to have been in Africa. In fact, Rossie and Maclatchy (2006) described a new genus (*Lomorupithecus*) of catarrhine in Uganda that, they say, may be the oldest catarrhine in Africa at between 19 and 20 M.Y.A. The Old World monkeys were rare relative to the primitive hominoids, but their numbers increased through the Miocene. By the late Miocene, the cercopithecoids were relatively much more common than the hominoids, the situation that exists among extant catarrhines. In Europe, *Pliopithecus* (also of the family Pliopithecidae) dates from the middle Miocene (12.5–13 M.Y.A.), and interestingly, the postcranial remains suggest some adaptations for suspension from the arms, although it did not have the prehensile tail of some New World monkeys. All of the pliopithecoids became extinct in the Pliocene apparently with no descendants.

Two families represent the line of Old World monkeys in the Miocene that actually led to significant descendants: the victoriapithecids (which are extinct) and the cercopithecids. The victoriapithecids appear in northern and eastern Africa at about 19 M.Y.A., and predate the probable split between the two Old World monkey subfamilies: the colobines and the cercopithecines, which occurred around 15 M.Y.A. (Sterner et al., 2006). They may represent an ancestral line to all Old World monkeys, or they could represent a separate line that became extinct without being ancestral to any of the extant Old World monkeys. *Victoriapithecus* (Figure 10.2) is a small monkey that exhibits bilophodont molars (like all current Old World monkeys) and some postcranial features that are similar to living terrestrial monkeys (Benefit and McCrossin, 1997). It likely ate fruits and seeds.

By 9 M.Y.A., the first true colobine fossil is seen in Africa, and fossils of colobines from Europe and Asia appear soon afterwards. We will talk a bit more about the cercopithecoids in the next chapter, as they and other monkeys flourish in the Plio-Pleistocene.

FIGURE 10.2 *Victoriapithecus* cranium showing catarrhine characteristics.

HOMINOIDS

Almost 30 genera and many more species of Miocene hominoids have been described. Although most Miocene fossil hominoids are known from teeth and jaws only, as more postcranial and cranial material are being discovered, it is apparent that these hominoids exhibit even more diversity than the dentition alone had indicated (Brunet et al., 2002; Kelly and Pilbeam, 1986; Kordos and Begun, 1997).

The apes of the early Miocene were very primitive, and except for their teeth (they had thick enamel and low cusps, similar to extant apes), they did not greatly resemble later apes. These primitive apes gave way to a radiation of apes of a more modern aspect in the middle Miocene.

Virtually all the primitive apes of the early Miocene have been found in East Africa, although a discovery was made in Namibia in 1992. Most of the species were likely to have been forest living and arboreal, although there is some diversity in locomotor behavior. Some were quite large; for example, *Proconsul major,* which was female gorilla–sized, was likely primarily an arboreal quadruped (from the skeletal morphology—see Nakatsukasa, 2004), although it may have been at least partially terrestrial. Observe the casts of any *Proconsul* species you have in your lab or look at Figures 10.3, 10.4, 10.5, and 10.6. *P. africanus* was about the size of a large female baboon. The specimen pictured (RU7290) is nearly complete, though the cranium and mandible were slightly deformed in the process of fossilization. The dentition is ape-like, but the remainder of the specimen exhibits none of the specializations (or derived characters) characteristic of living apes (except for the lack of a tail). For this reason, hominoids of the early Miocene are often referred to as "dental apes." *P. africanus* was a robust quadruped that probably ate mostly fruit in a rain forest or woodland habitat. Like the propliopithecids of the Oligocene, *Proconsul* and other primitive "dental

FIGURE 10.3 *Proconsul africanus. Drawing, after A. C. Walker and M. Pickford, "New Postcranial Fossils of Proconsul africanus and Proconsul nyanzae." In:* New Interpretations of Ape *and* Human Ancestry, *R. Ciochon and R. Corruccini (eds.), 1983, Plenum Press*

FIGURE 10.4 *Proconsul africanus. Photo, D. L. France; cast from National Museums of Kenya.*

FIGURE 10.5 *Proconsul africanus,* maxilla. *Photo, D. L. France; cast from National Museums of Kenya*

FIGURE 10.6 *Proconsul africanus,* mandible. *Photo, D. L. France; cast from National Museums of Kenya*

FIGURE 10.7 *Kenyapithecus wickeri,* mandible (left) and maxilla (right) fragments. *Photo, D. L. France; casts from Werner-Gren Foundation*

apes" of the early Miocene cannot be said to be specifically ancestral to specific later hominoids, although the genus is quite variable in size, general morphology, and dietary patterns. It has been said by some researchers that because *Proconsul* is just a dental ape with postcranial remains that are not particularly ape-like, they should be in their own superfamily, Proconsuloidea, but many researchers still place this fossil in the Hominoidea superfamily. *Micropithecus,* which is the smallest ape (at 6 to 8 pounds) ever uncovered (extinct or extant), is also in the family Proconsulidae (Fleagle and Simons, 2005).

As we have stated, the ancestors to the African hominoids are still an enigma. *Kenyapithecus* of the middle Miocene (about 14 M.Y.A.) consists of a few jaw fragments that contain a few teeth (Figure 10.7). Dentally, *Kenyapithecus* resembles *Sivapithecus* but probably predates the African great ape/hominin split (Simons, 1995). It has thick molar enamel, a large mandible, and large premolars.

Sivapithecus, Kenyapithecus, Ouranopithecus, and *Gigantopithecus* share the following characteristics:

- Teeth have thick enamel. In fact, the enamel of *Ouranopithecus* has been termed "hyperthick" by Kay and Ungar (1997).
- Molars are wide, have low cusps, and are large relative to anterior teeth.
- Mandibles are deep, with a heavy buttress.

These characteristics are similar to *Australopithecus* (a hominin discussed in Chapter 11) and were thought to be evidence that one of them was ancestral to the later hominins, although they are now thought to be better explained by parallel evolution (Simons, 1995).

Living primates that eat tough foods such as seeds and nuts have thick-enameled molars and low cusps similar to those of *Sivapithecus.* Studies of the postcranial remains of *Sivapithecus* reveal that they had begun to show anatomical patterns characteristic of living hominoids. They seem to have possessed generalized ape bodies underlying generalized locomotor and postural capabilities (Rose, 1983). These hominoids have usually been found at fossil sites (whether in Africa or southern Eurasia) that indicate that they were not tropical rain forest animals. Rather, paleobotanical and paleontological evidence from these sites indicate that they lived in mixed habitats of seasonal woodlands interspersed with open grasslands. The smaller animals were more arboreal, whereas the larger ones must have exhibited a considerable terrestrial component in their locomotor behavior.

A partial face of *Sivapithecus indicus* that resembles the face of an orangutan (see Figures 10.8 and 10.9) was recovered in Pakistan. In fact, the resemblances are so striking that most experts believed that *Sivapithecus* was ancestral to *Pongo* (Andrews, 1983; Pilbeam, 1984). Thus, paleoanthropologists had identified one Miocene genus that was probably in or close to the lineage that led to a living ape, although analysis of postcranial material indicates little similarity to the modern orangutan (Kelly, 1995).

However, *Lufengpithecus*, discovered in southern China and dated at about 9–5 M.Y.A. does show postcranial aspects similar to the orangutan. The genus is represented by many teeth, crania, mandibles, and recently some postcranial material, including a femur and some finger bones (Xu and Lu, 2007). It has a very narrow interorbital distance, oval orbits, and curved phalanges like extant orangutans (Harrison et al., 2008). In many ways, it is also very similar to *Sivapithecus*, and because *Sivapithecus* fossils date to around 12 M.Y.A., *Sivapithecus* may be ancestral to *Lufengpithecus* and to *Pongo* (modern orangutans) (Chaimanee et al., 2003).

Because of the dental characteristics, dates, and other similarities, a large species of *Sivapithecus* is also thought to have been the ancestor to *Gigantopithecus*. *Gigantopithecus* is the largest primate ever to have lived (Figures 10.10–10.12). The 8-million-year-old *Gigantopithecus gigantus* (*G. bilaspurensis*) was gorilla-sized.

FIGURE 10.8 Chimpanzee (left), *Sivapithecus indicus* (center), orangutan (right). *Photo, William Sacco and David Pilbeam*

FIGURE 10.9 *Sivapithecus indicus* maxilla. *Photo, D. L. France; cast from National Museums of Kenya*

FIGURE 10.10 *Gigantopithecus gigantus. Photo, D. L. France; cast from University of Pennsylvania*

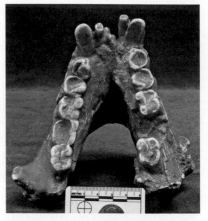

FIGURE 10.11 *Gigantopithecus blacki. Photo, D. L. France; cast from University of Pennsylvania*

FIGURE 10.12 *Gigantopithecus blacki* (left) and gorilla (right). *Photo, D. L. France; cast (left) from University of Pennsylvania; cast (right) from France Casting*

FIGURE 10.13 *Dryopithecus fontani,* mandible. *Photo, D. L. France; cast from University of Pennsylvania*

However, a younger species, *G. blacki* from China of about middle Pleistocene age (about 1 M.Y.A.) was two to three times the size of a gorilla (this is based on dentition only) (Figures 10.10 and 10.11)! Jaws and teeth are all we know of this, but they were so large that the animals must have been entirely terrestrial.

Dryopithecus (Figure 10.13) was the first fossil ape to be described in the scientific literature (Lartet, 1856). This specimen was found in southern France, and *Dryopithecus* species of middle Miocene age have been found throughout southern Europe. Its dental enamel is thin, and Galbany et al. (2005) suggest that microwear on its teeth indicate that it ate abrasive, tough foods. The thin dental enamel is different from most of the hominoids from this time period, and its descendants are not clearly known.

There is no record of hominoids in Africa between about 13 M.Y.A. and 10 M.Y.A., although there is fossil evidence of hominoids in Europe and Asia. A partial face with the upper dentition of *Ouranopithecus* was found in Greece and dated between 9.6–8.7 M.Y.A. It exhibits some similarity in dentition and facial form (including a big brow ridge with a frontal sinus) to the African apes and to hominins (De Bonis et al., 1990; Kordos and Begun, 1997; De Bonis and Koufos, 1994; Kay and Ungar, 1997, Smith et al., 2004).

Chororapithecus teeth have been discovered in Kenya, and date to about 10.5–10 M.Y.A. (Bernor, 2007). While *Ouranopithecus* (9.6–8.7 M.Y.A. in Greece) was thought to perhaps be an ancestor to modern apes and possibly the common ancestor between apes and humans, some believe that *Chororapithecus* is so similar to gorillas in their dental morphology that it was likely the gorilla ancestor. If that is true, then it pushes the ape/human split farther back in time.

Also in Kenya, *Nakalipithecus*, dated to 9.9–9.8 M.Y.A. displays some similarities to *Ouranopithecus*, although it has fewer derived characters. It might be an ancestor to *Ouranopithecus and* be a common ancestor to apes and humans (Kunimatsu et al., 2007).

GIBBONS AND SIAMANGS

The earliest hylobatid (gibbon and siamang) ancestor is now thought to be *Yuanmoupithecus* (Chatterjee, 2006; Harrison et al., 2008). It has been discovered in China and dated to about 9 M.Y.A. The biomolecular data places the gibbon-great ape divergence at about 15–18 M.Y.A., so the dates are appropriate. Also, remember that gibbons and siamangs today live in Borneo and Java, and this fossil shows some of the postcranial traits needed for the brachiating locomotion.

We will now leave the evolution of our primate relatives to concentrate on the evolution of the hominins.

EXERCISE 10.1   NAME _____   SECTION _____   DATE _____

Miocene Hominoid Evolution

1. Is it reasonable to expect that mutation rates are relatively constant over long periods of time?

    What events would significantly alter the mutation rates of a species?

2. Aside from the primitive hominoids of the early Miocene, what other group of primates that we have discussed is close to the divergence of the Old World monkeys and apes and might be ancestral to both?

3. How would a paleoprimatologist identify a cercopithecoid fossil?

FIGURE 10.14 *Proconsul africanus,* maxilla. *Photo, D. L. France; cast from National Museums of Kenya*

FIGURE 10.15 *Proconsul africanus,* mandible. *Photo, D. L. France; cast from National Museums of Kenya*

FIGURE 10.16 Mandible of chimpanzee. *Photo, D. L. France*

4. Compare the upper and lower jaws of *Proconsul africanus* (Figures 10.14 and 10.15) to an extant chimpanzee mandible (Figure 10.16). Make a list of the dental similarities of the two forms.

FIGURE 10.17 *Aegyptopithecus. Photo, J. C. Fleagle and R. F. Kay,* "New Interpretations of the Phyletic Position of Oligocene Hominoids," *in* New Interpretations of Ape and Human Ancestry, *R. Ciochon and R. Corruccini (eds.), 1983, Plenum Press.*

5. How is the skull of *P. africanus* (Figures 10.14 and 10.15) more derived than the skull of *Aegyptopithecus* (Figure 10.17) of the Oligocene?

FIGURE 10.18 Chimpanzee (left), *Sivapithecus indicus* (center), orangutan (right). *Photo, William Sacco and David Pilbeam.*

6. Compare the face of *Sivapithecus sivalensis* (= *indicus*) (GSP15000) (Figure 10.18) with an orangutan cranium. What are some of the similarities between this 8-million-year-old fossil face and the face of the extant orangutan?

7. What part or parts of the postcranial skeleton would be especially useful in identifying a hominin?

8. The early hominins appear to be bipedal but have small brains. Which would you consider to be more important in the identification of a fossil as "hominin"—a large brain or evidence of bipedalism? Why?

9. How would you organize or classify the Miocene hominoids into a cladogram (tree)? Do they relate to extant primates? Of course, a definitive solution is not possible at this time, but by using the disparate pieces of the puzzle we have given, you can make educated guesses about the appearance of the missing pieces.

10. Given the extremely large mandibles discovered for *Gigantopithecus*, what characteristics would the rest of the body have exhibited?

REEXAMINING THE ISSUES

- The Miocene is the epoch in which ancestors are seen for later lesser apes (gibbons and siamangs) and great apes.
- We will likely find increasing evidence for the last common ancestor for great apes and hominins in the Miocene.
- The oldest catarrhine appeared in Africa in the Miocene, and by the late Miocene the cercopiths were abundant.

OBJECTIVES

1. How can we recognize a fossil as a hominin?

2. Where did humans first appear?

3. Did we last share a common ancestor with the chimpanzee?

In previous chapters, we have investigated the basic differences between primates and other mammals, and we have examined many of the hominoids through the Miocene. We are not leaving the Miocene entirely, however, as fossil hominins have been discovered in deposits dated to 6 or 7 M.Y.A.

INTRODUCTION

As might be expected, becoming human does not happen overnight. In previous chapters, we talked about mosaic evolution, in which the characteristics we attribute to primates that live today did not appear fully developed and all at the same time. Instead, some fossils have some attributes (but perhaps not all) of the extant hominoids and hominins. How can we say that a fossil is a hominin? Probably the most important clues are changes that signal bipedalism, and in particular obligate bipedalism, which means that the individual is bipedal because other modes of locomotion are either impossible or are not biomechanically sensible (e.g., a healthy adult human *can* walk on his hands and feet, but it would take much more energy and would be much more difficult than walking bipedally). In addition to saving energy walking as an obligate biped, it has been suggested that it is easier to see over tall grasses on the savannah, and walking frees the hands for carrying loads (i.e., carrying tools or food) (Preuschoft, 2004; Wang and Crompton, 2004).

FIGURE 11.1 A nearly complete cranium of *Sahelanthropus* from Chad, dating to 7–6 M.Y.A.
Photo, Copyright Mission Paléoanthropologique Franco-Tchadienne

We also look for differences in dental morphology, particularly a reduction in size of all teeth and evidence that the lower premolars are not sectorial. The reduction in the size of the dentition is accompanied by a reduction in the size of the face. We also look for an increase in the size and complexity of the brain relative to the size of the body, and a foramen magnum that moves more to the center of the basicranium (concomitant with an upright posture and expansion of the brain).

In the past few years, an explosion of discoveries from this general time period has created interesting concerns in the categorization (and naming) of fossils. Should we continue to add more genera with fewer species within each, or should we "lump" more species (with more morphological variation) into fewer genera? All researchers would not agree upon the classification schemes presented in this chapter, but they are probably the most parsimonious. Of course, as more discoveries are made, the taxonomic classifications may change.

PRE-*AUSTRALOPITHECUS* HOMININS

Exciting discoveries of hominin fossils within the past decade have dramatically changed our view of early hominin evolution. In 2002, a collection of fossils was described from Chad (central Africa) (Brunet et al., 2002; Vignaud et al., 2002; Brunet et al., 2005). These fossils have been dated by associated fauna at between 6 and 7 million years old, by radioactive isotope (beryllium nuclide) to between 6.8 and 7.2 M.Y.A., and have been named *Sahelanthropus tchadensis* (commonly called "Chad Man") (Figure 11.1). These hominins display a combination of derived and primitive characters, including a small brain, smaller canines than the great apes (it also shows wear on the occlusal surface or tip, which means it is unlikely to have had a sectorial lower first premolar like an ape), a large and continuous supraorbital torus (an ape-like characteristic), large central incisors (ape-like), and intermediate enamel thickness. Its foramen magnum is more toward the back of the cranium than in a typical hominin, but farther forward than in apes. The postcranial characteristics suggest bipedality (Guy et al., 2005; Cobb, 2008; Crompton et al., 2008). These finds are important for several reasons. First, if the suggested dates are accurate, and if this is a hominin (and it appears that it is), then this discovery pushes the dates for a hominin back by about a million years. Also, it extends the geographical distribution of early hominins beyond what has been described to date. In addition, this discovery would push the likely dates of divergence from the common hominoid ancestor to an earlier date (and earlier than suggested by Steiper and Young, 2006—see Figure 10.1 in Chapter 10).

A different fossil has also been unearthed recently and is also dated to about 6 M.Y.A. (by radiometric dating). This fossil has been dubbed *Orrorin tugenensis* and was discovered in the Tugen Hills of central Kenya. It is represented by many skeletal and dental elements, exhibiting many characteristics similar to *Sahelanthropus*. Femur and other lower limb elements show clear bipedalism (Richmond and Jungers, 2008, Galik et al, 2004). The foramen magnum is relatively forward on the cranium, but cranial and dental elements are thought by several researchers (White et al., 2009) to be more primitive than the next hominin on our list, *Ardipithecus ramidus*.

Ardipithecus ramidus

A virtual explosion of information about a 4.4-million-year-old-assembly of fossils has recently been published (see *Science* 326(64), 2009, an entire issue exploring *Ardipithecus ramidus*). These individuals (more than 100 specimens have been recovered to date) lived in the Afar Rift region in northeastern Ethiopia. *A. ramidus* has a relatively small brain (between 300–350 cm^3), which is smaller than the australopiths and a little smaller than *Sahelanthropus* (estimated at a little less than 400 cm^3). Its canines are small relative to chimpanzees, and the cheek teeth are not as enlarged as in later australopithecines (Suwa et al., 2009a and b). Lovejoy (2009) infers from the small canines that there was little need for the aggressiveness between males implied by large canines and significant sexual dimorphism. Could this mean that there was cooperation between males for providing food for a group?

Because the canines and the cheek teeth are relatively small, the face in *Ardipithecus* is smaller than in *Australopithecus,* and it does not project as far forward. The dental enamel is relatively thin (thinner than the Miocene anthropoids, with the possible exception of *Dryopithecus*). The foramen magnum is placed more forward than in apes (Suwa et al., 2009a and b).

The pelvis and foot are consistent with bipedalism, but there was a big toe that was able to grasp objects (or tree limbs) (Haile-Selassie, 2001; Semaw et al., 2005; White et al., 2009; Suwa et al., 2009; Lovejoy et al., 2009a through d; also other authors in the volume *Science* 326(64) 2009).

With the hominin characteristics of *Sahelanthropus, Orrorin,* and *Ardipithecus*, as well as the dates assigned to these fossils, it is interesting to think about what this means in terms of the last common ancestor between chimps and humans, or, indeed, if there was a side branch leading to more modern hominins. Most researchers still believe that at least one australopithecine is in the line leading to *Homo*, so we will now look at the evidence in *Australopithecus*.

AUSTRALOPITHS

The australopiths are represented by two closely related genera, *Australopithecus* and *Paranthropus*, which lived between about 4.2 M.Y.A. and 1 M.Y.A. Fossils of these genera have been discovered in East Africa, South Africa, and Central Africa. Although *Paranthropus* looks more primitive (with a big brow ridge, large face, and a sagittal crest), it is actually the more derived genus. *Australopithecus* is the more primitive in morphology and therefore thought to be more in line with humans.

Australopithecus anamensis

Slightly more recent fossils with thick enamel on their teeth have been discovered relatively recently in northern Kenya, Ethiopia, and Tanzania. These are currently named *Australopithecus anamensis* (Figure 11.2), and all fossils but one are dated between 4.17 and 4.07 M.Y.A. (White et al., 2006). As with many other fossils, these show a mosaic of primitive and derived characters. The postcranial remains strongly suggest bipedality, but the face is still strongly projecting. In addition, the dentition is more ape-like in many ways, including large canines and teeth that are in a parallel dental arcade. However, the enamel is relatively thicker than in ape dentition (Macho et al., 2005, think that they were adapted to eating hard-tough foods), and the molars are wider (relative to length) than in *A. ramidus*. They are more primitive than the slightly more recent *Australopithecus afarensis*. Ward et al. (2001) believe that *A. anamensis* could be ancestral to *A. afarensis*. However, Senut (2002) believes that because of the postcranial morphology, *A. anamensis* should be considered ancestral to the Hominine lineage and separate from *Australopithecus afarensis* or *Ardipithecus ramidus*.

FIGURE 11.2 *Australopithecus anamensis. Photo, National Museum of Ethiopia, Addis Ababa. Photo © 2005 Tim D. White/Brill Atlanta*

Australopithecus afarensis

Beginning in the 1970s, specimens of *A. afarensis* were discovered at Hadar, Ethiopia, and Laetoli, Tanzania. Radiometric dates of these sites are roughly between 3 and 4 M.Y.A.

A. afarensis (Figures 11.3, 11.4, 11.5, and 11.6) exhibits a number of primitive as well as derived characters. The most striking derived characters are the adaptations of the pelvis and foot for habitual bipedal locomotion. On the other hand, *A. afarensis* retained longer, more curved metatarsals and pedal phalanges (Figure 11.6). On the basis of detailed analyses of foot remains, however, others argue that *A. afarensis* was clearly bipedal and did not use the trees to a great extent (Latimer and Lovejoy, 1990a, b). They argue that primitive characters such as long, curved phalanges are retentions from a common ancestor with the apes, although this idea is now being debated (see Ward, 2002, for an interesting discussion). It is possible that the locomotor behavior of *A. afarensis,* given its post-cranial morphology, could have included the trees as well as the savannah. The important footprints at Laetoli, Tanzania, indicate a bipedal gait (Day and Wickens, 1980).

The cheek teeth of *A. afarensis* and all australopithecines were very large relative to body size. The canines were smaller than in male apes, but they are still large, pointed teeth. In many of the specimens, there appears to be a diastema, and the lower first premolar is semisectorial (creating a cutting surface against the upper canine). Also, Rak, Ginzburg and Geffen (2007) think that the morphology of the mandible suggests some derived traits (similar, they say, to the morphology of a gorilla) that should cast doubt on it being ancestral to humans. Body weight estimates of *A. afarensis* range from 30 kg to 80 kg (66–176 lb) (Conroy, 1990), and there is a variation in

FIGURE 11.3 *Australopithecus afarensis. Photo, D. L. France; cast from Institute of Human Origins*

FIGURE 11.4 *A. afarensis* maxilla. *Photo, D. L. France; cast from Institute of Human Origins*

FIGURE 11.5 *A. afarensis* mandible. *Photo, D. L. France; cast from Institute of Human Origins*

FIGURE 11.6 Pedal phalanges of modern human (top), *A. afarensis* (center), chimpanzee (bottom). *Drawing, from R. L. Susman et al., "Arboreality and Bipedality in the Hadar Hominids,"* Folia Primat., *1984, 43:113–156*

morphology as well (Alemseged et al., 2005; White 2009). Cranial capacity is estimated to be approximately 400 cc (Holloway, 1983). Some argue that fossil specimens from Laetoli and Hadar represent two species (Falk, 1986; Falk and Conroy, 1983; Olson, 1981). The paleoanthropologists who originally described *A. afarensis* maintain that it was a highly sexually dimorphic species (Johanson and White, 1979), although Lee (2005) suggested that sexual dimorphism in this species is probably patterned differently than in living humans or apes or in the pre-*Australopithecus* hominins. A specimen at Hadar attributed to *A. afarensis* was dated to 3 M.Y.A., which is one of the most recent and largest individuals from that species (Drapeau et al., 2005). They concluded that the morphological differences in the arm and hand indicate that the ability to manipulate objects was more important than being arboreal.

An almost complete skeleton found near Hadar sites was dated at about 3.3 M.Y.A. (Alemseged et al., 2006). It is a very well preserved child, estimated to be about 3 years of age when it died. It is said to be female by the size of the teeth, but it is almost impossible to accurately assess sex even in a modern 3-year-old child, and the sexual dimorphism in this population is still not well understood. The cranium is nearly complete, and there are even foot bones that attest to a likely bipedal stance.

Australopithecus bahrelghazali was first discovered in 1993 by M. Brunet in a riverbed in Chad and is dated between 3.0 and 3.5 M.Y.A. It is similar in morphology (there is not much as yet for comparison, however) to *Australopithecus afarensis* and is classified with *afarensis* by some.

Kenyanthropus platyops

Discovered west of Lake Turkana, Kenya, by Maeve Leakey's team in 1999, *Kenyanthropus* is dated to approximately 3.5 M.Y.A., which makes it contemporary with *A. afarensis*. *Kenyanthropus* is represented by a temporal bone, two partial maxillae, isolated teeth, and a largely complete cranium (Leakey et al., 2001). It has a narrower second molar than does *A. ramidus* and thick enamel. Also, it differs from the australopithecines in facial morphology (in summary, this species has a somewhat flatter face—a derived feature). The size of the cranium is between that of *A. afarensis* and *A. africanus* (Leakey et al., 2001). Further information about this specimen must wait until further publications.

Australopithecus garhi

Australopithecus garhi, which was named in 1999 (Asfaw et al., 1999), was discovered in Ethiopia and was dated to approximately 2.5 M.Y.A. The cranium exhibits a large, projecting face, relatively large front teeth, and very large back teeth. The dental arcade is slightly parabolic, and there is marked postorbital constriction. The limb proportions are unusual, in that the forelimbs and hindlimbs are long.

Using craniodental characteristics, Strait and Grine (2004) have suggested that *Australopithecus anamensis* and *A. garhi* should be allocated to new genera and that they are likely not in the line leading directly to *Homo*.

Paranthropus (*Australopithecus*) *aethiopicus*

Paranthropus aethiopicus (or *Australopithecus aethiopicus*) has been described from Omo, Ethiopia, and Lake Turkana, Kenya. The specimen at Omo was discovered first, in 1967, but the more famous specimen, WT 17000, or the "Black Skull" (named because the deposits turned the fossil black), was discovered in 1986 west of Lake Turkana (Walker et al., 1986). The "Black Skull" (Figure 11.7) is dated at approximately 2.5 M.Y.A. and has a small cranial capacity (~410 cc). It also had a marked postorbital constriction (similar to the other robust *Paranthropus* species) and a large sagittal crest. The dental enamel was thick, however, and it had a parabolic dental arcade. The anterior dentition was small relative to the larger premolars and molars.

Paranthropus (*Australopithecus*) *boisei*

Paranthropus boisei (or *Australopithecus boisei*) has been discovered at Omo in Ethiopia, Koobi Fora in Kenya, and Olduvai Gorge in Tanzania. These fossils have been dated to 2.3 to 1.2 M.Y.A. and have several features in common (and also several features in common with the robust South African forms). The anterior dentition is reduced (incisors and canines), the molars and premolars are large, the enamel is thick (Figure 11.8), and the mandible is very large. In addition, there is a large sagittal crest (for large chewing muscles) and significant postorbital constriction in these forms. The brain size is similar to that of apes, although postcranially and cranially, the skeleton shows adaptations for bipedalism.

THE SOUTH AFRICAN AUSTRALOPITHECINES

Australopithecus africanus

The first australopithecine, discovered in South Africa, was the Taung child (Dart, 1925) (Figures 11.9 and 11.10). Although the specimen was that of a young child (judged from dental eruptions), many features were evident. The foramen magnum was farther forward than in apes, and the dentition was more hominin-like than ape-like (wider molars and smaller canines). The cranial capacity, however,

FIGURE 11.7 WT-17000. The "Black Skull." *Photo, D. L. France; cast from National Museums of Kenya*

FIGURE 11.8 *Paranthropus/ Australopithecus boisei,* maxilla. *Photo, D. L. France; casts from Werner-Gren Foundation*

FIGURE 11.9 *A. africanus:*
Taung. *Photo, Courtesy
of P. Tobias, University of the
Witwatersrand*

FIGURE 11.10 *A. africanus:*
Taung mandible. *Photo, D. L.
France; cast from University of
Pennsylvania*

was more similar to that of an ape. This specimen was named *Australopithecus africanus* ("southern ape of Africa").

Other fossils that have been named *Australopithecus africanus* have been found at Makapansgat and at Sterkfontein, both in South Africa. These many fossils are dated at about 2.3 to 3.0 M.Y.A. and have several features in common. They have a projecting face and some postorbital constriction. Also, they have canines that do not project much beyond the tooth row, and they have no diastema. The teeth exhibit thick enamel, although they have relatively parallel tooth rows. Postcranially, they have relatively long arms, but they have the modifications in the spinal column and lower limb bones that suggest bipedalism.

A new fossil was discovered in the late 1990s at Sterkfontein. The specimen is largely complete and is dated to 3.5 M.Y.A., although a more recent publication (Partridge et al., 2003) puts the date at about 4 M.Y.A. and at about the same time period as *A. anamensis*. The skull and parts of the arm and leg bones have been uncovered. This fossil is a complete adult, so continued analysis has the potential to yield significant information about *Australopithecus africanus* in South Africa.

Paranthropus (Australopithecus) robustus

The other species found in South Africa are named either *Paranthropus robustus* or *Australopithecus robustus*. This more robust form (most of the differences from the more gracile *A. africanus* are in the cranium and mandible) has been found in deposits dated from 2.0 to 1.0 M.Y.A. (Figures 11.11a and b, and Figures 11.12a and b). The most striking difference is in the presence of a large sagittal crest for the attachment of large chewing muscles. In addition, the molars and premolars are large relative to the incisor size and to the size of the body, and the teeth have thick enamel. The mandible is very large. There is a marked postorbital constriction, and the brain size is comparable to that of apes,

a
b

FIGURE 11.11a and b *A. africanus.* *Photo, D. L. France; cast from Werner-Gren Foundation*

FIGURE 11.12a and b *P. robustus. Photo, D. L. France; cast from University of Pennsylvania*

though there are modifications in the skeleton for bipedalism (see Figure 11.13 for a modern femoral neck compared to that of *Paranthropus robustus*).

Sites in South Africa that have yielded the robust form of paranthropine/australopithecine include Swartkrans, Kromdraai, and a new find at Drimolen (Keyser, 2000). All of these sites have fossils that are similar to each other but are somewhat dissimilar to the robust forms discovered in East Africa.

FIGURE 11.13 Proximal right femora: Modern human (left), *P. robustus* (right). *Photo, D. L. France; original bone (left), cast from University of Pennsylvania (right)*

COMPARISON OF EAST AND SOUTH AFRICAN PLIOCENE FOSSILS

There have been no undoubted specimens of *A. africanus* found in East Africa. However, there is no doubt that a hyperrobust species, *Paranthropus/Australopithecus boisei*, lived in East Africa from 2.5 M.Y.A. to just about 1 M.Y.A. *P. boisei* has been found at several East African fossil sites. It is very similar to *P. robustus* of South Africa. The dentition of the robust forms represents the continuation of dental trends first observed in the Miocene: a reduction of the anterior dentition, enlargement of the cheek teeth with thick enamel, and thickening of the jaws. The premolars of *boisei/robustus* are referred to as molariform premolars because of the molar-like form and function of these teeth (see Figure 11.18 later in this chapter). These large, thick-enameled cheek teeth probably provided the surface area for grinding small, tough food that needs little slicing and cutting, and are accompanied by small anterior teeth. Compare the relative sizes of the teeth of a robust australopithecine (Figure 11.18) to *Australopithecus africanus* (Figure 11.14).

Estimates of the cranial capacities of the australopithecine specimens run from just under 400 cc to more than 500 cc. When body size is considered, these cranial capacities are not much more than those of the extant apes. Brain expansion, so characteristic of our lineage, began with the first appearance of our genus.

The interpretations of the relationships between the Pliocene hominins vary. *Ardipithecus ramidus, Australopithecus anamensis,*

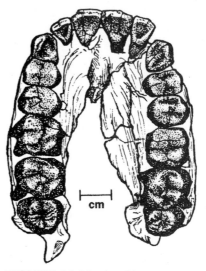

FIGURE 11.14 *A. africanus. Drawing, from C. S. Larsen and R. M. Matter,* Human Origins: The Fossil Record, *3rd ed., 1985, copyright © 1985 Waveland Press. Reprinted by permission of the publisher*

and *Australopithecus afarensis* occur in the fossil record before 3 M.Y.A., and one or more may be in the line leading to the later australopithecine forms or even to a later *Homo* line. The hominin forms that are found in deposits from the Miocene (*Sahelanthropus tchadensis, Orrorin tugenensis,* and *Ardipithecus ramidus*) may take that line millions of years before the Pliocene. Were there other australopithecines in the hominin lineage that led to modern humans? Did *A. afarensis* lead more directly into *Homo?* Were the Miocene hominins the ones in the ancestral line to *Homo*?

The Early Hominins

FIGURE 11.15 *Australopithecus afarensis*, pelvis. *Photo, D. L. France; cast from Institute of Human Origins*

FIGURE 11.16 *Australopithecus africanus os coxa*. *Photo, D. L. France; cast from Werner-Gren Foundation*

1. Observe the remains of an *A. afarensis* pelvis in your laboratory or as shown in Figure 11.15. Pelvic remains of a later species, *A. africanus* (Figure 11.16), are very similar to those of *A.afarensis*.

   a. Name similarities of the *A. afarensis* pelvis to that of modern humans.

   Primarily bipedal locomotion, wide pelvis gait more human-like

   b. How are they different?

   c. What does this mean in terms of biomechanical differences?

FIGURE 11.17 *A. afarensis,* maxilla. *Photo, D. L. France; cast from Institute of Human Origins*

FIGURE 11.18 *A. afarensis,* mandible. *Photo, D. L. France; cast from Institute of Human Origins*

2. Using the criteria of ape and human dentition from previous chapters, analyze the dentition of *A. afarensis* (Figures 11.17 and 11.18). In what ways is the dentition ape-like? In what ways is it humanlike?

FIGURE 11.19 Pedal phalanges of modern human (top), *A. afarensis* (center), chimpanzee (bottom).
Drawing, from R. L. Susman et al., "Arboreality and Bipedality in the Hadar Hominids," Folia Primat., *1984, 43:113–156*

3. Compare the phalanges of *A. afarensis* (Figure 11.19) to those of apes and humans. How are they ape-like? How are they human-like?

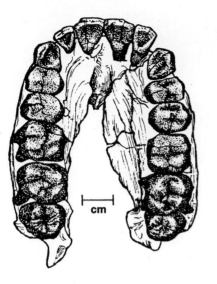

FIGURE 11.20 *A. africanus.*
*Drawing, from C. S. Larsen and
R. M. Matter,* Human Origins: The Fossil
Record, *3rd ed., 1985, copyright © 1985
Waveland Press. Reprinted by permission
of the publisher*

4. Compare the dentition of *A. africanus* (Figure 11.20) with that of the more ancient *A. afarensis* (Figures 11.17 and 11.18). In what ways can the dentition of *A. afarensis* be said to be more primitive than that of *A. africanus*? Based on this evidence, do you believe *A. afarensis* is a good ancestral candidate for *A. africanus*?

FIGURE 11.21 Proximal right femora: Modern human (left), *P. robustus* (right). *Photo, D. L. France; original bone (left), cast from University of Pennsylvania (right)*

5. Observe the proximal femur of *Paranthropus robustus* (Figure 11.21). How is it different from the proximal femur of humans?

FIGURE 11.22 *A. africanus:* Taung mandible. *Photo, D. L. France; cast from University of Pennsylvania*

FIGURE 11.23 *A. africanus:* Taung. *Source: Courtesy of P. Tobias, University of the Witwatersrand*

6. Observe the dentition of the Taung child (Figures 11.22 and 11.23). All but the molars (one in each quadrant) are deciduous. The first permanent molar erupts at about age 6 years in modern humans and at about age 3 in chimpanzees (Schultz, 1937). How old do you think the Taung child was at death? Why?

7. Develop a likely ancestor-descendant chart with the fossils from this chapter.

8. Which of the fossils are most likely in the line of evolution leading to modern humans?

9. What does it mean to the Pliocene ancestral/descendant relationships that *Kenyanthropus* has thicker enamel and a narrower second molar than does *Ardipithecus*?

REEXAMINING THE ISSUES

- The current evidence indicates that hominins first appeared in the Miocene and developed much more modern morphological characteristics in the Pliocene.
- The very early hominin species have been discovered in central and eastern Africa.
- Bipedalism seems to have developed first in the hominin line, and increased brain size followed.

CHAPTER 12

●

The Genus *Homo*

OBJECTIVES

1. When did humans begin to develop a significantly larger brain?

2. Did Neanderthals live at the same time as some anatomically modern humans?

3. Did modern humans develop in Africa and migrate from there, or did modern humans evolve independently from *Homo erectus* in all areas of the Old World?

The evolutionary theories of the genus *Homo* are some of the most fascinating in paleoanthropology and some of the most varied. New genetic evidence combined with fossil discoveries is shedding light on many of the ancestral relationships among species of *Homo*, while dispelling some of our old beliefs.

INTRODUCTION

By the time we reach the genus *Homo*, pretty much everyone agrees that the hominins were bipedal, although at the *Homo* stage, there is a refinement of the striding gait. The more interesting aspect of evolution at this stage is in the increasing size and complexity of the brain. After seeing relatively little increase in brain size in the pre-*Australopithecus* and *Australopithecus* species, we see exciting changes through the more recent species. Along with that, there is evidence of culture and more sophisticated tool use (chimpanzees make and use tools, so the earlier hominins must have used tools). Early in the *Homo* line, we see migration of groups of people out of Africa to Europe, Asia, and Indonesia, and perhaps different species of our genus living at the same places at roughly the same time.

In this chapter, you will see different phylogenetic hypotheses concerning the relationships of the first-known hominins (Figure 12.1),

FIGURE 12.1 Phylogenetic trees.

FIGURE 12.2 OH 7 mandible.
Photo, D. L. France; cast from Werner-Gren Foundation

FIGURE 12.3 KNM-ER 1470.
Photo, D. L. France; cast from National Museums of Kenya

although many more have been proposed. At the end of this chapter, you will be asked to develop a phylogenetic tree.

HOMO HABILIS

This species received its designation in the early 1960s when most of a mandible (Figure 12.2), skull fragments, and some postcranial materials were discovered at Olduvai Gorge and classified as *H. habilis* ("handy man"—because the hand bones exhibit features characteristic of a precision grip) (Leakey et al., 1964). These were considered to be in the genus *Homo* primarily because of more human-like dentition and a brain larger than that of australopithecines.

A few fossil fragments found in South Africa (at Sterkfontein and Swartkrans) (Curnoe and Tobias, 2006) probably represent an early *Homo* species contemporaneous with *Paranthropus robustus* more than 2 M.Y.A. The existence of early *Homo* in East Africa dates to approximately 2.4 M.Y.A., which makes *Homo habilis* roughly contemporaneous with australopithecines in East Africa as well. The most recent fossils of this early *Homo* species in East Africa date to approximately 1.44 M.Y.A., which, as we will see, overlaps with *Homo erectus* in East Africa! We will see overlaps like this throughout this chapter, which leads us to wonder what were these hominins doing with, and to, each other?

Probably the most important *Homo habilis* specimen is KNM-ER 1470 (Figures 12.3 and 12.4). Some researchers (e.g., Wood, 1992) placed this individual with the australopithecines, or as its own separate species, *Homo rudolfensis* (Alexeev, 1986), but most now place it with *Homo habilis* (e.g., Blumenschine et al., 2003). This specimen is characterized by a larger brain (775 cm^3) than seen in *Australopithecus* species and by evidence of smaller premolars and molars (although they are larger than in later species). KNM-ER 1470 is from deposits dated at approximately 1.8 M.Y.A. Also in this region of East Africa, a maxilla attributed to *Homo habilis* has an assigned date of 1.44 M.Y.A. (which is within the dates assigned to *Homo erectus*) (Spoor et al., 2007).

H. habilis specimens show considerable morphological variation, perhaps as much as in modern *H. sapiens* (Miller, 2000). The discovery of an *H. habilis* specimen, OH62, has shown a more *Homo*-like cranial morphology, with a more *Australopithecus*-like postcranium (Johanson et al., 1987; Stringer, 1995). Haeusler and McHenry (2004), however, thought that the relative leg length of OH62 was more human-like. In 2009, C. Ruff studied the cross sections of the femur and humerus of OH62 and compared them to the corresponding area in humans, *Homo erectus*, and chimpanzees, and stated that the distribution of strength as indicated by the thickness of the cross sections was an indication of the locomotor behavior of the different species. He concluded that, while *Homo habilis* walked bipedally, there was evidence that the species was still partly arboreal, which could indicate that *Homo habilis* and *Homo erectus* lived in potentially different environmental niches at about the same time. Most of a foot attributed to *H. habilis* (OH8) indicates that they had feet much like our own bipedally adapted feet, but *H. habilis* is still generally believed to be a transitional species between the australopithecines and *H. erectus*.

While there is still some debate about the sophistication of the morphology of some *Homo habilis* skeletons, it appears that they were making stone tools at about this time (although it is difficult to always identify the manufacturer of a very primitive tool). These first 2 M.Y.A. stone tools were very crude (see Plummer, 2004, for discussion of early *Homo* tool use) (Figure 12.5). Gradually, stone tools and other artifacts left by populations of *Homo* became more complex. The culture of these ancient hominins must be increasingly considered in the study of their evolution as we approach the present day.

FIGURE 12.4 KNM-ER 1470.
Photo, D. L. France; cast from National Museums of Kenya

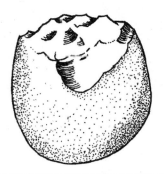

FIGURE 12.5 Oldowan tool.
Drawing, D. L. France

HOMO ERGASTER

H. ergaster is a somewhat controversial species designation. The hominins originally assigned to this species are in Africa and are roughly contemporaneous with *Homo erectus* from Asia. Is it an African form of the Asian *H. erectus*, or is it a species that shows characteristics more advanced than *H. habilis* and less advanced than *H. erectus*? The type specimen is KNM-ER 992, but another specimen often attributed to this genus and species is KNM-ER 3733 (Figures 12.6 and 12.7), which is dated at about 1.8 M.Y.A. Also, remains dated to 1.5 M.Y.A. in Israel have been tentatively identified as *Homo ergaster* (Belmaker et al., 2002).

A nearly complete skeleton of *H. erectus* (KNM-WT 15000) was found in Kenya in 1984 (Figure 12.8; Brown et al., 1985) and is thought to represent a young boy. The skeleton is placed in the

FIGURE 12.6 KNM-ER 3733. *Photo, D. L. France; cast from National Museums of Kenya*

FIGURE 12.7 KNM-ER 3733. *Photo, D. L. France; cast from National Museums of Kenya*

FIGURE 12.8 KNM-WT 15000. *Photo, National Museums of Kenya*

Homo ergaster species by some researchers, but in *Homo erectus* by most others. This 1.6-million-year-old individual showed incomplete union of the postcranial skeleton and erupted second molars. The bones are quite robust but are of a skeleton more advanced than *H. habilis* and relatively slightly different from *Homo sapiens*. The brain size has been estimated at about 880 cm³ (although this is an immature individual, so the adult size would have been slightly larger), and the arms and legs are within modern human limits.

In general, *Homo ergaster* is said to have a smaller brow ridge, a smaller area for muscle insertion on the occipital, and the crania are not as thick. Is this enough variation for a new species designation, or is there enough variation inherent in *Homo erectus* to account for this variation in the non-Asian fossils?

HOMO ERECTUS

The *H. erectus* (Figures 12.9 and 12.10 show the old fossil casts of *Homo erectus* from China) stage of human evolution lasted more than a million years (1.8 to 0.3 M.Y.A.) and is thought by Wood and Collard (1999) to be the earliest valid form of the genus *Homo*. If, as most

FIGURE 12.9 *Homo erectus pekinensis. Photo, D. L. France; cast from University of Pennsylvania*

FIGURE 12.10 *Homo erectus pekinensis. Photo, D. L. France; cast from University of Pennsylvania*

suggest, KNM-ER 3733 is actually *Homo erectus* and not *Homo ergaster*, it would be one of the earliest and most significant *Homo erectus* fossils found in East Africa. A well-preserved calvarium was also discovered east of Lake Turkana and dates to 1.55 M.Y.A. (Spoor et al., 2007). This cranium displays many of the typical *Homo erectus* characteristics, particularly of the Asian forms (described in the next paragraph), although it is closer in size to *Homo habilis*. At the same site, remember, a maxilla dated at 1.44 M.Y.A. is also attributed to *Homo habilis*. Other African *H. erectus* remains have been discovered in Olduvai Gorge (1.2 M.Y.A. to less than 1 M.Y.A.), Kenya, Algeria, Morocco, Ethiopia, and South Africa.

The features that characterize *H. erectus* include a reduction in premolars and molar size, an increase in brain size from *H. habilis,* and often some keeling of the midline of the cranium (this is similar to the keel of a ship in that the parietals form a mild ridge along the midline instead of a smoothly rounded form as in modern humans). Also, the cranium is usually wider at the base than at the top, whereas in modern humans, the widest part of the cranium is superior to that area. The supraorbital torus is pronounced, and the forehead is receding, although not as much as in the robust forms of *Australopithecus*. A study of the internal cranial features of a child from Java (attributed to *Homo erectus*) suggests that the brain developed differently in *Homo erectus* from *Homo sapiens* (Balzeau et al., 2005). A study of a South China (Hexian) *Homo erectus* suggests that the brain height, frontal breadth, cerebral height, frontal height, and parietal chord increased from *Homo erectus* times to modern, but there was little change in the length, breadth, frontal chord, and occipital breadth (Wu et al., 2006).

Comparisons of *H. erectus* (or *H. ergaster*) crania that are about 1.5 million years old (Figures 12.6 and 12.7) with those that are more recent than 0.5 M.Y.A. (Figures 12.9 and 12.10) have prompted some to argue that this is an example of stasis (e.g., Rightmire, 1981, 1985). Others argue that the cranial evolution found in *H. erectus* is an example of gradual morphological changes and that the more recent specimens are close to archaic *H. sapiens,* but the older specimens more closely resemble *H. habilis* and *Australopithecus* (Wolpoff, 1984).

A female pelvis from Chad has been assigned a date of 1.3 M.Y.A. (Simpson et al., 2008). This is exciting because it seems to show the sexual dimorphism in the pelvis that would allow a large-brained infant to develop significantly before leaving the womb.

Currently, *H. erectus* is thought to have migrated out of Africa between 2 and 1.5 M.Y.A. Sites in Java and China are now dated to as early as 1.8 M.Y.A. (Kaifu et al., 2005), and a mandible in the Republic of Georgia (Dmanisi) in the former Soviet Union is tentatively dated at about 1.7 M.Y.A. (Gabunia and Vekua, 1995; Spoor et al., 2007). Now a couple of crania from that region have been identified as *Homo ergaster* (or very early *Homo erectus*) and are argued to be the first to have migrated out of Africa (Gabunia et al., 2000). Even more information gained in 2006 (Rightmire et al., 2006) suggests that the

FIGURE 12.11 Acheulean hand axe. *Drawing, A. Blackstone*

FIGURE 12.12 Steinheim. *Photo, D. L. France; cast from University of Pennsylvania*

FIGURE 12.13 Steinheim. *Photo, D. L. France; cast from University of Pennsylvania*

specimens from the Republic of Georgia may be close to the origin of *Homo erectus*, although this idea is not accepted by everyone.

In Europe, the fossil hominin record for this time period is still fairly poor. A partial jaw and some teeth have been assigned a date of about 1.2 M.Y.A. (Carbonell et al., 2008) in Spain. Many hominin cultural remains have been found in Europe dating to around 0.8 to 0.3 M.Y.A., and the fossil remains that have been found (mostly teeth and partial crania) are either *H. erectus* or a very closely related species. Some place the European forms of *H. erectus* into the separate species *Homo heidelbergensis* (discussed in the next section).

A new tool type, the "Acheulian hand axe" (Figure 12.11), appears with the fossil remains of early *H. erectus* in East Africa. Acheulian stone tools are found in Africa, western Europe, and western India. Less advanced stone tools are found associated with eastern European and East Asian *H. erectus* remains. Sites in both France and China that are slightly younger than this age show that this *Homo* species used fire, lived in temporary camps, built temporary living shelters, and relied on gathering and hunting for subsistence.

HOMO HEIDELBERGENSIS

H. heidelbergensis is a transitional form between *H. erectus* and early archaic *H. sapiens,* and it seems to be gaining in popularity as a valid species designation. The characteristics are generally transitional between *Homo erectus* and Archaic *Homo sapiens* and include an increase in brain size, a reduction in cranial and postcranial robustness, a shift to the widest cranial breadth in the parietal region instead of near the cranial base, and a more rounded occipital region. The type specimen was discovered in 1907 at the Mauer region in Germany. The dates assigned to this species are generally thought to be between about 850 and 200 K.Y.A. An example of one of the early European forms is Steinheim (Figures 12.12 and 12.13), dated approximately 300–250 K.Y.A., in Germany. Also in Europe, sites in Spain have been yielding literally thousands of fossil fragments from as early as 850 K.Y.A. for one site (Gran Dolina) and from between 600 and 530 K.Y.A. from a cave nearby (Rightmire, 1998; Bischoff et al., 2007).

In Africa, one of the early archaic fossils has been discovered in Zambia. This site at Broken Hill has yielded a cranium and some postcranial remains that retain some characteristics of *H. erectus,* while exhibiting some characteristics of early *H. sapiens* (Figures 12.14 and 12.15). The brow ridges are still robust, the forehead is still receding, and there is still a large occipital torus, but the cranial base (particularly in the occipital region) is not as flat as in *H. erectus*. The cranial capacity is larger (~1280 cc), and the cranial bones are thinner than in *H. erectus*. Many are now putting this fossil in the *H. heidelbergensis* category.

FIGURE 12.14 Broken Hill; early archaic *Homo sapiens*. *Photo, D. L. France; cast from University of Pennsylvania*

FIGURE 12.15 Broken Hill; early archaic *Homo sapiens*. *Photo, D. L. France; cast from University of Pennsylvania*

Fossils from China have a mix of *Homo erectus*-like and *Homo sapiens*-like characteristics. Jinniushan (northeast China) has been dated to about 200 K.Y.A. (Tiemel et al., 1994; Rosenberg et al., 2006). The cranial capacity is approximately 1,260 cm³. There are great discussions about how the fossils from China relate to the fossils from the rest of the world, but they may be regional variants of *Homo heidelbergensis* (Rightmire, 2004).

ARCHAIC *HOMO SAPIENS*

Archaic *H. sapiens* (Neanderthals) fossils are found throughout Africa, Asia, Europe, and the Near East in deposits typically from about 75 to 10 K.Y.A. (although there are sites with fossils that are morphologically Neanderthal dating to around 130 K.Y.A.). These fossils represent a greatly varied group, and the interpretations surrounding the skeletal and cultural materials lead to various conclusions, as will be seen. The earlier fossils retain some *H. erectus* traits while moving toward some *H. sapiens* traits (some put the earlier fossils into a separate species: *Homo antecessor*), whereas the later fossils exhibit more of the anatomically modern (A.M.) *H. sapiens* traits, as might be expected.

The early archaic fossils in general are different from *H. erectus* in that they show larger brains, with the greatest width of the cranium now in the parietal region instead of near or below the ear (as in *H. erectus*). In fact, the cranial capacity is very large (actually larger as a group than modern humans, likely because there are fewer folds in the brain, although this is difficult to discern from endocranial characteristics). Neanderthals have long crania and a bun-shaped occipital bone. The brow ridges are still pronounced, but not as pronounced as in *H. erectus*. The forehead rises more vertically from the

FIGURE 12.16 La Chappelle aux Saints. *Photo, D. L. France; cast from University of Pennsylvania*

FIGURE 12.17 La Chappelle aux Saints. *Photo, D. L. France; cast from University of Pennsylvania*

brow ridges than in *H. erectus* (although this is not as pronounced as in modern *H. sapiens*). The face projects forward. The postcranial skeleton is large and robust. The premolar and molar sizes also continued to decrease.

The classic Neanderthal fossil is La Chapelle-aux-Saints in France (Figures 12.16 and 12.17). This individual had an extremely large cranial capacity (1,620 cm^3) and is thought to have lived about 50 K.Y.A. Interestingly, this individual seems to have been intentionally buried with some flint tools and some fragmentary nonhuman bones.

One of the oldest Neanderthal sites, and the oldest intentional burial site discovered to date is from Krapina, a site in Croatia (Figure 12.18a and b). Other sites in Israel (Tabun at Mt. Carmel), Iraq (at Shanidar), and Uzbekistan (Teshik-Tash) are populated by hominins that are morphologically like Neanderthal. An individual at Shanidar had massive antemortem blunt trauma (it shows signs of healing) to the cranium and elsewhere, and the fact that it shows signs of healing dictates that someone had taken care of the individual for a significant period of time. This is a significant indication of a cooperative culture.

In addition to definite signs of intentional burial and caring for the injured, Neanderthals showed other signs of group behavior and culture. They developed a new technique of making stone tools (the Levallois technique), which had more complex and varied tool kits than any hominin culture that had come before. More than 60 different types of scrapers, knives, points, and other stone tools have been identified in these cultural assemblages (e.g., Figure 12.19). This culture is referred to as Mousterian culture and/or Middle Paleolithic culture. Some studies (Richards et al., 2000; Bocherens et al., 2005) have suggested through isotope analysis that Neanderthals were large-animal predators (including wooly rhinoceros, wooly mammoth, bovines, large deer, horses) and not, as suggested by some, primarily scavengers.

Still, archaic *H. sapiens* culture is quite crude relative to the rich cultures that flourished in the Upper Paleolithic (around 30 to 10 K.Y.A.) that are associated with A.M. *H. sapiens* (although

a b

FIGURE 12.18 Krapina cranium. (a) Lateral view showing characteristic Neandertal traits. (b) Threequarters view.

Conard et al., 2004, suggest that Neanderthals may have contributed to the cultural artifacts of the Upper Paleolithic more than some believe). Anatomical evidence has been used to argue that classic Neanderthals were not capable of fully articulate speech, although the discovery of an anatomically modern hyoid bone from Israel, dated to around 60,000 years ago, sheds doubt on that claim.

DNA evidence from Krings et al. (1997) suggests that Neanderthals may have diverged from the line evolving into modern humans as long as 690 to 550 K.Y.A. However, some researchers believe that at least some Neanderthal populations were still sharing genes with more modern *H. sapiens* populations. A study by Currat and Excoffier in 2004 claims that because no Neanderthal mitochondrial DNA has been discovered in several thousands of Europeans, this suggests that there was virtually no interbreeding between Neanderthals and modern *Homo sapiens,* implying that the two populations were probably distinct biological species (see also Krause et al., 2007). The section on "Modern *Homo Sapiens*" discusses this issue further.

FIGURE 12.19 Mousterian tool. *Drawing, courtesy of A. Blackstone*

HOMO FLORESIENSIS

Homo floresiensis (Figure 12.20) was a surprising find (Brown et al., 2004; Morwood et al., 2004). Nicknamed the "Hobbit" after the small characters in *The Lord of the Rings,* this hominin stood only about 1 m (3 ft) tall and had a cranial capacity of about 380 cc (this is about the size of *Australopithecus*). It is placed at this point in this chapter because of its assigned date of about 18 K.Y.A., although there are some characteristics of the individuals that lead some to believe that it is not a relatively modern *Homo sapiens.* They lived on the island of Flores in Indonesia (east of Bali), and one explanation for the small size is that the people on this island may have been isolated for a very long time (perhaps since *H. erectus* times or even a little earlier), and that the population may have been a dwarfish subset of the *H. erectus* population (through genetic drift perhaps). Others have suggested that the type specimen (LB1) is a **microcephalic** (pathologically small brain size, usually resulting in mental retardation) individual (Weber et al., 2005), but Falk et al. (2005a, b) dispute this. Recently, Gordon et al. (2008) compared the size of the cranium with the size of the rest of the skeleton (a microcephalic would have a small cranium with a more normal postcranial skeleton) and decided that it is a normal but diminutive population with a head shape that is outside of the range of *Homo sapiens.* They believe that this population is more closely related in morphology to early *Homo erectus* from East Africa and/or Dmanisi or perhaps to *Homo habilis.* Argue et al. (2009) suggest that *H. floresiensis* emerged even before *Homo habilis.*

FIGURE 12.20 Cranium of adult female *Homo floresiensis* from Flores, Indonesia, dated 18,000 ya.

MODERN *HOMO SAPIENS*

There are basically three hypotheses used to explain the transition from archaic to A.M. *H. sapiens*. In 1987, the results of a mitochondrial DNA (mtDNA) study were published indicating that modern humans originated in Africa approximately 200 K.Y.A. (Cann et al., 1987). This study (called the "Out of Africa" theory) indicated that modern humans then moved to other areas of the Old World and replaced archaic *H. sapiens* populations everywhere (Stringer and Andrews, 1988), although the specific results from that study have been questioned.

The second hypothesis (called the "Multiregional Evolution" theory) (Wolpoff et al., 1994, 2001) suggests that archaic *H. sapiens* populations everywhere gradually evolved into A.M. *H. sapiens*. This theory states that A.M. humans originated in Africa and other areas, there was migration throughout the Pleistocene, and that interbreeding between populations would have mixed the traits and prevented speciation (Smith et al., 1989).

The third theory suggests that A.M. *H. sapiens* evolved in Africa and then migrated into Eurasia to genetically mix to some degree with the archaic *H. sapiens*. The disappearance of the archaic species, then, was the result of a combination of genetic mixing and replacement.

Templeton (2005) analyzed DNA sequences and postulated that the status of Neanderthal replacement by A.M. humans cannot be answered definitively, though there were probably three "out-of-Africa" major migrations (one at about 1.9 M.Y.A. with gene flow between African and Eurasian populations, the second at about 700 K.Y.A. with interbreeding with some Eurasian populations, and a third at 100 K.Y.A. with interbreeding but probably no total Eurasian replacement). Using mitochondrial DNA and Y chromosome DNA, researchers have discovered more variation in the DNA of African populations than in other areas of the world. Also, nine ancient but A.M. *H. sapiens* skeletons have had mtDNA sequencing (Caramelli et al., 2003, 2006; Serre et al., 2004), and they are different from the Neanderthal bones that have been sequenced.

Abundant fossils of Neanderthals and other archaic *H. sapiens* must be investigated to further analyze these theories. These fossils continue the morphological changes toward modern *Homo sapiens*. The brow ridges are relatively small, with a vertical frontal bone. There is a feature called a "canine fossa," which is a depression in the maxilla just above the canines. Also, there is a mental eminence (chin) for the first time in human evolution. Fossils that are transitional and occurred just before A.M. humans were discovered in Africa and date possibly as early as 200 K.Y.A. (the site of Omo Kibish in southern Ethiopia dates to 195 K.Y.A.) (McDougall et al., 2005). A group of individuals also from Ethiopia dates to 160 to

154 K.Y.A. and exhibited a mix of characteristics, not quite modern but beyond the Neanderthals. One adult (Figure 12.21) had a cranial capacity of 1,450 cm, which is well within the *Homo sapiens* range. White et al. (2003) placed these individuals into a new subspecies: *Homo sapiens idaltu.*

Fully A.M. fossils have been discovered in Africa in several localities dating from about 120 to about 80 K.Y.A. (e.g., Klasies River Mouth and Border Cave in South Africa).

Some information suggests that A.M. humans were in Israel about 100 K.Y.A. (Stringer, 1995) and therefore also predate Neanderthal populations. Skhūl Cave (Figures 12.22 and 12.23) in Israel has been dated at about 130 to 115 K.Y.A. Other fossils from Israel at Skhūl, Qafzeh (120 to 92 K.Y.A.), and Tabun (120 K.Y.A.) (Grun et al., 2005) suggest that anatomically modern humans were in these areas at the same time as Neanderthals, and Neanderthals, as a group, cannot be in the direct line to humans. A.M. *H. sapiens* have been thought to have been the only occupants of Europe by about 40 K.Y.A. (recently C14 dates of about 31 K.Y.A. have been given to modern human assemblages in the Czech Republic by Wild et al., 2005), but recent excavations in southwestern France and in southern Spain suggest that Neanderthals may have been in those areas as recently as 29 to 35 K.Y.A. It is currently believed that A.M. humans were living in western Europe by about 35 K.Y.A. (Cro-Magnon dates to about 30 K.Y.A. in southern France).

FIGURE 12.21 Herto cranium from Ethiopia, a well-preserved early modern *H. sapiens* cranium.

FIGURE 12.22 Skhūl V. *Photo, D. L. France; cast from University of Pennsylvania*

FIGURE 12.23 Skhūl V. *Photo, D. L. France; cast from University of Pennsylvania*

The data concerning archaic and A.M. *Homo sapiens* in China is interesting. Several sites in China have yielded A.M. humans. The upper cave at Zhoukoudian is dated at about 27 K.Y.A., and Tianyuan Cave near Zhoukoudian is dated at less than 40 K.Y.A. (Remember that Jinniushan had individuals with a mix of ancient and modern characteristics at around 200 K.Y.A.!) Wolpoff (1989) states that some of the traits are inconsistent with the "Out of Africa" theory because they are inconsistent with African traits.

Anatomically modern humans are exhibited in the fossil record on the north coast of Borneo by about 35 to 45 K.Y.A. (Barker et al., 2007), which may be contemporaneous with the settlement of Australia at about 50 K.Y.A., and Hudjashov et al. (2007) believe that the current residents of Australia are descendants from a single migration. Interestingly, individuals discovered from deposits dating to 14 to 9 K.Y.A. at Kow Swamp show much more archaic traits than do current native populations.

The culture of A.M. *H. sapiens* in the Upper Paleolithic was remarkable relative to the cultures of previous hominins. For the first time, musical instruments, sculpture, jewelry, paintings, needles, harpoons, and spear throwers (atlatls) appear on the fossil record. A.M. *H. sapiens* regularly buried their dead. Blade stone tools, which were much more varied and efficient than previous stone tools, appear in the Upper Paleolithic. The societies of the Upper Paleolithic truly represent a "cultural explosion" that has continued.

The Genus *Homo*

FIGURE 12.24 Lower dentition of *H. habilis.* *Photo, D. L. France; cast from Werner-Gren Foundation*

FIGURE 12.25 Lower dentition of *Australopithecus.* *Photo, D. L. France; cast from Institute of Human Origins*

1. Compare the lower dentition of *H. habilis* (Figure 12.24) with that of *Australopithecus* (Figure 12.25). How are they different?

FIGURE 12.26 *H. habilis*
(or *H. ergaster*) cranium.
*Photo, D. L. France; cast from
Kenya National Museums*

FIGURE 12.27 *H. habilis*
(or *H. ergaster*) cranium.
*Photo, D. L. France; cast from
Kenya National Museums*

FIGURE 12.28a *A. africanus.*
*Photo, D. L. France; cast from
Werner-Gren Foundation*

FIGURE 12.28b *A. africanus.*
*Photo, D. L. France; cast from
Werner-Gren Foundation*

FIGURE 12.29a *P. robustus.*
*Photo, D. L. France; cast from
University of Pennsylvania*

FIGURE 12.29b *P. robustus.*
*Photo, D. L. France; cast from
University of Pennsylvania*

2. Compare the *H. habilis* (or *H. ergaster*) cranium (Figures 12.26 and 12.27) with that of
   A. africanus and a robust species (Figures 12.28 and 12.29). How are they different?

*Habilis has a flatter face/smaller skull/larger
brain cavity/teeth are also smaller & eyes
are completely closed & forward facing*

FIGURE 12.30 *Homo erectus,* KNM-WT 15000. *Photo, National Museums of Kenya*

FIGURE 12.31 Proximal femur of modern human (left) and *Australopithecus* (right). *Photo, D. L. France; human bone (left) and cast from University of Pennsylvania (right)*

3. Compare the proximal femur of the 1.6 M.Y.A. *H. erectus* specimen (Figure 12.30) with those of *Australopithecus* and modern *H. sapiens* (Figure 12.31).

4. Do you notice any other differences in the *H. erectus* specimen in Figure 12.30 from those of modern humans?

FIGURE 12.32 Later *H. erectus* specimen. *Photo, D. L. France; cast from University of Pennsylvania*

FIGURE 12.33 Later *H. erectus* specimen. *Photo, D. L. France; cast from University of Pennsylvania*

5. Compare the crania of early *H. erectus* (or *H. ergaster*) specimens from Africa (Figures 12.26 and 12.27) with that of later *H. erectus* specimens (Figures 12.32 and 12.33). Would you support gradual morphological change, stasis, or something in between? What data might help in this assessment? Do you think that KNM-ER 3733 should be *H. ergaster*?

FIGURE 12.34 Steinheim skull. *Photo, D. L. France; cast from University of Pennsylvania*

FIGURE 12.35 Steinheim skull. *Photo, D. L. France; cast from University of Pennsylvania*

6. Observe the Steinheim skull (Figures 12.34 and 12.35) or any other non-Neanderthal specimen of archaic *H. sapiens*. Make a list of those characters that seem *erectus*-like and another list of those characters that seem *sapiens*-like. The cranial capacity of this specimen is about 1,000 cc.

7. Look at any Neanderthal postcrania you may have in your laboratory. Compare it with the appropriate postcrania of modern *H. sapiens*. What are the differences?

FIGURE 12.36 Unknown.
Photo, D. L. France; cast from University of Pennsylvania

8. Compare the mandible pictured in Figure 12.36 with those of other hominins discussed in this chapter. Based especially on the relative size of the cheek teeth to anterior teeth and the shape of the dental arcade, how would you classify this unknown?

FIGURE 12.37 Unknown.
Photo, D. L. France; cast from Werner-Gren Foundation

9. Compare the cranium pictured in Figure 12.37 with those of other hominins discussed in this chapter. How would you classify this unknown?

10. Do you believe that the relatively new species designations of *H. ergaster* and (although this designation was first proposed decades ago) *H. heidelbergensis* are valid, or should they be subsumed into another species? Why or why not?

11. Develop a phylogeny that explains the Plio-Pleistocene fossils so far discovered. State why you think your phylogeny is likely correct.

12. Why do you think *Homo floresiensis* is so different from other fossils that have been discovered?

REEXAMINING THE ISSUES

- The early genus *Homo* is fully bipedal and exhibits increased brain size and modification of the dentition and face.
- *Homo erectus* moved out of Africa and populated many areas of the Old World.
- New genetic information casts doubt on the theory that Neanderthals are in the line leading to modern humans.
- There is still much to learn about the lineages leading to all populations of humans as we know them today.

CHAPTER 13

●

Anthropometry, Nonmetric Traits, and Dermatoglyphics

OBJECTIVES

1. What can we learn from taking measurements on living people and skeletal remains?

2. What are the appropriate ways to take these measurements?

3. What are nonmetric traits, and why are we interested in them?

We could take an almost infinite number of measurements of bones and of living humans (and other primates) and describe each bone or individual we study. As important as this is, however, we have to use statistics to determine what these measurements and descriptions really mean. This chapter will first introduce the instruments and methods to record living human variation and the statistics appropriate to describe that variation. We will then move to measurements and analysis of skeletal remains, and a discussion of variation in remains that we do not necessarily measure. Finally, although fingerprint analysis is usually recognized as a technique used by law enforcement in forensic identification, anthropologists have also used dermal ridge analysis in their studies, making it appropriate to discuss in this book.

It is appropriate at this point to discuss the concept of human variation before we actually measure it. Everyone knows that humans vary greatly from individual to individual. Some of that variation can be explained by the effects of environment on the genetic predispositions in size (including stature and weight and the size of the skeletal elements), and morphology (in the soft tissue and skeleton) within populations and within the sexes. In some cases, differences can be measured between the sexes and between populations. As discussed in greater detail in Chapter 15, how those differences are explained and used or misused has become inextricably intertwined with the collection of the measurements or observations and the reports generated from the statistics. Your instructor may take the opportunity to discuss these issues at the end of study of this chapter (or when you study Chapter 15).

METRIC ANALYSIS: THE LIVING

The living body is measured with the tools shown in Figures 13.1, 13.2, and 13.3 in addition to flexible tapes and other equipment. The instrument used to measure skeletal material is shown in Figure 13.4.

FIGURE 13.1
Sliding calipers.
Photo, D. L. France

FIGURE 13.2
Spreading calipers.
Photo, D. L. France

FIGURE 13.3 Skin fold
calipers. *Photo, D. L. France*

FIGURE 13.4 Osteometric
board. *Photo, D. L. France*

Be sure you know how to use each of these instruments, as you will use them to demonstrate the variation in living individuals and also in skeletal material of humans and nonhumans.

The Living Body

Various measurements of the living body are useful to anthropologists, geneticists, physicians, and manufacturers of goods that fit on or around the body (clothing, car seats, and seatbelts, for instance). Measurements are useful in determining the inheritability of traits, the rate of growth at particular ages, the nutritional and health status of individuals, and so on. Measurements are also usually collected on infants and adolescents as they develop for comparison with national and world norms in measuring growth efficiency. You can take an almost infinite number of measurements on the human body, which are limited primarily by practicality in finding easily discovered and described landmarks.

MEASUREMENT DESCRIPTIONS

A. The following standard measurements are taken with spreading calipers:

1. **Head Length:** taken on the sagittal line, from between the brow ridges to the maximum measurement in the sagittal line of the occipital region (Figure 13.5).

2. **Maximum Head Width:** the maximum width of the head, above the supramastoid and zygomatic crests (Figure 13.6).

3. **Length of Nose:** from nasal root (or nasion) to tip of nose; no distorting pressure should be applied (Figure 13.7). Some spreading calipers will not accurately measure this; you may need to use sliding calipers. Use the rounded ends of the calipers.

FIGURE 13.5 Head length. *Photo, D. L. France*

FIGURE 13.6 Head width. *Photo, D. L. France*

FIGURE 13.7 Nose length. *Photo, D. L. France*

FIGURE 13.8 Width of nasal alae. *Photo, D. L. France*

4. **Width of Fleshy Alae of Nose:** the maximum width of alae; do not apply distorting pressure (Figure 13.8).

B. The following is taken with sliding or dial calipers.

5. **Length of Middle Finger:** of each hand. This should include only the combined lengths of the phalanges (do not include the metacarpal) (Figure 13.9).

C. The following are usually taken with an anthropometer rod or stadiometers.

6. **Standing Height:** taken in stocking feet to the vertex (highest point) of the head. The skull is in the Frankfort plane (a horizontal plane in which the lower border of the eye is on the same horizontal level as the upper border of the external auditory meatus).

7. **Sitting Height:** while the subject is sitting on a table, taken from the surface of the table to the vertex of the head (Figure 13.10).

FIGURE 13.9 Middle finger length. *Photo, D. L. France*

FIGURE 13.10 Sitting height. *Photo, D. L. France*

8. **Arm Length:** taken from the acromion process of the scapula to the styloid process of the ulna (each can be felt through the skin) (Figure 13.11).

D. The following are taken with a metal or fiberglass tape.

9. **Head Circumference**: the maximum circumference of the head, not including the brow ridges (Figure 13.12).

10. **Upper Arm Circumference:** at widest point in the middle of the biceps; arm is slightly bent, and lower arm is supported so that the muscle is not flexed.

E. **Skinfold Thickness:** taken on a subcutaneous fold without including muscle; the caliper is placed 1 mm below the hand gently pinching the tissue and perpendicular to the skinfold. Read the measurement within 3 seconds so that the pressure does not compress the subcutaneous tissue.

11. **Skinfold Thickness of Triceps Area:** taken approximately halfway down the arm while the arm is hanging relaxed at the side of the body (Figure 13.13).

12. **Subscapular Skinfold Thickness:** measured laterally just below the angle of the left scapula.

FIGURE 13.11 Arm length. *Photo, D. L. France*

FIGURE 13.12 Head circumference. *Photo, D. L. France*

FIGURE 13.13 Skinfold thickness. *Photo, D. L. France*

Measurement Record

Using the measurement instructions on the previous pages, complete this table for 10 individuals (5 males and 5 females), and keep track of which individual is which. Also keep track of whether the individual you have measured is left-handed or right-handed. You will use this information for exercises following a discussion of statistical techniques.

Measure	Individual (in cm)											
	1	2	3	4	5	6	7	8	9	10	$\bar{x}$	SD
Head length	__	__	__	__	__	__	__	__	__	__	__	__
Head width	__	__	__	__	__	__	__	__	__	__	__	__
Nasal length	__	__	__	__	__	__	__	__	__	__	__	__
Nasal width	__	__	__	__	__	__	__	__	__	__	__	__
Middle finger length R	__	__	__	__	__	__	__	__	__	__	__	__
Middle finger length L	__	__	__	__	__	__	__	__	__	__	__	__
Standing height	__	__	__	__	__	__	__	__	__	__	__	__
Sitting height	__	__	__	__	__	__	__	__	__	__	__	__
Arm length	__	__	__	__	__	__	__	__	__	__	__	__
Head circumference	__	__	__	__	__	__	__	__	__	__	__	__
Upper arm circumference	__	__	__	__	__	__	__	__	__	__	__	__
Triceps skinfold	__	__	__	__	__	__	__	__	__	__	__	__
Subscapular skinfold	__	__	__	__	__	__	__	__	__	__	__	__

STATISTICAL TESTS

We need to use some basic statistics to compare the data we just gathered as well as to compare measurements we will gather from skeletal remains. Following are a few of the basic statistical tests used to describe data, but first we must discuss a pattern of normal distribution of measurements (the normal distribution).

The normal distribution: a probability distribution depicted graphically by a bell-shaped curve symmetrical about the mean (Figure 13.14).

If the height of all individuals in a population were measured, those measurements would theoretically be arranged around the mean in a normal distribution. Because measurement of all individuals in a population is not usually possible, measurements are taken of a subset of that population (a sample). This sample is ideally taken at random from within the larger population, so that the sample is a true representation of the total population.

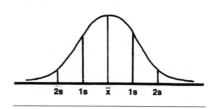

FIGURE 13.14 The normal curve.

Sample data:	Measurement A	Measurement B
Individual 1	10.0	1.2
2	10.3	3.8
3	11.1	1.9
4	10.9	2.2
5	10.5	3.2

Mean ($\overline{x}$): the average of a set of measurements, calculated by adding the terms and dividing their sum by the number of terms. The means of measurements of two data sets (e.g., the measurements of arm length of males and females) are usually compared to determine whether or not there is a difference between two samples. To determine the mean of one sample, follow this equation:

$$\text{Mean} = \frac{\text{sum of measurements}}{\text{number of measurements}}$$

The mean of Measurement A for the five individuals listed is

$$\frac{10.0 + 10.3 + 11.1 + 10.9 + 10.5}{5} = \frac{52.8}{5} = 10.56$$

Standard deviation: S (sample), σ (population) where y = measurement, and $\overline{y}$ = sample mean.

Mean: $\overline{x}$

$$\frac{\text{sum of measurements}}{\text{no. of measurements}}$$

$$\sqrt{\frac{\text{sum of } (y - \overline{y})^2}{\text{no. of measurements}}}$$

Standard deviation (S for sample, σ for population): a gauge of variation or spread within a set of measurements. When determining the mean of a sample, the same mean could be derived from measurements that are spread a great distance from the mean or from measurements that are all very close to the mean. The standard deviation is a description of the general pattern of measurements about the mean.

One standard deviation is about 68% of the total area.

Two standard deviations are about 95% of the total area.

The area within one standard deviation about the mean in a normal distribution is approximately 68% of the total area; the area within two standard deviations is approximately 95% of the total area.

$$\text{standard deviation} = \sqrt{\frac{\text{sum of } (y - \overline{y})^2}{\text{number of measurements}}}$$

where y is a measurement, and $\overline{y}$ is the sample mean.

The standard deviation of Measurement A for the five individuals above is

Meas. A	Mean	$y - \overline{y}$	$(y - \overline{y})^2$
10.0	10.56	−0.56	0.31
10.3	10.56	−0.26	0.07
11.1	10.56	+0.54	0.29
10.9	10.56	+0.34	0.12
10.5	10.56	−0.06	0.00

$$\text{standard deviation} = \sqrt{\frac{.31 + .07 + .29 + .12 + .00}{5}} = 0.40$$

Correlation coefficient :

$$r = \frac{S_{xy}}{(S_{xx})\,(S_{yy})}$$

Correlation coefficient (r): a measure of linear dependence or mutual relationship between two random variables, x and y. This is a useful statistical method to show cause and effect (where change in one variable will cause a change in another variable) or to simply show that two samples show a mutual relationship.

A correlation coefficient of 0 indicates two variables that show no mutual relationship, whereas a coefficient of 1 or −1 shows a direct relationship or dependency between the two variables.

The formula is

$$r = \frac{S_{xy}}{(S_{xx})\,(S_{yy})}$$

In this example, let Measurement A = x and let Measurement B = y.

$$S_{xy} = \text{Sum of } (x)\,(y) - \frac{(\text{sum of } x)\,(\text{sum of } y)}{n}$$

$$= 129.81 - \frac{(52.8)\,(12.3)}{5} = 0.07$$

	Meas. A	x^2	Meas. B	y^2	xy
	10.0	100.00	1.2	1.44	12.0
	10.3	106.09	3.8	14.44	39.14
	11.1	123.21	1.9	3.61	21.09
	10.9	118.81	2.2	4.84	23.98
	10.5	110.25	3.2	10.24	33.60
Sums	52.8	558.36	12.3	34.57	129.81

$$S_{xx} = \text{Sum of } x^2 - \frac{(\text{sum of } x)^2}{n}$$

$$= 558.36 - \frac{2787.84}{5} = +0.79$$

$$S_{yy} = \text{Sum of } y^2 - \frac{(\text{sum of } y)^2}{n}$$

$$= 34.57 - \frac{151.29}{5} = +4.31$$

So, for this sample

$$r = \frac{S_{xy}}{(S_{xx})(S_{yy})}$$

$$r = \frac{-0.07}{(+0.79)(+4.31)} = -.02$$

is a very slight negative correlation.

Chi-square (χ^2): a measure of the statistical significance of the deviation of a frequency of occurrences from an expected frequency. For example, the frequency of male to female students in a crowd is expected to be 50% males to 50% females, but if that frequency is actually observed to be 45% males and 55% females, is that deviation within the range of normal probability, or are the differences significant enough to be linked to a specific cause or event? This test will help you determine whether or not you have a "real" difference.

Chi-square (χ^2):

$$\chi^2 = \frac{(O - E)^2}{E}$$

O = Observed frequency

E = Expected frequency

Formula:

Let O = observed frequency

E = expected frequency

EXERCISE 13.2 NAME _____ SECTION _____ DATE _____

Statistical Analysis

1. What are the means of each sex in the measurements you took in Exercise 13.1?

2. What is the correlation between left hands and right hands in middle finger length?

3. How does middle finger length (left and right) correlate with handedness?

4. If you were to compare standing height for an individual in the morning and again in late afternoon, how do you think the measurements would compare? Why?

5. Pick one of the measurements, and have everyone in the class measure the instructor. How did your measurement results vary? This is interobserver error.

6. a. Pick one measurement, and measure the same individual each day for 2 or 3 days or each week for 2 or 3 weeks. How did your measurement results vary? This is intraobserver error.

   b. Why is the recognition of intraobserver error important in either setting up a research design or calculating results?

7. If you had a large sample of individuals of the same age for maximum height, and you found that the range of measurements was large, what would you expect some of the explanations for this variability to be?

8. Would you expect maximum head length to correlate more highly with head width or upper arm circumference? Would there be a difference? Why?

METRIC ANALYSIS: OSTEOMETRY

Osteometry, as the name implies, describes the measurement of bones. Data from these measurements can be helpful in documenting various aspects of human and nonhuman remains, including, but not limited to, age, sex, population affinity, height, and nutritional status or general levels of health, particularly when compared with other individuals or other populations. This section will focus on techniques for measuring cranial and postcranial bones, and the exercises will demonstrate how these measurements can describe individuals and populations.

Postcranial Measurements

Maximum length of long bone: with all except the tibia, this is the maximum measured length taken in the osteometric board (the osteometric board was shown earlier in Figure 13.4).
Tibia: the most prominent part of the lateral half of the lateral condyle to the distal end of the medial malleolus; this does not include the intercondylar eminence.
Bicondylar length of femur: both condyles are placed against one vertical end of the osteometric board, and the other vertical end of the osteometric board is placed against the head of the femur.

Indices

An index is the ratio of one measurement to another, expressed as a percentage. Indices have been used for decades in anthropometry, in both the living and the dead, and are still used even though multivariate statistics and other modern statistical techniques have made the index obsolete in some circumstances. An index is very useful for quick, preliminary investigations and also in describing evolutionary trends and general population variation. When using an index, however, note that a change in the value of an index can be the result of a change in any of its parts.

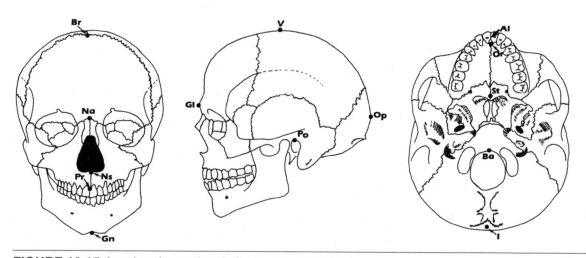

FIGURE 13.15 Landmarks on the skull. *Drawing, D. L. France*

CRANIAL LANDMARKS

(Bass, 1987) (see Figure 13.15)

Alveolare (Al):	The apex of the septum between the upper central incisors
Basion (Ba):	The midpoint of the anterior margin of the foramen magnum
Bregma (Br):	The intersection of the coronal and sagittal sutures
Glabella (Gl):	The most forward projecting point of the forehead in the midline at the level of the supraorbital ridges and above the nasofrontal suture
Gnathion (Gn):	Lowest median point on the lower border of the mandible
Inion (I):	An intersection in the midline with a line drawn tangent to the uppermost convexity of the right and left superior nuchal lines
Nasion (Na):	The midline point of intersection of the internasal suture with the nasofrontal suture; the point where the two nasal bones and the frontal bone meet
Nasospinale (Ns):	The midpoint of a line drawn connecting the two lower margins of the right and left nasal apertures
Opisthocranion (Op):	The most posterior point on the cranium not on the external occipital protuberance
Orale (Or):	A point on the hard palate where a line drawn tangent to the curves in the alveolar margin in back of the two medial incisor teeth crosses the midline
Porion (Po):	The uppermost lateral point in the margin of the external auditory meatus
Prosthion (Pr):	The most anterior point on the upper alveolar process in the midline
Staphylion (St):	The midpoint of a line drawn connecting the most forward points on the curves in the posterior margin of the palate
Vertex (V):	The uppermost point on the midline of the cranium when it is in the Frankfort plane

Cranial Measurements

Maximum cranial length:	From glabella to opisthocranion
Maximum cranial breadth:	The maximum measurement above the supramastoid crest
Basion-bregma height:	From basion to bregma (maximum height)
Porion-bregma height:	From porion to bregma
Bizygomatic breadth:	The maximum measurement spanning the zygomatic arches
Total facial height:	From nasion to gnathion
Upper facial height:	From nasion to alveolare
Nasal height:	From nasion to nasospinale
Nasal breadth:	Maximum breadth of the bony aperture
Palatal length:	From orale to staphylion
Palatal breadth:	Greatest transverse breadth between the inner borders of the alveolar arch at the second molars

Indices on the Cranium

A. **Cranial Index:** measures the shape of the cranium

$$\frac{\text{Cranial Breadth}}{\text{Cranial Length}} \times 100$$

(Martin and Saller, 1957; Bass, 1987):

Dolicocrany	Up to 74.9 (narrow or long-headed)
Mesocrany	75.0 to 79.9 (average)
Brachycrany	80.0 to 84.9 (round-headed)
Hyperbrachycrany	85.0 and up (even more rounded)

B. **Nasal Index:** measures the shape of the nasal (bony) aperture

$$\frac{\text{Nasal Breadth}}{\text{Nasal Height}} \times 100$$

(Martin and Saller, 1957; Bass, 1987):

Leptorrhiny	Up to 47.9 (narrow aperture)
Mesorrhiny	48.0 to 52.9 (average or medium)
Platyrrhiny	53.0 and up (broad aperture)

C. **Condylar Index:** measures the position of the foramen magnum (see landmark diagram)

$$\frac{\text{Basion to Opisthocranion}}{\text{Basion to Prosthion}} \times 100$$

D. **Palatal Index:** measures the shape of the palate (and hence of the mouth and lower face)

$$\frac{\text{Palatal Width}}{\text{Palatal Length}} \times 100$$

E. **Supraorbital Index:** measures the height of the skull

$$\frac{\text{Vertex to Superior Border of Eye}}{\text{Vertex to Inferior Border of Eye}} \times 100$$

F. **Nuchal Index:** measures the area given for the origin of nuchal muscles

$$\frac{\text{From Line Level with Inferior Border of Eye to Line with Inion}}{\text{From Vertex to Line with Inferior Border of Eye}} \times 100$$

Postcranial Indexes

A. **Brachial Index:** measures the relative lengths of the upper and lower arm (use the osteometric board for these measurements)

$$\frac{\text{Length of Radius}}{\text{Length of Humerus}} \times 100$$

B. **Crural Index:** measures the relative lengths of the thigh and leg bones (use the osteometric board for these measurements)

$$\frac{\text{Length of Tibia}}{\text{Bicondylar Length of Femur}} \times 100$$

C. **Intermembral Index:** measures the relative lengths of the upper and lower limbs

$$\frac{\text{Length of Humerus} + \text{Radius}}{\text{Bicondylar Length of Femur} + \text{Tibial Length}} \times 100$$

Skull Volume

Volumetric Method: to be used on complete, intact skulls

1. Plug holes and openings with cotton (except the foramen magnum).

2. Fill the cranium through the foramen magnum with suitable material (mustard seed or millet is often used).

3. Gently shake the skull to settle the seed.

4. When filled to the border of the foramen magnum, carefully empty the seed into a large volumetric cylinder. Record the volume.

Raw Data for Exercise 13.3

Following is a list of cranial measurements of maximum (glabello-occipital) length and maximum breadth for Questions 1 to 6 in Exercise 13.3.

No.	Cranium Length	Breadth	No.	Cranium Length	Breadth
1	16.4 cm	14.7 cm	11	18.5 cm	14.8 cm
2	17.1	13.8	12	18.7	13.8
3	17.6	13.8	13	18.6	13.8
4	19.1	14.3	14	17.2	13.1
5	19.7	14.0	15	19.8	13.6
6	17.6	12.6	16	18.5	13.3
7	18.9	13.7	17	16.0	12.6
8	18.7	13.3	18	17.9	14.0
9	17.4	13.4	19	17.5	12.7
10	16.1	13.8	20	17.6	12.9

Following is a list of humerus measurements from different populations to be used when answering Questions 7 to 11 in Exercise 13.3.

Population	Maximum Length No.	Mean	S.D.	Transverse Diameter of Head No.	Mean	S.D.
European American						
Male	84	32.64 cm	1.88	82	4.50 cm	0.23
Female	82	29.92	1.57	74	3.91	0.19
African American						
Male	87	33.53	1.87	81	4.50	0.24
Female	85	30.65	1.70	79	.95	0.21
Native American (Pueblo)						
Male	89	30.69	1.19	72	4.06	0.20
Female	68	28.59	1.43	63	3.60	0.17
Native American (Arikara)						
Male	96	31.79	1.25	84	4.33	0.19
Female	86	29.54	1.17	75	.83	0.16

Osteometrics

To answer the following questions, refer to the preceding raw data charts.

1. a. What is the range of glabello-occipital length?

   b. What is the range of maximum cranial breadth?

2. a. What is the mean glabello-occipital length?

   b. What is the standard deviation of the glabello-occipital length?

3. a. What is the mean maximum cranial breadth?

   b. What is the standard deviation of the maximum cranial breadth?

4. Does the glabello-occipital length show a correlation with the maximum cranial breadth?

   a. Is this a positive or negative correlation? What, in words, does this mean?

   b. What is the r value for the correlation?

   c. Draw a scattergram of the relationship between cranial length and breadth. Use a separate piece of paper.

   d. What reason would you suggest for this correlation?

   e. Would you also expect glabello-occipital length to be correlated with maximum cranial height?

   With nutritional levels in the diet?

   With the sex of the individual?

5. Why should you be concerned with the standard deviation of two samples when comparing their means?

6. If you had two measurements that were greatly different from the other measurements and if you had checked to make sure they were measured correctly, would you delete them or add them to your measurements? Why?

7. a. What is the approximate 95% range for the maximum humerus length measurements for European American males?

   b. For European American females?

   c. For African American males?

   d. For African American females?

8. Plot the means and one standard deviation on one histogram (bar graph) for maximum length of each of the populations. Use a separate piece of paper.

9. a. If you had a European American humerus that measured 31 cm in maximum length, and you were asked to judge its sex, what would you say?

   b. If that humerus measured 29.92 cm?

   c. If that humerus measured 24.0 cm?

10. Plot the means and one standard deviation on one histogram for transverse diameter of the humeral head of each of the populations. Use a separate piece of paper.

11. How does the overlap of the 68% (one standard deviation) ranges of the transverse diameter of the humeral head compare with the overlap for the maximum length? Which of the two measurements would you be more comfortable using to determine sex? How reliable is either of the measurements in determining sex? What about determining population affinity from these measurements?

12. Repeat the previous exercises for measurements taken from your laboratory on either skeletal populations or living subjects. What are the differences between the sexes in your measurements?

13. Would you expect a relatively high correlation between different size measurements within the same body?

NONMETRIC TRAITS

Nonmetric or discontinuous traits are not measured but are rather scored as present or absent (although some nonmetric traits are scored as small, medium, or large, and sometimes as trace to complete). These traits probably have a very high genetic component, although no simple Mendelian inheritance patterns have been discovered. When we use nonmetric traits, we assume that a predisposition occurs for the inheritance of these traits and that we can infer degrees of relatedness between individuals within and between populations by the shared frequency of traits. This comparison can be "spatial," in which two individuals within or between populations from about the same time period are compared, or the comparisons can be "temporal," in which individuals from different time periods are compared.

You can compare the frequency of a single trait between individuals, but multivariate (involving more than one variable in one test) statistics are now commonly used to analyze the additive effects of combinations of nonmetric traits. Univariate statistical tests can be performed quickly, but multivariate tests are performed with computers because of the complicated time-consuming nature of the computations.

Nonmetric traits are useful in part because most of the traits described seem to be less affected by environment than are metric measurements, although Trinkaus (1978) believes that environmental factors are responsible for the high level of asymmetry found in many bilaterally occurring traits.

The nonmetric traits described here (Figures 13.16 to 13.20) are chosen because of the low level of interobserver and intraobserver error. The frequencies for some of the traits are given; for more information, see Hauser and De Stefano (1989). Many nonmetric traits that are not listed here are also commonly scored.

FIGURE 13.16 Os japonicum. *Drawing, D. L. France*

FIGURE 13.17 Mandibular torus. *Drawing, D. L. France*

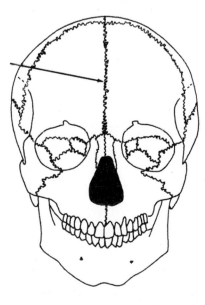

FIGURE 13.18 Metopic suture. *Drawing, D. L. France*

FIGURE 13.19 Ossicle at lambda. *Drawing, D. L. France*

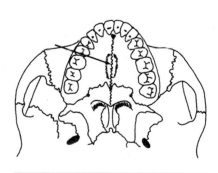

FIGURE 13.20 Palatine torus. *Drawing, D. L. France*

NONMETRIC TRAIT FREQUENCIES

Numbers refer to sides scored

	Combined Frequency	No.	Males %	Females No.	%	
Os japonicum						
North American Caucasians	1.4	154	2.6	124	0.0	(Corruccini, 1974)
North American Indians						
N.W. Coast	0.2	149	0.0	137	0.3	(Finnegan, 1972)
Arizona	0.2	245	0.0	347	0.3	(Birkby, 1973*)
African Americans	5.5	198	4.0	166	7.2	(Corruccini, 1974)
Japanese	8.8	282	7.1	174	11.4	(Mouri, 1976)
Indian (Uttar Pradesh)	0.4	Total N = 235				
Ainu	24.0	116	31.0	76	13.2	(Dodo, 1974)
Mandibular torus						
North American Caucasians	7.2	77	6.5	62	8.1	(Corruccini, 1974)
North American Indians						
N.W. Coast	17.5	Total N = 618				(Finnegan, 1972)
Arizona	28.6	282	34.6	387	4.0	(Birkby, 1973*)
African Americans	6.6	99	6.1	83	7.2	(Corruccini, 1974)
Japanese	29.2	151	26.7	90	33.3	(Mouri, 1976)
Indian (Uttar Pradesh)	30.4	Total N = 158**				
Metopic suture						
North American Caucasians	7.2	77	6.5	62	8.1	(Corruccini, 1974)
North American Indians						
N.W. Coast	2.8	149	2.0	137	3.6	(Finnegan, 1972)
Arizona	0.7	159	0.6	240	0.8	(Birkby, 1973*)
African Americans	2.2	99	2.0	83	2.4	(Corruccini, 1974)
Japanese	9.1	151	6.6	90	13.3	(Mouri, 1976)
Indian (Uttar Pradesh)	16.0	Total N = 119				
Ossicle at lambda						
North American Caucasians	10.1	77	9.1	62	11.3	(Corruccini, 1974)
North American Indians						
N.W. Coast	8.7	149	7.3	137	10.2	(Finnegan, 1972)
Arizona	25.8	116	19.8	178	29.8	(Birkby, 1973*)
African Americans	12.6	99	13.1	83	12.1	(Corruccini, 1974)
Japanese	6.9	119	9.2	84	3.6	(Mouri, 1976)
Indian (Uttar Pradesh)	23.5	Total N = 115				

Palatine torus

North American Caucasians	23.7	77	4.3	62	35.5	(Corruccini, 1974)
North American Indians						
N.W. Coast	14.8	149	9.3	137	20.4	(Finnegan, 1972)
Arizona	6.5	113	7.1	163	6.1	(Birkby, 1973*)
African Americans	15.4	99	11.1	83	20.5	(Corruccini, 1974)
Japanese	32.8	151	35.8	90	27.8	(Mouri, 1976)
Indian (Uttar Pradesh)	26.7	Total N = 116				

*Recalculated in Hauser and De Stefano, 1989

**combined males and females

RECORDING FORM

Use this recording form to score the nonmetric traits discussed in this chapter on the cranial material in your laboratory. You may also research other nonmetric and use those instead.

Individuals	1 L R	2 L R	3 L R	4 L R	5 L R	6 L R	7 L R	8 L R	9 L R	10 L R

EXERCISE 13.4 NAME _____ **SECTION** _____ **DATE** _____

Nonmetric Analysis

1. Can scientists extricate themselves from discussions of morality and social conscience when "doing" science?

   Is it possible for a scientist to be unaffected by the concerns of society at the time that the science is occurring (i.e., can the scientist escape from the "concerns of the day")?

   At what point in matters of social conscience should a scientist refuse to conduct research (give examples)? Has that point changed in history?

2. What are the means and standard deviations of the following traits listed in the table?

	Mean		S.D.	
	L	R	L	R
Os japonicum				
Mandibular torus				
Metopic suture				
Ossicle at lambda				
Palatine torus				

3. If you calculated the frequency of os japonicum in an unknown population to be 1.4%, would you be able to identify the population from which the population was genetically derived? Why or why not?

4. If you discovered os japonicum in an individual, would you be able to determine the group from which that individual came based on this trait alone? Why or why not?

5. The mandibular and palatine torus can be detected in the living. Calculate the frequency of occurrence of each of these traits in a large sample of your school colleagues. Are there significant differences in frequency with population affinity? Sex? If so, describe them.

6. Are there significant correlations in frequency of occurrence between any of the traits listed on the preceding chart? If so, describe them.

DERMATOGLYPHICS

The study of patterns of dermal ridges present on the fingers and palms of the hands and toes and soles of the feet of humans and other primates is called dermatoglyphics. These ridges even occur on the naked skin of the prehensile tail of some New World monkeys, and the presence of dermal ridges has a selective advantage in that they provide a surface of greater friction than if there were no ridges. The pattern of these ridges varies greatly, however, which is an indication that there are no strong selective advantages in favor of a particular pattern. Studies of fingerprint patterns in related individuals indicate that about 90% of the pattern is inherited (Brues, 1990), most likely through a complex polygenic mode, and because several congenital disorders that cause alterations of chromosomal numbers also have specific effects on dermal ridge patterns, these alleles probably occur on different chromosomes (Brues, 1990). There are some population differences between ridge patterns as well (Table 13.1).

Aside from the common practice of comparing unknown latent fingerprints at the scene of a crime to a collection of known individuals to identify who was at that particular location, there are other uses for studying dermal ridge patterns. Because of the high heritability of configurations, one can study familial inheritance patterns as well.

In classifying fingerprints, the patterns are initially grouped into three categories: arches, loops, and whorls (Figures 13.21 to 13.27). Along with this, the ridge count method is probably the most widely used for categorizing fingerprints.

Core: at the innermost ridge of the pattern, at the approximate center of the pattern.

Delta or triradius: the point at which three ridges diverge or the point nearest the center of the divergence of the type lines.

Type lines: the innermost ridges that surround the pattern area.

Ridge count: the number of ridges transecting a straight line drawn from the core to the delta.

Total ridge count: the total number of ridges on all fingers. In prints with whorls, only one ridge count per finger is added to the total.

Hints: Arches have no ridge count.

Loops have a single delta and hence a single line for a ridge count.

Whorls have two deltas, and therefore will have two lines drawn for ridge counts.

Loops can open (or flow if the delta is thought of as analogous to the delta of a river) toward the ulna (ulnar loops) or toward the radius (radial loops).

Table 13.1	Percentage Ranges of Types of Fingerprints Among Human Populations		
Group	Arches	Loops	Whorls
Africans	3–12%	53–73%	20–40%
Europeans	0–9%	63–76%	20–42%
East Asians	1–5%	43–56%	44–54%
Australian Aborigines	0–1%	28–46%	52–73%
Native Americans	2–8%	46–61%	35–57%
San (Bushmen)	13–16%	66–68%	15–21%
Adapted from Coon (1965, pg. 261)			

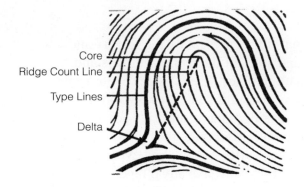

FIGURE 13.21 Print properties.
Drawing, The Science of Fingerprints,
Classification and Uses, *U.S. Government Printing
Office, Washington, D.C.*

FIGURE 13.22 Arch.
Drawing, The Science of
Fingerprints, Classification and
Uses, *U.S. Government Printing
Office, Washington, D.C.*

FIGURE 13.23 Loop.
Drawing, The Science of
Fingerprints, Classification and
Uses, *U.S. Government Printing
Office, Washington, D.C.*

FIGURE 13.24 Whorl.
Drawing, The Science of
Fingerprints, Classification and
Uses, *U.S. Government Printing
Office, Washington, D.C.*

FIGURE 13.25 Tented arch.
Drawing, The Science of
Fingerprints, Classification and
Uses, *U.S. Government Printing
Office, Washington, D.C.*

FIGURE 13.26 Double loop.
Drawing, The Science of
Fingerprints, Classification and
Uses, *U.S. Government Printing
Office, Washington, D.C.*

FIGURE 13.27 Central pocket
loop. *Drawing,* The Science of
Fingerprints, Classification and
Uses, *U.S. Government Printing
Office, Washington, D.C.*

Dermatoglyphics

FIGURE 13.28 Unknown.
Drawing, The Science of Fingerprints, Classification and Uses, *U.S. Government Printing Office, Washington, D.C.*

1. What is the type of fingerprint in Figure 13.28?

    What is the ridge count?

FIGURE 13.29 Unknown.
Drawing, The Science of Fingerprints, Classification and Uses, *U.S. Government Printing Office, Washington, D.C.*

2. What is the type of fingerprint in Figure 13.29?

    What is the ridge count?

FIGURE 13.30 Unknown.
Drawing, The Science of
Fingerprints, Classification and
Uses, *U.S. Government Printing
Office, Washington, D.C.*

3. What is the type of fingerprint in Figure 13.30?

    What is the ridge count?

4. Can the population from which an individual is derived be estimated by the type of print on that individual's fingers?

    Why or why not?

5. Use the following form to record the pattern of the prints from your fingers. The friction pads extend on the sides of the fingers toward the nail, so the fingers should be rolled from side to side on the inkpad and then on paper.

Digit	Left Hand Classification	Left Hand Ridge Count	Right Hand Classification	Right Hand Ridge Count
I (thumb)	_____	_____	_____	_____
II	_____	_____	_____	_____
III	_____	_____	_____	_____
IV	_____	_____	_____	_____
V	_____	_____	_____	_____

REEXAMINING THE ISSUES

- It is important to use the correct methods and instruments to measure skeletal elements and living individuals.
- It is important to understand the statistical tests employed to describe the relationships between individuals and populations in measured characteristics and in nonmetric traits.
- Variation in humans is an important consideration when deriving standards for age, sex, ancestry, stature, and so on.

CHAPTER 14

●

Abnormalities in the Skeleton: Pathology, Anomalies, and Intentional Modification

OBJECTIVES

1. What are the ways in which the skeleton reacts to disease processes?

2. How can we diagnose the direction of force in blunt trauma?

3. Can the skeleton be modified intentionally?

In this chapter, we will study some of the more common pathology and anomalies in the skeleton and in the dentition, although we certainly will not exhaust the topic as there are volumes of information written about these topics. The goal in this book is to merely touch on some examples you are most likely to see, with some clues about how to identify them as pathology, anomalies, intentional modification, or normal variation in the skeleton. The pathology more commonly associated with medicolegal (forensic) investigations will be explored further in Chapter 15.

Why do we study these processes? Obviously, it is important to know how to determine what happened to an individual during life or at about the time of death, but frankly, some of them are just interesting! In lectures about physical anthropology, students pay particular attention to the ways in which the skeleton is altered by disease pathogens, genetic abnormalities, and intentional modification (either by violence or by gentle pressures). We are all drawn to the abnormal.

We also need to study how a body reacts to various diseases because even if we cannot immediately identify the pathogen responsible, we still need to know how to accurately describe what is happening in the bone or tooth for later diagnosis (it is always important to precisely describe what a bone or tooth looks like because diagnoses can change but the description may not). Remember that this is one of the basic tenets of the scientific method.

INTRODUCTION

Throughout most of this book, we have investigated the normal human and nonhuman skeleton, so we should know by now how to recognize them. When something abnormal happens to bone and teeth, however, the classification into genus and species could be incorrect, or the abnormality may be so extreme that a bone may not even look like bone!

We will begin by investigating various pathological processes (i.e., processes that are harmful to the individual). We will then discuss a few anomalies commonly (and a few not-so-commonly) seen in the skeleton and teeth. These are not necessarily harmful to the individual, but they are unusual. We will complete the chapter by discussing some of the ways in which cultures or individuals intentionally modify their skeletons and teeth, both while the individual is alive and after death.

PATHOLOGY

Disease Agents

Infectious Processes Many of the manifestations of disease in present times are different from those seen in skeletal remains from even 100 years ago. The discovery of penicillin in 1929 and its general use during World War II, as well as the discovery of other antibiotics, have changed the course of medicine, so that in most cases, the bony changes that used to occur as a result of bacterial infections are not as severe, and most infections do not even get to the point at which they infect bone. However, antibiotic-resistant strains of bacteria have evolved in part because of the overuse and misuse of antibiotics for even minor infections (see Chapter 2 for the ways in which this could occur), so some infectious processes are progressing in the body more than they might have a few years ago. Having said that, however, the reactions to bacterial infections in bone are still usually not as severe as what were seen during, for example, the time of the American Civil War. Even so, anthropologists studying human remains still have to know what disease processes are likely to do to bone because we do not always look at modern human remains.

It is often difficult to diagnose the specific pathogen responsible for disease changes to bone, as bone can react to the entire disease spectrum in limited ways: the addition of new bone by osteoblastic activity, the destruction of existing bone by osteoclastic activity, or a combination of the two (see Chapter 4 for further discussions about osteoblastic and osteoclastic activity). In some cases, the osteoblasts and osteoclasts are both more active in different areas of the body, and in some cases the amount of bone is constant, but the shape of the bone may change relative to its normal morphology. Experienced anthropologists and pathologists will describe the changes seen in the entire skeleton, as the focal sites for bony change may be different for different pathogens or processes. As stated before, remember that it is more important to accurately describe the changes you see than to diagnose the specific pathogen (although it is tempting to try to make that diagnosis!).

Figure 14.1 shows the effects of a bacterial infection on a human humerus. This is obviously a pathogen that promotes osteoclastic activity, but interestingly, it also promotes osteoblastic activity, as the body is trying to react to the stress of the infection. The original bone shaft is essentially sequestered (like a jury in a trial is sequestered and not allowed to speak to anyone outside of the jury, and in fact this shaft of bone is called a **sequestrum**). The sequestrum is isolated from the rest of the body by a shell called an **involucrum**. Often the involucrum is penetrated by holes called **cloaca** (Figure 14.2), which are areas from which the pus from the infection exits the bone. Figure 14.3 shows a proximal tibia and fibula and a bacterial infection resulting from the amputation of the distal tibia and fibula during the Civil War after the soldier was shot in the lower leg. Note that there is no sequestrum or involucrum in this example (according to historical records, this individual's distal tibia and fibula were exposed and "unhealthy fluids" were flowing from the infected stump).

FIGURE 14.1 Infection in humerus. *Photo, D. L. France; materials curated by the National Museum of Health and Medicine*

FIGURE 14.2 Cloaca in proximal tibia (left). *Photo, D. L. France; material from National Museum of Natural History*

FIGURE 14.3 Proximal tibia and fibula showing infection. *Photo D. L. France; cast of original curated by the National Museum of Health and Medicine*

FIGURE 14.4 Effects of tuberculosis on thoracic vertebral column (right). Normal thoracic column is on the left. *Photo, D. L. France; diseased thoracic column from National Museum of Health and Medicine*

Figure 14.4 displays the effects of tuberculosis on thoracic vertebrae. Tuberculosis is an airborne disease that affects the lungs, and if it is not contained, it will spread to the surrounding soft and hard tissue (ribs, vertebrae). Because tuberculosis is obviously primarily an osteolytic process, as it progresses in the vertebral column, it makes the bodies of the vertebrae weaker, and they may ultimately collapse. As the disease wanes, the osteoclastic activity wanes, and the body may attempt to stabilize the vertebrae by osteoblastic activity (and in fact the vertebrae in Figure 14.4 are fused into one piece). Figure 14.5 may represent a tuberculosis lesion (this has been variously diagnosed) in the cranium.

The preceding osteoblastic and osteoclastic activity describes infections in bone, but the periosteum can also be affected by bacterial infections. When it is inflamed, it is called **periostitis**. It can be caused by something penetrating the skin and passing the pathogen to the periosteum, or it can be a more generalized infection that causes periostitis in multiple locations in the body. This can become quite severe and can spread to the underlying bone. Figure 14.6 shows an example of periostitis in a tibia.

Figure 14.7 represents a different kind of infection. Syphilis is caused by a treponemal organism (a spiral-shaped bacterium) that enters the body through skin or mucosal membranes. It can progress from soft-tissue infection in primary syphilis to tertiary syphilis, which attacks brain tissue and the skeleton, and obviously promotes osteoclastic activity.

FIGURE 14.5 Possible tuberculosis lesion in cranium. *Photo, D. L. France; material from San Diego Museum of Man*

FIGURE 14.6 Periostitis in tibia. *Photo, D. L. France; cast of original from San Diego Museum of Man*

FIGURE 14.7 Syphilis in cranial secton. *Photo, D. L. France; cast from specimen at National Museum of Health and Medicine*

Infections also result from tooth decay. If the bacteria within dental caries move into the pulp cavity, it can spread easily to the alveolus and beyond. Figure 14.8 shows a dental caries (cavity), while Figure 14.9 represents an abscess caused by dental decay.

Cancers Cancers are generally classified as either benign (or not rapidly spreading or life-threatening) or malignant (usually rapidly spreading and more dangerous to the individual). Cancers of bone more often start as a soft-tissue tumor that spreads to the bone (as a **metastasis**). A couple of forms of cancer of bone are shown here (Figures 14.10 and 14.11), but there are very many ways in which cancer of bone can manifest itself. They can be either primarily osteolytic or osteogenic.

Other Conditions Blood-supply problems or interruptions caused by anemia (possibly) or by other agents can result in more porotic bone than normal. When accompanied by a thickening of the bone, it is termed porotic hyperostosis. (Figure 14.12 shows a dramatic example of porotic hyperostosis.) Cribra orbitalia (Figure 14.13) is occasionally seen (particularly in younger individuals) and is probably an early example of porotic hyperostosis.

Developmental problems can arise in various ways. They can be caused by genetic abnormalities passed from the parents, but they can also arise from genetic abnormalities caused by abnormal conditions during the development of the fetus in the uterus. The latter can be caused by, for example, too much heat (pregnant women sitting in hot tubs during pregnancy is a recently recognized cause of some spinal abnormalities), altered chemistry in the blood (e.g., thalidomide was a drug used to decrease the effects of "morning sickness" in pregnancy, and often led to undeveloped or misshapen limbs), or other environmental problems.

FIGURE 14.8 Dental caries. *Photo, D. L. France; material from National Museum of Natural History*

FIGURE 14.9 Abscess caused by dental decay. *Photo, D. L. France; material from National Museum of Natural History*

FIGURE 14.10 Metastasis from sarcoma from lung. *Photo, D. L. France; material from National Museum of Natural History*

FIGURE 14.11 Cancer of the maxilla, an osteoclastic condition. *Photo, D. L. France*

FIGURE 14.12 Porotic hyperostosis. *Photo, D. L. France; specimen from National Museum of Natural History*

FIGURE 14.13 Cribra orbitalia. *Photo, D. L. France; material curated by the National Museum of Health and Medicine*

FIGURE 14.14 Anencephaly. *Photo: D. L. France; cast of specimen curated by the National Museum of Health and Medicine*

Problems in the developing skeleton can be as severe as anencephaly (Figure 14.14), in which the brain (and the cranium) does not develop *in utero,* and the child dies within a few days after birth (a child cannot survive this condition). Other developmental problems, including dwarfism (Figure 14.15), scoliosis (a lateral bending of the spine, as shown in Figure 14.16), or kyphosis (an anteroposterior bending of the spine), cleft palate (Figure 14.17), club feet, or missing or altered limbs, may not be fatal, but may have a serious impact on the quality of life of the individual.

Developmental problems can also occur after the birth of the infant. Chapter 4 discusses the effects of malnutrition and disease on the development of bones (with growth arrest lines) and teeth (with enamel hypoplasias). Rickets (Figure 14.18) is a condition in

FIGURE 14.15 Normal and dwarf femur. *Photo, D. L. France; materials curated by the National Museum of Health and Medicine*

FIGURE 14.16 Severe scoliosis. *Photo, D. L. France; cast of specimen curated by the University of Colorado*

FIGURE 14.17 Cleft palate. *Photo: D.L. France; material curated by the National Museum of Natural History*

FIGURE 14.18 Rickets in tibia. *Photo, D. L. France; material from National Museum of Natural History*

which calcium is not being applied to the growing skeleton, and the bones become curved (particularly if they support weight).

Mechanical Processes

Many types of mechanical insults are seen by osteologists, anthropologists, and pathologists. These include blunt trauma, sharp injuries, gunshot wounds, and even combinations of these forces. For example, one can often see a combination of blunt and sharp trauma to bone if a sharp instrument (such as a saber or hatchet) both cuts and fractures the bone. Victims of plane crashes or building explosions sometimes exhibit injuries from many different types of forces.

Bone is elastic in life (because of the organic component) and can "bounce back" from many mechanical forces, particularly if the stress is slow to build and contains little power. If the force contains a great deal of power applied quickly, bone will fracture before it has a chance to exhibit its elastic qualities. Slow-loading, or slower-impact forces produce more elastic response from bone before it fractures.

Fractures and Blunt Trauma Fractures in bone can, of course, be accidental as in a fall, for example, or they can be intentional. Fractures can be **incomplete**, in which the bone is not completely broken into two or more pieces (a "greenstick" fracture is this type of fracture and is particularly common in young individuals, in whom there is more organic component as the bone is growing and more bending is allowed before fracture). Fractures can also be a simple fracture or more complicated **comminuted** (fractured into many pieces) or **compound** (in which the broken ends of the bone erupt through the skin). Blunt trauma is, as its name implies, damage caused to bone or teeth by objects with relatively broad surfaces (as opposed to a sharp instrument). This is usually a relatively slow-loading force (i.e., it builds relatively slowly) and can cause significant deformation of the bone before the bone fractures. Often at least a portion of this deformation remains even after the bone is cleaned (which sometimes makes it more difficult to reconstruct the fragments).

Blunt trauma in tubular bone often results in the separation of wedge-shaped fragments of bone, as bone can withstand compression forces to a greater degree than it can withstand tensile forces (forces that pull bone apart) (see Figure 14.19 for an example). Be careful when trying to determine the direction of force in a tubular bone. It has been a common mistake in textbooks to describe the

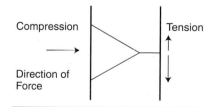

FIGURE 14.19 Reactions of tubular bone to stress. *Drawing, D. L. France*

FIGURE 14.20 Blunt trauma in cranium. *Photo, D. L. France; specimen from University of New Mexico*

results of force in a tubular bone as the same as a gunshot wound in either tubular bone or the cranium. See Figure 14.20 for an example of blunt trauma in the human cranium that resulted in plastic deformation and a complex fracture pattern.

Complex fracture patterns can sometimes contain clues as to which blow(s) occurred first, which occurred second, and so on (particularly in crania). Fracture lines in fresh bone usually radiate away from the point of initial impact, hence they are called "radiating fracture lines." Radiating fracture lines from multiple injuries usually do not cross each other but stop at other fractures or cranial sutures because the force transmitted through the radiating fracture lines is suddenly dissipated when it reaches a suture or another crack. (See Figure 14.21 for an example of this in plate glass. Although the fractures in this example are caused by gunshots, notice the interaction of the fracture lines.) Depending on the degree of force and the area of bone, concentric rings may also radiate away from the point of initial injury (this is like dropping a pebble into a pond). These are also helpful in identifying the initial point of contact even if you no longer have that part of the bone with the point of contact. This is also the way in which fresh bone injuries are distinguished from dry bone damage. Trauma to dry bone usually results in fractures with ragged edges and without the radiating fracture lines or concentric rings.

Degenerative changes in the skeleton can also lead to mechanical manifestations of force. They can be caused by disease, malnutrition, or old age, and are characterized by an imbalance in the osteoblastic/osteoclastic activities. Osteoporosis, for example, is a thinning of the cortical bone. It is caused by too much osteoclastic activity and is more prevalent in postmenopausal women. Figure 14.22 illustrates how thin the cortical bone in the distal femur of a 93-year-old woman can be (this was from a woman who donated her body to medicine). The cortical bone of this femur was so thin and brittle

FIGURE 14.21 Fracture interrupted by another fracture in glass. *Photo, D. L. France; demonstration by Wayne Bryant. Key: D = 2nd shot; M = 1st shot*

FIGURE 14.22 Osteoporosis in distal femur. *Photo, D. L. France*

that even mild pressure could fracture it. One hears often of an older woman "falling and breaking her hip." But actually, often the event occurs the other way around: a person may step off of a curb and the stress on the neck of the femur may be just enough with the thinner bones of osteoporosis that the femur will fracture at the neck (Figure 14.23). Degenerative joint disease can occur with increased age and/or with trauma. Figures 14.24a, b, and c are photographs of the knee joint of the woman from Figure 14.22, and illustrate what happens when the joint degenerates, the cartilage of the knee disintegrates, and bone moves against bone. When this occurs, the joint surfaces begin to break down (causing the ruffled appearance), and polishing (**eburnation**) begins as the reaction of bone rubbing on bone. Figure 14.25 shows increased bone growth along the spinal column. These areas of extra bone growth are called **osteophytes.**

Dislocations occur at any joint, depending on the relative stability of the joint and the strength of the ligaments and tendons surrounding the joint. Figures 14.26a and b show a long-term "unreduced" (i.e., it was not put back into proper position) dislocation at the shoulder. Notice the modifications of the scapula where the humeral head essentially created a new joint surface. Dislocations at the shoulder are more common than at the femoral head because the acetabulum is much deeper, and the ligaments (including the ligamentum teres) are so strong that it is much more difficult to

FIGURE 14.23 Fracture at neck of femur. *Photo, D. L. France; materials curated by the National Museum of Health and Medicine*

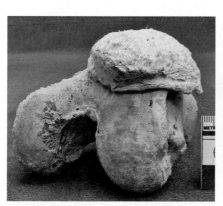

FIGURE 14.24a Arthritic knee of femur from Figure 14.22. *Photo, D. L. France*

FIGURE 14.24b Arthritic femur from Figure 14.22. Notice breakdown of joint surface. *Photo, D. L. France*

FIGURE 14.24c Posterior patella from same woman as in Figure 14.22. *Photo, D. L. France*

FIGURE 14.25 Sequence of osteophyte development in vertebrae. *Photo: D. L. France; specimens curated by the National Museum of Natural History*

FIGURE 14.26a Dislocated shoulder. *Photo: D. L. France; specimens curated by the National Museum of Natural History*

FIGURE 14.26b Glenoid fossa of dislocated shoulder. *Photo: D. L. France; specimens curated by the National Museum of Natural History*

displace. When it is dislocated, it is very difficult to reduce because the strong ligaments and tendons then hold the femoral head *out* of position.

Sharp Injury Cut marks are caused when a sharp object incises bone. On close inspection (with a dissection microscope or scanning electron microscope), cut marks typically are V-shaped, or have a series of V shapes (as if made by stone tools that have a series of parallel cutting edges along the worked edges). See Figure 14.27 for an example of the series of cuts caused by a stone tool. Vascular grooves (most often the grooves along the lateral aspects of the frontal bone) are often mistaken for cut marks, but they have a rounded or U shape in cross section (see Figure 14.28 for a photograph of a vascular groove). They are caused by gentle pressure of a blood vessel against the bone (the bone responds to gentle pressure by "molding" itself to that pressure—more about this later). Rodent tooth marks are also sometimes mistaken for cut marks on bone, but they are typically paired and have a square cross section (Figure 14.29).

FIGURE 14.27 Scanning electron micrograph of cuts made by stone knife (10X). *Photo, Colorado State University S.E.M. Laboratory*

FIGURE 14.28 Vascular groove on frontal bone. *Photo: D. L. France; specimens curated by the National Museum of Natural History*

FIGURE 14.29 Rodent tooth marks on bone. *Photo, D. L. France*

Sharp force injuries usually combine cuts with force, so that one sees a V cross section with compacted bone near the center of the cut and often lifted and somewhat displaced edges. These are often insults created by an axe, saber, or other relatively heavy sharp instrument.

Gunshot Wounds More will be said about the different types of gunshot wounds in Chapter 15, but they vary widely by the caliber (size) of the projectile (usually, but not always, a bullet), and they are projected by a wide variety of explosive forces. They are some-what predictable in that the missile usually creates a smaller opening at the entrance and a larger opening as it exits (i.e., the missile carries a "plug" of bone with it as it travels through the bone). With a round missile, one can liken the effect to the pattern of a small BB shot through a plate glass window. If the shot is coming from out-side the building, the cone of glass will be taken away from the side inside the building (see Figure 14.21). In this way, the direction of travel can often (but not always!) be determined by looking at the direction of beveling in the bone (see Figures 14.30 and 14.31).

FIGURE 14.30 Gunshot entry wound in cranium. *Photo, D. L. France*

Healing of Bone How do we determine whether or not an individ-ual has survived a mechanical insult to bone? In all of the preceding examples, the edges left by the insult are sharp. The body reacts to fractures by immediately forming a soft-tissue callus around the point of fracture, and the bone quickly (it is noticeable with a dissection microscope within a few days) reinforces this callus with a loosely woven bone bridge. The process of remodeling this quickly formed bone begins immediately and will proceed until the morphology of the bone approaches the normal condition. The edges of the fracture at this point are becoming smoother and more rounded. The fracture is stable within a few weeks (the physician requires a person to have a cast on the bone for about six weeks to be sure it is stable), depending on the health, age, and nutritional status of the individual. See Figures 14.32a and b for examples of healed fractures of bone. Although these are displaced fractures, the fracture site is healed and stable.

FIGURE 14.31 Gunshot exit wound in cranium. *Photo, D. L. France*

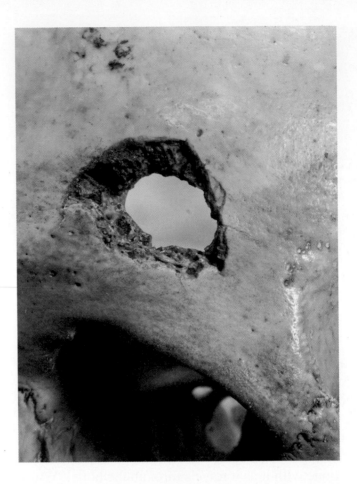

If a fractured bone is not stabilized and allowed to heal as described previously, sometimes the fractured ends never join, and they are allowed to constantly rub against one another. This can form a **pseudoarthrosis,** or false joint (like the dislocated shoulder shown earlier in Figure 14.26). The edges usually become rounded and sometimes show eburnation at the "joint" surface.

ANOMALIES

Anomalies are odd things that happen to bones and teeth that are not necessarily injurious to the individual. For example, some developmental problems with dentition may not even be known to the individual. Figure 14.33 shows an "occult" tooth obviously growing in the wrong direction. This individual also had a "pegged" tooth (a tooth that has an incompletely formed crown) and a cleft

FIGURE 14.32a Stable fracture, outside (above) and inside (below). Notice the original bone shaft segments. *Photo, D. L. France; materials curated by the National Museum of Health and Medicine*

FIGURE 14.32b Healed displaced fracture of clavicle. *Photo, D. L. France*

palate (shown in a more severe form in Figure 14.17), although not all occult teeth are accompanied by pathological conditions. Figure 14.34 shows a "pegged" tooth.

Figure 14.35 shows an anomaly on the occipital bone of a man from the island of Tinian. It has been variously described as "occupational" effects from the overuse of muscles that insert in this area, to a variation due to a genetic predisposition in this population. It could be a combination of both (Gary Heathcote, personal communication).

Osteomas are benign bone growths that can occur on the outside or the inside of the cranium. See Figure 14.36 for an example of a button osteoma on a cranium.

INTENTIONAL MODIFICATION

Cranial Modifications Just as the frontal bone yields to gentle pressure from the blood vessels that course along its surface, and just as the displaced fracture of a tibia will gradually remodel itself toward its original (and most efficient biomechanical) morphology, so too will the cranium and postcranium respond to gentle pressure. One of the most commonly seen cranial modifications in the southwestern United States is "cradleboard deformation" or the flattening of the rear of the cranium from the gentle pressure of the board onto which a baby is swaddled (see Figure 14.37). There is no indication

FIGURE 14.33 Occult teeth. *Photo, D. L. France; material from San Jose State University*

FIGURE 14.34 Pegged tooth. *Photo, D. L. France*

FIGURE 14.35 Anomalous bumps on occipital bone. *Photo, D. L. France; cast from material loaned from Gary Heathcote*

FIGURE 14.36 Osteoma. *Photo: D. L. France; specimens curated by the National Museum of Natural History*

FIGURE 14.37 Cradleboard modification in prehistoric Native American. *Photo, D. L. France*

FIGURE 14.38 Modification of frontal and occipital in prehistoric Native American from the Northwest United States. *Photo, D. L. France; cast from France Casting*

FIGURE 14.39 Wrapping modification of cranium in prehistoric Peruvian. *Photo, D. L. France; specimen from University of Wyoming*

that this cranial modification changes the IQ of the infant in any way, and in fact, the cranium can take on many shapes, as long as it is allowed to grow in some direction to accommodate the growing brain. Figure 14.38 shows a variation of this modification in a Northwest Coast (of the United States) Native American, in which there is a board on the occipital region as well as a board on the frontal region of the cranium. In this situation, the cranium is wider than usual. In Peru (and in other regions) a baby's head was wrapped in cloth, so that the posterior parietal and occipital bones were drawn toward the back of the cranium, making the cranium longer (see Figure 14.39). If the cranium is *not* allowed to grow in some direction to accommodate the developing brain, as in the pathological condition of **craniostenosis** (in which the sutures prematurely fuse), brain growth itself is stunted, and mental retardation can (and usually does) occur. See Figure 14.40 for an example of microcephaly, in which the cranial sutures are prematurely fused.

Surgical intervention is a form of intentional modification and includes **trephination** (Figure 14.41). Trephination is performed today as an emergency surgery designed to relieve pressure on the brain. Trephination was also performed in prehistoric societies and was once thought to have released "evil spirits" from the person.

FIGURE 14.41 Prehistoric trephination. Notice the relatively sharp edges and the area of reactive bone (at arrows) around wound, indicative of probable infection. *Photo: D. L. France; specimens curated by the National Museum of Natural History*

FIGURE 14.40 Microcephaly (left) compared to normal adult (right). Note the small and elongated cranium in the microcephalic. *Photos, D. L. France; casts of specimens from the University of Washington and University of New Mexico*

(It is interesting that if we do not understand cultural processes, we often jump to conclusions that involve religion or the supernatural with the assumption that those cultures didn't understand the biological aspects of the human body!) Most researchers now believe that trephination may have been performed in prehistoric societies to relieve symptoms of a previous injury.

Postcranial Modifications Probably the most well-recognized postcranial skeletal modification occurred in China, with "foot-binding," in which the foot was tightly bound, making the foot seem small and petite (see the shoes in Figure 14.42). Actually, the growing metatarsals were drawn caudally and toward the tarsals so that the foot was "folded." The women who bound their feet (or who had their feet bound) could wear tiny shoes, but they had difficulty walking.

Dental Modifications Dental modifications, such as filing, notching, staining, and adding implants of precious stones can occur in any culture, although certain of these are more prevalent in some cultures than in others. For example, the dark staining of the teeth with betel nut juice would obviously occur more often where there are, in fact, betel nuts (such as in New Guinea, Java, Bali, etc.). Figure 14.43 illustrates staining of the teeth by betel nut juice in an individual from Bali. Note also that the teeth were filed so that there is a horizontal groove in the teeth (Figure 14.44).

Unintentional modification of the dentition can also occur with the habitual use of tobacco pipes (particularly when pipe stems were made of ceramics), as shown in Figure 14.45. The teeth are worn down by the constant abrasion. Other notches can occur with holding yarn in the teeth while weaving, holding sewing needles in the teeth, and even by the habitual use of toothpicks. Figure 14.46 shows a tooth that has been notched on two surfaces.

FIGURE 14.42 Shoes used in foot binding. *Photo, D. L. France*

FIGURE 14.43 Teeth stained by betel nut juice. *Photo: D. L. France; specimens curated by the National Museum of Natural History*

FIGURE 14.44 Horizontal filing of teeth from individual in Figure 14.42. *Photo: D. L. France; specimens curated by the National Museum of Natural History*

FIGURE 14.45 Pipe stem groove. *Photo, D. L. France*

FIGURE 14.46 Notched tooth. *Photo: D. L. France; specimens curated by the National Museum of Natural History*

Postmortem Modifications Several cultures modify remains after death. Figure 14.47 shows a modified cranium and mandible from Tibet. Sometimes this modification/decoration was performed post-cranially as well. Figure 14.48 demonstrates a child's cranium that was incised after death.

FIGURE 14.47 Cranium from Tibet. *Photo: D. L. France; specimens curated by the National Museum of Natural History*

FIGURE 14.48 Postmortem incisions on cranium from New Guinea. *Photo: D. L. France; specimens curated by the National Museum of Natural History*

EXERCISE 14.1   NAME _____   SECTION _____   DATE _____

Abnormalities in the Skeleton

FIGURE 14.49 Unknown. *Photo, National Museum of Health and Medicine*

1. What processes are occurring in the bone pictured in Figure 14.49 (osteogenic or osteolytic)?

    Osteolytic

FIGURE 14.50 Unknown. *Photo, D. L. France; specimen from the University of New Mexico*

2. The cranium in Figure 14.50 illustrates blunt trauma. Did the individual survive this injury? How do you know?

    Looks like some osteoblastic healing may have occured therfore the individual must have survived

FIGURE 14.51 Unknown. *Photo, D. L. France; material from University of New Mexico*

3. Figure 14.51 is a photograph of the right mastoid process. Is this primarily an osteoblastic or osteoclastic pathogen? How do you know?

Bone seems to be degenerating therefore osteoclastic pathogen

FIGURE 14.52 Unknown. *Photo, D. L. France; materials curated by the National Museum of Health and Medicine*

4. Figure 14.52 is an example of trephination. Did this individual survive this surgery? How do you know?

The bone has a clean cut & no attempts to heal therfore the individual died before healing could take place

FIGURE 14.53 Unknown. *Photo, D. L. France*

5. What has happened to the cranium in Figure 14.53? How do you know?

Complex fracture pattern indicate several blunt blows to the head

FIGURE 14.54 Unknown. *Photo, D. L. France*

6.   Figure 14.54 shows a tibia that has been fractured by blunt trauma. From what direction did the force hit this bone? How do you know?

Tension in the bone created a small crack up top where the initial blow came from & the remaining stress snapped the bone at the bottom

FIGURE 14.55 Unknown. *Photo, D. L. France*

7.   How would you describe the distal femur in Figure 14.55?

Formation of new bone possibly caused by a osteoblastic pathogen

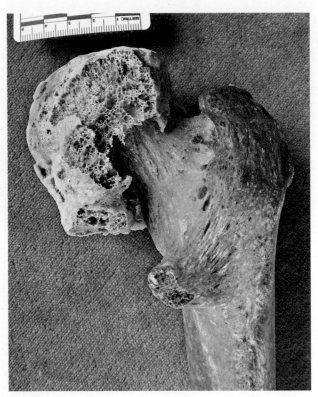

FIGURE 14.56a Unknown. *Photo, D. L. France*

FIGURE 14.56b Unknown.
Photo, D. L. France

8. Figures 14.56a and b show degenerative changes in what bone? What does the polishing in Figure 14.56b tell you?

The femur degenerating by a osteoclastic pathogen

REEXAMINING THE ISSUES

- The human skeleton has a wide range of normal variation, but anthropologists will also encounter a wide range of abnormal, unusual, or pathological conditions.

- It is important to understand that there are a limited number of ways in which the human skeleton can react to stresses while alive, and we must be aware of both what constitutes abnormal variation and how to describe it (which is more important than diagnosing the specific condition or pathogen responsible for that abnormal variation).

CHAPTER 15

Human Skeletal Variation and Forensic Anthropology

OBJECTIVES

1. How can we determine the age, sex, and ancestry of an individual from skeletal remains?

2. What information can we obtain from a partial skeleton that might help police solve a homicide?

3. Does "race" exist in humans?

Forensic anthropology is a rapidly growing subfield of anthropology, possibly in part because of the prevalence of forensic television programs that appeal to the "detectives" in all of us. With the growing interest in this field, there is an increasing need in colleges and universities (and even in high schools) to provide an introduction to forensics in a responsible way and to accurately represent what forensic scientists can do. This chapter will introduce the aspects of physical anthropology that are particularly relevant in forensic cases and almost all studies of human skeletal remains (archaeological finds, remains from a historic sites, etc.). In addition, some concepts and situations that arc more specific to the application of science to medicolegal cases not usually introduced in general physical anthropology training will be presented here.

INTRODUCTION

Forensic science is defined as the application of scientific methods to the law. Forensic physical anthropology is the application of physical anthropology to legal questions and is usually used in determining the identity and circumstances of death of an individual (with or without soft tissue). This is usually abbreviated as forensic anthropology, although that can literally mean the application of *any* subdiscipline of anthropology to the law.

The techniques used to assess age, sex, ancestry, stature (all of which are defined as parts of the biological profile of an individual), as well as the ways in which insults to the skeleton (disease, nutritional problems, trauma, etc.) are determined, are shared among the subfields within physical/biological anthropology. Those anthropologists who describe a skeleton in an archaeological site use many of the same techniques that a forensic anthropologist uses in describing a recent plane crash victim. There are some aspects of forensic anthropology that are not common to all anthropological investigations, however. The analysis of some gunshot wounds, cuts made by saw blades, time since death, and the concern about maintaining the chain of evidence are basic to forensic anthropology but not to the analysis of archaeological remains. Strictly speaking, the term "forensic anthropology" should be reserved for the analysis of remains that have forensic significance and are important in a medicolegal context.

Time is a standard measure of whether a case is a forensic case. In general terms, if a case occurred less than 50 years ago, there is a greater likelihood that the body can be identified, that evidence in the case will still be obtainable, and that a perpetrator will still be alive to be prosecuted. After 50 years (even though there is no statute of limitations on homicide), it is still important to identify the victim so that the family can be notified, although the possibility of obtaining evidence declines.

THE IMPORTANCE OF TAPHONOMY

Taphonomy is defined as anything that happens to a body after death. It includes various natural environmental factors (sun, temperature, elevation, scavenging, burial, etc.) as well as human-influenced factors (e.g., storage in a freezer versus storage in a cardboard box). These factors influence many things such as the decomposition patterns of a body and the location of bodies or body parts (e.g., scavenger versus river transport of elements). Recognition of taphonomic influences is extremely important in trying to determine time since death (or time since deposition in a certain environment), and in determining whether or not the evidence you think you have discovered on a body is important evidence or an artifact of the environment in which a body lay. The degree of decomposition in a body can help you determine whether or not the body is a forensic case or an archaeological case. The color, texture, smell, and weight are all important clues (see Figure 15.1 for an example of taphonomic influence on the color of bones). Are the bones dried out, bleached white, and cracking? Are the bones oily, and do they smell like decomposing tissue? Are the bones dried out and the color of dirt? Of these, which case is more likely an archaeological case that has been buried for hundreds of years? Why is the color different in a skeleton that has been buried for hundreds of

FIGURE 15.1 Copper staining on one side of the body is an example of taphonomic influence. *Photo, D. L. France; material from University of Tennessee*

years versus one that has been bleached white? We will come back to this issue later in this chapter.

Click!

Click for more information about forensic science and the proper handling of evidence.

THE DETERMINATION OF FORENSIC SIGNIFICANCE AND THE IDENTIFICATION PROCESS

The steps one goes through in the analysis of a potential forensic case starts with the determination of forensic significance. That process usually starts with determining whether or not the evidence is organic. To call in a forensic anthropologist, we would want to determine if the evidence is, or contains, bone. Is it human bone? Until the evidence is determined to be not forensically significant, it is important to follow proper protocol for the handling of evidence, which means that the evidence must be protected at every step.

Are the Materials Organic?

Often materials that are not even organic can look like human remains. For example, PVC pipe that is subjected to heat will some-times bubble slightly and fracture to look like portions of tubular bone that is burned to the calcined (or "white") stage (Figure 15.2 illustrates many pieces of PVC pipe affected by heat and fire in a building explosion and fire). How can you tell the difference? Burned bone has most if not all of the organic component destroyed, so only the inorganic component, which is extremely porous, remains (Figure 15.3 illustrates a bone that is burned to the point at which there is no organic component remaining). If you drip water on a piece of PVC or other plastic that has been melted and burned to look like bone, the drop of water will remain as a bead of water and roll off of the material. However, completely burned bone is "thirsty." Why? It has no organic matrix to withstand moisture, and the water soaks in quite quickly. In the past, archaeologists used this test when trying to determine whether they had dried bone or stone that looks like bone (actually, some archaeologists used to put the

FIGURE 15.2 Many fragments of PVC pipe mistaken for bone. *Photo, D. L. France*

questioned material to their tongue, and if it stuck to their tongue, it was bone!).

FIGURE 15.3 Calcined bone. *Photo, D. L. France*

Bone that burns to the point at which the organic component is destroyed is called calcined bone. It is white in color and very often cracks in a circular pattern. In tubular bone, that curved pattern can indicate the direction of travel of the burning. Use the "thumb" rule (Steve Symes, personal communication) in determining the direction of burn; that is, put your thumb so that it fits into the curved fracture pattern. When you pull your thumb away from the fire, that tells you the direction of the burn. See Figure 15.3 for an illustration of calcined bone and Figure 15.4 for an illustration of the curved fracture pattern.

If the Materials Are Organic, Are They Bone?

Some plant materials can look like bone, even to the point of having the internal structure that looks like trabecular bone (this is particularly true in reeds, which sometimes look like ribs). Sometimes it is a little tricky to tell the difference, but if you get a piece of reed wet, it will easily bend (that's how baskets are made), but bone has more mineral component and is more resistant to bending forces even when wet.

If the Materials Are Bone, Are They Human?

There are several ways to determine whether a bone is human, and we discussed some of them in Chapters 3 and 6. As discussed, morphological features are the easiest way to determine the species.

FIGURE 15.4 Burned bone with curved cracks. The arrow shows the direction of travel of burn. *Photo, D. L. France (S. Symes)*

Other ways to determine species (or at least whether the bone is likely human) are by histological methods, in which you take a thin section of bone and look at the microstructure. Artiodactyls (deer, antelope, etc.), for example, have **plexiform** bone as the primary structure. Plexiform bone cells look like "curved bricks" stacked on top of each other (see Figure 15.5). Humans, in contrast, have a series of rounded bone cells that are interspersed within a matrix (Figure 15.6), although other species, such as dog species, have variations of that pattern. DNA tests or antibody tests are other ways to distinguish human from nonhuman bone.

THE BIOLOGICAL PROFILE

After remains are determined to be human, we can then get to the features that help us determine the biological profile of the individual. The age, sex, ancestry, stature, and so on, are all part of a person's biological profile. We discussed other individualizing characteristics (such as anomalies, healed fractures, etc.) in the previous chapter, and we are also concerned with determining the circumstances surrounding the death of that person. We will investigate all of these topics in this chapter.

FIGURE 15.5 Plexiform bone. *Photo, D. L. France*

IMPORTANT NOTE: The diagnoses of age, sex, population affinity, and other features in skeletons are performed through statistical probabilities; that is, we state conclusions based on what has been seen in the majority of skeletons from similar populations.

FIGURE 15.6 Human bone cells. *Photo, D. L. France*

SOLVE THIS CASE!

Throughout this chapter, you will learn the information necessary to solve the identity of the individual in this forensic case. In addition, you will be able to provide information to the medical examiner about the circumstances surrounding the death of this person. This is not a real forensic case, though it is typical of many.

In the spring of this year, a body was discovered in the foothills of the Rocky Mountains by hikers who were out for the first hike of the season. The

FIGURE 15.7 Unknown cranium. *Photo, D. L. France*

body was covered by brush and had mostly decomposed (though some desiccated tissue remained). The hikers called the sheriff's office, and officers responded immediately to the scene. The medical examiner's office removed the body and called the forensic anthropologist (you).

Figures 15.7 through 15.13 are photographs of the remains (after cleaning). You will refer to these photographs and to others in the solution of this case.

FIGURE 15.8 Unknown pubis ventral surface. *Photo, D. L. France*

FIGURE 15.9 Unknown pubic symphysis. *Photo, D. L. France*

FIGURE 15.10 Unknown rib end. *Photo, D. L. France*

Squamosal suture

External auditory meatus

FIGURE 15.11 Right temporal region. *Photo, D. L. France*

FIGURE 15.12 Ribs. *Photo, D. L. France*

FIGURE 15.13 Left side of cranium. *Photo, D. L. France*

DETERMINATION OF SEX

One of the first steps in the determination of the biological profile is to determine the sex of the remains. In general, males are bigger than females: The bones are larger and the areas devoted to muscle attachment are larger and more rugged, just as in other primate species, most notably the gorillas and orangutans, and in many other mammals. This is, in part, **sexual dimorphism.** However, in order to use this size difference in sex determination, the researcher must be able to identify the population from which a skeleton came, as populations differ in average skeletal size and degree of sexual dimorphism and proportions. For example, the people of India have, on average, smaller skeletons than do Australian Aborigines. An adult male Asian Indian skeleton placed alongside a male (or many females) adult Australian Aborigine skeleton would, if judged on the basis of size, be misclassified as a female. A study performed on humeri of Arikara versus Pueblo (North American Native groups) misclassified almost 70 percent of the male Pueblo humeri on the basis of size alone, indicating that relatively great general size differences between these two populations could confuse sex differences (France, 1983). For this reason, particular morphological differences are usually more reliable than are general size differences, particularly if one is not sure from what population an individual is derived. We now turn to these differences in shape (see Figures 15.14 to 15.17 and Table 15.1). Size differences will be studied later.

The most reliable area for the determination of sex is, as one might guess, the pelvic girdle. This is the one area of the body for which a sexual difference has clear natural selection ramifications, for if the birth canal is not large enough in females for the fetus to pass, the infant (and perhaps the mother as well) will die, and the genes from the parents will

"Sex" and "gender" are often used interchangeably, but "sex" describes the biological characteristics while "gender" is the way in which an individual describes himself or herself.

Sexual dimorphism: variations in morphology attributed to the two sexes. The pelvic girdle is the most reliable area for determination of sex.

FIGURE 15.14 Male pelvic girdle. *Drawing, courtesy of Jayne Bellavia*

FIGURE 15.15 Female pelvic girdle. *Drawing, courtesy of Jayne Bellavia*

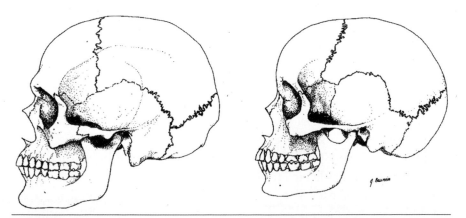

FIGURE 15.16 Cranium and mandible: male (left), female (right). *Drawing, courtesy of Jayne Bellavia*

Table 15.1   Sex-Determination Differences

Pelvic Girdle	Typical Male	Typical Female
A. Subpubic angle	Less than 90 degrees	More than 90 degrees
B. Pubic bone shape	Triangular	Rectangular
C. Ventral arc (see Sutherland and Suchey 1991)	Not well defined	Well defined
D. Subpubic angle shape	Convex	Concave
E. Pelvic outlet	Narrow mediolaterally	Wide mediolaterally
F. Greater sciatic notch	Less than 68 degrees	More than 68 degrees
G. Sacroiliac articulation	Relatively flat	Somewhat raised
H. Acetabulum	Large	Small
I. Obturator foramen	Oval	Triangular
J. Blade of ilium	More vertical	Flared
K. Sacrum	Small, narrower, more curved	Larger, wider, straighter

Cranium	Typical Male	Typical Female
A. Muscle attachment areas: mastoid process, etc.	More pronounced	Less pronounced
B. Superciliary arch/glabella	Raised, more pronounced	Less pronounced
C. Nuchal area	Rougher, more pronounced	Smoother, less pronounced
D. Frontal bone	Slanting	Globular
E. Superior margin of eye orbit	Rounded, blunt	Sharp
F. Palate	Deep	Shallow
G. Chin	More square	One midline point

Other Areas	Typical Male	Typical Female
A. Suprascapular notch on scapula	Often present	Often absent
B. Femur: angle of neck to shaft	Smaller angle	Greater angle
C. Femur: linea aspera	Raised/pronounced	Less pronounced

not be passed on to the next generation (although, of course, modern medical interventions through cesarean sections have circumvented much of the natural-selection pressures in societies in which they are performed). In females, the pubic bone is wider medio-laterally, the subpubic angle is wider (see Figure 15.15 and compare to Figure 15.14), and if a ventral arc (Sutherland and Suchey, 1991) is present (Figure 15.17), the individual is much more likely to be female. Other morphological

FIGURE 15.17 Ventral arc in classic female (above) and absence in classic male (below). *Photo, D. L. France*

differences between males and females are listed in Table 15.1. When the entire skeleton is available for inspection, the pelvic area is the most important for sex determination, but do not ignore the other areas of the skeleton. The more information you can gather, the better.

The preceding standards are for skeletons past adolescence; preadolescent sexing techniques are not very useful and are not as yet widely used. For a more thorough discussion of some of the techniques being studied, consult Krogman and Iscan (1986) and France (1998) for overviews or review forensic anthropology texts.

Size Differences in Sex Determination

It has been widely taught that the second best area for sex determination is the cranium and that measurements of the postcranium should be used largely if the cranium and pelvic girdle are not usable. However, if one knows the population from which a skeleton is derived, postcranial metric measurements can be highly reliable (see Table 15.2) (some researchers report an accuracy rate of over 90 percent in some measurements [cf. Dittrick and Suchey, 1986; France, 1983; Krogman and Iscan, 1986]). Cultural practices and differences in muscle use can reduce the reliability of both cranial morphological and postcranial metric dimorphic differences, however (France, 1986, 1990). For instance, a female who regularly lifts heavy weights will show less difference in upper arm measurements from a male who sits behind a desk and does no heavy lifting. In a culture in which burden baskets are carried on the female heads, the size of the mastoid process will increase so that a population would likely show less dimorphism for that trait.

Correction of Formulae Reported by Bass (1996)

In editions of *Human Osteology* by William Bass (1996, etc.), the entry concerning sex determination in the human humerus as studied by France (1983, 1985) is incorrect. When using Bass's reference, note that the *result of the regression formulae for females is higher than the cutoff, and those for males are lower than the cutoff, even though males are larger than females.*

Parturition Scars

Considerable interest has been shown in various features of the female pelvis thought to be remnants of parturition (birth). Suchey et al. (1979) studied 486 females aged 13 to 99 to determine the effect of parturition on the dorsal surface of the pubic bone and determined that the *number* of full-term pregnancies is only slightly correlated with the severity of the dorsal pitting, although it is likely that a pelvic girdle demonstrating bilateral dorsal pitting and preauricular sulci (a groove on the ilium just ventral to the auricular surface) belonged to a female who has given birth (see Figures 15.18 and 15.19). Interestingly, the age of the individual has a

Table 15.2 Size Differences in Sex Determination

This is not a complete list of sex-determination measurements. For more information, consult Bass (1996), Krogman and Iscan (1986), and Reichs (1997).

Transverse Diameter of Humeral Head (in centimeters)

Population	Sex	No.	Mean	S.D.	Min.	Max.	Cutoff	% Correctly Classified
African Americans*	M	81	4.50	.24	3.76	5.04	4.22	91.88%
	F	79	3.95	.21	3.35	4.40		
Euro-Americans*	M	82	4.50	.23	3.88	5.45	4.22	92.31%
	F	74	3.91	.19	3.45	4.41		
Native Americans								
Pecos Pueblo*	M	72	4.06	.20	3.40	4.54	3.84	89.64%
	F	63	3.60	.17	3.13	3.96		
Arikara*	M	84	4.33	.19	3.87	4.72	4.09	94.97%
	F	75	3.83	.16	3.42	4.26		
Central California	M	150	4.36	.22	4.12	89.5%		
Combined Horizons**	F	155	3.87	.18				

Articular Width of Distal Epiphysis of Humerus (in centimeters)

Population	Sex	No.	Mean	S.D.	Min.	Max.	Cutoff	% Correctly Classified
African Americans*	M	85	4.84	.26	3.97	5.65	4.48	93.53%
	F	85	4.13	.23	3.54	4.58		
Euro-Americans*	M	83	4.70	.25	4.13	5.33	4.37	92.12%
	F	82	4.04	.19	3.60	4.49		
Native Americans								
Pecos Pueblo*	M	83	4.13	.19	3.72	4.66	3.91	87.33%
	F	67	3.74	.15	3.39	4.02		
Arikara*	M	97	4.48	.21	3.82	5.03	4.27	83.06%
	F	86	4.07	.20	3.61	4.48		

Maximum Head Diameter of Femur (in centimeters)

Population	Sex	No.	Mean	S.D.	Min.	Max.	Cutoff	% Correctly Classified
African Americans ***	M	50	4.78	.24			4.50	90%
	F	58	4.19	.24				
Euro-Americans***	M	54	4.82	.23			4.50	90%
	F	53	4.22	.23				
Native Americans								
Central California	M	175	4.70	.25			4.46	88.7%
Combined Horizons**	F	171	4.22	.19				

*France, 1983.

**Central California Combined Horizon (Early Horizon, beginning circa 2500 B.C.E. through Late Horizon beginning after 500 A.D.) (Dittrick and Suchey, 1986).

***Compiled from Iscan and Miller-Shaivitz, 1986; and Krogman and Iscan, 1986.

FIGURE 15.18 Dorsal pitting on left pubic bone. *Photo, D. L. France*

FIGURE 15.19 Preauricular sulcus. *Photo, D. L. France*

positive correlation with the greater changes in the dorsal pitting, and nulliparous (meaning those who have not given birth) females under 30 more frequently have an absence of pitting than those over 30 (Suchey et. al 1979).

DETERMINATION OF AGE

The introduction to human growth and development was covered in some detail in Chapter 4, and to answer some of the questions in this chapter, you may have to review parts of Chapter 4 (particularly as the information relates to subadults). This chapter will use that information as clues to the diagnosis of age as part of the biological profile of an individual, and a few of the charts and illustrations will be repeated for your convenience.

Several methods are commonly used in the determination of the physiological age of a skeleton. Researchers hope that the physiological age will give an accurate estimate of chronological age, but as was discussed in Chapter 4, environmental, nutritional, and disease stresses will often cause changes in the skeleton that will mask the chronological age of the individual.

Subadults

Dental formation (Figure 15.20): Dental formation (mineralization) is more resistant to insults, such as disease and nutritional deficiencies, than are the formation and epiphyseal union of the body skeleton, and so are more reliable age indicators (see Saunders and Katzenberg, 1992; Hillson 2003 for good discussions of dental formation and eruption).

FIGURE 15.20 Dental eruption chart. *Courtesy, D. Ubelaker,* Human Skeletal Remains: Excavation, Analysis, Interpretation, *Washington: Taraxacum Press*

Dental eruption (Figure 15.20): The determination of the ages at which the deciduous and permanent dentition erupts is useful in identifying age to approximately 15 years. The third molar (wisdom tooth) erupts after this time but is so variable in age of eruption (if it erupts, as many never do), that it is not the most reliable age indicator. The chart shown for dental eruption times is based on a Native American population, so be aware that other populations may vary from these time frames.

Bone Growth

Table 15.3   Skeletal Age (in years): Appearance of Ossification Centers and Epiphyseal Fusion in Various Postcranial Bones (IU = In Utero)

Bone	Element	Appearance	Union	Notes
Clavicle	Diaphysis	Week 5 IU		
	Sternal epiphysis		17–30 for males, 16–33 females (Webb and Suchey, 1985)	
	Acromial epiphysis		19–20	
Sternum	Manubrium	Month 5 IU		
	Body sections	1: week 5 IU	All sections to manubrium 15–20 yrs.	
		2 & 3: by week 8 IU	Body section 2 fuses to 3 & 4 at 11–16 yrs.	
		4: after 1 yr	Body section 3 fuses to 4 at 4–10 yrs.	
Cervical vertebrae	Atlas	Week 7–10 IU	Three major sections 5–6 yrs.	
	Axis	Week approx. 8 IU	Major elements 9–10 yrs.	
	Axis dens tip	Approx. 2 years	To dens approx. 12 yrs.	
	C7–C3 (progressing cranially)	By month 4 IU	Neural arches 2–3 yrs.; arches to centrum 3–4 yrs.	
Thoracic vertebrae	Centrum and both neural arches	By week 10 IU	Fuse from caudally to cranially neural arches 1–3 yrs.; arches to centrum 5–6 yrs.	
Lumbar vertebrae	Centrum and both neural arches (progressing caudally)	By month 4 IU	Progressing caudally, arches 1–5 yrs.; arches to centrum 2–4 yrs.	

Table 15.3   (Continued)

Bone	Element	Appearance	Union	Notes
Ilium	Primary center	Months 2–3 IU		
	Iliac crest	12–13 yrs. in females; 14–15 yrs. in males	Completed 18–24 yrs. in females, 17–24 in males (Webb and Suchey, 1985).	
Ischium	Primary center	Months 3–5 IU	Fuses with pubis 4–8 yrs.	
	Ischial tuberosity	13–16 yrs.	Completed by 21–23 yrs.	
Pubis	Primary center	Months 4–6 IU	Fuses with ischium 4–8 yrs.	
Os coxa	All major elements		11–15 yrs. in females, 15–17 yrs. in males	
Sacrum**	Centra (center) for S1–S3	Month 3 IU	S1–3 centra to arches and alae 2–5 yrs.	
	Neural arches for S1–S3	Months 4–6 IU		
	Alae for S1–S3	Months 6–8 IU		
	Centra for S4, S5	Months 4–5 IU	S4, S5 centra to arches 2–6 yrs.	
	Neural arches for S4, S5	Months 6–8 IU		
	Sacral elements		At spinous processes 7–15, alae and centra approx. 12–20 yrs., years from S5 to S1; S1–S2 in the 20s	
	Auricular surface and lateral epiphyses	15–16 yrs.	to sacrum late teens	
Scapula	Body	Week 7–8 IU		
	Coracoid process	Birth–1 yr.	To body 16–17 yrs.	
	Acromion process	13–16 yrs.	18–20 yrs.	
	Inferior angle	15–17 yrs.	20–23 yrs.	
	Vertebral margin	15–17 yrs.	20–23 yrs.	
Humerus	Diaphysis	Week 7 IU		
	Head epiphysis	Birth–6 mos.	To diaphysis: 15–19 in females; 18–22 in males	
	Distal epiphyses	6 mos. to 2 yrs.	To diaphysis: 11–15 in females; 12–17 in males	
	Medial epicondyle	After 4 yrs.	To diaphysis: 13–15 in females; 14–16 in males	

continues

Table 15.3 (Continued)

Bone	Element	Appearance	Union	Notes
Radius	Diaphysis	Week 7 IU		
	Proximal epiphysis	Approx. 5 yrs.	To diaphysis: 11–15 in females; 14–17 in males	
	Distal epiphysis	1–3 yrs.	To diaphysis: 14–17 in females; 16–20 in males	
Ulna	Diaphysis	Week 7 IU		
	Proximal epiphysis	8–10 yrs.	To diaphysis: 12–15 in females; 13–17 in males	
	Distal epiphysis	5–7 yrs.	To diaphysis: 15–17 in females; 17–20 in males	
Hand	Carpals	After birth		
	Metacarpal diaphyses	Week 8–10 IU		
	Metacarpal distal epiphyses 2–5	10 months–2.5 yrs.	to diaphysis: 14–15 in females, 16–17 in males*	
	Phalanges vary			
Femur	Diaphysis	Week 7–8 IU		
	Head	Birth–1 yr.	To diaphysis: 12–16 in females; 14–19 in males	
	Greater trochanter	1–5 yrs.	To diaphysis: 14–16 in females; 16–18 in males	
	Lesser trochanter	7–12 yrs.	To diaphysis: 16–17 yrs.	
	Distal epiphysis	Week 36–40 IU (usually before birth)	To diaphysis: 14–18 in females; 16–20 in males	
Tibia	Diaphysis	Week 8 IU		
	Proximal epiphysis	Near birth	To diaphysis: 13–17 in females; 15–19 in males	
	Distal epiphysis	Approx. 2 yrs.	To diaphysis: 14–16 in females; 15–18 in males	
Fibula	Diaphysis	Week 8 IU		
	Proximal epiphysis	Approx. 4–5 yrs.	To diaphysis: 12–18 in females; 15–20 in males	
	Distal epiphysis	1–2 yrs.	To diaphysis: 12–16 in females; 15–18 in males	
Foot	Calcaneus	Varies: week 3–28 IU		
	Calcaneus posterior epiphysis	4–12 yrs.	Beg. 10–12 in females; 11–14 in males; and completed by 16 in females and 22 in males	

Bone	Element	Appearance	Union	Notes
	Metatarsal diaphysis Metatarsal distal epiphyses	Week 8–10 IU 2–3 yrs.	To diaphysis: 11–13 in females; 14–16 in males; and completed by 16 in females and 18 in males	

Table 15.3 (Continued)

* Scheuer and Black 2000
** Sacral elements fuse at spinous processes first, then lateral borders, and then centra.

Adults

Ectocranial and Endocranial Suture Closure As was discussed in Chapter 4, the use of ectocranial and endocranial suture closure for age determination is problematic because of the wide age ranges between individuals. However, a review of a sample (144 males and 51 females) of crania from people of various ancestries from the Los Angeles Coroner's Office (Baker, 1984) suggests the following general guidelines:

Endocranially

1. If all sutures are completely open, the individual is less than 36 years of age, usually less than 27.

2. If all sutures are completely closed, the individual is 26 or older.

Pubic Symphyseal Face The pubic **symphyseal face** (where the two pubic bones are joined through cartilage in the front of the pelvic girdle) in the young is characterized by an undulating surface that undergoes metamorphosis with advancing age. Several researchers have developed age-determination techniques based on the changing morphology of the symphyseal face. The first was developed by T. W. Todd (1920, 1921) using dissection-room cadavers. McKern and Stewart (1957) developed a technique using American males killed in the Korean War. Both of the samples from which these systems were derived have limitations in that the dissection-room sample used by Todd is based on individuals of uncertain age (Brooks, 1985, 1986), and the Korean War dead sample is predominantly young European American males, with few individuals over age 35.

Starting a little more than 20 years ago, J. M. Suchey, D. Katz, and S. T. Brooks developed a system based on a large sample of individuals for whom legal documentation of age was provided by death certificates. This autopsy-room sample was also more representative of the general population of North America because the majority of the individuals were born throughout the United States and Mexico. At autopsy bone segments were removed from victims of homicides, suicides, accidents, or unexpected natural deaths. This groundbreaking six-phase system has been used extensively around the world, and has been tested in different populations (which is to be expected—remember the scientific method). Within the past few years, several researchers have suggested modifications to the phase descriptions of the Suchey–Brooks system, as well as the addition of a seventh phase to describe older individuals (see Berg 2008; Djuric et al., 2007; Kimmerle et al., 2008; and Hartnett, 2010). K. Hartnett and L. Fulginiti (personal communication with K. Hartnett) examined more than 400 male and more than 200 female pubic bones (and ribs which will be discussed in the appropriate section) with known age at death. They developed somewhat different phase descriptions but incorporated many of the descriptions of the Suchey–Brooks research (although the sample sizes are low in some phases in the Hartnett system). The phase descriptions listed here are the descriptions from Brooks and Suchey (1990), although a few comments from Hartnett (2010) have been added in blue text, and the seventh phase from Hartnett has been included. The original publications should be consulted for exact descriptions of each system (consult Hartnett, 2010; Brooks and Suchey, 1990; Suchey et al., 1986; Suchey and Katz, 1998; and others)! Also, it should be recognized that further testing continues to be performed on each of these systems.

As illustrated in Figures 15.21 through 15.22. The top and bottom bones of the pairs are from two individuals and are two examples of a phase.

Rib Phases

Iscan et al. (1984, 1985) have selected and illustrated specific phases for age-related changes in the sternal end of the fourth right rib (Figures 15.23 to 15.28 and Table 15.4). As with all age determination techniques, this system has been tested, and some revisions to the phase descriptions have been suggested. Some believe that the methods might be applied with some revision to ribs other than the fourth. DiGangi et al. (2009) have also developed a system for the first rib.

FIGURE 15.21 Male pubic symphyses. *Photos, D. L. France*

FIGURE 15.22 Female pubic symphyses. *Photos, D. L. France*

SUCHEY–BROOKS PUBIC AGE PHASE DESCRIPTIONS

Phase I: The symphyseal face has a billowing surface (ridges and furrows) that usually extends to include the pubic tubercle. The horizontal ridges are well marked, and ventral beveling may be commencing. Although ossific nodules may occur on the upper extremity, *a key to the recognition of this phase is the lack of delimitation of either extremity (upper or lower).*

Phase II: The symphyseal face may still show ridge development. *The face has commencing delimitation of lower and/or upper extremities occurring with or without ossific nodules.* The ventral rampart may be in beginning phases as an extension of the bony activity at either or both extremities.

Phase III: The symphyseal face shows lower extremity and *ventral rampart in process of completion.* There is a continuation of fusing ossific nodules forming the upper extremity and along the ventral border. The symphyseal face is smooth or can continue to show distinct ridges. The dorsal plateau is complete. There is an absence of lipping of symphyseal dorsal margin and no bony ligamentous outgrowths.

Phase IV: The symphyseal face is generally fine-grained, although remnants of the old ridge-and-furrow system may still remain. *Usually the oval outline is complete at this stage, but a hiatus can occur in the upper ventral rim.* The pubic tubercle is fully separated from the symphyseal face by definition of the upper extremity. The symphyseal face may have a distinct rim. Ventrally, bony ligamentous outgrowths may occur on the inferior portion of pubic bone adjacent to symphyseal face. If any lipping occurs, it will be slight and located on the dorsal border. The ventral arc may be large and elaborate in females.

Phase V: *The symphyseal face is completely rimmed with some slight depression of the face itself, relative to the rim.* Moderate lipping is usually found on the dorsal border, with more prominent ligamentous outgrowths on the ventral border. There is little or no rim erosion. Breakdown may occur on superior ventral border. Ridges and furrows are absent on the face.

Phase VI: *The symphyseal face shows ongoing depression as the rim erodes.* Ventral ligamentous attachments are marked. In many individuals, the pubic tubercle appears as a separate bony knob. The face may be pitted or porous, giving an appearance of disfigurement with the ongoing process of erratic ossification. Crenulations may occur. The shape of the face is often irregular at this stage. The dorsal surface of the bone is rough and coarse. Projections are present at the medial aspect of the obturator foramen. Bone weight is a major deciding factor between phases 6 and 7.

Phase VII: The face and rim are very irregular in shape and are losing integrity. The rim is complete but is eroding and breaking down, especially on the ventral border. There are no ridges and furrows. The face is porous and macroporous. Distal lipping is pronounced. Bone quality is poor, and the bone is very light and brittle. The dorsal surface of the bone is roughened. The ventral surface of the body is roughened and elaborate. Projections are present at the medial wall of the obturator foramen. The pubic tubercle is elaborate and proliferative.

K. Hartnett (2010b) and L. Fulginiti recently completed a test of the Iscan-Loth rib age-determination system on a series of known individuals from Arizona and suggested some slight changes in the phase descriptions, primarily having to do with the weight and overall condition of the bone (it is commonly understood that the skeleton loses bone mass with increasing age in males and females, though particularly in menopausal females).

Table 15.4   Comparison of the Statistics of the Pubic Symphysis

Male Comparative Statistics

Suchey–Brooks*					Hartnett, K**				
Phase	N	Mean	SD	Range	Phase	N	Mean	SD	Range
1	105	18.5	2.1	15–23	1	14	19.29	1.93	18–22
2	75	23.4	3.6	19–34	2	14	22.14	1.86	20–26
3	51	28.7	6.5	21–46	3	36	29.53	6.63	21–44
4	171	35.2	9.4	23–57	4	69	42.54	8.8	27–61
5	134	45.6	10.4	27–66	5	90	53.87	8.42	37–73
6	203	61.2	12.2	34–86	6	34	63.76	8.06	51–83
7	0	na	na	na	7	96	77.00	9.33	58–97

Female Comparative Statistics

Suchey–Brooks*					Hartnett, K**				
Phase	N	Mean	SD	Range	Phase	N	Mean	SD	Range
1	48	19.4	2.6	15–24	1	5	19.80	1.33	18–22
2	47	25	4.9	19–40	2	5	23.20	2.38	20–25
3	44	30.7	8.1	21–53	3	25	31.44	5.12	24–44
4	39	38.2	10.9	26–70	4	35	43.26	6.12	33–58
5	44	48.1	14.6	25–83	5	32	51.47	3.94	44–60
6	51	60	12.4	42–87	6	35	72.34	7.36	56–86
7	0	na	na	na	7	56	82.54	7.41	62–99

*Brooks and Suchey (1990).
**Hartnett (2010).

Other Systems for Age Estimation

Although only the pubic symphysis and rib age-determination systems have been covered in detail in this book, many other areas of the dentition and skeleton should be used. The auricular surface of the ilium undergoes a metamorphosis with increasing age (see Lovejoy et al., 1985; Buckberry and Chamberlain, 2002; Igarashi et al., 2005). Lamendin et al. (1992) developed a technique for estimating adult age from dentition, which has since been tested on

FIGURE 15.23 Age-related changes at the costochondral junction of the fourth rib in males, phases 0–2. *Photos, M. Y. Iscan*

Phase Descriptions

Male Phase 0 (16 and Younger): The articular surface is flat or billowy with a regular rim and rounded edges. The bone itself is smooth, firm, and very solid (0a, 0b, 0c).

Male Phase 1 (17–19): There is a beginning amorphous indentation in the articular surface, but billowing may also still be present. The rim is rounded and regular. In some cases, scallops may start to appear at the edges. The bone is still firm, smooth, and solid (1a, 1b, 1c).

Male Phase 2 (20–23): The pit is now deeper and has assumed a V-shaped appearance formed by the anterior and posterior walls. The walls are thick and smooth with a scalloped or slightly wavy rim with rounded edges. The bone is firm and solid (2a, 2b, 2c).

Male Phase 3 (24–28): The deepening pit has taken on a narrow to moderate U-shape. Walls are still fairly thick, with rounded edges. Some scalloping may still be present, but the rim is becoming more irregular. The bone is still quite firm and solid (3a, 3b, 3c).

Male Phase 4 (26–32): Pit depth is increasing, but the shape is still a narrow to moderately wide U. The walls are thinner, but the edges remain rounded. The rim is more irregular with no uniform scalloping pattern remaining. There is some decrease in the weight and firmness of the bone; however, the overall quality of the bone is still good (4a, 4b, 4c).

Male Phase 5 (33–42): There is little change in pit depth, but the shape in this phase is predominantly a moderately wide U. Walls show further thinning, and the edges are becoming sharp. Irregularity is increasing in the rim. The scalloping pattern is completely gone and has been replaced with irregular bony projections. The condition of the bone is fairly good; however, there are some signs of deterioration, with evidence of porosity and loss of density (5a, 5b, 5c).

FIGURE 15.24 Age-related changes at the costochondral junction of the fourth rib in males, phases 3–5. *Photos, M. Y. Iscan*

FIGURE 15.25 Age-related changes at the costochondral junction of the fourth rib in males, phases 6–8. *Photos, M. Y. Iscan*

Male Phase 6 (43–55): The pit is noticeably deep, with a wide U-shape. The walls are thin with sharp edges. The rim is irregular and exhibits some rather long bony projections that are frequently more pronounced at the superior and inferior borders. The bone is noticeably lighter in weight, thinner, and more porous, especially inside the pit (6a, 6b, 6c).

Male Phase 7 (54–64): The pit is deep, with a wide to very wide U-shape. The walls are thin and fragile with sharp, irregular edges and bony projections. The bone is light in weight and brittle, with significant deterioration in quality and obvious porosity (7a, 7b, 7c).

Male Phase 8 (65 and older): In this final phase, the pit is very deep and widely U-shaped. In some cases, the floor of the pit is absent or filled with bony projections. The walls are extremely thin, fragile, and brittle, with sharp, highly irregular edges and bony projections. The bone is very lightweight, thin, brittle, friable, and porous. "Window" formation is sometimes seen in the walls (8a, 8b, 8c).

Female Phase 0 (13 and younger): The articular surface is nearly flat, with ridges or billowing. The outer surface of the sternal extremity of the rib is bordered by what appears to be an overlay of bone. The rim is regular with rounded edges, and the bone itself is firm, smooth, and very solid (0a, 0b, 0c).

Female Phase 1 (14–15): A beginning, amorphous indentation can be seen in the articular surface. Ridges or billowing may still be present. The rim is rounded and regular, with a little waviness in some cases. The bone remains solid, firm, and smooth (1a, 1b, 1c).

Female Phase 2 (16–19): The pit is considerably deeper and has assumed a V-shape between the thick, smooth anterior and posterior walls. Some ridges or billowing may still remain inside the pit. The rim is wavy, with some scallops beginning to form at the rounded edge. The bone itself is firm and solid (2a, 2b, 2c).

FIGURE 15.26 Age-related changes at the costochondral junction of the fourth rib in females, phases 0–2. *Photos, M. Y. Iscan*

FIGURE 15.27 Age-related changes at the costochondral junction of the fourth rib in females, phases 3–5. *Photos, M. Y. Iscan*

Female Phase 3 (20–24): There is only slight if any increase in pit depth, but the V-shape is wider, sometimes approaching a narrow U as the walls become a bit thinner. The still-rounded edges now show a pronounced, regular scalloping pattern. At this stage, the anterior or posterior walls may first start to exhibit a central, semicircular arc of bone. The rib is firm and solid (3a, 3b, 3c).

Female Phase 4 (24–32): There is a noticeable increase in the depth of the pit, which now has a wide V-shape or narrow U-shape with, at times, flared edges. The walls are thinner, but the rim remains rounded. Some scalloping is still present, along with the central arc; however, the scallops are not as well defined, and the edges look somewhat worn down. The quality of the bone is fairly good, but there is some decrease in density and firmness (4a, 4b, 4c).

Female Phase 5 (33–46): The depth of the pit stays about the same, but the thinning walls are flaring into a wider V-shape or U-shape. In most cases, a smooth, hard, plaque-like deposit lines at least part of the pit. No regular scalloping pattern remains, and the edge is beginning to sharpen. The rim is becoming more irregular, but the central arc is still the most prominent projection. The bone is noticeably lighter in weight, density, and firmness. The texture is somewhat brittle (5a, 5b, 5c).

Female Phase 6 (43–58): An increase in pit depth is again noted, and its V-shape or U-shape has widened again because of pronounced flaring at the end. The plaque-like deposit may still appear but is rougher and more porous. The walls are quite thin, with sharp edges and an irregular rim. The central arc is less obvious, and, in many cases, sharp points project from the rim of the sternal extremity. The bone itself is fairly thin and brittle, with some signs of deterioration (6a, 6b, 6c).

Female Phase 7 (59–71): In this phase, the depth of the predominantly flared U-shaped pit not only shows no increase but also actually decreases slightly. Irregular bony growths are often seen extruding from the interior of the pit. The central arc is still present in most cases but is now accompanied by pointed projections, often at the superior and inferior borders, yet may be evidenced anywhere around the rim. The very thin walls have irregular rims with sharp edges. The bone is very light, thin, brittle, and fragile, with deterioration most noticeable inside the pit (7a, 7b, 7c).

Female Phase 8 (70 and older): The floor of the U-shaped pit in this final phase is relatively shallow, badly deteriorated, or completely eroded. Sometimes, it is filled with bony growths. The central arc is barely recognizable. The extremely thin, fragile walls have highly irregular rims with very sharp edges and often fairly long projections of bone at the inferior and superior borders. "Window" formation sometimes occurs in the walls. The bone itself is in poor condition: extremely thin, light in weight, brittle, and fragile (8a, 8b, 8c).

FIGURE 15.28 Age-related changes at the costochondral junction of the fourth rib in females, phases 6–8. *Photos, M. Y. Iscan*

Table 15.5 Descriptive Statistics of Metamorphic Phases of Ribs

Iscan et al.*					Hartnet**				
Phase	N	Mean	SD	Range	Phase	N	Mean	SD	Range
0	10			<17	0	na	na	na	na
1	4	17.3	0.5	16.5–18.0	1	20	20.00	1.45	18–22
2	15	21.9	2.13	20.8–23.1	2	27	24.63	2	21–28
3	17	25.9	3.5	24.1–27.7	3	27	32.27	3.69	27–37
4	12	28.2	3.83	25.7–30.6	4	47	42.43	2.98	36–48
5	14	38.8	7	34.4–42.3	5	76	52.05	3.5	45–59
6	17	50	11.17	44.3–55.7	6	61	63.13	3.53	57–70
7	17	59.2	9.52	54.3–64.1	7	75	80.91	6.6	70–97
8	12	71.5	10.27	65.0–78.0	8	na	na	na	na

* Modified from Iscan et al. (1984), Table 2, and Iscan et al. (1985)
** Hartnet (2010)

Iscan et al.*					Hartnett**				
Phase	N	Mean	SD	Range	Phase	N	Mean	SD	Range
0	10			<14	0	na	na	na	na
1	1	14	na	na	1	7	19.57	1.67	18–22
2	5	17.4	1.52	16–20	2	7	25.14	1.17	24–27
3	5	22.6	1.67	20–24	3	22	32.95	3.17	27–38
4	10	27.7	4.62	24–40	4	21	43.52	3.08	39–49
5	17	40	12.22	29–77	5	32	51.69	3.31	47–58
6	18	50.7	14.93	32–79	6	18	67.17	3.41	60–73
7	16	65.2	11.24	48–83	7	71	81.20	6.95	65–99
8	11	76.4	8.83	62–90	8	na	na	na	na

*Modified from Iscan et al. (1984), Table 2, and Iscan et al. (1985).
**Hartnett (2010).

other populations (Prince and Ubelaker, 2002; Martrille et al., 2007; and others). Histological methods use thin cross sections of femora, ribs, and other bones to estimate age (Kerley and Ubelaker, 1978; Stout and Paine, 1992; Cho et al., 2002; and many others).

Old Age

The characteristics of older age (sometimes exaggerated by mechanical stress, as explored in Chapter 14) start by about age 30, at which time the maturation of the skeleton begins to turn to degenerative changes. In addition to the morphological changes seen in the pubic bones, ribs, auricular surface and ribs, pathological conditions such as **arthritis** and **osteophytosis** (see Figure 15.29 for osteophytosis) become more prevalent and pronounced, as does **osteoporosis**, which is increased porosity of the bone, particularly in postmenopausal women (see Figures 15.30a, b, and c). These degenerative changes can give corroborative evidence to determinations of older age but are not reliable by themselves, as injury and disease can cause many of these changes even in a younger skeleton.

FIGURE 15.29 Osteophyte development in vertebra. Note that in addition to the osteophytes, the vertebral bodies have partially collapsed. *Photo, D. L. France*

Dental Wear

The amount of wear on dentition has traditionally been used to determine the *relative* age of individuals within a population (see **seriation** later in this chapter). It should be stressed, however, that humans eat a variety of foods that promote wear at different rates and, consequently, dental wear should not be used to determine the absolute age of an individual, particularly when the dietary and other uses of the teeth in that individual are not known. For examples of teeth with moderate wear and more severe wear, see Figures 15.31a and b.

a   b   c

FIGURE 15.30a–c Progressive degenerative changes in the trabecular bone in the proximal femur.
Photo, D. L. France; material from the National Museum of Natural History

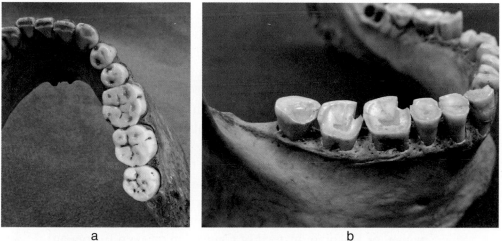

a   b

FIGURE 15.31a and b
Increased wear on mandibular dentition.
Photos, D. L. France

Seriation is a technique used when determining the relative age of many unidentified individuals within a population. In this technique, the remains are usually placed on a table and repositioned so that the bones and teeth show progression in the degree of morphological and/or degenerative changes from the youngest to the presumed oldest of the individuals. Sometimes a chronological age is assigned to the individuals based on this progression, but this should be done with extreme caution when the ages are intended to be used in modern populations to aid in personal identification. Some researchers have used seriated samples in the development of techniques of age determination, but these techniques should be used only with caution and with the full knowledge that they were not based on individuals of documented age.

DETERMINATION OF ANCESTRY

Anthropologists use biological clues to determine the social identity of an individual.

A controversy exists today in anthropology about whether or not "races" exist. For centuries, peoples in the world have been categorized into groups, the most recent titles of which are Caucasoid, Negroid, Mongoloid, and usually Australoid and Polynesian.

There are many reasons to discontinue the use of racial terminology in science. The terms used (as well as the identification of differences between groups in general) have made it easier in history for one group to attempt to demonstrate that its own individuals are more intelligent, more physically fit, and more deserving of the benefits of society than are individuals who are different. Racism has used these terms as its tools.

Racial terms have historically placed people into the four or five regularly named "racial groups," or pigeonholes, even when they do not fit physically. It is generally recognized (and often stated) that there is more variation *within* races as they are usually defined than *between* racial groups. There is a continuum in each characteristic (such as skin color, hair form, etc.) around the world that makes it impossible to categorize every individual in the world into the generally defined racial groups. It is more accurate to investigate traits as **clines** instead of absolute defining characteristics.

Cline: a gradient of frequency of traits in a population.

Forensic physical anthropologists, however, would be derelict in their duty if they ignored the morphological differences that can help to distinguish between individuals. When an anthropologist is asked to help in the identification of a set of remains, part of that identification must include a statement as to probable ancestry or race because this feature is included in the social identity of that person. Anthropologists use biological clues to determine the social identity of an individual. This identity was traditionally made in racial terms and was usually *made by the person himself or herself.* This identification of ancestry is changing, however, in that more of the world's inhabitants are identifying themselves according to the geographic or political location of their ancestors (i.e., German, Spanish, or Bosnian, instead of Caucasian or even European).

The question for forensic physical anthropologists then becomes: How closely can we estimate these more refined identities from the physical remains? The answer is that it depends. If a person identifies himself as an African American, it implies that the person's ancestors were from Africa but that he is himself currently living in America. The forensic anthropologist cannot, of course, determine the person's current place of residence by the bones alone, so we would be perhaps misleading the law enforcement official if we say that this is an "African American." It is, however, becoming more feasible to determine, with experience, statistical analysis, and computer programs, the probable ancestral background with more refinement, even to the point at which many forensic anthropologists can determine the regional ancestry of many Native American groups by looking primarily at the facial morphology. Many forensic physical anthropologists are now stating in their reports that, for instance, the remains are from an individual with European ancestry, or African ancestry, or even eastern European ancestry.

One thing must be stated, however. Even as forensic physical anthropologists are becoming more refined in their abilities to detect clues about ancestry in the skeletal morphology, it is important to realize that no matter what terms are used to describe the individuals we study, they too will (and should) object to the terms if they are misused. If any term is used maliciously, or with intent to create a political hierarchy between recognized groups, its use will increase suspicion and ill will between peoples. Reputable forensic physical anthropologists intend their use of the terms to be clues to the eventual identification of remains and nothing more.

Some have suggested that the concept of population physical differences should not be discussed because it might be too controversial and difficult to discuss. Conversely, it is clearly not appropriate to use the outdated terms of "Caucasoid, Mongoloid, and Negroid" because we can often be more specific about the ancestry of an individual. In the final analysis, the student must decide not only the appropriateness of the terms used but also whether it is legitimate and useful to have scientists endeavor to determine the identity of unidentified human remains and to allow them (and you) to research better methods of determining ancestry. Without that tool, the forensic physical anthropologist is less equipped to help in that identification process.

If we agree philosophically that it is important to study population differences, how do we do it? Should we study measurements we take on skeletal material from different populations and statistically evaluate whether or not they are significantly different between populations? Should we study nonmetric or *morphoscopic* (a term suggested by Ousley and Hefner, 2005) traits that we can see but upon which cannot necessarily perform a metric analysis? It has been argued for decades within forensic anthropology that professionals who are experienced at looking at traits and who know very well the natural variation within populations are likely as good or better at determining ancestry as those who are less experienced and rely on metric analysis, but the answer is more likely that one should use both. There have been many metric methods through the years, but the most sophisticated is *Fordisc*, which is a computer program developed at the University of Tennessee by Richard Jantz and Stephen Ousley in 1993 (now in *Fordisc 3*: Jantz and Ousley, 2005). It incorporates measurements taken by multiple researchers from skeletons around the world and attempts to match a set of measurements taken on an unknown skull with the same measurements representing a population in the world. Although Fordisc is an important tool in forensic anthropology, its application is beyond the scope of this book, so we will now turn to morphoscopic traits.

In Figures 15.32 through 15.34, there are some simple traits that have traditionally been used to assist with the determination of

Table 15.6 Features That Can Aid in the Determination of Ancestry Using the Skull

See also Bass, 1996; Brues, 1977; Dahlberg, 1951; Gill and Rhine, 1990; and Krogman, 1962.

Feature	African Ancestry	Australian Ancestry	European Ancestry	East Asian Ancestry
Central incisors	Blade	Trace	Rarely shoveled	Often shoveled
Cranial shape*	Dolicocranic	Dolicocranic	Mesocranic	Brachycranic
Nasal root (at root of nose)	Wide, rounded	Wide, depressed	Narrow, pinched	Medium, tented
Nasal aperture**	Platyrrhiny	Mesorrhiny	Leptorrhiny	Mesorrhiny
Zygomatic bone	Medium	Large	Retreating	Projecting
External auditory meatus (ear opening)	Round	Round	Round	Oval
Facial shape	Prognathic (lower face projects forward)	Prognathic (nonprojecting)	Orthognathic (lower face)	Medium

*The **cranial shape** is obtained from the **cranial index**, calculated from:

$$\frac{\text{Cranial breadth}}{\text{Cranial length}} \times 100$$

Up to 75 = Dolicocrany (long headed)

75–79.9 = Mesocrany (medium)

80–84.9 = Brachycrany (rounded)

85 and up = Hyperbrachycrany (very rounded) (Bass, 1987)

The **nasal aperture shape is obtained from the nasal index:

$$\frac{\text{Nasal breadth}}{\text{Nasal height}} \times 100$$

Up to 47.9 = Leptorrhiny (narrow)

48–52.9 = Mesorrhiny (medium)

53 and up = Platyrrhiny (wide) (Bass, 1987)

ancestry, but it should be remembered that no one trait (whether in the skeleton or soft tissue) can be used to successfully assess ancestry throughout the world. Most anthropologists use many traits to get a general idea (or the gestalt) of the unknown individual. In Figures 15.35 through 15.47, pay close attention to which traits each of the individuals from different populations exhibit, and then look at the overall face and profile. Note the similarities between groups and the differences between these individuals.

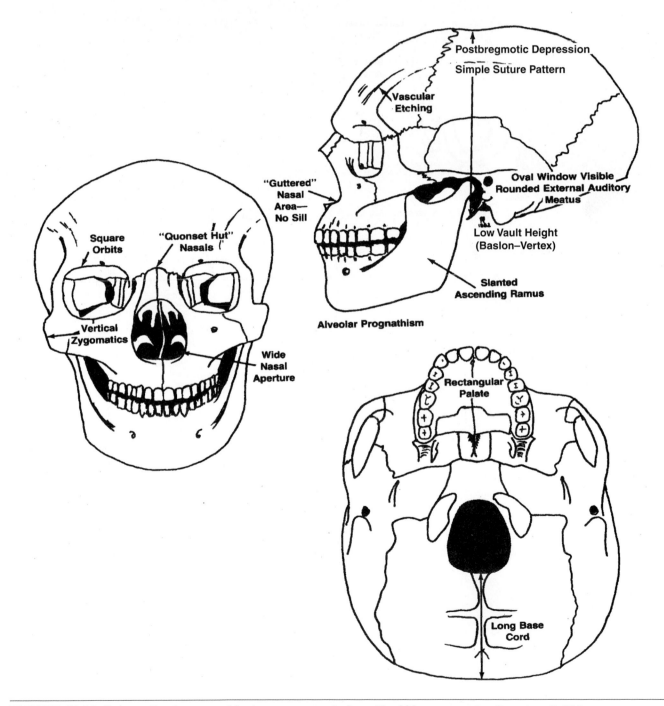

FIGURE 15.32 Schematic diagram of features commonly found in African ancestry. *Drawing, S. Rhine*

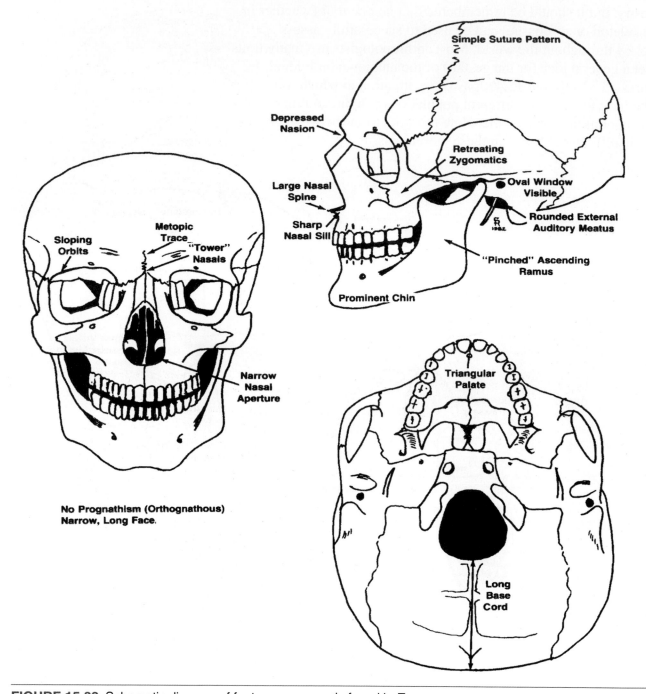

FIGURE 15.33 Schematic diagram of features commonly found in European ancestry. *Drawing, S. Rhine*

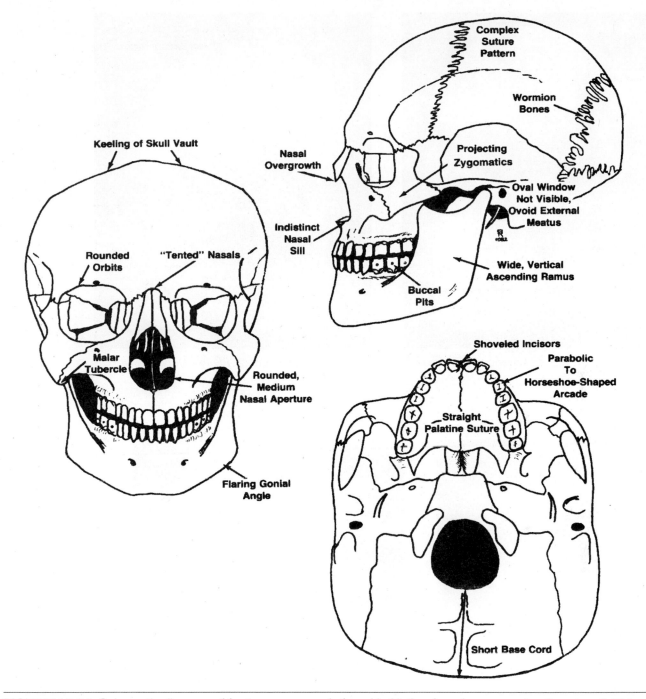

FIGURE 15.34 Schematic diagram of features commonly found in Native American ancestry. *Drawing, S. Rhine*

FIGURE 15.35 Native American (from southwestern part of United States). *Photos, D. L. France*

FIGURE 15.36 Mongolian male. *Photos, D. L. France; skull from National Museum of Natural History*

FIGURE 15.37 Mongolian female. *Photos, D. L. France; skull from National Museum of Natural History*

FIGURE 15.38 European male. *Photos, D. L. France; skull from National Museum of Natural History*

FIGURE 15.39 European American female. *Photos, D. L. France; cast*

FIGURE 15.40 Eskimo male. *Photos, D. L. France; skull from National Museum of Natural History*

FIGURE 15.41 New Britain male. *Photos, D. L. France; skull from National Museum of Natural History*

FIGURE 15.42a Australian female. *Photo, D. L. France of material from National Museum of Natural History*

FIGURE 15.42b Australian female, lateral view. *Photo, D. L. France of material from National Museum of Natural History*

FIGURE 15.43a Australian male. *Photo, D. L. France of material from National Museum of Natural History*

FIGURE 15.43b Australian male. *Photo, D. L. France of material from National Museum of Natural History*

FIGURE 15.44 Japanese male. *Photos, D. L. France; skull from National Museum of Natural History*

FIGURE 15.45 Japanese female. *Photos, D. L. France; skull from National Museum of Natural History*

FIGURE 15.46 African-American male. *Photo, D. L. France; skull from National Museum of Natural History*

FIGURE 15.47 African-American female. *Photo, D. L. France; cast*

ESTIMATION OF STATURE

The following measurements are lengths, measured in millimeters. The results are in inches; that is, measure the bone in millimeters, multiply that measurement by the "factor," and add the constant. Add the 90 percent PI number to the result, and then subtract it from the result for the stature range into which 90 percent of the measured individuals will fall. For example, if the femur length for a male of European ancestry is 454 mm, there is a 90 percent chance that his stature is:

$$0.10560 \,(454) + 19.39 = 67.33 \;+/-\; 2.8"$$

FURTHER TRAINING IN FORENSIC ANTHROPOLOGY

If you are interested in a career in forensic anthropology, it is important to obtain a Ph.D. and then to be certified as an expert by the American Board of Forensic Anthropology (A.B.F.A.). The A.B.F.A. is not a licensing board, and you do not have to have a license to practice forensic anthropology, but being board certified is important when you are being qualified as an expert in court. Anyone can testify in court if asked (and if you receive a subpoena, you must testify in court), but to testify as an expert in your field, you must be qualified as an expert in that courtroom. Being board certified in any

Table 15.7 Estimating Stature*

Factor	Bone Measurement, in mm	Constant	90% PI	N
Males of European Ancestry				
0.05566	Femur Max L + Tibia L	21.64	+/– 2.5"	62
0.05552	Femur Max L + Fibula L	22.00	+/– 2.6"	54
0.10560	Femur Max L	19.39	+/– 2.8"	69
0.10140	Tibia L	30.38	+/– 2.8"	67
0.15890	Ulna L	26.91	+/– 3.1"	62
0.12740	Humerus L	26.79	+/– 3.3"	66
0.16398	Radius L	28.35	+/– 3.3"	59
Females of European Ancestry				
0.06524	Femur Max L + Fibula L	12.94	+/– 2.3"	38
0.06163	Femur Max L + Tibia L	15.43	+/– 2.4"	42
0.11869	Femur Max L	12.43	+/– 2.4"	48
0.11168	Tibia L	24.65	+/– 3.0"	43
0.11827	Humerus L	28.30	+/– 3.1"	45
0.13353	Ulna L	31.99	+/– 3.1"	40
0.18467	Radius L	22.42	+/– 3.4"	38
Males of African Ancestry				
0.16997	Ulna L	21.20	+/– 3.3"	14
0.10521	Tibia L	26.26	+/– 3.8"	19
0.08388	Femur Max L	28.57	+/– 4.0"	17
0.07824	Humerus L	43.19	+/– 4.4"	20
Females of African Ancestry				
0.11640	Femur Max L	11.98	+/– 2.4"	18

*From Ousley, S., "Should We Estimate Biological or Forensic Stature?" *Journal of Forensic Sciences* 40(5): 768–773 (September 1995).

field means that you are more easily qualified as an expert in court because a certifying board states that you have the knowledge, training, and experience sufficient to make you an expert. For further information, search for the American Board of Forensic Anthropology on the web (its address is http://www.theABFA.org).

COMPARISON OF ANTEMORTEM TO POSTMORTEM CHARACTERISTICS

There are several ways to obtain a positive identification of remains. A positive identification is what it states: There are enough characteristics in common with the antemortem records that it is so unlikely that the remains could represent someone else that it represents a positive identification. If fingerprints remain on the body, and if enough points of comparison on a latent print (one made before death in, for example, a police fingerprint record) are the same as on the body, a positive identification can be made (see Chapter 13 for examples of how fingerprints are "typed"). Dental comparisons (dental radiographs before and after death) can also, with enough positive comparison points, be considered a positive identification. DNA (nuclear or mitochondrial, depending on the condition of the remains) can be obtained from the soft tissue or bones and can be compared to DNA obtained from antemortem sources (blood sources, hair from hairbrushes, epithelial cells from toothbrushes, etc.). Radiographs from antemortem sources can also be compared to postmortem radiographs (see Figure 15.48).

Medical interventions done before someone died can also be compared to postmortem information. For example, note the surgical plate used to stabilize the wrist in Figure 15.49, and in particular, note the serial number on the plate (Figure 15.50). Theoretically, one could trace this number through the manufacturer to the hospital, and ultimately to the patient, but sometimes the details of those records are not retained.

There is one complication with all of these techniques: You need to have antemortem information to compare with the postmortem tests. Postmortem DNA samples have to be compared to antemortem DNA samples to be effective as an identification tool. If you do not have the antemortem information, the postmortem information is ineffective. Sometimes the problem in obtaining antemortem data is that there is no hint of where to start looking for that data.

That is where the information from the anthropologist can help. The biological profile (age, sex, ancestry, idiosyncrasies) can help to narrow the search in the missing persons database. The popular technique of applying a face to a skull (variously called "facial reconstruction" or "facial approximation") is part science (in that the average tissue depths come from many measurements of tissue depths) and part artistic rendition (because the exact shape of the nose, the shape of the soft tissue surrounding the eyes, whether or not there are wrinkles on the face, and so on, are not precisely known from the morphology of the skull). The purpose of the facial approximation (Figure 15.51) is to publish the rendition of the face in newspapers and to show it on television to determine if someone will look at it and say "that looks like Uncle Joe who has been missing for 10 years." It should be used as the last-ditch attempt to narrow the search for a missing person and not as a means of positive identification.

FIGURE 15.48 Comparison of antemortem (left) and postmortem (right) radiographs. Arrows show corresponding vertebrae. *Photo, D. L. France*

FIGURE 15.49 Surgical intervention at the wrist. *Photo, D. L. France*

FIGURE 15.50 Surgical intervention at the wrist showing plate with serial number. *Photo, D. L. France*

FIGURE 15.51 Facial approximation technique. *Photo, Sergei Nikitin of his work*

EXERCISE 15.1   NAME _____   SECTION _____   DATE _____

Forensic Anthropology

1. What is the difference between time since death and time since deposition? How might there be a significant difference between those two in how a forensic case is investigated?

2. What are some of the taphonomic influences not mentioned in the text? How might they influence the body (with soft tissue or without soft tissue)?

3. Resolve the unknown individual from the forensic case presented in the first part of this chapter (pages 383-385). What is the age of this individual? The sex? The ancestry? Are there identifiable injuries? Be sure you can justify your responses with appropriate evidence.

FIGURE 15.52a Unknown pubic symphysis. *Photo, D. L. France*

FIGURE 15.52b Unknown pubic bone dorsal surface. *Photo, D. L. France*

4. Figure 15.52a and b show one pubic bone. Figure 15.52a shows the pubic symphysis, and 15.52b shows the dorsal surface.

   a. What is the sex of this individual?

   b. Using the Suchey–Brooks age determination system appropriate to the sex you assigned, to what phase did you assign this pubic bone?

   c. What is the approximate age of this individual?

FIGURE 15.53 Unknown. *Photo, D. L. France*

5. What happened to the individual represented in Figure 15.53? Be as specific as possible in your assessment.

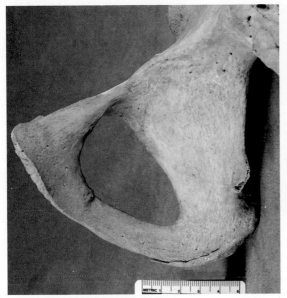

FIGURE 15.54a Unknown. *Photo, D. L. France*

FIGURE 15.54b Unknown. *Photo, D. L. France*

6. a. What is the sex of the individual represented in Figure 15.54a and b? What did you use to make this determination, and why?

    b. What is the approximate age of this individual? How do you know?

FIGURE 15.55 Unknown. *Photo, D. L. France*

7. What happened to the individual shown in Figure 15.55? Be as specific as possible.

FIGURE 15.56 Unknown cranium. *Photo, D. L. France*

8. Describe what happened to the individual in Figure 15.56. Be as specific as possible.

FIGURE 15.57 Shoveled incisor. *Photo, D. L. France*

9. Figure 15.57 shows a shoveled central incisor. To what population(s) does this individual possibly belong (only in terms of likelihood)?

10. Should forensic anthropologists determine the ancestry of an individual in a forensic case? Why or why not? What did you learn from comparing the skulls from Figures 15.35 to 15.47?

REEXAMINING THE ISSUES

- Determinations of aspects of the biologicprofile (age, sex, ancestry, stature, etc.) are based on statistical probabilities derived from studies of populations.

- It is as important to describe skeletal characteristics in a study or report as it is to diagnose what those characteristics mean.

- Forensic anthropology (and forensics in general) has exploded in popularity in recent years, but it is as important to demonstrate what *cannot* be done in forensics as it is to show what *can* be done (and in this chapter, what is and is not possible in investigations of the skeleton).

Glossary

Abducts draws away from.

Acetabulum on the os coxa, the point of articulation with the head of the femur.

Acheulian tools an early tool type that appears in association with *Homo erectus* remains.

Acromion process posterior projection on the superior scapula.

Adapids members of the Eocene family Adapidae, the fossils of which are found in Europe.

Adapoidea one of two Eocene superfamilies of euprimates (the other is Omomyoidea), the first recognizable primates. Adapoidea is thought to be more lemur-like although there are differences from modern lemurs.

Adaptive radiation rapid increase and spread of an evolving group of organisms that spread into and adapt to new ecological niches.

Adenine One of four chemical bases central to the structure of a DNA nucleotide.

Ad-lib sampling a technique in which primate behavior is recorded by observing any behavior of a group that is interesting and/or readily observable.

Afradapis an adipiform primate from the late Eocene in the Fayum Depression in northern Egypt.

Agglutination clumping of red blood cells as a result of the destruction of blood antigens by antibodies.

Ala one of the "wings" of the fleshy nose or bony sacrum.

Allele alternative form of a gene.

Alveolare the apex of the septum between the upper central incisors.

Ameloblasts cells that secrete enamel.

Amphiarthrosis (plural: amphiarthroses) a joint in which some movement is allowed.

Amphipithecids members of the Eocene family Amphipithecidae, the fossils of which are found in Asia.

Analogy characters that are morphological and functionally similar between species but are not shared by common descent.

Anatomical position body with arms by side, palms forward.

Anencephaly a pathological condition in which the full brain of a fetus does not develop.

Antemortem before death.

Anterior in front of (*similar to* Ventral).

Anthropoidea suborder of primates that includes monkeys, apes, and humans.

Antibodies proteins produced by the body in response to, and in an attempt to neutralize, a foreign antigen.

Antigens as used in this book, proteins that occur on the blood cells of an individual.

Apomorphic derived characters.

Appendicular the skeleton of the limbs.

Arboreal theory theory that the characters found on most primates are adaptations that allow primates to pursue an arboreal lifestyle.

Arthritis inflammation of a joint surface that can cause bony changes at and around the joint.

Articulation in osteology, where two bones move against each other.

Ascending ramus of the mandible, the vertical aspect of bone above the gonial angle to the condyles.

Assortative mating occurs when individuals mate more frequently and more consistently with those similar to themselves or dissimilar to themselves in those traits.

Atlas first cervical vertebra.

Auricular surface of the ilium, an area which articulates with the sacrum.

Australopithecus extinct genus of hominids that lived during the Plio-Pleistocene. This genus is usually divided into the gracile species *africanus,* the robust species *robustus, boisei,* and *aethiopicus,* and the very early species *afarensis* (see also *Paranthropus*)

Autosomes chromosomes that carry DNA for all characteristics except for the sex of the individual.

Axial the skeleton of the head and trunk.

Axis second cervical vertebra.

Basilar suture *see* Spheno-occipital synchondrosis.

Basion the midpoint of the anterior margin of the foramen magnum.

Bilophodont molars usually have four cusps situated in two parallel rows.

Binocular vision vision in which the visual field between the two eyes overlap, creating a greater depth of field.

Binomial in genetics, the mathematical equation consisting of two terms; in classification, a two-word scientific name consisting of a genus name and a species name.

Biological profile age, sex, ancestry, stature, and other aspects that characterize an individual.

Biped an animal that habitually walks on two legs.

Brachial index measures the relative lengths of the upper and lower arm.

Brachiator an animal that habitually swings under branches in arm-over-arm locomotion.

Brachycephaly having a round head (*brachycrany* in the dry cranium).

Bregma the intersection of the coronal and sagittal sutures.

Buccal in the mouth toward the cheek.

Calcaneus the largest bone of the ankle.

Callimiconidae primitive New World monkey family of Goeldi's marmoset.

Callitrichidae primitive New World monkey family of tamarins and marmosets.

Canine single-rooted teeth lateral to the incisors in the anterior mandible and maxilla.

Capitate one of the bones of the wrist.

Carpals the bones of the wrist.

Catarrhini anthropoid infraorder of Old World monkeys, apes, and humans.

Caudal toward the tail.

Cavity an open area.

Cebidae New World monkey family including squirrel, spider, capuchin, howler, and other monkey species.

Ceboidea anthropoid superfamily of New World monkeys.

Centromere The place where two sister chromatids are joined.

Cercopithecidae Old World monkey family that includes baboons, macaques, mangabeys, guenons, and others.

Cercopithecinae Old World monkey subfamily.

Cercopithecoidea Old World monkey superfamily.

Cervical vertebra one of the seven (the number sometimes varies) uppermost vertebrae, in the neck.

Chain of evidence/chain of custody the record of contact with and custody of evidence.

Characters morphological traits.

Chi-square a measure of the statistical significance of the deviation of a frequency of occurrences from an expected frequency.

Chondroblasts cartilage-forming cells.

Chondroclasts cartilage-removing cells.

Chromosome a thread-like collection of DNA molecules. Chromosomes carry genes.

Chromatid One of two identical copies of DNA comprising a replicated chromosome.

Clade a group of organisms related through a common ancestor.

Cladistics (cladism) classification based exclusively on genealogy, such that a group of species is all descended from a common ancestor.

Clavicle the collarbone, maintains a constant distance between the scapula and the sternum.

Cline a gradient of frequency of traits in a population.

Cloaca in osteology, an opening in the bone through which pus drains.

Coccygeal vertebra one of the most inferior vertebrae in the spinal column.

Codominant alleles alleles that, when paired in an organism, are both expressed (either additively or distinctively).

Codons the three-base code for amino acids on the messenger RNA chain.

Colobidae Old World monkey family that includes langurs and other colobine monkeys.

Comminuted fracture fracture into many pieces.

Compound fracture bone fracture in which the broken end(s) of the bone erupt through the skin.

Condylar index measures the position of the foramen magnum.

Condyle rounded process at the point of articulation with another bone.

Coracoid process anterior projection on the superior scapula.

Core in dermatoglyphics, the centralmost ridge at the approximate center of a ridge pattern.

Coronal plane the plane through the body parallel to the coronal suture (dividing anterior from posterior).

Coronal suture on the cranium, posterior to the frontal bone, coursing laterally.

Coronoid process the area of the mandible that is the insertion of the masseter muscle (one of the muscles of chewing).

Correlation coefficient a measure of linear dependence or mutual relationship between two random variables.

Costal referring to a rib.

Costal facets/pits facets on thoracic vertebrae for the articulation of ribs.

Costochondral cartilage at the sternal end of the ribs.

Coxa *see* Os coxa.

Cranial toward the head.

Craniostenosis premature fusion of the sutures of the cranium.

Crest a projecting ridge.

Crossing over the exchange of genetic information between homologous chromosomes during the first meiotic division.

Crown the part of a tooth above the gum line; covered by enamel.

Crural referring to the leg or thigh.

Crural index measures the relative lengths of the thigh and leg bones.

Cuboid one of the bones of the ankle.

Cytosine one of four chemical bases central to the structure of a DNA nucleotide.

Deciduous teeth subadult teeth.

Delta point in dermatoglyphics where three ridges diverge, or the point nearest the center of divergence of the type lines (also called triradius).

Dens *see* Odontoid process.

Dental formula a count of the number and kinds of teeth an animal has, given for ¼ of the mouth. The human adult formula is 2:1:2:3, which indicates two incisors, one canine, two premolars, and three molars.

Deoxyribonucleic acid large molecules composed of four chemical bases: adenine, guanine, cytosine, and thymine, as well as phosphates and sugars. These are the genetic codes for the assembly of amino acids, which are building blocks of proteins.

Dependent variables variables that can be controlled in the experiment.

Derived characters that evolve from more primitive characters, and are usually acquired by few members of an evolutionary group (they are not found in earlier ancestors).

Dermatoglyphics the study of the ridge patterns on the skin of the hands and feet.

Diaphysis primary centers of bone growth; the shafts of long bones.

Diastema in general, a gap. In primates this usually refers to a gap in the mandibular teeth that makes room for the maxillary canines.

Distal away from the center of the body. In the mouth, this term refers to the direction away from the anterior midline.

DNA *see* Deoxyribonucleic acid.

DNA typing a means of identification (in any plant or animal with DNA) using genetic codes.

Dolicocephaly having a long head (*dolicocrany* in the dry cranium).

Dominant allele an allele that is phenotypically expressed in the heterozygote and that prevents the expression of the recessive allele.

Dorsal in back of (*similar to* Posterior).

Dryopithecus an extinct genus of hominoids from the Miocene.

Eburnation polishing of bone caused by bone rubbing on bone.

Ectocranium outside the cranium.

Endochondral bone bone formed from a cartilage matrix that is derived from specialized mesenchymal cells.

Endocranium inside the cranium.

Enzyme a protein that accelerates a specific chemical reaction in a living system.

Epiphysis secondary centers of bone growth at the ends of long bones. These centers eventually unite with the diaphysis, at which time longitudinal growth ceases at that location.

Ethmoid bone paired bone on the medial eye orbit.

Eukaryotic cells that have a discrete nucleus and other organelles contained within a plasma membrane.

Euprimates modern primates.

Evolutionary classification classifications based on descent from a common ancestor, as are clades, but also take into account different rates of evolution in different lineages.

External outside of.

External auditory meatus the bony opening of the ear.

Facet a smooth, small point of articulation.

Fayum a primate site in Egypt that has yielded several Oligocene fossil forms.

Femur the bone of the thigh.

Fibula the small bone of the leg, lateral to the tibia.

First cuneiform one of the bones of the ankle.

Focal sampling the researcher records the behavior of a specific animal.

Fontanelle membranous space between cranial bones in fetal life and infancy.

Foramen a hole or opening.

Foramen magnum "big hole" on the base of the cranium in the occipital bone. This is where the spinal nerves (cord) enter the cranium.

Foramen ovale opening on the sphenoid bone (near posterior margin of greater wing.

Forensic physical anthropology sometimes shortened to forensic anthropology, this is the application of physical/biological methods to answer medicolegal questions.

Forensic science the application of scientific methods to the law.

Fossa a pit, depression, or cavity.

Founder effect a case in which a newly isolated sample from the original population soon diverges genetically from the parent population.

Fovea capitis a pit on the head of the femur that connects the femur to the acetabulum and through which blood is carried to the femur.

Frankfort plane a standard position of reference in which the upper border of the external auditory meatus is on a horizontal plane with the lower border of the eye.

Frontal bone a bone on the anterosuperior portion of the cranium.

Gametes sex cells (sperm or ova) that contain half of the chromosomes of the adult of that species.

Gene section of DNA responsible for the ultimate synthesis of a specific gene product, usually a polypeptide chain of amino acids; portion of DNA with a detectable function.

Gene flow a movement of genes from one population to another.

Gene pool the total complement of genes in a population.

Genetic drift an effect of sampling error and chance fluctuations in gene frequency; a function of population size.

Genome a complete set of chromosomes (and genes) inherited as a unit from one parent.

Genotype the genetic constitution (gene makeup) of an organism.

Gigantopithecus a genus of very large Miocene to Pleistocene hominoids.

Glabella the most forward-projecting point of the forehead in the midline at the level of the supraorbital ridges, and superior to the nasofrontal suture.

Glenoid process (or fossa) on the lateral scapula, this is the point of articulation of the scapula with the head of the humerus.

Gnathion lowest median point on the lower border of the mandible.

Gradistic classifications based on gross anatomy and behaviors.

Greater multangular one of the bones of the wrist.

Greater sciatic notch a deep incurve on the posterior ilium.

Guanine one of four chemical bases central to the structure of a DNA nucleotide.

Hamate one of the bones of the wrist.

Haplorhini primate suborder that includes all higher primates, including tarsiers.

Hardy–Weinberg equilibrium an expression of predicted genetic equilibrium that would occur under ideal conditions.

Harris lines (growth arrest lines) areas of slowed bone growth resulting in a line of dense bone cells.

Hemizygous used in reference to males in sex-linked traits, as most of these traits are contained on the X chromosome, and have no corresponding locus on the Y chromosome.

Heterozygote an organism with unlike members of any given pair or series of alleles at a particular locus (example: AA or BB).

Hominidae human family.

Hominids common term to describe humans and other upright bipeds in the fossil record.

Hominin modern humans and extinct bipedal relatives.

Hominoid common term to describe lesser apes, great apes, and humans.

Hominoidea Old World superfamily in which apes and humans are classified.

Homo the genus into which humans are categorized.

Homo erectus the hominid species which occurred between *H. habilis* and *H. sapiens*.

Homo habilis the hominid species that occurred between *Australopithecus* and *Homo erectus*.

Homo sapiens the genus and species of modern and archaic humans.

Homologous chromosomes chromosomes that carry genetic information for the same trait, though not necessarily the same codes for that trait. For instance, one chromosome may carry the dominant code for a trait, the homologous chromosome may carry the recessive code for the same trait, but they both code for the same trait.

Homology characters that are morphologically and functionally similar between species resulting from common descent.

Homozygote an organism whose chromosomes carry identical members of a given pair of alleles (example: AA or BB or aa).

Humerus the bone of the arm, and the largest bone of the upper limb.

Hylobatidae hominoid family that includes gibbons and siamangs.

Hyoid bone small bone suspended below the mandible by many muscles acting on the tongue, pharynx, and neck.

Iliac crest the rounded superior margin of the ilium.

Ilium the upper bone of the os coxa.

Incisor single-rooted tooth at the anterior of mouth in both maxilla and mandible, central to canines.

Incomplete fracture fractures in which the bone is not completely broken.

Independent variables the subjects of the hypothesis that, by definition, are not controlled.

Inferior lower.

Inion an intersection in the midline with a line drawn tangent to the uppermost convexity of the right and left superior nuchal lines.

Intermembral index measures the relative lengths of the upper and lower limbs.

Interspecies variation variation between species.

Internal inside of.

Intramembranous bone bones that are transformed from mesenchymal tissues, including some bones of the cranial vault, facial bones, mandible, and clavicle.

Intraspecies variation variation within species.

Involucrum a shell surrounding a sequestrum in an infected bone.

Ischial tuberosity a large prominence on the posterior ischium.

Ischium the inferoposterior bone of the os coxa.

Karyotype The summary of the chromosomes within a nucleus often viewed as an image.

Knuckle-walking locomotor mode of chimpanzees and gorillas in which the animal walks on the knuckles of the front limbs and on the soles of the feet.

Labial in the mouth, toward the lips.

Lacrimal bone on the medial eye orbit.

Lambdoidal suture on the posterior cranium, between the occipital and parietal bones.

Lateral to the side, away from the midline.

Lateral malleolus a downward-projecting process of bone on the lateral fibula.

Leg in popular language, refers to the entire lower limb; in anatomical terms it refers to the area defined by the tibia and fibula.

Lemuroidea prosimian superfamily of lemurs, found today only on Madagascar.

Leptorrhiny narrow nasal aperture.

Lesser multangular (trapezoid) one of the bones of the wrist.

Levallois technique a technique of tool manufacture associated with Neanderthal remains.

Ligament strong connective tissue that holds bones in proximity at a joint.

Ligamentum teres strong ligament that maintains the close contact between the head of the femur and the acetabulum.

Linea aspera long raised and roughened line coursing longitudinally on the posterior femur. This is the point of insertion of muscles of the thigh.

Lingual in the mouth, toward the tongue.

Locus location on a chromosome for a particular trait.

Longitudinal coursing or placed lengthwise (*opposite of* Transverse).

Lorisoidea prosimian superfamily of lorises found in Africa and southern Asia.

"Lucy" a specimen of *Australopithecus afarensis* found in Hadar, Ethiopia, in 1974.

Lumbar vertebra one of the bones of the spinal column in the lower back.

Lunate bone   one of the bones of the wrist.

Mandible   bone of the lower jaw.

Mandibular condyles   the articular surfaces of the mandible that articulates with the cranium at the temporomandibular joint.

Mandibular foramen   on the medial side of the mandible, a foramen that allows passage of the mental nerve and blood vessels on either side of the midline.

Manubrium   the most superior portion of the sternum, usually fused to the rest of the sternum in the adult.

Masseter muscle   one of the muscles of chewing.

Mastoid process   a downward-projecting process of bone on the temporal bone, onto which the sternocleidomastoid muscle inserts.

Maxilla   bone of the lower face on the cranium.

Mean   the average of a set of measurements, calculated by adding the terms and dividing their sum by the number of terms.

Meatus   a canal.

Medial   toward the midline.

Medial malleolus   a downward-projecting process of bone on the medial tibia.

Meiosis   the process of cell division that results in half of the full complement of chromosomes for gametes, or sex cells.

Mendel's Principle of Segregation   *see* Principle of Segregation.

Mental eminence   chin.

Mental foramen   foramen on the mandible (paired) on the lateral aspect.

Mesenchymal cells   unspecialized cells in the embryo that give rise to all connective tissue, including cartilage, bone, and teeth (as well as some other types of cells).

Mesial   in the mouth, direction toward the anterior midline.

Mesocephaly   having a medium-shaped head (in between long and round) (*mesocrany* in the dry cranium).

Mesorrhiny   nasal aperture of medium size.

Metacarpals   the five bones of the palm.

Metaphysis   location of bone growth between the diaphysis and epiphysis.

Metastasis   the spread of a cancerous growth to areas of the body other than where it originated.

Metatarsals   the five bones of the main part of the foot.

Metopic suture   between the two halves of the frontal bone in very young individuals, usually missing or only a remnant in the adult.

Microcephalic   pathologically small brain size, usually resulting in mental retardation.

Mitochondrial DNA   deoxyribonucleic acid that occurs outside the nucleus of the cell, in the mitochondria, and is therefore passed from generation to generation only by females.

Mitosis   cell replication and division in which the two resulting cells each have a full complement of genetic information.

Molar   multiple-cusped and multiple-rooted tooth in distal part of mouth.

Molecular clock   calculation from biomolecular data of the time of separation of evolutionary taxa.

Mollison's craniophore   an apparatus that places the cranium in the Frankfort plane.

Monosomy   the absence of one of a pair of chromosomes in a daughter cell.

Mousterian tool   Upper Paleolithic stone tools associated with Archaic *Homo sapiens* and *Homo neandertalensis*.

Mutation   an actual alteration in genetic material. This is the basic creative force in evolution and the only way to produce entirely new variation in a population. This is a change in DNA.

Nasal bone   paired bones on the medial aspect of the nose.

Nasion   the midline point of intersection of the internasal suture with the nasofrontal suture; the point where the two nasal bones and the frontal bone meet.

Nasospinale   the midpoint of a line drawn connecting the two lower margins of the right and left nasal apertures.

Natural selection   a process that acts on population variation. Natural selection is differential net reproductive success, in which individuals best adapted to an environment will pass on their genetic information to the next generation.

Navicular   one of the bones of the wrist (also called scaphoid), and also one of the bones of the ankle.

Neanderthals   once thought of as a population of archaic *Homo sapiens* in Europe, most paleoanthropologists place Neanderthals in their own species that is transitional from *Homo erectus* to *Homo sapiens*.

Neck   of a tooth, the constricted area just below the crown.

Niche   the environment to which a species is adapted, including diet, habitat preference, activity pattern, and other features.

Nondisjunction   failure of chromosome pairs to separate correctly during cell division.

Nonmetric traits   traits that are not measured but are scored as present or absent (though sometimes scored as small, medium, or large).

Normal distribution   a probability distribution depicted graphically by a bell-shaped curve symmetrical about the mean.

Notharctids   members of the Eocene family Notharctidae, the fossils of which are found in North America.

Nuchal   referring to the neck (cervical area of the body).

Nuchal index   measures the area given for the origin of nuchal muscles.

Nucleotide   one genetic base (*see* Deoxyribonucleic acid) attached to a sugar and phosphate group.

Occipital bone   bone of the posterior inferior portion of the cranium.

Occipital condyles   area of articulation between the occipital bone and the atlas (first cervical) vertebra.

Occlusal   the chewing surface of the teeth.

Odontoblasts   dentin-forming cells.

Odontoid process   a prominence on the second cervical vertebra around which the first cervical vertebra rotates.

Oldowan tool   the earliest recognized stone tool.

Omomyoidea   one of two Eocene superfamilies of euprimates (the other is Adapoida), the first recognizable primates. Omomyoidea is thought to be more tarsier-like.

Opisthocranion   the most posterior point on the cranium not on the external occipital protuberance.

Orale   a point on the hard palate where a line drawn tangent to the curves in the alveolar margin in back of the two medial incisor teeth crosses the midline.

Origin of a muscle   area of its attachment to bone that remains relatively fixed during the contraction of that muscle.

Os coxa   one of the bones of the hip, consisting of the fused ilium, ischium, and pubis (os pubis) (also called innominate).

Ossification centers   the points at which osteoblasts initially invade the cartilage to lay down bone.

Osteoblasts   bone-forming cells.

Osteoclasts   bone-destroying cells.

Osteocyte   bone cell.

Osteophyte   a bony projection (sometimes called a bone spur) that occurs along a joint surface, often in reference to bony outgrowths along the vertebral borders.

Osteophytosis   a condition characterized by multiple osteophytes.

Osteoporosis   increased porosity of bone.

Palatal index   measures the shape of the palate.

Palatine bone   paired bone on the posterior palate.

Parietal bone   paired bone on the laterosuperior portions of the cranium.

Parturition scars   remnants in the female pelvic girdle as a result of having given birth. One example of this is dorsal pitting on the dorsal surface of the pubic bone.

Pascal's triangle   a short-hand method of determining coefficients in binomial equations.

Patella   kneecap, a large sesamoid bone.

Pentadactyly   five digits.

Perimortem   at or around the time of death.

Periosteum   thin soft-tissue layer surrounding bone.

Periostitis   an inflammation of the periosteum.

Phalanges   the bones of the fingers and toes.

Phenotype   characteristics of an individual visually observed or discernable by other means.

Phylogenetic classification scheme   a classification scheme based on evolutionary relationships, usually including a time line.

Phylogeny   the study of evolutionary lines of descent.

Piezoelectric effect   a slight electric charge produced in the bone that may produce more bone.

Pisiform   one of the bones of the wrist.

Platyrrhini   an infraorder of Anthropoidea of New World monkeys.

Platyrrhiny   wide nasal aperture.

Pleisomorphic   primitive characters.

Plexiform bone   bone cells that are similar to stacked curved bricks when viewed in microscopic cross section.

Polar bodies   during oogenesis (production of eggs during meiosis), those nonviable cells that give up their cytoplasm for the one viable gamete produced (also, in another context, a big white bear).

Polymerase chain reaction (PCR)   a method for making multiple copies of a particular DNA sequence.

Pongid   common term to describe apes.

Pongidae   hominoid family of apes.

Porion   the most anterior point on the upper alveolar process in the midline.

Posterior   behind, toward the back (*similar to* Dorsal).

Postmortem   after death.

Premolar   tooth between canine and molar (also called bicuspids). There are no deciduous premolars in humans.

Primates   the order of mammals to which prosimians, monkeys, apes, and humans belong.

Primitive   characters that are found with phylogenetically older organisms, and are usually shared with many organisms in an evolutionary group.

Principle of Independent Assortment   members of different homologous chromosomes separate independently into gametes. The way in which one set of homologous chromosomes separates into cells has no effect on other homologous chromosome separations.

Principle of Segregation   parental traits do not blend in the offspring during meiosis. Homologous chromosomes, carrying the genes for each of those traits, separate into two different cells.

Process   any outgrowth or prominence of bone.

Proconsul   an extinct genus of early Miocene hominoid.

Prognathism   projection of the lower face.

Prokaryotic   prokaryotic cells lack a nucleus and other organelles that are within the plasma membrane.

Pronation   rotation of the hand and forearm so that the palm faces dorsally or toward the body. Some primates can perform the same action with the foot.

Prosimian   common term for Prosimii, the suborder of primates which includes lemurs, lorises, and tarsiers.

Prosthion   the most anterior point on the upper alveolar process in the midline.

Proximal   toward the center of the body.

Pseudoarthrosis   false joint caused by unreduced dislocation or unstable fracture.

Pubic symphysis   the face of the pubic bone at its medial side.

Pubis (or os pubis)   the anterior bone of the os coxa.

Punctuated equilibria   slow evolutionary rates of change punctuated by spurts of sudden significant change.

Punnett square   a short-hand tool used to calculate offspring genotypes from specific parental genotypes.

Quadruped   animal that habitually walks on four limbs.

Radius   the lateral bone of the forearm.

Ramapithecus   an extinct genus of hominoid of the Miocene, now considered likely to be a female *Sivapithecus*.

Recessive allele   an allele that is not expressed when paired with a dominant allele.

Ribosomes   organelles made of ribosomal RNA (ribonucleic acid) responsible for protein synthesis.

Ridge count   the number of ridges transecting a straight line drawn from the core to the delta.

Root   of a tooth, that area below the neck of the tooth that is contained within the tooth socket of the mandible or maxilla.

Sacral vertebra   bone of the spinal column in the lower back, all fused together in the adult to form the sacrum.

Sacrum   fused vertebrae (usually five) between the os coxae.

Sagittal section   any section of the body parallel to the midsagittal plane.

Sagittal suture   on the cranial midline, coursing in an anteroposterior direction, separating the parietal bones.

Scan sampling   in recording primate behavior, method in which the researcher records the behavior of a group of primates or an individual primate at regular time intervals.

Scapula   the shoulder blade, a triangular flat bone on the upper back.

Scapular spine   The raised surface on the dorsal scapula that leads to the acromion process.

Scaphoid   another term for navicular in the carpals.

Second cuneiform   one of the bones of the ankle.

Sectorial lower first premolar   single-cusped premolar that forms a cutting complex with the upper canine, found in modern pongids and some monkeys.

Semilunar notch   on the proximal ulna, articulates with the distal humerus.

Semiorder   taxonomic classification between suborder and order.

Sequestrum   a part of bone that is isolated from the rest of the bone (and body) by an involucrum.

Seriation   a technique of placing remains "in series," usually for age determination.

Sesamoid bone   a bone encased in tendon. The patella is the largest sesamoid bone in the human body.

Sex linked   genes that occur on the chromosomes that determine an individual's sex.

Sexual dimorphism   variations in morphology attributed to the two sexes.

Shoveled incisors   incisors shaped like a shovel when viewed from the edge of the tooth toward the gum line.

Sinus   bone cavity lined with mucous membranes.

Sivapithecus   an extinct genus of hominoid of the Miocene.

Slow quadrumanos climbing   locomotion found only in orangutans, in which they use their forelimbs and hindlimbs to grasp branches and other supports as they move slowly through the trees.

Slow quadrupedal climbing   locomotion found only in pottos of Africa and lorises of South Asia, in which they move slowly on four limbs.

Sphenoid bone   bone in the interior cranium that is also visible in the lateral eye orbit, and lateral and inferior cranium.

Spheno-occipital synchondrosis   (often called basilar suture, though it is not a suture), between the occipital and sphenoid bones on the base of the cranium.

Squamosal suture   between the parietal and the temporal bones.

Standard deviation   a gauge of variation or spread within a set of measurements.

Staphylion   the midpoint of a line drawn connecting the most forward points on the curves in the posterior margin of the palate.

Stasis   situation in evolutionary history in which there is no morphological change in an organism for long periods of geologic time.

Sternum   breastbone, at the anterior thorax, that consists of the manubrium, body, and xiphoid process.

Strepsirhini   primate suborder that includes lemurs and lorises.

Superciliary arch   *see* Supraorbital torus.

Superficial   near the surface.

Superior   above, top.

Superior nuchal line   superiormost point of attachment of the nuchal muscles on the occipital bone. This becomes a raised crest in some animals.

Supination   turning of the palm of the hand upward.

Supraorbital index   measures the height of the skull.

Supraorbital torus   also called superciliary arch or brow ridges, a rounded process of bone above the eye orbits.

Suture   form of articulation found on a cranium.

Symphyseal face   on the pubis, where the two pubic bones are joined through cartilage in the front of the pelvic girdle.

Synapomorphs   derived characters shared among members of an evolutionary group.

Synarthrosis (plural: **synarthroses**)   joints in which the bones are so tightly bound by cartilage that there is virtually no movement between them (such as at the sutures of the cranium).

Synovial fluid   fluid the consistency of egg whites that lubricates some joints.

Talus   one of the bones of the ankle.

Taphonomy   the events that happen to a body after death. This includes the environment, time, scavengers, and so on.

Tarsals   the seven bones of the ankle.

Tarsiioidea   prosimian superfamily of tarsiers, found in southern Asia.

Temporal bone   paired bone on the lateral inferior portions of the cranium.

Temporal line   point of origin of the temporal muscle.

Temporal muscle   a major muscle of mastication (chewing), which originates on the temporal line of the temporal bone and inserts on the mandible.

Temporomandibular joint   the joint at which the mandible articulates with the cranium.

Tendon   tough fibrous tissue at the end of the insertion of a muscle that attaches that muscle to bone.

Third cuneiform   one of the bones of the ankle.

Thoracic vertebra   one of the spinal column bones of the thoracic (chest) region.

Thymine   one of four chemical bases central to the structure of a DNA nucleotide.

Tibia   the largest bone of the leg (in anatomical terms, in which "leg" refers to only the part of the lower limb defined by the tibia and fibula). The tibia is the second largest bone of the leg (in the popular definition of "leg," which includes the upper and lower leg).

Tibial tuberosity   point of insertion of the patellar tendon on the anterior proximal tibia.

Total ridge count   the total number of ridges on all fingers. In prints with whorls, only one ridge count per finger is added to the total.

Torus   an elevation or prominence.

Trait   a distinguishing characteristic or quality of a phenotype (example: hair color, blood type, tongue rolling, etc.).

Transverse   any crosswise section.

Transverse process   lateral projections of vertebrae. There are costal facets/pits on the transverse processes of the thoracic vertebrae.

Trapezium   *see* Greater multangular.

Trapezoid   *see* Lesser multangular.

Trephination (or **trepination**)   a surgical technique whereby a section of bone is removed, usually from the cranium. Modern trephination involves drilling a burr hole in the cranium to relieve pressure on the brain.

Triplets   the three-base code for amino acids on the DNA chain.

Triquetrum   one of the bones of the wrist.

Trisomy   an extra chromosome in a daughter cell resulting in three chromosomes instead of two.

Tubercle   a small, knob-like projection on bone.

Tuberosity   a large, rough eminence or projection on bone.

Type lines   the innermost ridges that surround the pattern area in dermatoglyphics.

Ulna   the medial bone of the forearm.

Ventral   in front (*similar to* Anterior).

Vertebra   a bone of the spinal column.

Vertex   the uppermost point on the midline of the cranium when it is in the Frankfort plane. In general terms, vertex means top or highest point.

Vertical clinging and leaping   locomotor mode found in some prosimians, in which the animal pushes off of a vertical tree limb with powerful hindlimbs, turns in midair, and lands feet first on another tree limb.

Visual predation theory   theory originally proposed by M. Cartmill, that the first primates developed characteristics that allowed them to prey on insects on the terminal branches of the lower layers of tropical rain forests.

Vomer bone   bone on the inferior cranium, posterior and superior to the palatine bones.

Xiphoid process   the most inferior portion of the sternum, often ossified in the adult.

Zygomatic arch   paired arches on the lateral cranium, made up of projections from the zygomatic (malar) bone anteriorly and the temporal bone posteriorly.

Zygomatic bone   paired bones of the lateral face on the cranium.

Bibliography

Alemseged, Z., F. Spoor, W. H. Kimbel, R. Bobe, D. Geraads, J. G. Wynn 2006 "A Juvenile Early Hominin Skeleton from Dikika, Ethiopia." *Nature* Sep 21; **443**(7109): 296–301.

Alemseged, Z., J. G. Wynn, W. H. Kimbel, D. Reed, D. Geraads, R. Bobe 2005 "New Hominin from the Basal Member of the Hadar Formation, Dikika, Ethiopia, and Its Geological Context." *J Hum Evol* **49**(4): 499–514.

Alexeev, V. P. 1986 *The Origin of the Human Race.* Moscow: Progress.

Andrews, P. J. 1983 "The Natural History of *Sivapithecus*." In: R. Ciochon and R. Corruccini (eds.), *New Interpretations of Ape and Human Ancestry*, New York: Plenum, pp. 441–463.

Anemone, R. L. 1990 "The VCL Hypothesis Revisited: Patterns of Femoral Morphology among Quadrupedal and Saltatorial Prosimian Primates." *Am J Phys Anthropol* **83**: 373–393.

Anemone, R. L., H. H. Covert 2000 "New Skeletal Remains of Omomys (Primates, Omomyidae): Functional Morphology of the Hindlimb and Locomotor Behavior of a Middle Eocene Primate." *J Hum Evol* **38**(5): 607–633.

Ankel-Simons, F., J. G. Fleagle, P. S. Chatrath 1998 "Femoral Anatomy of Aegyptopithecus zeuxis, an Early Oligocene Anthropoid." *Am J Phys Anthropol* **106**(4): 413–424.

Argue, D., M. J. Morwood, T. Sutikna, et al. 2009 "*Homo floresiensis*: A Cladistic Analysis." *J. Hum. Evol.* Nov; **57**(5): 623–39.

Arnason, U., A. Gullberg, A. Janke 1998 "Molecular Timing of Primate Divergences as Estimated by Two Nonprimate Calibration Points." *J Mol Evol* **47**: 718–727.

Asfaw, B., T. White, O. Lovejoy, B. Latimer, S.Simpson, G. Suwa 1999 "*Australopithecus garhi*: A New Species of Early Hominid from Ethiopia." *Science* **284**: 629–635.

Bacon, A. M., M. Godinot 1998 "Morphological Functional Analysis of the Femora and Tibiae of Quercy 'Adapis': Recognition of Five Morphological Types." *Folia Primatol (Basel)* **69**(1): 1–21.

Baker, R. K. 1984 *The Relationship of Cranial Suture Closure and Age Analyzed in a Modern Multi-Racial Sample of Males and Females.* M.A. Thesis, California State University, Fullerton.

Balzeau, A., D. Grimaud-Herve, T. Jacob 2005 "Internal Cranial Features of the Mojokerto Child Fossil (East Java, Indonesia)." *J Hum Evol* **48**(6): 535–553.

Barker, G., H. Barton, et al. 2007 "The Human Revolution in Lowland Tropical Southeast Asia: The Antiquity and Behavior of Anatomically Modern Humans at Niah Cave (Sarawak, Borneo)." *Journal of Human Evolution* **52**: 243–261.

Bass, W. M. 1987 *Human Osteology: A Laboratory and Field Manual* (3rd ed.). Columbia, Mo.: Missouri Archaeological Society Special Publication No. 2.

Bass, W. M. 1996 *Human Osteology: A Laboratory and Field Manual* (4th ed.). Columbia, Mo.: Missouri Archaeological Society Special Publication No. 2.

Beard, K. C., J. Wang 2004 "The Eosimiid Primates (Anthropoidea) of the Heti Formation, Yuanqu Basin, Shanxi and Henan Provinces, People's Republic of China." *J Hum Evol* **46**(6): 789.

Belmaker, M., E. Tchernov, S. Condemi, O. Bar-Yosef 2002 "New Evidence for Hominid Presence in the Lower Pleistocene of the Southern Levant." *J Hum Evol* **43**(1): 43–56.

Benefit, B. R., M. L. McCrossin 1997 "Earliest Known Old World Monkey Skull." *Nature* **388**: 368–371.

Berg, G. E. 2008 "Pubic Bone Age Estimation in Adult Women." *Journal of Forensic Sciences* **53**: 569–577.

Bernor, R. L. 2007 "New Apes Fill the Gap." *Proceedings of the National Academy of Sciences* **104**(50): 19661–19662.

Birkby, W. H. 1973 *Discontinuous Morphological Traits of the Skull as Population Markers in the Prehistoric Southwest.* Ph.D. Dissertation, University of Arizona, Tucson.

Bischoff, J. L., R. W. Williams, R. J. Rosebauer, et al. 2007 "High-Resolution U-Series Dates from the Sima de los Huesos Hominids Yields 600+/-66 kyrs: Implications for the Evolution of the Early Neanderthal Lineage." *Journal of Archaeological Science* **34**: 763–770.

Bloch, J. I., D. C. Fisher, K. D. Rose, P. D. Gingerich 2001 "Stratocladistic Analysis of Paleocene Carpolestidae (Mammalia, Plesiadapiformes) with Description of a New Late Tiffanian Genus." *Journal of Vertebrate Paleontology*: **21**(1): 119–131.

Bloch, J. I., D. M. Boyer 2002 "Grasping Primate Origins." *Science* Nov. 22; **298**(5598): 1606–10.

Bloch, J. I., P. D. Gingerich 1998 "Carpolestes simpsoni, New Species (Mammalia, Proprimates) from the Late Paleocene of the Clarks Fork Basin, Wyoming." *Contrib. Mus. Paleontol. Univ. Mich.* **30**: 131.

Bloch, J. I., M. T. Silcox 2001 "New Basicrania of Paleocene-Eocene Ignacius: Re-evaluation of the Plesiadapiform-Dermopteran Link." *Am J Phys Anthropol* **116**(3): 184–98.

Bloch, J. I., M. T. Silcox 2006 "Cranial Anatomy of the Paleocene Plesiadapi form Carpolestes simpsoni (Mammalia, Primates) Using Ultra High-Resolution X-Ray Computed Tomography, and the Relationships of Plesiadapiforms to Euprimates." *J Hum Evol* **50**(1): 1–35.

Blumenschine, R. J., C. R. Peters, F. T. Masao, et al. 2003 "Late Pliocene Homo and Hominid Land Use from Western Olduvai Gorge, Tanzania." *Science* **299**: 1217–21.

Bocherens, H., D. G. Drucker, D. Billiou, M. Patou-Mathis, B. Vandermeersch 2005 "Isotopic Evidence for Diet and Subsistence Pattern of the Saint-Cesaire I Neanderthal: Review and Use of a Multi-Source Mixing Model." *J Hum Evol* **49**(1): 71–87.

Brooks, S. T. 1985 Personal communication.

Brooks, S. T. 1986 "Comments on 'Known' Age at Death Series." Presented in conjunction with "Skeletal Age Standards Derived from an Extensive Multi-Racial Sample of Modern Americans," by J. Suchey and D. Katz, at the Fifty-Fifth Annual Meeting of the American Association of Physical Anthropologists, Albuquerque, New Mexico.

Brooks, S. T., J. M. Suchey 1990 "Skeletal Age Determination Based on the Os Pubis: A Comparison of the Acsadi-Nemeskeri and Suchey-Brooks Methods." *Hum Evol* **5**(3): 227–238.

Brown, F., J. Harris, R. Leakey, A. Walker 1985 "Early *Homo erectus* Skeleton from West Lake Turkana, Kenya." *Nature* **316**: 788–792.

Brown, P., T. Sutikna, et al. 2004 "A New Small-Bodied Hominin from the Late Pleistocene of Flores, Indonesia." *Nature* **431**(7012): 1055–1061.

Brues, A. M. 1977 *People and Races.* New York: Macmillan.

Brues, A. M. 1990 *People and Races.* Reissued by Waveland Press, Prospect Heights, IL.

Bruner, E., G. Manzi 2005 "CT-Based Description and Phyletic Evaluation of the Archaic Human Calvarium from Ceprano, Italy." *Anat Rec A Discov Mol Cell Evol Biol* **285**(1): 643–658.

Brunet, M., F. Guy, D. Pilbeam, et al. 2002 "A New Hominid from the Upper Miocene of Chad, Central Africa." *Nature* **418**: 145–151.

Brunet, M., F. Guy, D. Pilbeam, et al. 2005 "New Material of the Earliest Hominid from the Upper Miocene of Chad." *Nature* **434**: 752–755.

Buckberry, J. L., A. T. Chamberlain 2002 "Age Estimation from the Auricular Surface of the Ilium: A Revised Method." *American Journal of Physical Anthropology* **119**: 231–239.

Campbell, B. G. 1976 *Human Evolution: An Introduction to Man's Adaptations* (2nd ed.). New York: Aldine.

Campbell, B. G. 1985 *Human Evolution: An Introduction to Man's Adaptations* (3rd ed.). New York: Aldine.

Cann, R. L., M. Stoneking, A. C. Wilson 1987 "Mitochondrial DNA and Human Evolution." *Nature* **325**: 31–36.

Caramelli, D., C. Lalueza-Fox, et al. 2003 "Evidence for Genetic Discontinuity Between Neandertals and 24,000-Year-Old Anatomically Modern Humans." *Proceedings of the National Academy of Sciences* **100**: 6593–6597.

Caramelli, D., C. Lalueza-Fox, et al. 2006 "A Highly Divergent mtDNA Sequence in a Neandertal Individual from Italy." *Current Biology* **16**(16): R630–R632.

Carbonell, E., J. M. Bermuda de Castro, et al. 2008 "The First Hominin of Europe." *Nature* **452**: 465–469.

Carlson, B. M. 2004 *Human Embryology and Developmental Biology.* St. Louis: Mosby.

Cartmill, M. 1972 "Arboreal Adaptations and the Origin of the Order Primates." In: R. Tuttle (ed.), *Functional and Evolutionary Biology of Primates,* Chicago: Aldine, pp. 97–122.

Cartmill, M. 1974 "Rethinking Primate Origins." *Science* **184**: 436–443.

Cartmill, M. 1992 "New Views on Primate Origins." *Evol Anthropol* **1**: 105–111.

Cela-Conde, C. J., F. J. Ayala 2003 "Genera of the Human Lineage." *Proc Natl Acad Sci USA* **100**(13):7684–7689.

Chaimanee, Y., D. Jolly, M. Benammi, P. Tafforeau, D. Duzer, I. Moussa, J. J. Jaeger 2003 "A Middle Miocene hominoid from Thailand and Orangutan Origins." *Nature* **422**: 61–65.

Chatterjee, H. J. 2006 "Phylogeny and Biogeography of Gibbons: A Dispersal-Vicariance Analysis." *International Journal of Primatology* **27**(3): 699–712.

Chatterjee, H. J., S. Y. Ho, I. Barnes, C. Groves 2009 "Estimating the Phylogeny and Divergence Times of Primates Using a Supermatrix Approach." *BMC Evolutionary Biology* **9**: 259 (doi:10.1186/1471-2148-9-259).

Cheng, Z., M. Ventura, X. She, P. Khaitovich, T,. Graves, K. Osoegawa, D. Church, P. DeJong, R. K. Wilson, S. Pääbo, et al. 2005 "A Genome-Wide Comparison of Recent Chimpanzee and Human Segmental Duplications." *Nature* **437**: 88–93.

Cho, J., S. D. Stout, R. W. Madsen, M. A. Streeter 2002 "Population-Specific Histological Age-Estimating Method: A Model for Known African-American and European-American Skeletal Remains." *Journal of Forensic Sciences* **47**(1): 12–18.

Ciochon, R. L., G. F. Gunnell 2002 "Chronology of Primate Discoveries in Myanmar: Influences on the Anthropoid Origins Debate." *Am J Phys Anthropol Suppl* **35**: 2–35.

Clark, W. E. Le Gros 1959 *The Antecedents of Man.* New York: Harper & Row.

Cobb, S. N. 2008 "The Facial Skeleton of the Chimpanzee-Human Last Common Ancestor." *J Anat* **212**(4): 469–85.

Conard, N. J., P. M. Grootes, F. H. Smith 2004 "Unexpectedly Recent Dates for Human Remains from Vogelherd." *Nature* **430**: 198–201.

Conroy, G. C. 1990 *Primate Evolution.* New York: Norton.

Conroy, G. C., B. Senut, D. Gommery, M. Pickford, P. Mein 1996 "New Primate Remains from the Miocene of Namibia, Southern Africa." *Am J Phys Anthropol* **99**: 487–492.

Coon, C. S. 1965 *The Living Races.* New York: Alfred A. Knopf.

Corruccini, R. S. 1974 "An Examination of the Meaning of Cranial Discrete Traits for Human Skeletal Biological Studies." *Am J Phys Anthropol* **40**: 425–446.

Crompton, R. H., E. E. Vereecke, S. K. Thorpe 2008 "Locomotion and Posture from the Common Hominoid Ancestor to Fully Modern Hominins, with Special Reference to the Last Common Panin/Hominin Ancestor." *J. Anat.* **212**(4): 501–43.

Curnoe, D., P. V. Tobias 2006 "Description, New Reconstruction, Comparative Anatomy, and Classification of the Sterkfontein Stw 53 Cranium, with Discussions about the Taxonomy of Other Southern African Early Homo Remains." *J Hum Evol* **50**(1): 36–77.

Currat, M., L. Excoffier 2004 "Modern Humans Did Not Admix with Neanderthals during Their Range Expansion into Europe." *PLoS Biol* (12).

Czarnetzki, A., T. Jakob, C. M. Pusch 2003 "Palaeopathological and Variant Conditions of the Homo heidelbergensis Type Specimen (Mauer, Germany)." *J Hum Evol* **44**(4): 479–495.

Dahlberg, A. A. 1951 "The Dentition of the American Indian." In: W. S. Laughlin (ed.), *The Physical Anthropology of the American Indian*, New York: Viking Fund, pp. 138–176.

Dart, R. 1925 "*Australopithecus africanus*: The Man Ape of South Africa." *Nature,* **115**: 195–199.

Day, M. H., E. H. Wickens 1980 "Laetoli Pliocene Hominid Footprints and Bipedalism." *Nature* **286**: 385–387.

De Bonis, L., G. Bouvrain, D. Geraads, G. Koufos 1990 "New Hominid Skull Material from the Late Miocene of Macedonia in Northern Greece." *Nature* **345**: 712–714.

De Bonis, L., G. D. Koufos 1994 "Our Ancestors' Ancestor: *Ouranopithecus* is a Greek Link in Human Ancestry." *Evol Anthropol* **3**: 75–83.

Delson, E. 1995 "Evolution of Old World Monkeys." In: S. Jones, R. Martin, and D. Pilbeam (eds.), *The Cambridge Encyclopedia of Human Evolution,* Cambridge, U.K.: Cambridge University Press, pp. 217–222.

Dene, H. T., M. Goodman, W. Prychodko 1976 "Immunodiffusion Evidence on the Phylogeny of the Primates." In: M. Goodman, R. E. Tashian, and J. H. Tashian (eds.), *Molecular Anthropology,* New York: Plenum, pp. 171–195.

Day, M. H., E. H. Wickens 1980 "Laetoli Pliocene Hominid Footprints and Bipedalism." *Nature* **286**:385–387.

DiGangi, E. A., J. D. Bethard, E. H. Kimmerle, L. W. Konigsberg 2009 "A New Method for Estimating Age-at-Death from the First Rib." *American Journal of Physical Anthropology* **138**(2): 164–176.

Djuric, M., D. Djonic, S. Nikolic, D. Popovic, J. Marinkovic 2008 "Evaluation of the Suchey-Brooks Method for Aging Skeletons in the Balkans." *Journal of Forensic Sciences* **52**: 21–23.

Dittrick, J., J. M. Suchey 1986 "Sex Determination of Prehistoric Central California Skeletal Remains Using Discriminant Analysis of the Femur and Humerus." *Am J Phys Anthropol* **70**: 3–9.

Dodo, Y. 1974 "Non-Metrical Cranial Traits in the Hokkaido Ainu and the Northern Japanese of Recent Times." *J Anthropol Soc Nippon* **82**: 31–51.

Dominy, N. J., J. C. Svenning, W. H. Li 2003 "Historical Contingency in the Evolution of Primate Color Vision." *J Hum Evol* **44**(1): 25–45.

Drapeau, M. S., C. V. Ward, W. H. Kimbel, D. C. Johanson, Y. Rak 2005 "Associated Cranial and Forelimb Remains Attributed to Australopithecus afarensis from Hadar, Ethiopia." *J Hum Evol* **48** (6):593–642.

Eldredge, N., S. J. Gould 1972 "Punctuated Equilibria: An Alternative to Phyletic Gradualism." In: T. J. M. Schopf (ed.), *Models in Paleobiology,* San Francisco: Freeman, Cooper, pp. 82–115.

Falk, D. 1986 "Evolution of Cranial Blood Drainage in Hominids: Enlarged Occipital/Margina Sinuses and Emissary Foramina." *Am J Phys Anthropol* **70**: 311–324.

Falk, D., G. C. Conroy 1983 "The Cranial Venous Sinus System in *Australopithecus afarensis.*" *Nature* **306**: 779–781.

Falk, D., C. Hildebolt, K. Smith, et al. 2005a "The Brain of LB1, Homo floresiensis." *Science* **308**: 242–245.

Falk, D., C. Hildebolt, K. Smith, et al. 2005b "Response to Comment on The Brain of LB1, Homo floresiensis." *Science* **310**: 236.

Finnegan, M. 1972 *Population Definition on the Northwest Coast by Analysis of Discrete Character Variation.* Ph.D. dissertation, University of Colorado, Boulder.

Fleagle, J. G. 1976 "Locomotion and Posture of the Malayan Siamang and Implications for Hominoid Evolution." *Folia Primatol* **26**: 245–269.

Fleagle, J. G. 1988 *Primate Adaptation and Evolution.* San Diego: Academic.

Fleagle, J. G. 1999 *Primate Adaptation and Evolution.* San Diego: Academic.

Fleagle, J. G., and R. F. Kay "New Interpretations of the Phyletic Position of Oligocene Hominoids." In: R. Ciochon and R. Corruccini (eds.), *New Interpretations of Ape and Human Ancestry,* New York: Plenum, 1983.

Fleagle, J. G., E. L. Simons 1995 "Limb Skeleton and Locomotor Adaptations of Apidium phiomense, an Oligocene Anthropoid from Egypt." *Am J Phys Anthropol* **97**: 235–289.

Floud, R., K. Wachter, A. Gregory 1990 *Height, Health and History: Nutritional Status in the United Kingdom 1750–1980.* Cambridge: Cambridge University Press.

France, D. L. 1983 *Sexual Dimorphism in the Human Humerus.* Unpublished Ph.D. Dissertation, University of Colorado, Boulder.

France, D. L. 1986 "Osteometry at Muscle Origin and Insertion in Sex Determination." *Am J Phys Anthropol* **76**: 515–526.

France, D. L. 1990 "A Cautionary Note in the Cross-Cultural Use of the Mastoid Process in Sex Determination." *Adli Tip Dergisi J Forens Med Istanbul* **6**(1–2): 149–156.

Franzen, J. L., P. D. Gingerich, J. Habersetzer, J. H. Hurum, W. von Koenigswald, B. Holly Smith 2009 "Complete Primate Skeleton from the Middle Eocene of Messel in Germany: Morphology and Paleobiology" *PLoS ONE* **4**(5): e5723. (Published online 2009 May 19. doi: 10.1371/journal.pone.0005723.)

Gabunia L., A. Vekua 1995 "A Plio-Pleistocene Hominid from Dmanisi, East Georgia, Caucasus." *Nature* **373**: 509–512.

Gabunia, L., A. Vekua, D. Lordkipanidze, et al. 2000 "Earliest Pleistocene Hominid Cranial Remains from Dmanisi, Republic of Georgia: Taxonomy, Geological Setting, and Age." *Science* **288**: 1019–1025.

Galbany, J., S. Moya-Sola, A. Perez-Perez 2005 "Dental Microwear Variability on Buccal Tooth Enamel Surfaces of Extant Catarrhini and the Miocene Fossil Dryopithecus laietanus (Hominoidea)." *Folia Primatol* (Basel) **76**(6): 325–41.

Galik, K., B. Senut, M. Pickford, et al. 2004 "External and Internal Morphology of the BAR 1002'00 Orrorin tugenensis Femur." *Science* **305**: 1450–1453.

Gardner, E. J. 1975 *Principles of Genetics* (5th ed.). New York: Wiley.

Gargett, R. H. 1989 "The Evidence for Neandertal Burial." *Curr Anthropol* **30**: 157–190.

Garn, S. M., S. T. Sandusky, N. N. Rosen, F. Trowbridge 1973a "Economic Impact on Postnatal Ossification." *Am J Phys Anthropol* **38**: 1–3.

Garn, S. M., J. M. Nagy, S. T. Sandusky, F. Trowbridge 1973b "Economic Impact on Tooth Emergence." *Am J Phys Anthropol* **39**: 233–238.

Gebo, D. L., M. Dagosto, K. C. Beard, T. Qi 2001 "Middle Eocene Primate Tarsals from China: Implications for Haplorhine Evolution." *Am J Phys Anthropol* **116**(2): 83–107.

Gebo D. L., M. Dagosto, K. C. Beard, X. Ni 2008 "New Primate Hind Limb Elements from the Middle Eocene of China." *J Hum Evol,* Dec; **55**(6): 999–1014. Epub 2008 May 13.

Gill, G., S. J. Rhine (eds.) 1990 *Skeletal Attribution of Race: Methods for Forensic Anthropology.* Albuquerque: Maxwell Museum of Anthropology, Anthropological Papers No. 4.

Gingerich, P. D. 1990 "African Dawn for Primates." *Nature* **346**. 411.

Gingerich, P. D., R. D. Martin 1981 "Cranial Morphology and Adaptations in Eocene Adapidae. II. The Cambridge Skull of Adapis Parisiensis." *AJPA* **56**(3): 235–257.

Godinot, M. 1994 "Early North African Primates and Their Significance for the Origin of Simiiformes (=Anthropoidea)." In: J. G. Fleagle and R. F. Kay (eds.), *Anthropoid Origins,* pp. 235–95. New York: Plenum.

Godinot, M., M. Mahboubi 1992 "Earliest Known Simian Primate Found in Algeria." *Nature* **357**: 324–326.

Gordon, A. D., L. Nevell, B. Wood 2008 "The *Homo Floresiensis* Cranium (LB1): Size, Scaling, and Early *Homo* Affinities." *Proc Natl Acad Sci USA* Mar 25; **105**(12): 4650–5.

Gould, S. J., N. Eldridge 1977 "Punctuated Equilibria: The Tempo and Mode of Evolution Reconsidered." *Paleobiology* **3**: 115–151.

Greulich, W. W., S. I. Pyle 1959 *Radiographic Atlas of Skeletal Development of the Hand and Wrist.* Stanford, CA: Stanford University Press.

Grun, R., C. Stringer, F. McDermott, et al. 2005 "U-Series and ESR Analyses of Bones and Teeth Relating to the Human Burials from Skhul." *J Hum Evol* **49**(3): 316–334.

Gunnell, G. F. 1997 "Wasatchian-Bridgerian (Eocene) Paleoecology of the Western Interior of North America: Changing Paleoenvironments and Taxonomic Composition of Omomyid (Tarsiiformes) Primates." *J Hum Evol* **32**(2–3): 105–132.

Gunnell, G. F. 2002 "Notharctine Primates (Adapiformes) from the Early to Middle Eocene (Wasatchian-Bridgerian) of Wyoming: Transitional Species and the Origin of Notharctus and Smilodectes." *J Hum Evol* **43**(3): 353–380.

Guy, F., D. E. Lieberman, D. Pilbeam, et al. 2005 "Morphological Affinities of the Sahelanthropus tchadensis Late Miocene Hominid from Chad Cranium." *Proc Natl Acad Sci USA* **102**: 18836–18841.

Haeusler, M., H. M. McHenry 2004 "OH62 Leg Length Body Proportions of *Homo habilis* Reviewed." *J Hum. Evol* **46**(4): 433–465.

Haile-Selassie, Y. 2001 "Late Miocene Hominids from the Middle Awash, Ethiopia." *Nature* **412**: 178–181.

Harcourt-Smith, W. E., Aiello, L. C. 2004 "Fossils, Feet and the Evolution of Human Bipedal Locomotion." *J Anat* **204**(5): 403–416.

Harrison, T., X. Ji, et al. 2008 "Renewed Investigations at the Late Miocene hominoid Locality of Leilao, Yunnan, China." *American Journal of Physical Anthropology* **135**(S46): 113.

Hartnett, K. 2010 "Analysis of Age-at-Death Estimation Using Data from a New, Modern Autopsy Sample, Part I: Pubic Bone." *Journal of Forensic Sciences,* accepted for publication in 2010.

Hartnett, K. 2010 "Analysis of Age-at-Death Estimation Using Data from a New, Modern Autopsy Sample, Part II: Sternal End of the Fourth Rib. *Journal of Forensic Sciences,* accepted for publication in 2010.

Hauser, G., G. F. De Stefano 1989 *Epigenetic Variants of the Human Skull.* Stuttgart: E. Schweizerbartsche.

Heathcote, G. 2006 Personal communication.

Hershkovitz, P. 1977 *Living New World Monkeys (Platyrrhini) with an Introduction to Primates,* Vol. 1. The University of Chicago Press.

Hillson, S. 2003 *Dental Anthropology.* Cambridge: Cambridge University Press.

Hodgson, J. A., K. N. Sterner, L. J. Matthews, A. S. Burrell, R. A. Jani, R. L. Raaum, C. Stewart, T. R. Disotell 2009 "Successive Radiations, Not Stasis, in the South American Primate Fauna." *PNAS* **106**(14): 5534–5539.

Holloway, R. L. 1983 "Cerebral Brain Endocast Pattern of *Australopithecus afarensis* Hominid." *Nature* **303**: 420–422.

Hooker, J. J., D. E. Russell, A. Phelizon 1999 "A New Family of Plesiadapiformes (Mammalia) from the Old World Lower Paleocene." *Palaeontology* **42**(3): 377–407.

Hoppa, R. D., T. N. Garlie 1998 "Secular Trend on the Growth of Toronto Children During the Last Century." *Annals of Human Biology* **25**: 553–561.

Hudjashov, G., T. Kivisild, P. A. Underhill, P. Endicott, J. J. Sanchez, A. A. Lin, P. Shen, P. Oefner, C. Renfrew, R. Villems, P. Forster 2007 "Revealing the Prehistoric Settlement of Australia by Y Chromosome and mtDNA Analysis." *Proceedings of the National Academy of Sciences, USA* **104**: 8726–8730.

Igarashi, Y., K. Uesu, T. Wakebe, E. Kanazawa 2005 "New Method for Estimation of Adult Skeletal Age at Death from the Morphology of the Auricular Surface of the Ilium." *American Journal of Physical Anthropology* **128**: 324–339.

International Human Genome Sequencing Consortium 2004 "Finishing the Euchromatic Sequence of the Human Genome." *Nature* **431**(7011): 931–45.

Iscan, M. Y., S. R. Loth, R. K. Wright 1984 "Age Estimation from the Rib by Phase Analysis: White Males." *J Forens Sci* **29**: 1094–1104.

Iscan, M. Y., S. R. Loth, R. K. Wright 1985 "Age Estimation from the Rib by Phases Analysis: White Females." *J Forens Sci* **30**: 853–863.

Iscan, M. Y., P. Miller-Shaivitz 1986 "Sexual Dimorphism in the Femur and Tibia." In: K. J. Reichs (ed.), *Forensic Osteology: Advances in the Identification of Human Remains,* Springfield, IL: Charles C. Thomas, pp. 101–111.

Janecka, J. E., W. Miller, T. H. Pringle, F. Wiens, A. Zitzmann, K. M. Helgen, M. S. Springer, W. J. Murphy 2007 "Molecular and Genomic Data Identify the Closest Living Relative of Primates." *Science* **318**(5851): 792–794.

Johanson, D., F. Masao, G. Eck, et al. 1987 "New Partial Skeleton of *Homo habilis* from Olduvai Gorge, Tanzania." *Nature* **327**: 205–209.

Johanson, D. C., T. D. White 1979 "A Systematic Assessment of Early African Hominids." *Science* **203**: 321–330.

Jolly, C. J., F. Plog 1988 *Physical Anthropology and Archeology* (5th ed.). New York: McGraw-Hill.

Kaifu, Y., H. Baba, F. Aziz, E. Indriati, F. Schrenk, T. Jacob 2005 "Taxonomic Affinities and Evolutionary History of the Early Pleistocene Hominids of Java: Dentognathic Evidence." *Am J Phys Anthropol* **128**(4): 709–726.

Katz, D., J. M. Suchey 1986 "Age Determination of the Male Os Pubis." *Am J Phys Anthropol* **69**: 427–435.

Kay, R. 1984 "On the Use of Anatomical Features to Infer Foraging Behavior in Extinct Primates." In: J. Cant and P. Rodman (eds.), *Adaptations for Foraging in Nonhuman Primates,* New York: Columbia University Press, pp. 21–53.

Kay, R. F., V. M. Campbell, J. B. Rossie, M. W. Colbert, T. B. Rowe 2004 "Olfactory Fossa of Tremacebus Harringtoni (Platyrrhini, Early Miocene, Sacanana, Argentina): Implications for Activity Pattern." *Anat Rec A Discov Mol Cell Evol Biol* **281**(1): 1157–1172.

Kay, R. F., P. S. Ungar 1997 "Dental Evidence for Dietin Some Miocene Catarrhines with Comments on the Effects of Phylogeny on the Interpretation of Adaptation." In: D. R. Begun, C. Ward and M. Rose (eds.), *Function, Phylogeny and Fossils: Miocene Hominoids and Great Ape and Human Origins,* New York: Plenum, pp. 131–151.

Kelly, J. 1995 "Evolution of Apes." In: S. Jones, R. Martin, and D. Pilbeam (eds.), *The Cambridge Encyclopedia of Human Evolution,* Cambridge, U.K.: Cambridge University Press, pp. 223–230.

Kelly, J., D. Pilbeam 1986 "The Dryopithecines: Taxonomy, Comparative Anatomy, and Phylogeny of Miocene Large Hominoids." In: D. Swindler and J. Erwin (eds.), *Comparative Primate Biology,* Vol. 1, Systematics, Evolution, and Anatomy, New York: Alan R. Liss, pp. 361–411.

Kerley, E. R., D. H. Ubelaker 1978 "Revisions in the Microscopic Method of Estimating Age at Death in Human Cortical Bone." *American Journal of Physical Anthropology* **49**: 545–546.

Keyser, A. W. 2000 "New Finds in South Africa." *National Geographic* May: 76–83.

Kim, U. K., E. Jorgenson, H. Coon, M. Leppert, N. Risch, D. Drayna 2003 "Positional Cloning of the Human Quantitative Trait Locus Underlying Taste Sensitivity to Phenylthiocarbamide." *Science* **299**(5610): 1221–5.

Kimmerle, E. H., L. W. Konigsberg, R. L. Jantz, J. P. Baraybar 2008 "Analysis of Age-at-Death Estimation Through the Use of Pubic Symphyseal Data." *Journal of Forensic Sciences* **53**: 558–568.

Kirk, E. C., E. L. Simons 2001 "Diets of Fossil Primates from the Fayum Depression of Egypt: A Quantitative Analysis of Molar Shearing." *J Hum Evol* **40**(3): 203–229.

Kitchin, F. D., W. H. Evans, C. A. Clarke, R. B. McConnel, P. M. Sheppard 1959 "PTC Taste Response and Thyroid Disease." *BMJ* **1**: 1069–1074.

Klar A. J. 2003 "Human Handedness and Scalp Hair-Whorl Direction Develop from a Common Genetic Mechanism." *Genetics* **165**(1): 269–76.

Kordos, L., D. R. Begun 1997 "A New Reconstruction of RUD77, a Partial Cranium of *Dryopithecus brancoi* from Rudabanya, Hungary." *Am J Phys Anthropol* **103**: 227–294.

Krause, J., C. Lalueza-Fox, et al. 2007 "The Derived FOXP2 Variant of Modern Humans was Shared with Neandertals." *Current Biology* **17**: 1908–1912.

Krings, M., A. Stone, R. W. Schmitz, H. Krainitzki, M. Stoneking, S. Paabo 1997 "Neandertal DNA Sequences and the Origin of Modern Humans." *Cell* **30**: 19–30.

Krogman, W. M. 1939 "A Guide to the Identification of Human Skeletal Material." *FBI Law Enforce Bull* **8**(8): 3–31.

Krogman, W. M. 1962 *The Human Skeleton in Forensic Medicine.* Springfield, IL: Charles C. Thomas.

Krogman, W. M., M. Y. Iscan 1986 *The Human Skeleton in Forensic Medicine* (2nd ed.). Springfield, IL: Charles C. Thomas.

Kumar, S., A. Filipski, V. Swarna, A. Walker, S. B. Hedges 2005 "Placing Limits on the Molecular Age of the Human-Chimpanzee Divergence." *Proc Natl Acad Sci USA* **102**(52): 18842–18847.

Kunimatsu, Y., M. Nakatsukasa, Y. Sawada, T. Sakai, M. Hyodo, H. Hyodo, T. Itaya, H. Nakaya, H. Saegusa, A. Mazurier, M. Saneyoshi, H. Tsujikawa, A. Yamamoto, E. Mbua 2007 "A New Late Miocene Great Ape from Kenya and Its Implications for the Origins of African Great Apes and Humans." *PNAS Proceedings of the National Academy of Sciences* **104**(49): 19220–19225.

Lamendin, H., E. Baccino, J. F. Humbert, J. C. Tavernier, R. M. Nossintchouk, A. Zerilli 1992 "A Simple Technique for Age Estimation in Adult Corpses: The Two Criteria Dental Method." *Journal of Forensic Sciences* **37**: 1373–1379.

Lartet, E. 1856 "Note Sur la Decouverte Recent d'un Machoire de Singes Superieurs." *C R Acad Sci Paris* 43.

Latimer, B., C. O. Lovejoy 1990a "Hallucal Tarsometatarsal Joint in *Australopithecus afarensis*." *Am J Phys Anthropol* **83**: 135–143.

Latimer, B., C. O. Lovejoy 1990b "Metatarsophalangeal Joints of *Australopithecus afarensis*." *Am J Phys Anthropol* **83**: 13–23.

Leakey, L. S. B., P. V. Tobias, J. R. Napier 1964 "A New Species of the Genus *Homo* from Olduvai Gorge." *Nature* **202**: 7–9.

Leakey, M. G., F. Spoor, F. H. Brown, et al. 2001 "New Hominin Genus from Eastern Africa Shows Diverse Middle Pliocene Lineages." *Nature* **410**: 433–440.

Lee, S. H. 2005 "Patterns of Size Sexual Dimorphism in Australopithecus afarensis: Another Look." *Homo* **56**(3): 219–232.

Lovejoy, C. O. 2009 "Reexamining Human Origins in Light of *Ardipithecus ramidus*." *Science* **326**(5949): 74, 74e1–74e8.

Lovejoy, C. O., B. Latimer, G. Suwa, B. Asfaw, T. D. White 2009a "Combining the Prehension and Propulsion: The Foot of *Ardipithecus ramidus*." *Science* **326**(5949): 72, 72e1–72e8.

Lovejoy, C. O., R. S. Meindl, T. R. Pryzbeck, R. P. Mensforth 1985 "Chronological Metamorphosis of the Auricular Surface of the Ilium: A New Method for the Determination of Adult Skeletal Age at Death." *American Journal of Physical Anthropology* **68**: 15–28.

Lovejoy, C. O., G. Suwa, L. Spurlock, B. Asfaw, T. D. White 2009d "The Pelvis and Femur of *Ardipithecus ramidus*: The Emergence of Upright Walking." *Science* **326**(5949): 71, 71e1–71e6.

Lovejoy, C. O., S. W. Simpson, T. D. White, B. Asfaw, G. Suwa 2009b "Careful Climbing in the Miocene: The Forelimbs of *Ardipithecus ramidus* and Humans Are Primitive." *Science* **326**(5949): 70, 70e1–70e8.

Lovejoy, C. O., G. Suwa, S. W. Simpson, J. H. Matternes, T. D. White 2009c "The Great Divides: *Ardipithecus Ramidus* Reveals the Postcrania of Our Last Common Ancestors with African Apes." *Science* **326**(73): 100–106.

Macho, G. A., D. Shimizu, Y. Jiang, I. R. Spears 2005 "Australopithecus anamensis: A Finite-Element Approach to Studying the Functional Adaptations of Extinct Hominins." *Anat Rec A Discov Mol Cell Evol Biol* **283** (2): 310–318.

Mangold, J. E., T. J. Payne, J. Z. Ma, G. Chen, M. D. Li 2008 "Bitter Taste Receptor Gene Polymorphisms Are an Important Factor in the Development of Nicotine Dependence in African Americans." *J Med Genet* **45**(9): 578–82.

Marivaux, L., P. O. Antoine, S. R. Baqri, M. Benammi, Y. Chaimanee, J. Y. Crochet, D. de Franceschi, N. Iqbal, J. J. Jaeger, G. Metais, G. Roohi, J. L. Welcome 2005 "Anthropoid Primates from the Oligocene of Pakistan (Bugti Hills): Data on Early Anthropoid Evolution and Biogeography." *Proc Natl Acad Sci USA* **102** (24): 8436–41.

Marivaux, L., Y. Chaimancee, S. Ducrocq, et al. 2003 "The Anthropoid Status of a Primate from the Late Middle Eocene Pondaung Formation (Central Myanmar): Tarsal Evidence." *Proc Natl Acad Sci USA* **100** (23): 13173–13178.

Marivaux, L., J. L. Welcomme, S. Ducrocq, J. J. Jaeger 2002 "Oligocene Sivaladapid Primate from the BugtiHills (Balochistan, Pakistan) Bridges the Gap Between Eocene and Miocene Adapiform Communities in Southern Asia." *J Hum Evol* **42** (4): 379–388.

Martin, N. G. 1975 "No Evidence for a Genetic Basis of Tongue Rolling or Hand Clasping." *J Hered* **66**: 179–180.

Martin, R., K. Saller 1957 *Lehrbuch der Anthropologie.* Stuttgart: Gustav Fischer.

Martin, R. D. 1990 *Primate Origins and Evoution: A Phylogenetic Reconstruction.* Princeton, NJ: Princeton University Press.

Martrille, L., D. H. Ubelaker, C. Cattaneo, F. Seguret, M. Tremblay, E. Baccino 2007 "Comparison of Four Skeletal Methods for the Estimation of Age at Death on White and Black Adults." *Journal of Forensic Sciences* **52**: 302–307.

Matsui, A., F. Rakotondraparany, I. Munechika, M. Hasegawa, S. Horai 2009 "Molecular Phylogeny and Evolution of Prosimians Based on Complete Sequences of Mitochondrial Dnas." *Gene* **44**(1–2): 53–66.

Mayr, E. 1970 *Populations, Species and Evolution.* Cambridge, MA: Harvard University Press.

Mayr, E. 1981 "Biological Classification: Toward a Synthesis of Opposing Methodologies." *Science* **214**: 510–516.

McDougall, I., F. H. Brown, et al. 2005 "Stratigraphic Placement and Age of Modern Humans from Kibish, Ethiopia." *Nature* **433**(7027): 733–736.

McKern, T. W., T. D. Stewart 1957 "Skeletal Age Changes in Young American Males, Technical Report EP-45." Natick, MA: U.S. Army Quartermaster Research and Development Center.

Miller, J. M. 2000 "Craniofacial Variation in Homo habilis: An Analysis of the Evidence for Multiple Species." *Am J Phys Anthropol* **112**(1): 103–128.

Miller, E. R., G. F. Gunnell, R. D. Martin 2005 "Deep Time and the Search for Anthropoid Origins." *Am J Phys Anthropol Suppl* **41**: 60–95.

Moffat, A. S. 2002 "Primate Origins: New Fossils and a Glimpse of Evolution." *Science* **295**: 613–615.

Mourant, A. E. 1954 *The Distribution of the Human Blood Groups.* Oxford: Blackwell.

Mourant, A. E., A. C. Kopec, K. Domaniewska-Sobczak 1958 *The ABO Blood Groups.* Springfield, IL: Charles C. Thomas.

Mouri, T. 1976 "A Study of Non-Metrical Cranial Variants of the Modern Japanese in the Kinki District." *J Anthrop Soc Nippon* **84**: 191–203.

Moya-Sola, S., M. Kohler, D. M. Alba, I. Casanovas-Vilar, J. Galindo 2004 "*Pierolapithecus catalaunicus*, a New Middle Miocene Great Ape from Spain." *Science* **306** (5700): 1339–1344.

Nakatsukasa, M. 2004 "Acquisition of Bipedalism: The Miocene Hominoid Record and Modern Analogues for Bipedal Protohominids." *J Anat* **204** (5): 385–402.

Napier, J. R., A. C. Walker 1967 "Vertical Clinging and Leaping—A Newly Recognized Category of Primate Locomotion." *Folia Primatol* **6**: 204–219.

Olson, S. L., D. T. Rasmusson 1986 "Paleoenvironment of the Earliest Hominoids: New Evidence from the Oligocene Avi of Egypt." *Science* **233**: 1202–1204.

Olson, T. R. 1981 "Basicranial Morphology of Extant Hominoids and Pliocene Hominids: The New Material from the Hadar Formation, Ethiopia and Its Significance in Early Human Evolution and Taxonomy."

In: C. B. Stringer (ed.), *Aspects of Human Evolution,* London: Taylor and Francis, pp. 99–128.

Orlando, L., S. Calvignac, C. Schnebelen, C. J. Douady, L. R. Godfrey, C. Hänni 2008 "DNA from Extinct Giant Lemurs Links Archaeolemurids to Extant Indriids." *BioMed Central Evol Biol* 8:121.

Ousley, S. 1995 "Should We Estimate Biological or Forensic Stature?" *J Forens Sci* 40 (6): 768–773.

Ousley, S. D., J. T. Hefner 2005 "The Statistical Determination of Ancestry." Proceedings of the 57th Annual Meeting of the American Academy of Forensic Sciences; Feb 21–26; New Orleans, LA. Colorado Springs, CO: American Academy of Forensic Sciences.

Partridge, T. C., D. E. Granger, M. W. Caffee, R. J. Clarke 2003 "Lower Pliocene Hominid Remains from Sterkfontein." *Science* 300 (5619): 607–612.

Pilbeam, D. 1984 "The Descent of Hominoids and Hominids." *Sci Am* 250: 84–96.

Plummer, T. 2004 "Flaked Stones and Old Bones: Biological and Cultural Evolution at the Dawn of Technology." *Am J Phys Anthropol Suppl* 39: 118–164.

Poux, C., O. Madsen, E. Marquard, D. R. Vieites, W. W. de Jong, M. Vences 2005 "Asynchronous Colonization of Madagascar by the Four Endemic Clades of Primates, Tenrecs, Carnivores, and Rodents as Inferred from Nuclear Genes." *Syst Biol* 54 (5): 719–730.

Preuschoft, H. 2004 "Mechanisms for the Acquisition of Habitual Bipedality: Are There Biomechanical Reasons for the Acquisition of Upright Bipedal Posture?" *J Anat* 204 (5): 363–384.

Prince, D. A., D. H. Ubelaker 2002 "Application of Lamendin's Adult Aging Technique to a Diverse Skeletal Sample." *Journal of Forensic Sciences* 47: 107–116.

Rae, T. C. 2004 "Miocene Hominoid Craniofacial Morphology and the Emergence of Great Apes." *Ann Anat* 186 (5–6): 417–241.

Rak, Y., A. Ginzburg, E. Geffen 2007 "Gorilla-Like Anatomy on *Australopithecus Afarensis* Mandibles Suggests *Au. Afarensis* Link to Robust Australopiths." *Proc. Natl. Acad. Sci. USA* 104(16): 6568–72.

Rasmussen, D. T., G. C. Conroy, E. L. Simons 1998 "Tarsier-Like Locomotor Specializations in the Oligocene Primate Afrotarsius." *Proc Natl Acad Sci USA* 95(25): 14848–14850.

Reichs, K. J. (ed.) 1997 *Forensic Osteology: Advances in the Identification of Human Remains.* Springfield, IL: Charles C. Thomas.

Rhine, J. S., Kris Sperry 1991 "Radiographic Identification by Mastoid Sinus and Arterial Pattern." *J Forens Sci* 36 (1): 272–279.

Richards, M. P., P. B. Pettitt, E. Trinkaus, F. H. Smith, M. Paunovic, I. Karavanic 2000 "Neanderthal Diet at Vindija and Neanderthal Predation: The Evidence from Stable Isotopes." *Proc Natl Acad Sci USA* 97(13): 7663–7666.

Richmond, B. G., W. L. Jungers 2008 "Orrorin Tugenensis Femoral Morphology and the Evolution of Hominin Bipedalism." *Science* 319(5870): 1662–1665.

Rightmire, G. P. 1981 "Patterns in the Evolution of *Homo erectus*." *Paleobiology* 7: 241–246.

Rightmire, G. P. 1985 "The Tempo of Change in the Evolution of Mid-Pleistocene *Homo*." In: E. Delson (ed.), *Ancestors: The Hard Evidence,* New York: Alan R. Liss, pp. 255–264.

Rightmire, G. P. 2004 "Brain Size and Encephalization in Early to Mid-Pleistocene *Homo*." *Am J Phys Anthropol* 124(2): 109–123.

Rightmire, G. P., D. Lordkipanidze, A. Vekua 2006 "Anatomical Descriptions, Comparative Studies and Evolutionary Significance of the Hominin Skulls from Dmanisi, Republic of Georgia." *J Hum Evol* 50(2): 115–141.

Roede, M. J., J. C. Van Wieringen 1985 "Growth Diagrams 1980—Netherlands Third Nation-Wide Survey." *Tijdschr Soc Geneeskd* 63(Suppl 1): 1–34.

Roos, C., J. Schmitz, H. Zischler 2004 "Primate Jumping Genes Elucidate Strepsirrhine Phylogeny." *Proc Natl Acad Sci USA* 101: 10650–10654.

Rose, M. D. 1983 "Miocene Hominoid Postcranial Morphology: Monkey-like, Ape-Like, Neither or Both?" In: R. Ciochon and R. Corruccini (eds.), *New Interpretations of Ape and Human Ancestry,* New York: Plenum, pp. 405–417.

Rosenberg, K. R., L. Zune, C. B. Ruff 2006 "Body Size, Body Proportions, and Encephalization in a Middle Pleistocene Archaic Human from Northern China." *Proc Natl Acad Sci USA* 103(10): 3552–3556.

Ross, C. F. 2000 "Into the Light: The Origin of Anthropoidea." *Annual Review of Anthropology* 29: 147–194.

Rossie, J. B. 2005 "Anatomy of the Nasal Cavity and Paranasal Sinuses in Aegyptopithecus and Early Miocene African Catarrhines." *Am J Phys Anthropol* 126(3): 250–267.

Rossie, J. D., L. Maclatchy 2006 "A New Pliopithecoid Genus from the Early Miocene of Uganda." *J Hum Evol* 50(5): 568–586.

Rossie, J. B., X. Ni, K. C. Beard 2006 "Cranial Remains of an Eocene Tarsier." *Proc Natl Acad Sci USA* 103(12): 4381–4385.

Ruff, C. 2009 "Relative Limb Strength and Locomotion in *Homo habilis*." *Am J Phys Anthropol* 138(1): 90–100.

Sargis, E. J., D. M. Boyer, J. I. Bloch, M. T. Silcox 2007 "Evolution of Pedal Grasping in Primates." *J Hum Evol* 53(1):103–7.

Saunders, S. R., M. A. Katzenberg, (eds.) 1992 *Skeletal Biology of Past Peoples: Research Methods.* New York: Wiley-Liss.

Scheuer, L., S. Black 2000 *Developmental Juvenile Osteology.* New York: Academic.

Schultz, A. H. 1937 "Proportions, Variability and Asymmetries of the Long Bones of the Limbs and the Clavicles in Man and Apes." *Hum Biol* 9: 281–328.

Schultz, A. H. 1973 "The Recent Hominoid Primates." In: A. Montagu (ed.), *The Origin and Evolution of Man: Readings in Physical Anthropology,* New York: Thomas Y. Crowell.

Seiffert, E. R., E. L. Simons, Y. Attia 2003 "Fossil Evidence for an Ancient Divergence of Lorises and Galagos." *Nature* 422(6930): 421–424.

Seiffert, E. R., E. L. Simons, T. M. Ryan, Y. Attia 2005 "Additional Remains of *Wadilemur elegans,* a Primitive Stem Galagid from the Late Eocene of Egypt." *Proc Natl Acad Sci USA* 102(32): 11396–11401.

Seiffert, E. R. J. M. G. Perry, E. L. Simons, D. M. Boyer 2009 "Convergent Evolution of Anthropoid-Like Adaptations in Eocene Adapiform Primates." *Nature* 461: 1118–1121.

Semaw, S., S. W. Simpson, J. Quade, et al. 2005 "Early Pliocene Hominids from Gona, Ethiopia." *Nature* 433(7023): 301–305.

Senut, B. 2002 "From Apes to Humans: Locomotion as a Key Feature for Phylogeny." *Z Morphol Anthropol* 83(2–3): 351–360.

Senut, B., M. Pickford, D. Grommercy, et al. 2001 "First Hominid from the Miocene (Lukeino Formation, Kenya)." *C R Acad Sci Paris* 332: 137–144.

Serre, D., A. Langaney, M. Chech, M. Teschler-Nicola, M. Paunovic, P. Mennecier, et al. 2004 "No Evidence of Neandertal mtDNA Contribution to Early Modern Humans." *PLoS Biology,* 2: 313–7.

Sibley, C. G., J. E. Ahlquist 1984 "The Phylogeny of the Hominoid Primates as Indicated by DNA-DNA Hybridization." *J Mol Evol* 20: 2–15.

Sibley, C. G., J. E. Ahlquist 1987 "DNA Hybridization Evidence of Hominoid Phylogeny: Results from an Expanded Data Set." *J Mol Evol* 26: 99–121.

Silcox, M. T. 2003 "New Discoveries on the Middle Ear Anatomy of Ignacius Graybullianus (Paromomyidae, Primates) from Ultra High Resolution X-Ray Computed Tomography." *J Hum Evol* 44(1): 73–86.

Simons, E. L. 1990 "Discovery of the Oldest Known Anthyropoidean Skull from the Paleogene of Egypt." *Science* 247: 1567–1569.

Simons, E. L. 1995 "The Fossil History of Primates." In: S. Jones, R. Martin, and D. Pilbeam (eds.), *The Cambridge Encyclopedia of Human Evolution,* Cambridge, U.K.: Cambridge University Press, pp. 199–208.

Simons, E. L. 1998 "The Prosimian Fauna of the Fayum Eocene/Oligocene Deposits of Egypt." *Folia Primatol* 69 (Suppl 1): 286–294.

Simons, E. L. 2001 "The Cranium of Parapithecus grangeri, an Egyptian Oligocene Anthropoidean Primate." *Proc Natl Acad Sci USA* 98(14): 7892–7897.

Simons, E. L., T. M. Bown 1985 "Afrotarsius Chatrathi, 1st Tarsiiform Primate (Questionable Tarsiidae) from Africa." *Nature* 313: 475–477.

Simpson, S. W., J. Quade, et al. 2008 "A Female *Homo Erectus* Pelvis from Gona, Ethiopia." *Science* 322: 1089–1092.

Smith, F. H., A. B. Falsetti, et al. 1989 "Modern Human Origins. *Yearbook of Physical Anthropology* 32: 35–68.

Smith, T. M., L. B. Martin, D. J. Reid, L. de Bonis, G. D. Koufos 2004 "An Examination of Dental Development in *Graecopithecus Freybergi* (=*Ouranopithecus Macedoniensis*)." *Journal of Human Evolution* 46: 551–577.

Spoor F., M. G. Leakey, P. N. Gathogo, F. H. Brown, S. C. Antón, I. McDougall, C. Kiarie, F. K. Manthi, L. N. Leakey 2007 "Implications of New Early *Homo* Fossils from Ileret, East of Lake Turkana, Kenya." *Nature* 448(7154):688–91.

Stauffer, R. L., A. Walker, O. A. Ryder, M. Lyons-Weiler, S. B. Hedges 2001 "Human and Ape Molecular Clocks and Constraints on Paleontological Hypotheses." *J Hered* 92(6): 469–474.

Steiper, M. E., N. M. Young 2006 "Primate Molecular Divergence Dates." *Molecular Phylogenetics and Evolution* 41(2): 384–394.

Steiper, M. E., N. M. Young 2008 "Timing Primate Evolution: Lessons from the Discordance Between Molecular and Paleontological Estimates." *Evolutionary Anthropology* 17: 179–188.

Steiper, M. E., N. M. Young, T. Y. Sukarna 2004 "Oligocene Estimate for the Hominoid-Cercopithecoid Divergence." *Proc Natl Acad Sci USA* **101**(49): 17021–17026.

Sterner, K. N., R. L. Raaum, Y. P. Zhang, C. B. Stewart, T. Disotell 2006 "Mitochondrial Data Support an Odd-Nosed Colobine Clade." *Mol Phylogenet Evol* **40**(1): 1–7.

Stout, S. D., R. R. Paine 1992 "Histological Age Estimation Using Rib and Clavicle." *American Journal of Physical Anthropology* **87**: 111–115.

Strahan, T., A. Read 2004 *Human Molecular Genetics* (3rd ed.). New York: Garland Publishing.

Strait, D. S., Grine F. E. 2004 "Inferring Hominoid and Early Hominid Phylogeny Using Craniodental Characters: The Role of Fossil Taxa." *J Hum Evol.* **47**(6): 399–452.

Stringer, C. 1995 "Evolution of Early Humans." In: S. Jones, R. Martin, and D. Pilbeam (eds.), *The Cambridge Encyclopedia of Human Evolution,* Cambridge, U.K.: Cambridge University Press, pp. 241–251.

Stringer, C. B., P. Andrews 1988 "Genetic and Fossil Evidence for the Origin of Modern Humans." *Science* **239**(4845): 1263–1268.

Suchey, J. M., S. T. Brooks, R. D. Rawson 1982 "Aging the Female *Os Pubis.*" American Academy of Forensic Sciences, Annual Meeting, Orlando, Florida.

Suchey, J. M., D. Katz 1998 "Applications of Pubic Age Determination in a Forensic Setting." In: K. J. Reichs (ed.), *Forensic Osteology: Advances in the Identification of Human Remains,* Springfield, IL: C. C Thomas, pp. 204–236.

Suchey, J. M., D. V. Wisely, D. Katz 1986 "Evaluation of the Todd and McKern-Stewart Methods for Aging the Male os pubis. In: K. J. Reichs (ed.), *Forensic Osteology: Advances in the Identification of Human Remains* Springfield, IL: C. C Thomas, pp. 33–67.

Suchey, J. M., D. V. Wiseley, R. F. Green, T. T. Noguchi 1979 "Analysis of Dorsal Pitting in the *Os Pubis* in an Extensive Sample of Modern American Females." *Am J Phys Anthropol* **51**(4): 517–540.

Sussman, R. W. 1991 "Primate Origins and the Evolution of Angiosperms." *Am J Primatol* **23**: 209–223.

Sutherland, L. D., J. M. Suchey 1991 "Use of the Ventral Arc in Pubic Sex Determination." *Journal of Forensic Sciences* **36**: 501–511.

Suwa, G., B. Asfaw, R. T. Kono, D. Kubo, C. O. Lovejoy, T. D. White 2009 "The *Ardipithecus Ramidus* Skull and Its Implications for Hominid Origins." *Science* **326**(5949): 68e1–7.

Suwa, G., R. T. Kono, S. W. Simpson, B. Asfaw, C. O. Lovejoy, T. D. White 2009 "Paleobiological Implications of the *Ardipithecus Ramidus* Dentition." *Science* **326**(5949): 94–9.

Szalay, F. S. 1981 "Phylogeny and the Problem of Adaptive Significance: The Case of the Earliest Primates." *Folia Primatol* (Basel) **36** (3–4): 157–82.

Szalay, F. S. 2000 In: E. Delson, I. Tattersall, J. A. Van Couvering, and A. S. Brooks (eds.), *Encyclopedia of Human Evolution and Prehistory* (2nd ed.), New York: Garland.

Szalay, F. S., E. Delson 1979 *Evolutionary History of the Primates.* New York: Academic.

Tabuce, R., M. Mahboubi, P. Tafforeau, J. Sudre 2004 "Discovery of a Highly-Specialized Plesiadapiform Primate in the Early-Middle Eocene of Northwestern Africa." *J Hum Evol* **47**(5):305–321.

Tabuce, R., L. Marivaux, R. Lebrun, M. Adaci, M. Bensalah, P. Fabre, E. Fara, H. G. Rodrigues, L. Hautier, J. Jaeger, V. Lazzari, F. Mebrouk, S. Peigné, J. Sudre, P. Tafforeau, X. Valentin, M. Mahboubi 2009 "Anthropoid versus Strepsirhine Status of the African Eocene Primates *Algeripithecus* and *Azibius*: Craniodental Evidence." Proceedings of the Royal Society B. December 7, 2009; 276:4087-4094; published online before print September 9, 2009 (doi:10.1098/rspb.2009.133).

Tanner, J. M. 1962 *Growth at Adolescence* (2nd ed.). Oxford: Blackwell Scientific.

Tanner, J. M. 1978 *Foetus into Man—Physical Growth from Conception to Maturity.* London: Open Books.

Tarling, D. 1980 "The Geologic Evolution of South America with Special Reference to the Last 200 Million Years." In: R. Ciochon and A. Chiarelli, (eds.), *Evolutionary Biology of the New World Monkeys and Continental Drift,* New York: Plenum, pp. 1–41.

Tattersall, I. 1970 *Man's Ancestors: An Introduction to Primate and Human Evolution.* Levittown, NY.

Tattersall, I. 1970 *Man's Ancestors: An Introduction to Primate and Human Evolution.* London: J. Murray.

Templeton, A. R. 2005 "Haplotype Trees and Modern Human Origins." *Am J Phys Anthropol Suppl* **41**: 33–59.

Thewissen, J. G., S. T. Hussain, M. Arif 1997 "New Kohatius (Omomyidae) from the Eocene of Pakistan." *J Hum Evol* **32**(5): 473–7.

Tiemel, Chen, Yang Quan, and Wu En 1994 "Antiquity of *Homo sapiens* in China." *Nature* **368**: 55–56.

Todd, T. W. 1920–21 "Age Changes in the Pubic Bone" *Am J Phys Anthropol* **3**: 285–334; **4**: 1–70.

Trinkaus, E. 1978 "Bilateral Asymmetry of Human Skeletal Non-Metric Traits." *Am J Phys Anthropol* **49**: 15–318.

Turanov, A. A., A. V. Lobanov, D. E. Fomenko, H. G. Morrison, M. L. Sogin, L. A. Klobutcher, D. L. Hatfield, V. N. Gladyshev 2009 "Genetic Code Supports Targeted Insertion of Two Amino Acids by One Codon." *Science* **323**(5911): 259–61.

Vignaud, P., P. Duringer, H. T. Mackaye, et al. 2002 "Geology and Palaeontology of the Upper Miocene Toros-Menalla Hominid Locality, Chad." *Nature* **418**: 152–155.

Walker, A., R. E. Leakey, J. M. Harris, F. H. Brown 1986 "2.5-M.yr. *Australopithecus boisei* from West of Lake Turkana, Kenya." *Nature* **322**: 517–522.

Walker, A., C. Walker, M. Pickford 1983 "New Postcranial Fossils of *Proconsul africanus* and *Proconsul nyanzae*." In: R. Ciochon and R. Corruccini (eds.), *New Interpretations of Ape and Human Ancestry,* New York: Plenum.

Wang, W., R. H. Crompton 2004 "The Role of Load-Carrying in the Evolution of Modern Body Proportions." *J Anat* **204**(5): 417–430.

Wang, W., R. H. Crompton, T. S. Carey, et al. 2004 "Comparison of Inverse-Dynamics Musculo-Skeletal Models of AL 288-1 Australopithecus afarensis and KNM-WT 15000 Homo ergaster to Modern Humans, with Implications for the Evolution of Bipedalism." *J Hum Evol* **47**(6): 453–478.

Ward, C. V. 2002 "Interpreting the Posture and Locomotion of Australopithecus afarensis: Where Do We Stand?" *Am J Phys Anthropol Suppl* **35**:185–215.

Ward, C. V., M. G. Leakey, A. Walker 2001 "Morphology of Australopithecus anamensis from Kanapoi and Allia Bay, Kenya." *J Hum Evol* **41**(4): 255–368.

Weber, J., A. Czarnetzki, C. M. Pusch 2005 "Comment on the Brain of LB1, Homo floresiensis." *Science* **310**(5746): 236.

White, T. D., B. Asfaw, et al. 2003 "Pleistocene Homo Sapiens from Middle Awash, Ethiopia." *Nature* **423**(6941): 742–747.

White, T. D. B. Asfaw, Y. Beyene, Y. Haile-Selassie, C. O. Lovejoy, G. Suwa, 2009 "*Ardipithecus Ramidus* and the Paleobiology of Early Hominids." *Science* **326**(5949): 64, 75–86.

White, T. D., G. WoldeGrabriel, B. Asfaw, S. Ambrose, Y. Beyene, R. L. Bernor, J. R. Boisserie, B. Currie, H. Gilbert, Y. Haile-Selassie, W. K. Hart, L. J. Hlusko, F. C. Howell, R. T. Kono, et al. 2006 "Asa Issie, Aramis and the Origin of *Australopithecus*." *Nature* **440**(7086): 883–9.

Wild, E. M., M. Teschler-Nicola, W. Kutschera, P. Steier, E. Trinkaus, W. Wanek 2005 "Direct Dating of Early Upper Paleolithic Human Remains from Mladec." *Nature* **435**(7040): 332–335.

Wildman, D. E., M. Uddin, G. Liu, L. I. Grossman, M. Goodman 2003 "Implications of Natural Selection in Shaping 99.4% Nonsynonymous DNA Identity between Humans and Chimpanzees: Enlarging Genus Homo." *Proc Natl Acad Sci* **100**: 7181–7188.

Wolpoff, M. H. 1984 "Evolution in Homo erectus: The Question of Stasis." *Paleobiology* **10**: 389–406.

Wolpoff, M. H. 1989 "Multiregional Evolution: The Fossil Alternative to Eden." In: P. Mellars and C.B. Stringer (eds.), *The Human Revolution.* Princeton, NJ: Princeton University Press. pp. 62–108.

Wolpoff, M., A. G. Thorne, et al. 1994 "Multiregional Evolutions: A World-Wide Source for Modern Human Populations." In: M. H. Nitecki and D.V. Nitecki (eds.), *Origins of Anatomically Modern Humans.* New York: Plenum Press. pp. 175–199.

Wood, B. 1992 "Origin and evolution of the genus Homo." *Nature* **355**: 783–790.

Wood, B., M. Collard 1999 "The Human Genus." *Science* **284**(5411): 65–71.

Wu, X., L. A. Schepartz, D. Falk, W. Liu 2006 "Endocranial Cast of Hexian Homo erectus from South China." *Am J Phys Anthropol,* Jan. 19 Epub ahead of print.

Xu, Q., Q. Lu 2007 *Series Monograph III: Lufengpithecus—An Early Member of Hominidae.* Beijing: Science Press.

Yoshiura, K., A. Kinoshita, T. Ishida, A. Ninokata, T. Ishikawa, T. Kaname, M. Bannai, K. Tokunaga, S. Sonoda, R. Komaki, M. Ihara, V. A. Saenko, G. K. Alipov, I. Sekine, K. Komatsu, H. Takahashi, M. Nakashima, N. Sosonkina, C. K. Mapendano, M. Ghadami, M. Nomura, D. S. Liang, N. Miwa, D. K. Kim, A. Garidkhuu, N. Natsume, T. Ohta, H. Tomita, A. Kaneko, M. Kikuchi, G. Russomando, K. Hirayama, M. Ishibashi, A. Takahashi, N. Saitou, J. C. Murray, S. Saito, Y. Nakamura, N. Niikawa 2006 "A SNP in the ABCC11 Gene Is the Determinant of Human Earwax Type." *Nat Genet* **38**(3): 324–30.

Index